History of Colorado

By Hubert Howe Bancroft

(From Vol. XX of *History of the Pacific States of North America*,
The History Company, San Francisco, 1890)

WESTERN REFLECTIONS
PUBLISHING COMPANY®

Western Reflections Publishing Company
Lake City, Colorado

A Reprint Published by
Western Reflections Publishing Co.
P. O. Box 1149
951 N. Highway 149
Lake City, Colorado 81235

www.westernreflectionspub.com
westref@montrose.net

ISBN 978-1-932738-66-7

Bancroft History of Colorado

Prologue

Hubert Howe Bancroft might be called "The Western Historian's Historian," as he was the first and perhaps the greatest collector, publisher, and documenter of Western History (from Alaska all the way down to South America). He began his career in 1852 as a bookseller in San Francisco. He soon had the largest book and stationery business west of Chicago and collected a variety of Western history materials and artifacts. During this time he did research for *Works of Hubert Bancroft*, a thirty-nine volume set – five volumes on Native Americans, twenty-eight volumes on the history of the Pacific States, five volumes of essays, with the final volume an autobiography and perspective on life.

Almost all of the work was written by several dozen assistants hired for this purpose, but to whom he gave absolutely no credit. At first his work was boycotted because of this unethical practice; however, eventually it became known as one of the great works on the history of the American West. Bancroft's *History of Colorado* is a portion of Volume XX, which also includes the histories of Nevada and Wyoming. These were grouped together because they were "commonly termed the silver and centennial states." Bancroft's work on Colorado remains one of the primary sources of history for that state.

In the Preface to Volume XX Bancroft sets the stage for his history:

> In the same year that witnessed the discovery of the Comstock lode occurred the great migration to Pikes peak, when, in the summer of 1859, an army of 150,000 men traversed the plains between the Missouri and the base of the Rocky Mountains. Of these at least one third turned back, discouraged by evil reports, and of those who arrived on the ground probably less than 20,000

remained as permanent settlers. But here was the nucleus of a population, and that of the best material for empire-building—men resolute of will, inured to hardship, and with all the energy and adaptability of the typical pioneer. Assuredly there was no lack of resources in this great and goodly region, with its magnificent soil and climate, its majestic canon and river systems, its series of natural parks, its gardens of the gods, its virgin forests, and its untold mineral wealth.

Hubert Howe Bancroft was born on May 5, 1832, in Granville, Ohio. He left home at age sixteen to work at his brother-in-law's bookstore in Buffalo, New York. After the discovery of gold, Bancroft went to California in 1852 with a consignment load of his brother-in-law's books. Following his brother-in-law's death, Bancroft opened his own store in Crescent City, California, and then opened a print shop, publishing company, and bookstore in San Francisco in 1858. His business was an immediate success. By 1867, Bancroft was wealthy enough to retire, but instead started his *"Works"* in 1869. Some 6,000 sets were eventually sold.

Bancroft sold his enormous collection of 60,000 books, unpublished manuscripts, maps, photographs and drawings, pamphlets, oral histories, and notes to the University of California in 1905. This collection formed the nucleus of the Bancroft Library – now known throughout the world. Although Bancroft's work was at first downplayed because of his failure to give proper credit for the authorship, by the time he died on March 2, 1918, he and his works were very well respected.

Because his set on *The History of the Pacific States* now sells for thousands of dollars, very few readers have ever heard of this work, little less read it. Western Reflections Publishing Company is delighted to make Bancroft's *History of Colorado* portion available to both historians and the general public.

CONTENTS

HISTORY OF COLORADO

CHAPTER IV.
Progress of Settlement
1859-1860

CHAPTER V.
Organization of Government
1858-1861

CHAPTER VI.
Political Affairs
1861-1886

CHAPTER VII.
Indian Wars
1860-1880

CHAPTER VIII.
Material Progress
1859-1875

CHAPTER IX.
Further Development
1875-1886

CHAPTER X.
Agriculture and Stock Raising
1861-1886

CHAPTER XI.
Denver and Arapahoe County
1859-1886

CHAPTER XII.
Counties of Colorado
1859-1886

CHAPTER XIII.
Counties of Colorado Concluded
1859-1886

CHAPTER XIV.
Later Events
1886-1888

HISTORY OF COLORADO.

CHAPTER I.

PHYSICAL FEATURES.

Mountain System—Primeval Waters—Upheaval, Evaporation and Glacial Action—Dry Rivers—Flora and Fauna—Primitive Man— Cañons and River Systems—Series of Parks—Climate—Soil— Forests—Geological Formations—Minerals and Metals—Gold and Silver—Coal and Iron—Precious Stones—Land and Water Elevations.

In the gradual upheaval of the continent from a deep sea submersion, the great Sierra Madre, or mother range, of old Mexico first divided the waters, and presented a wall to the ocean on the west side. The San Juan range of Colorado is an extension of the Sierra Madre, and the oldest land in this part of the continent. Then at intervals far apart rose the Sangre de Cristo range, the Mojada or Greenhorn range, and lastly the Colorado, called the Front range because it is first seen from the east; and northeast from this the shorter upheavals of Wind river and the Black hills, each, as it lies nearer or farther from the main Rocky range, being more or less recent.

The longer slope and greater accessibility of the mountains on their eastern acclivity has come from the gradual wash and spreading out of the detritus of these elevations in comparatively shallow water, while yet the ocean thundered at the western base of the mother range. The salt waters enclosed by the barrier of the Rocky mountains, and subdivided afterward by the later upheavals into lesser seas, were carried off through the cañons which their own mighty force, aided by other activities of nature, and

by some of her weaknesses, opened for them.   For
uncounted ages the fresh water of the land flowed
into the inland seas, and purged them of their saline
flavor, washing the salts and alkalies into the bed of
the ocean on the west, where after the emergence of
the Sierra Nevada, and the elevation of the interven-
ing mountains of the great basin, they largely remained,
having no outlet.   Gradual elevation and evaporation,
with glacial action, completed the general shaping of
the country.   Subsequent elemental and volcanic
action has left it with four parallel mountain ranges,
from which shoot up 132 peaks, ranging from 12,000
to 14,500 feet above sea level, and from 9,000 to
10,000 feet above the general level of the state, with
many lesser ones; with large elevated valleys called
parks, walled about with majestic heights, covered
with luxuriant grasses, threaded by streams of the
purest water, beautified by lakes, and dotted with
groups of trees; with narrow, fertile valleys skirting
numerous small rivers, fringed with cottonwood and
willow; with nobler rivers rushing through rents in
the solid mountains thousands of feet in depth, and
decorated by time and weather, with carvings such as
no human agency could ever have designed, their wild
imagery softened by blended tones of color in harmony
with the blue sky, the purple-gray shadows, and the
clinging moss and herbage; with forests of pine, fir,
spruce, aspen, and other trees, covering the mountain
sides up to a height of 10,000 or 12,000 feet; with
wastes of sand at the western base of the Snowy range,
or main chain, and arid mesas in the southeast, where
everything is stunted except the enormous cacti; with
grassy plains sloping to the east, made gay with an
indigenous flora, and other grassy slopes extending to
the mountains toward the west, each with its own
distinctive features.   It is, above all, a mountain
country; and with all its streams, which are numerous,
it is a dry one.   In the summer many of its seeming
water-courses are merely arroyos—dry creek beds;

others contain some water flowing in channels cut twenty or more feet down through yellow clay to a bed of shale; and still others run through cañons, with narrow bottoms supporting rich grass, and willow, thorn, cherry, currant, and plum trees. Sloping up from these may be a stretch of rolling country covered sparsely with low, spreading cedars; or a table-land, with colonies of prairie-dogs scattered over it, and moving about upon it herds of wild horses, buffaloes, deer, and antelopes. Up in the mountains are meadows, having in their midst beaver-dams overgrown with aspens, and little brooks trickling from them. Several other fur-bearing animals are here, also. In still other localities are fine trout streams, and game about them is abundant, elks, mountain sheep, bears, lynxes, wolves, panthers, pumas, wild-cats, grouse, pheasants, ptarmigans, and birds of various kinds having their habitat there.

But these were not the first inhabitants of these mountains. In the bed of one of the ancient seas west of the San Juan mountains, before mentioned, in a deposit three thousand feet thick, now hardened into rock, are the fossil skeletons of the first vertebrates of the American continent, species until recently unknown to science. As their bones are very numerous, being scattered over three thousand square miles, it is safe to conclude that Colorado supported a vast amount of animal life at that period when the rivers now dry washed down their remains to that ancient receptacle.

Here, too, about the shores of this primeval lake, which was encircled by upturned ridges of white gypsum and sandstone of various colors, yellow, vermilion, gray, and blood red, on sharp ridges, with precipitous sides, sometimes hundreds of feet high, dwelt the first men who inhabited this region of whom there is any trace. Their dwellings were of unhewn stones, cemented with a mortar containing a large portion of volcanic ashes. Their form was oval, like a bee-hive,

and they enclosed usually a cedar stump, the use of
which is purely conjectural. So numerous were these
dwellings, that the population must have been dense
which occupied them; yet all were in these inaccessible situations. About them were scattered a few
domestic implements, including large water-jars sunk
in the ground, and some arrow-heads. But as no
water can now be found within twenty-five miles of
the cliff-dwellings, a long time must have elapsed to
account for the change of climate which has taken
place. Why this ancient people found it necessary or
desirable to dwell on the top or in the face of the
cliffs is unanswerable, unless we accept the almost in-
credible theory that, like the lake-dwellings of Switzerland, these houses were erected when the water of
the now dried-up lake reached up to them. This belief might go far to account for the great number of
bones of animals found in the lake bed, for they must
have subsisted upon animal food. The few human
bones found have been fossilized, which is in itself
evidence of the long period of time since they were
clothed in flesh.

I should be afraid to say this primitive race were
capable of comparing the beauties of the great cañons
over which modern Coloradans grow enthusiastic; or
that they would understand what to-day is meant by
Garden of the Gods, the place being conspicuous for
the absence of both garden and gods; yet more striking, perhaps, than the Olympic mount, as here we
have, if the imagination be strong enough, sandstone
columns sculptured by the elements into the simili-
tude of giant human forms, divinely tall if not divinely
fair. Of the eight or more principal cañons which
were opened for the waters in the infancy of this
early world, the most wonderful and beautiful are
west of the main range; and Black cañon, on Gunnison river, which is a branch of Grand river, itself
a branch of the great stream of the west, with the
longest and deepest cañon in the world, is the grand-

est of them all. So many aspects has it that any mood may be satisfied in regarding its varied features. The walls have an average width of three hundred feet, the rock being stratified, and continuing for miles. In places it rises one, two, or three thousand feet, with level summits, surmounted by a second wall of prodigious height. The level of the Gunnison river at Mountain creek, above the cañon, is 7,200 feet above the sea, that of the mesa on the north side 8,000, the wall of the cañon here being 1,600 feet, and a little lower, on the opposite side, 1,900. Still further down, the wall rises 3,000 feet, the lower 1,800 being of gneiss rock. The elevation of the mesa at this point is 9,800 feet. But these figures represent only height and depth; they convey no impression of the gorge itself, which sometimes narrows down to the width of the river, and is all gloom and grandeur, and again broadens out into a park, with waterfalls dashing down its inclosing walls, needles of highly-colored sandstone pointing skyward, trees growing out of the clefts in the palisades, huge rocks grouped fantastically about, curious plants sheltering in their shadows, and the brilliant, strong river darting down in swift green chutes between the spume-flecked boulders, dancing in creamy eddies, struggling to tumble headlong down some sparkling cataract, making the prismatic air resound with the soft tinkle as of merry laughter. Again, it surges along in half shadows, rushing as if blinded against massive abutments, to be dashed into spray, gliding thereafter more smoothly, as if rebuked for its previous haste, but always full of light, life, and motion. The grandeur, beauty, and variety of the views in Black cañon make doubly interesting the reflection that through this channel poured the waters of that great primal sea which once spread over western Colorado. A rival to it is the cañon of the Uncompahgre, in the same division of the state; and on the eastern slope are those of Boulder, Clear, and Cheyenne creeks, and the Platte and Arkansas rivers.

The western slope is drained entirely, excepting some small streams falling into the San Luis lakes, by the affluents of the Rio Colorado of the west. All of the principal of these, except the main river and some of the branches of Green river, have their sources in the Rocky ranges, in the state of Colorado, most of them in the Park, the Saguache, the Elk, or the San Juan mountains. The Grand river rises in the Middle park, and after receiving the tributaries that drain Egeria park, and the northern slopes of the Elk mountains, cuts its way in mighty cañons through the plateaus of western Colorado, while its two chief affluents, the Gunnison and Rio Dolores, with their branches, drain all the western slopes lying between latitude 37° 30′ and 39° north. In the extreme southwest the Rio San Juan and its tributaries perform this office for a large extent of country.

On the east side of the great divide, the South Platte river, with about forty tributaries, rises well up among the peaks of the Front, or Colorado, range, and flowing north-northeast and easterly, drains a large extent of country, while the North Platte, rising in the Park range, drains the whole of tke North park toward the north. The eastern slope of Colorado is watered and drained by the royal river Arkansas, with its sixty or more tributaries, some of which are of considerable volume. It heads in the high region of the Saguache range, interlacing with springs of the Grand river, quite as the Columbia and the Missouri rise near each other farther north. Republican river, an affluent of the Kansas, itself having four tributaries, flows northeast down the long descent to its union with the main stream, near its junction with the Missouri, and in the south the Rio Grande del Norte, starting from the summits of the same range which feeds the Gunnison branch of Grand river on the opposite side, flows toward the gulf of Mexico. Such is the river system of Colorado.

The series of high valleys, to which in Colorado are given the name of parks, and of which I have spoken, are of various dimensions. North park has a diameter of thirty miles, and an elevation of 8,500 feet. Middle park has a length of sixty-five miles by a breadth of forty-five, with an altitude of 8,000 feet. South park is but little less in size, and is 842 feet more elevated than its neighbor. San Luis park, still further south, is nearly as large as all the other three just named, and has an altitude of 7,500 feet. In it are the San Luis lakes. These elevated valleys are separated from each other, and surrounded by the several mountain chains, and their spurs or cross-ranges, except San Luis, which is opened toward the east. Through them course the tributary streams which feed the great rivers. Egeria, Estes, Animas, and Huerfano parks are small valleys of great beauty, at a general elevation of 8,000 feet.

What, then, shall be said of this country so grandly organic and so interesting in its cosmical history? That it illustrates the condition of the lower valleys and plains when they shall be as old as these oldest lands in America? For with all its numerous streams as I have said, Colorado is a dry country. The air has little humidity in it. The summer heat of the plains is excessive by day, but owing to the altitude the nights, even in midsummer, are cool. The summer mean temperature ranges from 64.6° to 69.2°, and the winter mean from 31.3° to 32.8°. The maximum heat of summer ranges from 93° to 99°, with from six to thirty days above 90°; and the minimum of winter from 3° to 12°, with from six to ten days when the mercury is below zero; which gives an extreme range for the year from 96° to 110°; and the rainfall averages 18.84 inches. With a surface composed of mountains and plains, ranging in altitude from about 3,000 to more than 14,000 feet above the level of the sea, Colorado possesses many varieties of climate.   The sharp extremes of heat and cold are perceptible to the senses only in a limited degree, on account of the large preponderance of sunny days and the dryness and tonic properties of the atmosphere, which is at once healthful, bracing, and exhilarating. The winter is the season of greatest charm, for then the bright sunshine gives balminess to the air, while in the blue dome of the sky is no cloud to stain its purity.

From the small amount of moisture distributed over the surface, and the great general elevation, it is natural that the agricultural area should be limited, and that only by a good system of irrigation could the soil be made to produce food enough to supply a dense population.   Yet the soil is exceedingly rich with its mineral constituents of plants, and also deep, and must yield, when supplied with water, large and fine crops of cereals.   On the eastern slopes of the state, in the parks, and west of the mother range, are grazing lands for countless herds of herbivorous animals. By and by all this will be changed; the herds will give way to the superior demands of the soil, a way meanwhile having been found to overcome the sterility of nature.

The effect of climate is visible in the forests of Colorado, which cover perhaps a tenth part of the area.   The trees are not majestically tall and straight, like those of the more northern and western regions, but squat and branching, and of no great size. Neither are they in any great variety, but they will serve for fuel and lumber as well as the trees of many of the trans-Missouri states.

To find out where the natural wealth of this wonderful and beautiful country is hidden we must search beneath the soil and break open the rocks.   The geology of the plains is cretaceous, or post-cretaceous, with the exception of areas of tertiary formation in the northern portion and on the Arkansas divide. At the base of the mountain the strata are turned up, forming hog-backs in which the cretaceous and Jura trias are exposed, coal being found in the latter. All this is very simple; but in the mountains all the formations known are represented, and the arrangement is complex. The Front, most of the Park, all of the Mojada, and part of the Sangre de Cristo ranges are of granite and allied metamorphic rocks. The southern portion of the Sangre de Cristo is carboniferous, with here and there an intruded volcanic rock. The San Juan mountains are volcanic, with an area of quartzite peaks in their midst, and flanking the range on the south is an area of carboniferous and cretaceous rocks, while the Elk mountains are a medley of volcanic peaks thrown up among the silurian and carboniferous, flanked by cretaceous areas.

The North and Middle parks rest upon the tertiary formation, through which have been thrust up mountains of volcanic rock, while South park is an indescribable jumble, and San Luis is of recent formation. Volcanic rock overlies the high plateau on White river, in the western part of the state, beneath which may be found every formation down to the tertiary. Still further west and north the plateaux are tertiary. The Uintah mountains, which project into the state, consist of cretaceous, Jura trias, carboniferous, and silurian. In some places small groups of igneous upheavals have been pushed up through the sedimentary rocks. South of the San Juan mountains a large tertiary area is enclosed by cretaceous beds. And so on. Granite, gneiss, and sandstone might be said to be country rock, with impure limestone, slates, shales, and trachyte. It would seem hopeless to search for treasure with so confusing a stone guide-book to take our directions from. The younger world in Colorado has been resentfully pushed aside and overflowed by the older in so rude and violent a manner that much labor must be expended in fitting together again the dislocated strata and reading the story they should

teach. First by accident, and afterward by search,
the clue was discovered which led to the knowledge
of the mineral wealth of this portion of the Rocky
mountains, for so long a time unsuspected.

The minerals of Colorado were not easy to come at.
Gold, which was found in gneiss principally, existed
in many refractory combinations, with sulphur and
iron, with copper and sulphur, with zinc, tellurium,
and other metals and minerals. If it were free
milling it contained silver, and sometimes lead. In
the trachyte mines of the south-west there was a
chloridized combination of gold, silver, iron, maganese
and gray copper. Silver, which was found in both
gneissic and granite rocks, was chiefly in the form of
a compound sulphuret of silver and lead called argentiferous galena, but existed also in combinations with
carbonates of lead, carbonates and sulphurets of copper, zinc, tellurides of gold, nickel, iron, copper, man-
ganese, antimony, arsenic, and sometimes in the form
of a chloride, or as horn silver.

Nor was there any rule of nature known to mineralogists which applied to the situation of mines in
Colorado, and old traditions were entirely at fault.
Gold, which had always been found in placers washed
down from the mountain veins, or in fissure veins of
granite, or at the deepest, silurian rocks, filled with
fragments of quartz or conglomerate, among which
grains of gold were mingled, or deposited by water,
was here found in metamorphic rocks, and also in the
tertiary.

Silver, too, was equally eccentric in its situations.
One of its remarkable deposits, found in the Leadville region, was in horizontal flat veins, from a few
inches to a foot in thickness, separated from each
other by layers of barren rock of a depth of a few
hundred feet—blanket lodes they are called. They
extended quite through lofty heights, cropping out
on either side; but whether they were so deposited

or were formed in the rocks, which by some convulsion of the mountains were split open and turned over, is still conjectural. Almost equally surprising was it to find silver in trachyte rocks, or enveloping pebbles and bowlders like a crust, or still more remarkable, in fine threads or wires. These were problems for the scientists, as the modes of extracting the metals from their matrices was for the practical metallurgist.

The trend of the fissure veins in Colorado is northeast and south-west. They have in general clearly defined walls, some of them remarkably smooth and regular, and correspond in direction with the cleavage of the eruptive rocks, and with the dikes which extend long distances across the plains. There is another cleavage of the metamorphic rocks in a southeast and north-west direction, which was made at an earlier period than the cleavage of the eruptive rocks, as is shown by the eruptive material overlying the metamorphic in large areas, a combination of facts which seems to fix the age of the deposit of the ores in fissures at a date more recent than the cleavage of the metamorphic rock. In a few instances short veins are found running east and west, or north and south; but though sometimes rich, they soon pinch out.

Coal in immense quantities has been formed in Colorado. It is of several geologic eras, some of it merely lignite, some beds petroleum-bearing, and in the western portion of the state anthracite in large areas. Iron is placed in juxtaposition, as also limestone, hydraulic lime, and a variety of rocks used in building or manufacturing. Of the different crystals of quartz which are scattered liberally over the country the varieties are numerous, though none more valuable than carnelian, chalcedony, onyx, jasper, sardonyx, chrysoparse, and trope, rose-quartz, black-quartz, moss-agate, and aventurine.

After all, nothing interests many of us like the mountains, which will always draw men from the

ends of the earth that they may climb as near to
heaven as may be by their rocky stairs. Take a
position on Gray's peak—there are really two of them
shooting up from a single base in the midst of a wil-
derness of mountains—which is won by ascending
from the plains to the timber-belt, then following the
course of rapidly descending creeks to where no trees
can grow, but scant grass and lowly flowering plants
have the zone to themselves; higher still to the belt
of starving mosses; and yet higher among great
blocks of loose, broken rock with patches of snow
between them, and chilly springs in their shadows;
and then to the windy pinnacle above the snow !

The view begins nowhere and ends nowhere. It is
infinite. Mountains beyond mountains, unbounded
plains belittled to look like parks, the great South
park like a pleasure ground, range after range westward, silvered with the lingering snow, although it is
August—for we must not attempt the high peaks
before the summer heat has done its utmost to modify
the climate at their altitude. Among the more
western mountains stand some covered with almost
perpetual snow, and one which fixes the eye on account of the snow-field having taken the form of a
cross, that symbol of life eternal alike among pagan
and Christian philosophers, and which could have
found no more fitting place to be displayed than on
these everlasting hills. Yet here more than almost
anywhere are the evidences of change which we call
decay, the proof that eternity is but a comparative
term. Gorge and ledge, shattered cliff, and weird
shapes in stone, furrows cut by avalanches, torrents
hurrying down from the melting snow-drifts, washing
earth and gravel into the basins below, generations of
forest fallen like slain warriors on a hard fought field.
all point to a continual transformation, and show that
the most heaven-inspiring heights are destined to lower
their proud heads before time and the elements, that
the grandeur of the past and the present is constantly

passing away. Lower, this consciousness becomes less oppressive, until it is lost in the enjoyment of what the decay of the higher zone has done for the lower. Tiny parks, gem-like lakes, green groves, beds of flowers, miniature presentments of the grander valleys, forests, and lakes still farther down.

In a general way one mountain is like another; yet they have their differences, dependent upon the kind of rock of which they are formed, its hardness, friableness, stratification, color, and condition of upheaval. The variety of rocks and their singular displacement gives a corresponding variety to the mountain scenery. In one place is a cluster of low cones, broken down and rounded, so grouped as to resemble the rim of a mighty peak broken roughly off; in another an almost smooth round top, and in its immediate neighborhood a needle-like peak. The other features of each are likely to correspond somewhat to the character of the summits, which are approached either by circuitous trails, by long slope after slope, or by wild ravines leading from bench to bench, but everywhere grand and impressive scenery meets the eye. Many are the passes by which the mother range may be crossed, but only seven are below 10,000 feet, five are over 12,000, and one is 13,000 feet above sea-level. Some of the high mountains to which names have been given, none of which are less than 14,000 feet high, are Blanca, Harvard, Massive, Gray's, Rosalie, Torrey, Elbert, La Plata, Lincoln, Buckskin, Wilson, Long's, Quandary, Antero, James, Shavano, Uncompahgre, Crestones, Princeton, Bross, Holy Cross, Baldy, Sneffles, Pike's, Castle, Yale, San Luis, Red Cloud, Wetterhorn, Simpson, Æolus, Ouray, Stewart, Maroon, and Cameron. Of those over 13,000 feet which have received names, Handie lacks but three feet of belonging to the first class, then Capital, Horseshoe, Snowmass, Grizzly, Pigeon, Blaine, Frustrum, Pyramid, White Rock, Hague, R. G. Pyramid, Silver Heels, Hunchback, Rowter, Homestake, Ojo, Spanish

Peaks, Guyot, Trinchara, Kendall, Buffalo, Arapahoe, and Dunn. The nomenclature of these peaks betrays its unromantic, unscientific, undescriptive, and often commonplace origin, the accident of a mineral discovery by prospectors frequently giving the appellative; for the precious metals lie far up among the eruptive rocks, and the gnomes of these lofty peaks are often the Smiths and the Joneses.

The lakes of Colorado, with the exception of the San Luis group, lie from eight to eleven thousand feet above sea, and may therefore be reckoned a part of the mountain scenery. At the foot of the Saguache range, near the source of the Arkansas, are the Twin lakes, one three and a half miles by two and a half in extent, the other one third as large, and both furnishing delicious trout, while the surrounding mountains abound in game. Not far distant, at the foot of Mount Massive, set in terraces of the mountain, surrounded by gently sloping shores, is a group of silvery sheets of purest water, which pass under the collective and inappropriate name of Evergreen lakes, one lake being five hundred feet above the principal group, of which it is a feeder, and the lower and larger single lake occupying a terrace to itself. None are large, this one being but about fifty acres in extent, but all are highly picturesque, with clear water which lets the speckled trout be plainly seen. The middle terrace furnishes some rare mineral springs, the water of which bubbles sparklingly out of the earth around the lake, adding to the other attractions of the place. The view overlooks the valley of the Arkansas river, with clumps of trees upon its banks contrasting with the bright mineral stains upon its banks, while above all towers the background of ever-present mountains.

On the west side of Front range, in the edge of Middle park, occupying the trough of a glacier basin, is Grand lake, in the immediate shadow of Roundtop mountain, which, with other high peaks, guards its solitudes. It is three miles long by two in breadth, and hundreds of feet in depth. On its dark face are mirrored the surrounding mountains and the clouds that crown them. Down from the gorges sweep windy currents which would make navigation dangerous. So awe-inspiring is it that the Indians fear to approach, leaving it to our irreverent race to violate the God-like loneliness of the place.

Chicago lakes, the highest yet discovered, being 11,500 feet above the sea, are near the headwaters of Chicago creek, on the eastern flank of the Rocky or mother range. They are two in number, and, like Grand lake, surrounded by peaks, and of unknown depth, but are of small area. Their origin was undoubtedly the same. San Luis lake, in the lower and more extensive San Luis park, is the only large body of water in Colorado, and has the additional peculiarity of being without any outlet, although receiving the water of sixteen tributaries. It is situated in the middle of the park, and extends sixty miles north and south. About its borders are vast deposits of peat. Stories are told of a subterranean lake in Colorado, ten acres in extent, covered with eighteen inches of soil, which has a corn-field on it; and if one digs a hole, and drops a hook and line, a fish without eyes or scales, but otherwise resembling a perch, is caught. In a country so abounding in minerals, springs with medical qualities, both hot and cold, should be looked for, and here, indeed, we find them. They are of all ingredients and proportions, and with the invigorating air of the mountains make the state a vast sanitarium.

Time was when, if you believed travellers' tales, the great American desert stretched up to the foot of the Stony mountains, and all was unfruitful and forbidding. How, little by little, this obloquy was removed, and Colorado made known to the world in its true and very different character, it is my pleasant task to relate.

CHAPTER II.

DISCOVERY AND OCCUPATION.

1541-1853.

PROBABLY the inquisitive and not well-behaved followers of Coronado, in their marches from New Mexico in search of Quivira, did not set foot within the present limits of Colorado. If they did, they have left no record of their explorations, and no sign of them remains; and though they affirm having found structures similar to the ruins which exist in southern Colorado, they found them in what is now New Mexico. The expedition of the Spanish captain, in 1541, at the instance of a native of fabled Quivira, brought him possibly across the extreme southeast corner of the state; but since the guides complained that in his march he went too far east, it is hardly probable. Changing his course, he found Quivira, an Indian village not different from those we may see to-day, in latitude 40°, but far out on the plains, among the northern tributaries of the Arkansas. A few persons, priests and their attendants, remained with the Indians; some of them in time returned to Mexico, and some died by the hands of their converts. Many narrators, who have hastily glanced over an account given by some previous writer as careless as themselves, state confidently that Coronado was the first European in Colorado, and so he would have been had he been there at all.[1]

About the middle of the eighteenth century considerable interest was manifested by the authorities of New Mexico in the country to the north of Santa Fé, and Cachupin, who was governor for a long time in the last half of the century, set on foot one or more expeditions, the object of which was to ascertain the true character and value of the minerals to be found in what is now known as the San Juan country. After these came the expedition of Juan María Rivera in 1761, which was prosecuted as far as the Gunnison river. He was accompanied by Don Joaquin Lain, Gregorio Sandoval, Pedro Mora, and others. There is no doubt that a number of expeditions, of only local importance, were made into what is now Colorado, both east and west of the continental divide. About fourteen years after Rivera's tour, Padre Junípero Serra, president of the California missions, urged the ecclesiastics of New Mexico to undertake the exploration of a route from Santa Fé to the coast of upper California. With this object in view, Padre Francisco Silvestre Velez Escalante, ministro doctrinero of Zuñi, and Padre Atanacio Dominguez, visitador comisario of New Mexico, organized an expedition in 1776, which consisted, besides themselves, of Pedro Cisneros, alcalde mayor of Zuñi, Bernardo Miera y Pacheco, capitan miliciano of Santa Fé, Don Joaquin Lain, who having accompanied Rivera, was official guide of this expedition, and

---

[1] Greenhow, who is usually well informed, says Quivira was probably the region about the headwaters of the Arkansas and Platte rivers, but Coronado's route would not have brought him so far west and north. *Or. and Cal.*, 63. Some of the Spanish writers have committed serious blunders in geography, making the sea visible from Quivira. See *Hist. North Mex. States.* Inman, *Stories of the Santa Fé Trail*, 11–59, has an account of Coronado's march, and gives his course quite correctly. This is a well written and captivating series of legends and tales of the great historic highway of the plains, by Henry Inman of Kansas, 1881.

five soldiers, Lorenzo Oliveras, Lucrecio Muñiz, Andrés Muñiz, Juan de Aguilar, and Simon Lucero.

They set out from Santa Fé July 29th, and proceeded to Abiquiú on the Rio Chama, from whence they took a north course to the Rio San Juan, reaching it three leagues below the junction of the Navajo August 5th. The place of contact was called Neustra Señora las Nieves, and, although not the first place named in Colorado, as we shall see, is the first whose date is unquestioned. From Nieves they took a course north-west, across the several affluents of the San Juan, which lay between them and the Rio de Nuestra Señora de los Dolores, the names of which have been retained to the present as Piedra Parada, Pinos, Florida, and Las Animas. The eastern section of the La Plata range was called by Escalante Sierra de la Grulla. The La Plata river he called the San Joaquin, and in the cañon, says his narrative, were the mines sought for by Cachupin's explorers, and which gave the name to the mountains, supposed to contain silver.

Escalante's descriptions of the country passed over avoid dwelling upon the exceeding roughness of this region, dwelling rather upon the beauty and fertility of the small valleys, the grandeur of the forests of pine which grew upon the high benches and mountain sides, and the abundance of water, even that which fell from the clouds, of which he complained a little. At the Rio Mancos, or San Lázaro, he again heard reports of mines. At the Rio Dolores he beheld ruined habitations high up in the south bank. On this river he met with some difficulty in travelling, being sometimes at a distance from the stream, and at other times apparently confined to its cañon. The stations or camps along the Dolores were named Asuncion, Agua Tapada, Cañon Agua Escondida, Miera Labarinto (in honor of the capitan), and Ancon San Bernardo. At the latter place he found some Utes, from whom he obtained a guide; and observing three paralyzed women of the tribe at the junction of a small stream with the Dolores, he named it the Paraliticas. It was at this point, or near it, that he left the cañon of the river, and came out in Gypsum valley, or Cajon del Yeso, still so called. Climbing upon a mesa, he travelled six leagues north-east to the next station, San Bernabé. Six leagues north from this point brought him, through a cañon, to the San Miguel, or, as he called it, Rio San Pedro. Encamping at stations on the north side named San Luis, San Felipe (where were traces of Rivera's passage), Fuenta de la Guia, and passing through the cañada Honda, which was doubtless the Uncompahgre park, to Ojo de Lain (named in honor of the official guide), he reached the Uncompahgre river, spelled by him Ancapagari, and named Rio San Francisco. Escalante gives the distance travelled from the San Miguel to the Uncompahgre as twenty-four and a half leagues, which is proof conclusive, if any other than descriptions were needed, of his long detour through the Uncompahgre country. His first station beyond was San Agustin. The distance from the crossing of the Uncompahgre, in a north-east course, was ten leagues to the Gunnison river, which he said was called by the natives Tomichi, but which was called by him San Javier. His probable crossing of the Gunnison was near the junction of the south and north forks. To this region Rivera's explorations had reached, and farther down a cross had been cut in the rock of the river bank. Four leagues up the Gunnison, in a north-east direction, he came to a stream, which he named Santa Rosa ; and proceeded further, in the same course, to Rio Santa Mónica, which corresponds to the north branch of the north fork of the Gunnison. Following the direction of this stream, he came to the Rio San Antonia Mártir, which is the Divide creek of the present. Even the two buttes, known as the North and South Mam, are named San Silvestre (after Escalante himself), and Nebuncari. The

Mam creek of the present day was at that time called
Santa Rosalía.   Near here he forded the San Rafael
or Grand river, the course of the travellers seeming
to lead over Book cliffs, and thence north-west to
White river, called by them San Clemente, where
they arrived September 9th, about at the point where
it crosses the boundary of Utah, having spent a little
more than two months on the journey, and travelled

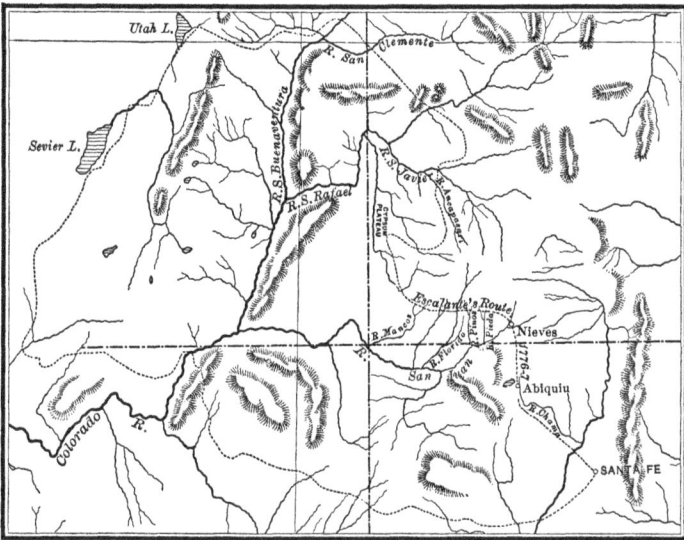

ESCALANTE'S ROUTE.

from the Dolores $86\frac{1}{2}$ leagues.   In two places on his
route Escalante mentioned other roads, and especially
that there was a shorter way from the Gunnison to
the Grand river than the one he was taking.   He
crossed this road near the stream he called Santa
Rosalía.   Beyond White river he found hills of
loose slate, passed through a long cañon, on the wall
of which were painted three shields and a spear, and
two warriors in combat ; saw veins of metal, and
found buffalo trails, from which he named this defile
Arroyo del Cíbolo.   At Green river he found a group

of six large cottonwood trees, and one lone tree. On one of these Lain carved his name and the date, 1776, with a cross above and below. The company returned from Utah by a more southern route, and the Spanish trail was established not far north of the 37th parallel in Colorado, crossing southern Utah, and thence southwest to Los Angeles. A trail to Salt Lake was, however, established at a later period, which crossed the boundary of Colorado and Utah on the south side of Rio Dolores, which was surveyed as late as 1857 by Captain J. N. Macomb for the United States Government.[2]

In the beginning of the seventeenth century France claimed the sovereignty of the country, and during that period several expeditions were undertaken toward the Spanish frontier, a not very clearly defined boundary.[3] The most important of these was conducted by Monsieur La Salle, who first having in 1682 explored the Mississippi from the Illinois region to the gulf of Mexico, and named the region contiguous Louisiana, in 1685 took formal possession of Texas, and founded a colony or two near the gulf, on the Guadalupe and Colorado rivers. But La Salle was assassinated, and the only effect of his settlement was to carry the western boundary of Louisiana as far west as these rivers.[4] In the mean time the country west of the Mississippi had again changed hands, Spain claiming it from 1762 to 1800, when it was retroceded to France, and sold by the first Napoleon to the United States three years afterward. Still the boundary was unsettled, and in 1806 an arrangement was entered into between the Spanish and American authorities that the former should not cross the Sabine, nor the latter approach to it, To prevent collisions,

[2] *Dominguez and Escalante, Diario y derrotero para descubrir el camino desde Santa Fé á Monterey.* In *Doc. Hist. Mex.*, 2d ser., i. 375-558. See also *Hist. Utah*, this series.

[3] Among these few are mentioned one by Col Wood in 1654, and another by Capt. Bolt in 1670; but they were productive of nothing in particular.

[4] *U. S. Laws and Docs*, 1817, 5.

orders were given not to survey the public lands west of the meridian of Natchitoches, or Red river.

But the curiosity of the new proprietors of Louisiana concerning the regions toward the Rocky mountains could not be restrained; and President Jefferson, also desiring to know something of them, encouraged exploration. It happened that Zebulon Montgomery Pike, son of Zebulon Pike of New Jersey, an officer in the revolutionary army, who at the age of twenty had been appointed an ensign in his father's company, and was a lieutenant at twenty-six, was serving under General Wilkinson in the west, at the time when Lewis and Clarke were fitting out their expedition to the head waters of the Missouri and Columbia in 1804.

General Wilkinson, whose military duties included keeping peace with the Indians, thought to serve his country and gratify the president by sending young Pike to explore the upper Mississippi, under the pretence of communicating with Indian tribes in that region. To this end, in August 1805, a keel-boat seventy feet long, manned by a crew of one sergeant, two corporals, and seventeen privates, under Lieutenant Pike, left St Louis to discover the source of the Mississippi, being provisioned for four months. He had started late for such an undertaking, encountering many difficulties, and performing the last part of the journey with sledges drawn by his men. On the last of January 1806 he reached the utmost source of the great river, arriving at a fort of the Northwest Fur company, by whose officers he was generously entertained. He returned to St Louis about the last of April.

General Wilkinson had meanwhile found cause for another expedition, having on his hands some rescued captives of the Kaw nation, who lived on the Osage river, a southern branch of the Kansas, and whom he had promised to restore to their people. On this errand, possibly, Pike set out July 15th, after a brief rest at home with his family.

His party consisted of one lieutenant, one surgeon, one sergeant, two corporals, sixteen privates, and an interpreter, besides fifty-one Indians of all ages, and both sexes. He ascended the Missouri in two boats, taking six weeks to this part of the journey, which brought him to the Osage river. Here he landed his expedition, purchased horses, loaded them with provisions and presents, and set out north-westward across the plains, delivering his Indian wards to their people as previously agreed upon. Having performed this part of his duty, he entered upon the more interesting one of exploration. Crossing the country to the Arkansas river he ascended that stream, finding the plains black with buffaloes. At two o'clock on the afternoon of the 15th of November he first discerned a small blue cloud, which being viewed with a spy-glass he perceived to be a mountain. A half hour later the range came into view, and his men gave "three cheers for the Mexican mountains."

It was already too late in the autumn for mountain travel, but Pike knew nothing of fear or discouragement. Pressing eagerly forward for yet another week, he at length reached the most eastern ridge of the Colorado range, thinking to come to the base of the peak which bears his name; but finding, when with great toil and suffering from struggling through snow that he was still distant fifteen miles from this mountain, he relinquished the attempt, his men being without proper clothing, and having quite worn out their stockings. Before beginning the ascent Pike had established a depot at or near the mouth of Fontaine-qui-Bouille, where he left most of his party; thence he moved camp nearer to the foot of the Sangre de Cristo range, about where Cañon city now stands. The cold was severe, and many of the men were frostbitten. Leaving these in camp he began exploring for a river by which he might return to the Mississippi, it having been specially charged upon him to discover if possible the sources of the Red river.

Coming to the South park by the present route from Cañon City, he called the first stream he reached the Platte, in which curiously enough he was correct; but in his wanderings striking the head of Grand river, he believed it to be the Yellowstone. Other errors were entered on his chart, given in chapter XV of my *Arizona and New Mexico.* The geography of the west was very vague as yet; and toiling about in the mountains with the mercury below zero was but a poor way to improve it.

But in the South park he made a discovery that white men and Indians had been there before him, and that recently. Not wishing to fall into the hands of Mexicans or Indians, he retreated toward the south, and became entangled among the cañons of the upper portion of the Arkansas river, but finally reached camp with only one horse able to travel. After a little rest he again set out, this time on foot, in search of Red river, and crossing the Arkansas, violated the terms of the recent arrangement by entering Mexican territory. Marching up the Wet Mountain valley, leaving disabled men by the way in improvised shelters, he moved straight to and up the Sangre de Cristo range, and from its summits looked down on San Luis park and the Rio Grande del Norte, which he believed to be the Red river. Greatly rejoiced, he descended to the valley, erected a fortified camp, and sent back a detachment of his little party to pick up the stragglers.

Not long did he enjoy his dreams of success. The Mexican authorities had been on the lookout for his expedition, which had become known to them, and a few days after completing the above arrangements he was politely arrested by a squad of Mexican soldiers, and persuaded to accompany them to Santa Fé, El Paso, and subsequently to Chihuahua, more than a year being consumed in this courteously managed captivity, during which the most valuable portion of his papers were lost, and his command scattered. They were finally returned to the United States through Texas.

One thing pertinent to the subsequent history of Colorado, Lieutenant Pike discovered during his detention in New Mexico. An American, James Pursley, of Bairdstown, Kentucky,[5] whom he met there, showed him lumps of gold brought by himself from the South park; and he learned that the traces of white men and Indians seen by him, and which had turned him southward, related to gold discoveries in that region.[6] In 1807 Pike was permitted to return home, and in the second year of the war of 1812 was killed at the assault on Toronto, after having been previously promoted to the rank of brigadier-general.[7] The peak which bears his name was measured by him, on the base of a mile, and on the presumption that the plains were 8,000 feet above sea-level. He made the height of the mountain to be 18,581 whereas it is really but 14,147. Most early explorers exaggerated the height of mountains, whether purposely or not.

[5] Pursley went up the Platte in 1803 or 1804, and was conducted by Indians to Santa Fé. A French creole, La Lande, took some goods up the Platte in 1804 for his employer, Morrison, a merchant of Kaskaskia; but he took the goods to Santa Fé, and established himself in business, where he remained. *Barber's Hist. West. States*, 549.

[6] W. B. Vickers, in *Hayden's Great West*, 98, says there is no evidence to show that there were any settlers in Colorado previous to 1843, or any knowledge of the treasures hidden in the soil or rocks at that time. This is a hasty conclusion. The Spanish-Mexicans would conceal as much as possible any such knowledge from Americans; but it existed. The American referred to above discovered the gold on the head of the Platte while a captive in the hands of the Indians; and he assured Pike he had been frequently solicited to go and show a detachment of Mexican cavalry where to find it, but refused. It was probably this detachment which had just left the park when Pike arrived in it. Appendix to *An Account of an Expedition to the Sources of the Mississippi, and Through the Western Part of Louisiana, etc;, in the Years 1805, 1806, and 1807; Philadelphia, 1810.* I have seen it stated that old deserted shafts had been found in southern Colorado, together with some copper vessels, the writer attributing these evidences of mining to the ancients who inhabited the ruined cities and the cliffs; but these people used only stone implements, and clearly knew nothing of mining. The prospect holes were undoubtedly made by the Mexicans about the beginning of the century.

[7] *James Parton,* in *The Discoverer of Pike's Peak,* MS., 7, an abridgement of Parton's account of Pike's expeditions. See also *Denver Rocky Mountain Herald,* Aug. 21, 1875.

Probably the cold had something to do with the reported altitude of Pike's peak.[8]

No further official explorations of the country at the base of the Rocky mountains were ordered until after the treaty of the 22d of February, 1819, by which the boundary between the possessions of Spain and the United States was definitely settled,[9] giving to the latter the northern two thirds of the present state of Colorado, with all the country north of the Arkansas river. Immediately after the confirmation of the Florida treaty, Secretary-of-war Calhoun ordered an expedition more complete in equipment than any which had preceded it, comprising besides military officers a number of men of science. The company, commanded by Major Stephen H. Long, left Pittsburgh May 30, 1819, and proceeded by a steam-vessel, constructed especially for the purpose, to St Louis, and thence by land travel to Council Bluffs, on the Missouri, where they wintered. In the following June, Long explored the Platte valley to the junction of the north and south forks, where he took the di-

[8] From the original *Pike's Expedition*—for a biographical notice of which see my *History of the Northwest Coast*—come scores of accounts which follow, such as is found in the *Colorado Gazetteer* for 1871. This book, which contains besides a brief history of the state, a comprehensive account of its mining, agricultural, commercial, manufacturing interests, and climate, will be frequently referred to for statistics on these subjects. Notice of Pike's expedition is found in *Thomas B. Corbett's Colorado Directory of Mines*, 1879, p. 34. This also is an important book of reference, containing a description of the mines and mills, and the mining corporations. *The Northwest*, by Samuel J. Parker, son of Samuel Parker, explorer and missionary to the Oregon country in 1835, is a manuscript history of the north-west country, compiled partly from the father's writings and partly from the accounts of other explorers. It is, like the other missionary writings, very bitter against the fur companies. A writer in *Harper's Magazine*, xli. 372, gives a good brief account of Pike's expeditions.

[9] *U. S. Laws and Treaties, 1815–21*, vi. 614–29. This boundary, which was changed by conquest and purchase, subsequently gave the U. S. the Florida territory east of the Mississippi. West of the Mississippi the line began at the mouth of the Sabine river, continuing north along the west bank of that stream to the 32d degree of north latitude, thence due north to the Red river, which it followed up to the degree of longitude 23 west from Washington, running thence due north again to the Arkansas river, which it followed to its source in latitude 42° north, and thence it was drawn westward on that parallel to the 'South sea.' It will be seen that this boundary supposed the Arkansas river to be two degrees longer than it really was, and left the actual boundary from central Colorado northward to the 42° still in doubt.

rection of the southern branch, which brought him to the South park by a route different from that of Pike's. The high peak first seen by Lieutenant Pike received the name of E. James, botanist of the expedition,[10] he being the first man known to have reached a summit of the Colorado mountains. He also measured it, and made it almost as much too low as Pike had made it too high.[11] Long descended the valley of the Arkansas to the Mississippi, having gained much valuable geographical information of the country explored. But his account was not one pleasing to the secretary of war, or to the government. He represented the whole country drained by the Missouri, Arkansas, Platte, and their tributaries as unfit for cultivation, and uninhabitable in consequence. He found all between the 39th and 49th parallels, and for five hundred miles east of the Rocky mountains, a desert of sand and stones, whereupon this region was represented on maps as the Great American desert. The report of Long was a stumbling-block in the way of the advocates of the American claim to Oregon in congress for many years, for no sooner did an advocate of that claim open his mouth than he was reminded of Major Long's scientific observations and explorations, and asked what value could attach to a desert. This impression was to some extent the key which kept Colorado a locked treasure-house until Oregon and California had both been settled, and proved to be rich agricultural countries, even where they had appeared as much deserts as Colorado.

It should be borne in mind that small parties of adventurers, like Pursley, had already penetrated the Rocky mountains in advance of either of the above-

---

[10] The name of Pike has been retained, but to James and Long were given peaks elsewhere. For Long's note on the subject see *Long's Exped. Rocky Mountains*, ii. 45. Another peak has been named after Lieut Graham of Long's party, and the hot springs on the Arkansas after Captain Bell. *Col. Gazetteer*, 21; *Frémont's Explor. Exped.*, 30.

[11] James called Pike's peak 11,500 feet high. Frémont in 1843, made it 14,300. Its present received measurement was made in 1862 by Parry, whose careful examination of the country entitles his work to credit.

named expeditions,[12] and that previous to that of Long's, a number of traders had established posts on

[12] See *Hist. Northwest Coast*, this series. A little work by David H. Coyner, first published in 1847, and republished in Cincinnati in 1859, called *The Lost Trappers*, gives a particular account of the wanderinge of a company of 20 men who left St Louis in 1807, intending to cross the Rocky mountains. The leader was Ezekiel Williams, and this was the first overland expedition to the Pacific of the kind ever undertaken. It proceeded to the Mandan village under the guidance of a chief of that tribe, Big White, who had accompanied Lewis and Clarke to Washington, and was returning to Fort Mandan. From this point Williams's party proceeded by land to the mouth of the Yellowstone, up which they travelled looking for beavers. Soon after finding a locality where beavers were plenty in the streams and buffaloes upon the plains, a hunting party of ten men went out, but were set upon by Indians, whom they believed to be Blackfoot, and five of them slain, the other five escaping to camp. The company at once set off again southward until they fell in with the Crows, by whom they were so well treated that a man named Rose, who had joined the party at St Louis, but whose character as an outlaw was not known to Williams, determined to remain among them, and did so until 1823, being the first white man who had a residence in the Yellowstone country. He returned as guide to Fitzpatrick and Sublette, and afterward joined the American Fur company, but was ever one of those unprincipled men who gave to the trappers the unsavory character dwelt upon by the Parkers. Williams' party, now reduced to 14 members, proceeded in a direction toward the South pass, and when upon the headwaters of the north Platte were attacked by Crows and sustained another loss of five men. In the first attack one Indian had been killed; in this fight, for which the company were prepared by the the theft of their horses, twenty or more of their enemies were killed. The party now reduced to ten, their horses being gone, hastened on foot out of the vicinity of the battle-ground, caching their furs and such things as they could not carry on a long march, and moved southward, wandering about until spring, when they found themselves on the sources of the south Platte, and of course in Colorado. One after another of them were cut off by the Comanches until only three remained, Williams, James Workman, and Samuel Spencer, who determined to return to St Louis if they could. But as often happens, misfortune had made them not only reckless, but at enmity with one another; and the three wanderers separated, Williams journeying down the Arkansas, which he mistook for Red river, in a canoe, and by travelling at night arrived safely among the Kansas, who directed him to Fort Cooper, on the Missouri. Here he found an Indian trader of the U. S., C. Cibley, about to pay the Indians their annuities, and who first compelled the Kansas to return to Williams several packages of furs they had stolen from him after his departure from their village. In the following year, 1809, Williams returned to the mountains with a party and recovered the furs cached by his company on the Platte. Workman and Spencer in the meantime had made their way to the Arkansas, which they also mistook for the Red river, and in following which toward its source they discovered the trail of Pike's party of the year before, who had cut in the rocks the name of Red river, which confirmed them in their error. Hoping to find that its headwaters were in a range by crossing which they would find themselves at Santa Fé in New Mexico, they followed up this stream, coming in sight of Pike's peak, which they said seemed so high 'that a cloud could not pass between its top and the sky.' They became entangled among the mountains and cañons of Colorado, passing many weeks in endeavoring to find the sources of the Rio Grande Del Norte, but coming instead to the Rio Colorado, which they followed—believing it would take them to Santa Fé—until they came to a crossing and a plain trail, which they resolved to follow. Meeting a Mexi-

the Arkansas and other rivers,[13] forerunners of the more powerful fur companies. A profitable trade was also carried on between the merchants of St Louis and the inhabitants of New Mexico, of which all of Colorado south of the Arkansas river was a part. The Indians on the Santa Fé route—the Comanches of the plains—gave traders and travellers much trouble; and in 1823 the government ordered an escort, commanded by Captain Riley, to meet the Santa Fé train, and conduct it to the Missouri frontier.[14] He advanced to the crossing of the Arkansas, and conducted it to Independence, the eastern terminus of the Santa Fé trail, the first military expedition by United States troops west of the Missouri and north of Texas. Four years afterward Fort Leaven-

can caravan bound to Los Angeles, California, two days afterward, they joined it, and the following spring returned with it to Santa Fé, where they remained trading for 15 years. When Workman and Spencer set out to descend the Colorado it was by canoe. From the description given by them to the author of the Lost Trappers, I think they were upon the Gunnison branch of the Colorado, and that it was the black cañon which interrupted their navigation. The crossing of the Spanish trail could not have been far from the present crossing of the Salt Lake road. At all events, they were the first Americans to float upon the waters of this stream, or, so far as I have discovered, to cross the Rocky mountains south of Lewis and Clarke's pass.

[13] Manuel Lisa, a Mexican, enjoyed a monopoly of the Indian trade west of the Missouri at the beginning of the century under a grant of the Mexican government. Peter Choteau, a rival trader and U. S. agent for the Osages, managed to separate a part of that nation from their adherence to Lisa, and established a post among them on the Verdigris branch of the Arkansas in 1808. It was, however, removed in 1813, and it was not for ten years afterward that a regular fur trade to the Rocky mountains was begun.

[14] This was in consequence of the capture of the previous year's train from Santa Fé, commanded by Capt. Means, who, with several of his men, was killed. Coyner relates that in 1823 the Mexican government, having banished several citizens of importance for alleged treasonable designs, permitted them to go to the U. S. with the annual Santa Fé train, and sent as an escort a company of 60 men, Mexicans and Pueblo Indians, under Capt. Viscarro, who was to conduct the exiles along the road until he met Capt. Riley. When near the Cimarron river, 60 miles from the crossing of the Arkansas, he was attacked, and 8 or 10 of his command killed. Viscarro himself is accused of cowardice. The Pueblos and two Americans named Barnes and Wallace fought and pursued the Comanches, inflicting severe loss upon them. The company hoping to meet Riley at the Arkansas, yet fearing that he might be gone, sent a detachment, consisting of the Pueblos, Wallace, Barnes, and Workman, to overtake him. They found he had moved away from the river, but overtook him in two days' travel, and detained him until the train came up, after which they were under the protection of American troops, and Viscarro with his depleted force turned back to Santa Fé. Coyner's Lost Trappers, 170-86.

worth was established on the west bank of the Missouri, twenty miles above the mouth of the Kansas river, and near enough to the Santa Fé trail to afford protection to travellers. For many years this was the initial point of expeditions west and northwestward, as all books of travel show. In 1829 Major Riley, with four companies, escorted a caravan as far as Bent's fort, on the Arkansas. Captain Wharton was on the trail in 1834, and Captain Cook in 1843.

The establishment of a fort in the Indian country did not precede but followed the adventures of private individuals and associations in the public territory of the United States, to which I have already referred. Among those who followed their pursuits in Colorado were the Bents, St Vrain, Vasquez, Bridger, Carson, Lupton, Pfeiffer, Nugent, Pattie, Baker, Beckwourth, Sarpy, Wiggins, the Gerrys, Chabonard, and others. Bonneville's company of trappers and explorers passed through the Arkansas country in 1834.[15]

[15] See *Victor's River of the West*, 157, and *Hist. Northwest Coast*, this series. It is difficult to give satisfactory accounts of men who lead a wandering life in an unsettled country. Only scraps of information are preserved, whose authenticity may well be questioned. From the best information obtainable the following biographies have been gathered: James P. Beckwourth was born in Virginia of a negro slave mother and an Irish overseer. His white blood impelled him to run away from servitude in or about 1817, and he joined a caravan going to New Mexico. Some years afterward he was in the service of Louis Vasquez in Colorado, and subsequently so ingratiated himself with the Crows that they made him head chief, an office in which he used to give the American Fur company much trouble. Later in life he severed his connection with savagery, and became interpreter and guide to government expeditions. He resided for a time in a valley of the Sierra Nevada, but being implicated in certain transactions which attracted the notice of the vigilants, fled and went to Missouri. When the migration to Colorado was at its height in 1859, he proceeded to Denver, and was taken into partnership with Vasquez and his nephew. Being tired of trade, he went to live on a farm, and took a Mexican wife; but fell out with her, and finally relapsed into his former mode of savage life, dying about 1867. *Montana Post*, Feb. 23, 1867. Bridger, Carson, Pattie, and others have been frequently spoken of in other volumes of this series. The last named came to the mountains of Colorado in 1824 with a company of 120 men. He was a youth at the time. The company fell apart, and drifted in various directions through New Mexico and Arizona. Pattie and a few companions descended the Colorado, and reached the coast at San Diego, naked and starving. They were arrested by the Mexican authorities and imprisoned, suffering much; but Pattie, on account of his knowledge of the Spanish language, was employed as an interpreter, and escaped back to the states. James Baker came out, probably with Bridger, and roved about in the mountains until he finally settled on Clear creek, four miles north of Denver, I do not

No forts of importance were erected within the present limits of Colorado before 1832, when the Bent brothers erected Fort William on the north branch of the Arkansas river, eighty miles northeast from Taos, and one hundred and sixty from the mountains.[16] They traded with the Mexicans and the Co-

know exactly at what date; but he is recognized as the first American settler in Colorado. He had an Indian wife and half-caste children grown to manhood in 1859. The occupation of the country displeased him, and he left Clear creek for the mountains of Idaho, where he ended his days. O. P. Wiggins, a Canadian, formerly a servant of the Hudson's Bay Co., came to Colorado in 1834, and was employed by the American Fur Co., and stationed at Fort St John. He became a wealthy citizen of Colorado. Peter A. Sarpey was one of the French families of St Louis. He had one trading-post in Colorado, and another at Bellevue in Nebraska; a small, wiry, mercurial-dispositioned man, who lived among savages simply to make money, which furthered no enterprises and purchased no pleasures such as a man of good family should value. Col Ceran St Vrain began trading to New Mexico in 1824, working up into American territory a few years later, where he built a fort named after himself. He died at Mora in New Mexico, in October 1870, to which country he returned on the ·decline of the fur trade. Godfrey and Elbridge Gerry were lineal descendants of Gov. Elbridge Gerry, one of the signers of the declaration of independence. They came to the Rocky Mountains while quite young men, and spent their lives on the frontier. After settlement began, Godfrey built an adobe residence on the Platte, and kept a station of the Overland Stage Co. During the Indian disturbance of 1864 his station was besieged—it went by the name of Fort Wicked—for days by a large force of the savages, who endeavored to fire the buildings. With no help but his own family he successfully resisted all their attempts to reduce his fort, and killed many of the besiegers. The Indians also conspired to capture Elbridge Gerry and his large band of horses, but his Indian wife having discovered the plot, informed him of it, and he, too, saved his life and property. These brothers were among the earliest settlers in Colorado. *Byers' Hist. Col.*, MS., 61-8. Elbridge Gerry died in 1876. Kit Carson, Bill Williams, Pfeiffer, the Autobeas brothers, John Paisel, and Roubideau were all noted mountaineers. Carson rendered himself a second time famous during the civil war. He died at Fort Lyon in June 1868. *Denver Rocky Mountain News*, June 3, 1868. Williams was killed by the Utes in south-western Colorado in 1850. *Folsom* (Cal.) *Telegraph*, Oct. 28, 1871. And so died many a brave man. But none who went to the mountains in those early times were better known than the Bent family of St Louis. There were six brothers, John, Charles, William, Robert, George and Silas. Robert and George died in 1841. Charles was the first American governor of New Mexico, and was killed in the massacre at Taos in March 1847. Silas, the youngest, was a member of the expedition to Japan under Perry, and made a report to the Geographical Society of New York concerning the warm current from the Japan sea, which touches the coast of North America. The other brothers were fur traders, and William was subsequently government freighter. He died May 19, 1869, the last of the original firm. *Colorado Paper*, in *Montana Democrat*, June 17, 1869; *Arkansas Val. Hist.*, 830.

[16] It is related, and is probably true, that Maurice, a French trader from Detroit, built a fortification on Adobe creek in Arkansas valley in 1830, which would give him precedence in point of time. He collected a Mexican settlement, and erected 13 adobe cabins around a square or plaza, in Mexi-

manches, Cheyennes, Arapahoes, and Utes. Fort William, after which the other trading-posts were modelled, consisted of an enclosure 150 by 100 feet in extent, surrounded by an adobe wall seven feet thick and eighteen feet high. At the north-west and south-east corners stood bastions ten feet in diameter and thirty feet high, with openings for cannon and small arms. A partition wall divided the interior, two-thirds of which was devoted to the necessary shops, storehouses, and dwellings, the remaining third being a corral in which the horses and mules were secured from theft at night. In the east wall was a large gate, with heavy plank doors, opened only on certain occasions. Adjoining the wall on the west was a wagon-house, made to shelter a dozen or more large wagons used in conveying goods from and peltries to St Louis. The tops of the houses were flat and gravelled, and served for a promenade in the evenings, like the house-tops of Egypt. There were about sixty persons employed in the affairs at Fort William, and many were the dangers they incurred and adventures they encountered;[17] for the region was the common ground of several of the most warlike tribes of the plains. Here, too, at different times were entertained travellers of every description and rank for a period of more than twenty years. In 1852 Bent blew up Fort William and moved his goods down the

can fashion, one of which was used as a church. In 1838 the Sioux and Arapahoes attacked the place, and were fought by the Utes, whose assistance had been sought. The battle was a bloody one, resulting in the victory of the Utes. This Mexican settlement was not entirely broken up until 1846. *Arkansas Val. Hist.*, 545–6. Among those earliest in the service of the fur companies were Bill Williams, John Smith, a young man of good education from Philadelphia, Ben. Ryder, C. de Bray, Metcalfe, and William Bransford, who later lived in Las Animas county.

[17] *Farnham's Travels in the Great Western Prairies*, 35. The author of this book was at Fort William in 1839, and wrote accurately of what he saw. He says: 'In the months of June, August, and September there are in the neighborhood of those traders from 15,000 to 20,000 savages, ready and panting for plunder and blood. If they engage in battling out old causes of contention among themselves the Messrs Bent feel comparatively safe in their solitary fortress. But if they spare each other's property and lives there are great anxieties at Fort William; every hour of day and night is pregnant with danger.'

Arkansas to the mouth of Purgatoire river, where he erected a new fort, which was leased to the government in 1859, when it was occupied by troops and called Fort Wise, after the governor of Virginia.

Another trading-post erected in 1832 was that of Louis Vasquez, five miles north-east of the site of Denver, at the junction of Vasquez fork or Clear creek with the Platte river. A nephew of Vasquez resided with him at the fort from 1832 to 1836, and was one of the first settlers in Colorado. Fort Sarpy was erected soon after the two above named, and was situated on the Platte, five miles below Vasquez's post. Five miles below Sarpy's post was another fort, whose name has been forgotten, and fifteen miles further down the river was Fort Lancaster, erected by Lupton, which in 1886 was in a good state of preservation. Fort St Vrain, ten miles below Lupton, at the confluence of the Cache le Poudre river with the Platte, was erected in 1838. The Bent brothers also had a post on the Platte before reaching the junction of the next stream below. So thickly clustered rival establishments in the first ten or fifteen years of trade in the Rocky mountains. Five miles above Fort William toward the mountains was El Pueblo, a Mexican post, although owned in part by Americans, and constructed very much on the plan of Fort William. It was not, like the others, a trading establisment, but a farming settlement, intended to supply the trading-posts with grain, vegetables, and live stock. The proprietors irrigated their farm with water from the Arkansas, and were undoubtedly the first agriculturists in this region; but as they neglected to water their potions of alcohol sufficiently at the same time, their enterprise did not flourish as it should, even in 1838.[18]

[18] Stone, *General View*, MS., 20–21, mentions a Col Boone, who had a trading post known as Hardscrable in the Arkansas valley, contemporary with St Vrain and others. Another post was on the site of Trinidad in Las Animas county. The St Vrain mentioned here, I have no doubt, was one of the family of that name which became possessed of a grant to certain lead

Somewhere between 1840 and 1844 another settlement was made on Adobe creek, further up the Arkansas on the south side, in what was later Frémont county. It was under the patronage of an association of traders, among whom were Bent, Lupton, St Vrain, Beaubien, and Lucien B. Maxwell, Beaubien having charge, and being the owner of a large grant of land from the Mexican government. The settlement was broken up in 1846 by the Indians.

A feature of the period to which I have just alluded was the obtaining of grants from the Mexican authorities for the purpose of colonization and development. As I have shown, success had not attended their efforts, but the grants were valid notwithstanding. The Vigil and St Vrain grant embraced nearly all of what is now Colorado south of the Arkansas river and east of the mountains, excepting the Nolan grant, a tract fifteen miles wide by forty miles in length, lying south of Pueblo. Under the treaty of 1848 the title to these lands was undisturbed, except that the United States government thought best to cut them down to eleven square leagues each, as enough to content republican owners. I shall have occasion to refer again to them in this history. On the Vigil and St Vrain grant James Bonney in 1842 founded the town of La Junta.

In 1841 the first immigrant wagon bound to the Pacific coast passed up the Platte valley, and taking the North fork, crossed the Rocky mountains into Oregon by the South pass; and soon it became the usual route instead of that by the Arkansas valley, being safer from Indian depredations. But whatever route was taken, no settlers came in these days from the United States to make their homes in the Rocky mountains; and even the hunters and trappers, whose

mines in 'upper Louisiana' by authority of the Baron de Carandolet, surveyor-general of Louisiana in 1796. This was James Ceran St Vrain, and the mines were in Tennessee.

numbers had once been that of a respectable army, were being killed off by the Comanches or absorbed by the half civilization of the Mexican border.

The first government expedition since Long's was set on foot in 1842 under Frémont, but did not more than touch Colorado this year. Returning in 1843–4, some explorations were made of this portion of United States territory. The only persons encountered in the Rocky mountains by Frémont [19] at this time were the few remaining traders and their former employés, now their colonists, who lived with their Mexican and Indian wives and half-breed children in a primitive manner of life, usually under the protection of some defensive structure called a fort. [20]

The first American families in Colorado were a part of the Mormon battalion of 1846, who, with

[19] Enough has been said about Frémont's expeditions elsewhere. He made no important discoveries in Colorado, those which he did make being noted under other heads. His expedition was very completely furnished. He left the Platte with a part of his command after reaching Fort Laramie, and following the South fork, came in sight of Long's peak July 8, 1842. He continued up the valley as far as St Vrain's fort, 17 miles east of that mountain, where he remained for three days only, returning on the 12th to rejoin his company. In 1843 he took a different route to the mountains, via the valley of the Kansas river and Republican fork, crossing thence to the Smoky Hill fork, and proceeding almost directly west to Fort St Vrain by the well-worn trails of the fur companies. From St Vrain, where he arrived July 4th, he continued up the Platte, seeing Pike's peak covered with new-fallen snow on the morning of the 10th. Crossing the divide between the Platte and Arkansas, he arrived on the 17th at Fontaine-qui-Bouille, or Soda Springs, near the eastern base of the peak, the same which Long had named after Capt. Bell. On the 19th he left this spot, and descending the river to the eastern fork, which was hastily surveyed, the party returned to Fort St Vrain, whence they proceeded north to Fort Laramie. Frémont mentions the fort called El Pueblo, and explains that the inhabitants were, at that time at least, a number of mountaineers, principally Americans, who had married Mexican women, and occupied themselves in farming and carrying on a desultory trade with the Indians. In 1844 he returned by a course which took him through the north-west corner of the state, through North park, which he called New park, through the South park, and to the Arkansas river, by which route he reached St Louis in the autumn. *Explor. Exped.*, 116. His 3d and last expedition in 1848 was a disastrous one, in which he lost most of his men, animals, and stores in an attempt to cross the mountains to Grand river in the dead of winter.

[20] Captain Gunnison in 1853 noticed a small settlement in the Culebra valley, and on the banks of the Costilla, where he found a little farming, wheat, corn, beans, and watermelons being among the productions. Six Mexican families were settled on the Greenhorn river, and at Sangre de Cristo pass an American named Williams was herding some stock. *Beckwith in Pac. R. R. Rept*, ii. ch. iii

their wives and children, resided at Pueblo from September to the spring and summer of the following year, when they joined the Mormon migration to Salt Lake. A number of persons later living in Utah were born at Pueblo in 1846–7.[21]

A number of houses [22] were erected by them for

[21] See *Hist. Cal.* and *Hist. Utah,* this series. From *Tyler's Mormon Battalion,* 126, 'I take the following names of persons who were quartered at Pueblo during this period: Gilbert Hunt, Dimick B. Huntington, Montgomery Button, John Tippets, Milton Kelley, Nicholas Kelley, Norman Sharp, James Brown, Harley Morey, Thomas Woolsey, S. C. Shelton, Joseph W. Richards, James T. S. Allred, Reuben W. Allred, Marvin S. Blanchard, James W. Calkins, David Garner, James H. Glines, Schuyler Hulett, Elijah E. Holden, Charles A. Jackson, Barnabas Lake, Melcher Oyler, Caratat C. Roe, John Sessions, John P. Wriston, Elam Ludington, John D. Chase, Franklin Allen, Erastus Bingham, William Bird, Philip Garner, Harmon D. Persons, Lyman Stephens, Dexter Stillman, William Walker, Charles Wright, Orson B. Adams, Alexander Brown, Jesse J. Brown, William E. Beckstead, William H. Carpenter, Isaac Carpenter, John Calvert, Francillo Durphy, Samuel Gould, John C. Gould, Jarvis Johnson, Thurston Larson, Jabez Nowlan, Judson A. Persons, Richard Smith, Milton Smith, Andrew J. Shupe, James Shupe, Joel J. Terrill, Solomon Tindall, David Wilkin, David Perkins, John Perkins, Thomas S. Williams, Arnold Stephens, Joshua Abbott, Jonathan Averett, William Costo, Abner Chase, James Davis, Ralph Douglas, William B. Gifford, James Hirous, Lorin E. Kenney, Lisbon Lamb, David S. Laughlin, Peter J. Meeseck, James Oakley, William Rowe, John Steel, Abel M. Sargent, William Gribble, Benjamin Roberts, Henry W. Sanderson, Albert Sharp, Clark Stillman, John G. Smith, Myron Tanner, Almon Whiting, Edmund Whiting, Ebenezer Hanks, Samuel Clark, George Cummings, Luther W. Glazier, J. W. Hess, Charles Hopkins, Thomas Karren, David Miller, William A. Park, Jonathan Pugmire, Jr, Roswell Stephens, Bailey Jacobs. These were detached and sent to Pueblo on account of sickness; first detachment from the crossing of the Arkansas, and a second one from Santa Fé. Those who had families were ordered to send them to Pueblo, except such as were retained for laundresses; but as their names are given but once, and that before the division, it is impossible to give the number of women who wintered in Colorado. There were 34 married women with the battalion, with children of all ages, to the number of 60 or 70. There were also several men, not enlisted, with the families, as John Bosco, David Black, James P. Brown, and others. Milton Kelley, Joseph W. Richards, John Perkins, Norman Sharp, Arnold Stephens, M. S. Blanchard, Milton Smith, Scott, and Abner Chase, died in Pueblo, or on the road to that place. The first white American born in Colorado was Malinda Catherine Kelley, daughter of Milton and Malinda Kelley, in Nov., soon after the death of her father, whose first child she was. Subsequently Mrs Fanny M. Huntington, wife of Captain Dimick B. Huntington, gave birth to a child, which died in a few hours. Eunice, wife of James P. Brown, bore a son, John; Mrs Norman Sharp a daughter; Albina, wife of Thomas S. Williams, a daughter, Phebe. A child of Capt. Jefferson Hunt, by his wife, Celia, died and was buried at Pueblo, and probably others, whose names have been forgotten; but from this record it is easy to imagine the remainder of a sad story of privation, death, and burial in a savage land, and children born to sorrow.

[22] See *Stone's Gen. View,* MS.; *Byers' Hist. Colo,* MS. The detachment sent from Santa Fé built 18 rooms 14 feet square, of timbers cut in the woods. *Tyler's Hist. Mormon Battalion,* 171. The first detachment may have built others.

winter quarters, and here were born, married,[23] and buried a number of their people. Driven out of Illinois at the point of the bayonet, seeking homes on the western side of the continent, they had accepted service under the government, which had failed to protect them in their direst need, for the sake of being provisioned and having their families transported across the continent. Of their strange history the winter in Pueblo was but an incident.[24] Another portion of General Kearny's army, under Colonel Price and Major Emory, travelled up the Arkansas as far as Bent's fort, where it turned off to Santa Fé by the Raton pass. This force consisted of 1,658 men, including Doniphan's 1st regiment of Missouri mounted volunteers.

Meanwhile there were no real military establishments in the whole region west and north-west of Fort Leavenworth; although, to protect the Oregon immigration, a chain of posts across the continent had been much talked of in congress; and it had been announced that Frémont's explorations were ordered with the design of establishing a permanent overland route, and selecting the sites for the posts which were to guard and render it safe. I have shown in my history of Oregon that this was not actually done before 1849, the intervention of the war with Mexico diverting the army to that quarter. But measures were taken early in March 1847 to select locations for two United States forts between the Missouri and the Rocky mountains, the sites selected being those now occupied by Kearney City and Fort Laramine, the latter being

[23] Almira, daughter of Capt. Nelson Higgins, was married to John Chase at Pueblo.

[24] I have noticed some erroneous statements concerning the Mormon battalion in my Colorado manuscripts. It was commanded in the first place by a regular officer, Col James Allen, 1st dragoons, though it was an infantry force. He died soon after the battalion left Leavenworth, and the command was taken by Lieut A. J. Smith, who reported to Col Doniphan at Santa Fé, the whole being under the command of Gen. Kearny. From Santa Fé to Los Angeles Col P. St George Cook commanded the battalion. See *Hist. Cal.* and *Hist. Utah*, this series.

purchased from the American Fur company.[25] The work of constructing and garrisoning these forts progressed slowly,[26] and it was not until some months after the close of the Mexican war that troops were stationed at them, although in 1847–8 there was a considerable force kept moving on the plains. In 1850 Fort Massachusetts was erected on Ute creek, at the west base of the main chain of the Rocky mountains, near Sangre de Cristo pass; the site being chosen the better to intercept the raiding bands of Utes, and was occupied, although the situation proved unhealthful, until 1857, when the present Fort Garland was substituted.[27]

In 1853 congress passed an act authorizing a survey of railroad routes from the Mississippi river to the Pacific ocean, that between the 38th and 39th parallels being entrusted to Captain J. W. Gunnison, of the Topographical engineers. Captain Gunnison began his survey at the mouth of the Kansas river, proceeded westward to Bent's fort, up the Arkansas to the Apishapa and Huerfano affluents, through Sangre de Cristo pass into San Luis park, the Saguache valley, and Cochetopa pass, down the Gunnison branch of the Colorado to its junction with Grand river, thence westward across the Wasatch range, in Utah, as far as the valley of Sevier lake and river, where he, with several of his party, was murdered October 26th[28] by Pah Utes. Gunnison's

[25] Fort Laramie was sometimes called Fort John. Byrse in his *Hist. Colo,* MS., 66, says it was St John, and that the government changed its name to Laramie. But it was known to travellers as Laramie a number of years before the purchase; and in *Bonneville's Adventures* it is called Fort William, probably after William Sublette, who built it in 1834, in conjunction with Robert Campbell. They sold it the following year to Milton Sublette and James Bridger, who went into partnership with the American Fur Company. There is a more complete account of Fort Laramie in my *History of Wyoming,* this vol. Hastings, in his *Or. and Cal.,* 136, mentions F't John as being one mile south of Fort Laramie.

[26] Rept of W. L. Marcy, sec. war, in *Niles' Reg.,* Dec. 13, 1848.

[27] Fort Garland is located in latitude 27° 35' north; longitude 27° 20' west; with an altitude of 7,805 feet. The reservation comprises 4 square miles, and lies between Sangre de Cristo and Ute creeks in San Luis park. *Surgeon-gen. Circ.,* 1870–4, 257; *Beckwith,* in *Pac R. R. Rept,* ii. 38.

[28] Gunnison had an escort of a dozen mounted riflemen, Co. A, under Capt. Morris. On the morning of Oct. 25th Gunnison, with F. Creutzfeldt

survey of the mountain passes of Colorado rendered it conclusive that there was no route equal to that travelled by the immigration through the great depression about the 42d parallel;[29] although the apprehension of obstruction from snow in this latitude continued to govern the views of those in authority, and in spite of the survey of the Northern Pacific railroad line, until the civil war forced the abandonment of the more southern routes.

botanist, R. H. Kern topographer, William Potter guide, John Bellows, and a corporal and 6 men, left camp to explore the vicinity of Sevier lake. On the next morning, most of the party being at breakfast, the Indians fired upon them from a thicket, and stampeding the horses, prevented their escape. Only 4 out of the 12 survived the attack. The corporal, who was able to mount, gave the first information to Capt. Morris, and the escort arrived on the scene of the massacre that evening too late to collect the remains of the murdered, which had been mangled by the savages, though not scalped, and torn and almost devoured by wolves during the night. *Beckwith* in *Pac R. R. Rept*, ii. 73–4; *Olympia Wash. Pioneer*, Jan. 21, 1854. See *Hist. Utah*, this series.

[29] See *Hist. Northwest Coast*, this series. The other government expeditions which have surveyed Colorado have been those military reconnoissances connected with railroads and mail routes. In 1854 Steptoe, on his way to Oregon with 300 troops, surveyed the country from New Mexico to Salt Lake City, and expended $25,000 in improving the route from that place to the southern California coast by the way of the Rio Vírgen and Muddy river and the Cajon pass. *U. S. Ex. Doc.*, 34th cong. 1st sess., i. pt 2, 504–7. The overland mail was carried over this route for several years, or until the war with the south compelled the adoption of the central route. In 1857 the government sent out an expedition under William M. Magraw to locate a wagon-road through the South pass. It was accompanied by a corps of scientific men, who made collections of the plants, minerals, and animals of the country. *Smithsonian Rept*, 1858, 50. Congress had at different times made appropriations for the exploration of the Rocky mts in the interest of science, and especially of geology. An expedition to the lower Yellowstone, under the command of G. K. Warren, of the U. S. Eng. corps, as early as 1856, was the first to become interested in the marvellous reports of the Yellowstone country through the medium of the fur-traders. James Bridger offered to guide the command to the head of the river, but the undertaking was not entered upon at that time. Warren had planned an expedition to Yellowstone lake for the years of 1859–60, but was superseded in command by Col Reynolds of his corps. Prof. F. V. Hayden was connected with the expedition of 1856, and had charge of the geological department in 1859–60; but Reynolds failed to make the passage of the Wind River mts, from which side he made his approach. At the same time a small party under Cook and Folsom, by approaching by the valley of the Yellowstone, crossed the divide into the geyser basin of the Madison river, but not until after W. W. De Lacy, as I have shown in my *History of Montana*, had penetrated to that spot from the head of Snake river, in 1863. In 1870 the sur.-gen. of Montana, Henry D Washburne, with a party of settlers reached the upper geyser basin, at the head of the Yellowstone, and N. P. Langford, one of the party, published an account of the discoveries made by the expedition in the May and June numbers of *Scribner's Magazine* for 1871. An army officer who accompanied the excursion in command of a small escort—Lieut G. C. Doane, 2d cav. —made an official report to Gen. Hancock, who forwarded it to the

sec of war, Belknap. These revelations of the wonders of the Rocky mts greatly stimulated research. Under the direction of the sec. of the int., Delano, the geological survey was resumed in 1871 in the mountain regions, Prof. Hayden being in charge. He proceeded from Odgen to Fort Hall, and thence to Fort Ellis, Montana, where he obtained an escort and made the long-contemplated visit to the geyser basin, of which there is a description in his report for 1871, being the 5th of the series. In the following year Hayden, with his photographer, W. H. Jackson, made a tour through a part of Colorado, and in his report for 1872 gave a brief general sketch of the scenery and the geological features, with analyses of the mineral springs; but his explorations were confined principally to the country north of the 41st parallel. In 1873 and 1874 the survey of Colorado was prosecuted with zeal. The headquarters of the company was at Denver, but it was separated into 7 divisions to prosecute specifically the work of the topographical, geological, botanical, zoölogical, archæological, paleontological, and photographical branches of the service, which in all respects was of great value to the country and to science at large. Hayden's report for 1874 contains, besides the strictly scientific history of the state, many interesting observations on the conditions of the country and its development at this date. All of his reports are written in a popular style, which enables the least studious reader to find some charm in them. *Daly's Address Am. Geog. Soc.*, 1873, 9–12, 55–6. In 1880 Hayden published a volume of general and scientific information concerning the intramontane states and territories which he called *The Great West*, containing over 500 pages, and made up of selected matter from other sources, with some descriptive matter from his own, in which 75 pages are devoted to Colorado. In 1873 an expedition was thrown into the field by the war department, under the general charge of Lieut George M. Wheeler, the primary object being to discover the most available routes for the transport of troops and wagons between interior posts, and incidentally to conduct researches in geology, zoölogy, botany, archæology, and other special branches of science. The expedition was in the field three years, and a part of it in Colorado most of the time. The force for 1875 was divided into two sections, one under the immediate direction of Wheeler, to start from Los Angeles for the survey of southern Cal. and Arizona, and another under Lieut William L. Marshall, to start from Pueblo for the survey of the southern part of Colo. and New Mex. I have referred in my *History of Nevada* to Wheeler's work in that state. Marshall's route from Pueblo meandered the sage plains east of the mountains, rounded the base of Pike's peak, through the Sangre de Cristo pass to Conejos, on the Conejas branch of the Rio Grande del Norte, where the real work of the expedition for Colo. began. The topography of the whole country west of the 100th meridian and between the parallels was secured by triangulation, and a series of maps made which omitted no faintest trail or smallest stream. Wheeler's publications consist of reports, maps, and photographs, and are of great geographical value. In 1867 the government ordered the geological survey of the 40th parallel, and the explorations were placed in charge of Clarence King, a man of many attainments, to whose work and that of his party I have referred in my *History of Nevada*. A large octavo volume published in 1870 at Washington on mining industry contains chapters on gold and silver mining in Colorado, by James D. Hague, with general and particular histories of the most noted mines and mineral districts, with illustrations, the whole being of much interest and value.

CHAPTER III.

GOLD DISCOVERIES.

1853-1859.

Mythological Mines—Men from Georgia—The Cherokees—Hicks and Russell—The Lawrence Party—Other Companies—Auraria versus Denver—The Town Builders—Early Merchants and Manufacturers—First Guide Books and Journals—Gold Discoveries on Boulder Creek and Clear Creek—Russell and Gregory—Central City and Fair Play—Pioneer Biography.

Up to 1853 Colorado's scant population still lived in or near some defensive establishment, and had been decreasing rather than increasing for the past decade, owing to the hostility of the Indians.[1] The great wave of population which rolled westward after the gold discoveries in California had its effect on this intermediate territory. Traditions of gold nuggets carried in shot-pouches of mountaineers are of early date, a Frenchman named Duchet[2] being one of the careless finders of the royal metal, "away back in the thirties." These stories were wafted abroad, and piqued the curiosity of the California bound pilgrims, who prospected, as opportunity offered, anywhere along the branches of the Platte river.[3] A party of Cherokees being en route to California, looking not only for gold, but for a new country in which to locate their people who had been invited to sell their

[1] Frémont, in his *Explor, Exped.*, 1843-4, mentions the taking of Roubideau's fort, on the Uintah branch of Green river, in northwestern Utah, by the Utes, soon after he passed it in 1814. The men were all killed and the women carried into captivity. Bent's fort was also captured subsequently, and the inmates slaughtered. The absence of the owners alone prevented their sharing the fate of their employés.

[2] *Hollister's Mines of Colorado*, 6; *Stuart's Montana*, 68-9.

[3] *Colorado Rem. in San Juan*, MS., 1.

(363)

lands in Georgia, taking the Arkansas valley route, and the trail by the Squirrel creek divide to the head of Cherry creek, made the discovery that gold existed in the streams of this region.   The party continued on to California, and returned in time to Georgia, where they attempted to organize an expedition for the Rocky mountains.   The news came to the ears of W. Green Russell, a miner of Dahlonega, Georgia, who also projected an expedition to this region.

In the meantime a Cherokee cattle trader from Missouri, named Parks, in driving his herds along the trail, and having had his eyes sharpened by the report of the previous company of his people, discovered gold in 1852, on Ralston creek, a small affluent of Vasquez, or Clear creek.[4]   A column of troops marching through the country a few years later made a similar discovery, on Cherry creek, on the southwest corner of the present state of Colorado; and in 1857 other troops made the same report concerning Cherry creek in the Platte region.[5]   Still, but little gold was found, and no excitement followed at that time.

Early in the spring of 1858 the Cherokees organized for a prospecting expedition to the vicinity of Pike's peak.   W. Green Russell joined their company with a party of white men.   Some difficulties occurring in passing through the country of the Osages, part of the Cherokees turned back.   The expedition, as finally organized for the plains, consisted of twelve white persons and thirty Indians, among whom were George Hicks, Sen.,[6] leader of the company, George Hicks, Jr, John Beck, who had organized the expedition, Ezekiel Beck, Pelican Tigre, and others.   The

[4] *Pabor's Colo. as an Agricultural State*, 21-22; *King's Geol. Explor.*, iii. 487-92.

[5] *Richardson's Hist. Gunnison County*, MS., 4; *Gilpin's A Pioneer of 1842*, MS., 3; *Corbett's Legis. Manual*, 36; *Hayden's Great West*, 99-100; *Harper's Mag.*, xli. 373-4.

[6] Hicks was a lawyer by profession, had served on the bench as judge, and was a notable man among the Cherokees.

white persons were George McDougal, brother of Governor McDougal of California, who had a trading post on Adobe creek, a Mr Kirk, wife and two children, Levi Braumbaugh, Philander Simmons, a mountaineer of a dozen years' experience, and Messrs Brown, Kelly, Johns, Taylor, and Tubbs. Kelly had a Cherokee wife, who with her sister accompanied him. The company left the Missouri frontier May 12th, and arrived at Bent's new fort in good season; but the winter had been severe and the spring late,[7] which made travelling difficult. Nor were their labors rewarded that season, though they prospected from the head of the Arkansas to the Platte, and thirty miles to the north; and only Russell remained, with half a dozen men, who ultimately found diggings where they took out fair wages, on a dry creek putting into the Platte seven miles south of the mouth of Cherry creek.

The fame of the Cherokee expedition spread through the Missouri river towns, and soon other companies were on the road to the mountains, without waiting for confirmation of the rumored discoveries. A company left Lawrence, Kansas, soon after the passage of the Hicks and Russell parties, consisting of fifty men, two of whom, Holmes and Middleton, had families, and went by the Arkansas valley route to the foothills of the Front range. At Pueblo they found a few Mexicans, and at Fountain City a mixed settlement of Americans and Mexicans, presided over by George McDougal. The company prospected southward as far as the Sangre de Cristo pass, some crossing the mountains to Fort Massachusetts for supplies. Returning northward along the base of the mountains, they remained two or three months in the Garden of the Gods at the foot of Pike's peak, which a party, including Mrs Holmes, ascended, this woman, being

---

[7] Simmons relates that in the Squirrel creek pineries they found the deserted camp of Capt. Marcy, who, on his way to join Jonnson's army, lost several men and a large number of sheep by the cold and snow encountered here. *Arkansas Val. Hist.*, 548.

the pioneer of her sex upon this lofty summit. Their
camp at this place was called by them Red rocks.

While in this vicinity, the Lawrence company laid
out a town at the site of Colorado springs, which they
called El Paso, from its location at the mouth of the
Ute pass of the mountains. Some of the company
took land claims along the Fontaine-qui-Bouille river,
above El Paso town site, covering portions of the
site where Colorado City now stands. · But as no one
came to purchase lots, and as no gold had been found
in the vicinity, El Paso town company became restless, and moved northward to the Platte, a number
of them encamping five miles above the present city
of Denver, where they again laid out a town, putting
up eighteen or twenty cabins, and calling it Montana.[8]
Here the company finally disbanded. Part of them
again engaged in a real estate venture, laying out the
town of St Charles, the site of which embraced 1,280
acres of the ground now occupied by Denver, possession of which was subsequently acquired by the
Denver people.[9] The greater portion of the Lawrence company returned to Kansas, some in the
autumn and others in the following spring. A few
wintered at Pueblo,[10] and while there were joined by
other companies [11] from the Missouri border.

[8] There was also a place called The Eleven Cabins, 14 miles below Denver,
on the Platte, but of its history I learn nothing, except the name of the
builder, John Rothrack, of Pa.

[9] The would-have-been founders of St Charles were Frank M. Cobb, Ad-
nah French, William Smith, and William Hartley. Cobb returned later in
the autumn to Kansas, leaving Charles Nichols in charge of the new town.
On his reappearance on Cherry creek in 1859, he found the Denver company
in possession. Cobb mined for three years, and was sutler from 1861 to 1865
to the army in the south, after which he went to Worcester, Mass., where he
was engaged in business until 1869, when he embarked in cattle raising and
mining in the Gunnison country. He was born at Minot, Maine.

[10] Among those who returned to Pueblo to winter were George Peck, Middleton, wife and child, and one McClellan. They returned to the states in
the spring, and to Colorado in the autumn of 1859. Peck, with a brother,
went to farming on the Goodnight rancho, where he remained till 1865, at
which time he engaged in mercantile business in the east. In 1872 he returned once more to Colorado, settling at Las Animas, where he again engaged in farming and cattle raising. In 1880 he was elected probate judge
for Bent county. He married Mary E. Rice in 1871. *Arkansas Val. Hist.*,
877–8.

[11] Few of the names of the Lawrence party have been preserved. John
T. Younker was one of those who remained. He was a native of Ohio, born

Meanwhile several other parties had set out from various points along the Missouri, arriving at Cherry creek in the autumn, by the route up the Platte. Foremost among these was a little company from Mills county, Iowa, consisting of D. C. Oakes,[12] H. J. Graham, George Pancoast, Abram Walrod,[13] and Charles Miles. They arrived on the 10th of October on the site of Denver, and after paying a visit to W. Green Russell at Placer camp, pitched their tents at this place.

Two weeks later a company of fifteen men arrived on Cherry creek, encamping on the west side of the stream. Among them was Henry Allen from Council Bluffs, Iowa, a practical surveyor, whose talent and instruments were soon called into the service of town companies. Small parties continued to arrive every few days, encamping for the most part on the west side of Cherry creek, which suggested, of course, a town ; and Auraria was duly organized in the latter part of October, with Allen as president of the company. The town plat was surveyed by him, assisted by William Foster. The first building erected was by Anselm H. Barker.[14] To add to the population,

Aug. 28, 1833, and bred a farmer. From farm life he went to school teaching, and next to telegraphy. He emigrated to Kansas just in time to become involved in the troubles there, joining the free state men, and fighting 'border ruffians.' After the failure of the Lawrence company to find gold, he took a land claim on the Platte, five miles from Denver, where he resided until 1879, when he removed to the city. In 1867 he married Annie R. Thompson.

[12] D. C. Oakes was born at Carthage, Maine, April 3, 1825. At the age of six years he removed with his parents to Gillion, Ohio, four years later to Ind., and the following year to Iowa. In 1849, his parents having died, young Oakes accompanied Abram Walrod to Cal., and mined on American river in partnership with A. R. Colton. Returning home after a few years of life in the mines, he married, and settled at Glenwood, Iowa, as a contractor and builder, remaining there until 1858, when he started for Pike's Peak. From this time his life is a part of the history of Colorado. *Denver Hist.*, 538.

[13] Abraham Walrod was born in N. Y., Jan. 22, 1825, bred a farmer, and educated at the common schools. In 1843 he removed to Iowa, and in 1849 accompanied D. C. Oakes to Cal., working in the mines for two years. On returning to Iowa he settled at Glenwood, whence he came to Colo in 1858, and engaged in mining. In 1852 he married Emily A. Cramblet of Ill. His daughter Mary was the first white girl born in Denver. *Denver Hist.*, 644–5.

[14] Barker was a native of Ohio, born in Gallia county, Nov. 23, 1822, and bred a farmer and blacksmith. He married Aug. 7, 1843, and removed to

the settlers at Montana were persuaded to move their
cabins to Auraria [15] and become incorporated with the
prospective city, [16] every settler being allowed as many
lots as he would build upon.

Iowa soon after.   In 1857 he again removed to the new town of Plattsmouth
in Neb., whence he came to Colorado, where he remained and worked at his
trade.   Among his discoveries was the Total Eclipse mine at Leadville.   He
was sergeant-at-arms of the constitutional convention of 1876.
    [15] Auraria was named after a town in Lumpkin county, Georgia, by some
persons from that mining region.   Some authorities state that it was named
after some person, for which assertion I find no ground.   There were many
miners from Georgia who would wish to compliment their former residence
or preserve their home memories in this way.   I quote *Byers' Hist. Colo.*, MS.,
17; *Sopris' Settlement of Denver*, MS., 1.   In *Hollister's Mines of Colorado*,
10, it is said that J. L. Russell of Auraria, Geogia, named the place.
    [16] Richard Sopris, one of the Auraria town company, was born in Bucks
co., Pa., June 26, 1813.   He was bred a farmer, and learned the trade of a
carpenter.   On the 5th of June, 1837 he married Elizabeth Allen, of Trenton,
N. J., and removed to Ind., changing his residence frequently, as he took
canal and railroad contracts in various parts of the state.   He arrived at
Cherry creek Feb. 1, 1859, in company with Parks.   He took an active part
in public affairs in Colorado; was a capt. in the first Colo inf.; first president
of the Colorado Agricultural society; for two years sheriff of Arapahoe
county, 1864–6; assisted in building the railroads of the state; and has been
mayor of Denver, and president of the Pioneer association.   I found him intelligent and reliable authority on Colorado affairs, and his contribution of
The Settlement of Denver, MS., very important.   His family consisted in 1884
of five sons and three daughters.
    Andrew J. Williams was a native of N. Y., born Nov. 22, 1833.   When
the Pike's peak gold fever broke out he left for the mountains in the autumn
of 1858, in company with Charles H. Blake—after whom Blake street,
Denver, was named—having four wagons drawn by four yokes of oxen each,
carrying merchandise.   They arrived Nov. 1st with the first stock of goods,
and erected the first store in Auraria, or West Denver.   In Dec. they joined
the Denver town company, and helped to survey the ground, removing to
the east side of the creek in the spring of 1859, where they erected the first
hotel, a log house, 110 by 32 feet, and roofed with canvas, situated on Blake
street near 15th street.   It was burned in 1863.   In 1859 Williams engaged
in freighting and contracting in Colorado and New Mexico, which he followed until 1865.   He also bought large herds of cattle which he drove to
Colorado from Texas, making good profits.   He became one of the incorporators and directors of the Exchange bank in 1876, and president in 1878.
    Judson H. Dudley, born in N. Y., April 8, 1834, in 1857 went to Neb.,
and from there to Pike's peak, where he arrived October 20, 1858, and assisted
in organizing the town company of Auraria, of which he was vice-president.
Subsequently he joined the Denver company.   On the breaking out of the
war he was appointed quartermaster with the rank of major.   He was owner
of the Moose mine, and manager of the reduction works at Dudley for five years.
    William Cole, a native of N. Y., was born Feb. 16, 1836, and educated at
a common school.   After a brief experience as a salesman in a mercantile establishment, he travelled through several of the western states, and being
caught by the current setting toward the new gold region, found himself on
the 20th of October, 1858, at Cherry creek, and when Auraria was being organized joined the town company.   Then he went to Missouri to purchase
beef and stock cattle, and soon after obtained contracts for furnishing the
government posts.   In 1865 he engaged in stock raising on a large scale.
With Williams & Co. he built 40 miles of the Kansas Pacific railroad.

Some time during the winter there arrived at
Auraria a party from Leavenworth, which had come
by the Arkansas route. It consisted of Richard E.
Whitsitt,[17] George William Larimer, William Larimer, Jr, Charles A. Lawrence, Folsom Dorsett, M.
M. Jewett, E. W. Wynkoop, Hickory Rogers, and
H. A. P. Smith, the last three having been picked up
at Pueblo by the Leavenworth party. Immediately
on viewing the situation of Auraria, and the relation
of Cherry creek to all the routes of travel, these new-
comers jumped the town site of St Charles on the
opposite or east side of the creek, and organized a
company to build a town, which was to be called Denver, after the governor of Kansas. A number of the
Auraria company joined the Denver company, and

John D. Howland, another of the Auraria company, was a native of
Zanesville, Ohio, born May 7, 1843, and educated at Marietta college. In
1857 he took up his residence among the Sioux, in order to paint mountain
scenery. He enlisted in the 1st Colo Cavalry, serving four years, and then
went to Europe. On returning from abroad he made his home in Colorado,
acting as secretary of the peace commission to the northern Sioux in 1867,
and serving as a government scout for a number of years. After this he
gave himself up to his art, having his studio in Denver.

George C. Schleier, a native of Baden, Germany, who immigrated to the
U. S. in 1833 at the age of six years, was one of a party of 30 which left
Leavenworth in Sept. 1858, arriving at Auraria Dec. 1st, where they wintered. In Schleier, Teutonic phlegm and American enterprise were happily
united, making him a typical pioneer. He acquired a fortune by these
qualities, and became an influential citizen of his adopted state. D. C.
Collier, Frank Dorris, George Le Baum, and Cyrus Smith were members of
this Leavenworth company, which travelled the Arkansas route.

Matthew L. McCaslin, a native of Pa, wintered at Auraria in 1858-9.
He went to Gold hill the following summer, where he mined for four years,
after which he settled on a land claim on St Vrain creek, where he secured
750 acres of land. He is a wealthy cattle owner.

William R. Blore, of English and German parentage, was born in N. Y.,
July 27, 1833, and removed to Pa in childhood. In 1856 he went to Neb.,
and thence to Colorado, being one of the Auraria town company. After
putting up some buildings he went to Gold run, and in company with Mc-
Caslin and Horsfal, discovered the famous Horsfal lode at Gold hill. He
became president of the Gold Hill Mining co. in 1860, and realized a fortune.

George R. Williamson was another pioneer of 1858. He was born July
14, 1824, removed to Nebraska, and was elected sheriff of Decatur county in
1856. Thence he went to the Pike's peak country. In 1861-2 in company
with H. C. Norton he built the Bear cañon toll road. In 1875 he discovered
and located the Yellow Pine mine, and the Nucleus, Gray Copper, and Duroc
lodes, in Sugar Loaf district. They yielded him over half a million dollars.

[17] Whitsitt was a native of Ohio, born March 30, 1830. He was bred to
mercantile pursuits, and removed to Kansas on the organization of that territory, settling at Leavenworth, where he operated in real estate. This probably suggested to him the course he took in Colorado. *Denver Hist.*, 631.

when the founder of St Charles returned from a visit
to Kansas in the spring he was compelled to take
shares in the new company or lose all, his agent having already been overpowered.   The first secretary of
the company was P. T. Basset.   He was followed by
Whitsitt, who was secretary, treasurer, and donating
agent until a grant was obtained from the government, all the deeds passing through his hands.   The
town was surveyed by E. D. Boyd, Larimer and A.
J. Williams carrying the chain.   It was this surveying which was assumed to give the new company the
superior right.   Larimer built the first house [18] after
a stockade occupied by William McGaa.[19]   It was
a log cabin 16 by 20 feet, with a ground floor,[20]
and probably a turf roof.   It stood near the corner
of Larimer and Fifteenth streets.   The second
house was erected by Moin and Rice, carpenters and
wagon-makers, on Fifteenth street, opposite Larimer,
which goes to show that this part of town became
the business centre.

The first trader in Denver was John Smith, who
was acting as agent for Elbridge Gerry, one of the
brothers before mentioned as a wealthy fur-trader.
When Blake and Williams opened their stock of
goods, Gerry hastened from Fort Laramie and took
charge of the business.[21]   A tin-shop was the third

[18] *Sopris' Settlement of Denver*, MS., 3.   There is some doubt about the
builder of the first house in Denver.   Like so many first things, it has several claimants.   David C. Collier, a native of Mina, N. Y., born Oct. 13,
1832, a descendant of puritan ancestors, a student of Oberlin college, in
Ohio, is one of those who built the first house on the east side of Cherry
creek.'   *Clear Creek and Boulder County Hist.*, 444.   Collier drove an ox-team
from Leavenworth, and was the first lawyer who offered his professional services in Colorado.   He erected several houses in Denver.   He explored a considerable portion of Gilpin and Clear Creek counties, White and Uncompahgre rivers, and the head waters of the Del Norte and Arkansas rivers,
and also the San Juan country.   In 1862 he removed to Central city, and
besides practising law, edited the *Register*.   He was connected with the
educational interests of Colorado as supt of the public schools for Gilpin
county.
[19] *Hollister's Mine of Colorado*, 16.
[20] The first building having a wooden floor was at the store of Wallingford
and Murphy, at the corner of Larimer and 17th street.   *Moore's Early Days
in Denver*, MS., 3.
[21] *Denver Rocky Mountain Herald*, Jan. 8, 1876.

business place opened, kept by Kinna and Nye, who had brought a small stock of tin and sheet-iron to make into such articles as were required by miners. They began business in Auraria in November, but were soon induced to remove to Denver. The first stove in Colorado was made by them out of sheet-iron for Blake and Williams' public hall, known as Denver hall, for which they were paid $150. On Christmas 1858 a train of six large wagons belonging to Richard Wooten and brother arrived from New Mexico, loaded with provisions, and these goods being placed on sale, made the third trading establishment, and the last before immigration began in 1859. The next large stock of goods which arrived belonged to J. B. Doyle and Fred Z. Salomon, and came from 'the States.' It consisted of twelve large wagon-loads of groceries, provisions, boots and shoes, and miners' tools. A warehouse was erected in Auraria, and an active rivalry in trade was carried on between the two towns, Denver soon after receiving almost as large a stock from New Mexico, belonging to St Vrain and St James, whose store was on Blake street, and was the largest in Denver at the time. It furnished women's and children's shoes, the first offered in Colorado.

Women and children were not reckoned among the inhabitants of the Pike's peak mining region in 1858, although there were five of the former who saw the beginning of Denver. They were Mrs and Miss Rooker from Salt Lake ; Mrs H. Murat ;[22] Mrs Smoke, who afterward went to Montana ; and Mrs Wooten, a native of Mexico. To these were added in August 1859 Mrs W. N. Byers, Mrs Henry Allen, and two daughters. Before winter of that year there were many of all classes in Denver. The first child

[22] H. Murat, commonly called 'the count,' was a lineal descendant of Marshal Murat, king of Naples. The countess washed, and the count shaved men's beards—occupations more useful than noble personages usually engage in. He later became an inmate of the Arapahoe county hospital. *Byers' Hist. Colo*, MS., 82.

born in the town was a half-caste son of McGaa,[23] one
of the original town company, who voted to name it
after his friend, the governor of Kansas, and to give
him a share in the town site.[24]

The destiny of east Denver as against Auraria
was settled in the autumn of 1859 by the arrival of
two trains from Leavenworth, aggregating thirty
wagons, loaded with merchandise, belonging to Jones
and Cartwright, who opened stores on Blake
street. "Now," said the Denver partisans, "no more
Mexican trash for free Americans. No more one
hundred per cent. The trade is ours, and Denver is
saved." They made good their word, as it afterward
proved—all but the one hundred per cent.[25]

[23] McGaa went by the name of Jack Jones among mountain men. It is
said by Moore in his *Early Days in Denver*, MS., 9, that he was the son of
an Irish baronet, but Byers, in *Hist. Colo*, MS., 73, says he was an American.
At all events he was an educated man, and a good writer. He was a friend
and guide of Gen. J. W. Denver, and a shrewd business man. But he fell
into dissipated habits, and lost his standing. The town company hastened
his final end by changing the name of McGaa street to Holladay street in
honor of Ben Holladay. This insult broke his heart. At least, so says
Moore, quoted above. McGaa died about 1866.

[24] Denver did not visit the place, or claim his lots in accordance with the
terms of the grant, until 1882, when his share had been taken possession of,
and divided among some of the other members of the company. He would
not disturb titles, as the property had passed to innocent purchasers.

[25] I find mention of a number of the pioneers of 1858 belonging to the settlement of Denver who have not been here recorded. William M. Slaughter,
from Plattsmouth, Neb., later mayor of Central City, was one of the early
arrivals. John J. Reithmann, born in Lausanne, Switzerland, in 1838, came
to the U. S. at the age of 10 years, and was educated in the public schools of
Indianapolis, where he was employed in the bank of the capital. In 1858
the family removed to Council Bluffs, from which place he soon after emigrated with his brother, L. D. Reithmann, to Colorado. They did not go to
Cherry creek, but the latter wintered at a place known as Rough and Ready,
2½ miles below the mouth of Cherry creek, on the Platte, while the former
returned to Council Bluffs, carrying the first mail between Colorado and Iowa.
In the spring of 1859 he recrossed the plains to Denver, where he engaged in
manufacturing crackers; and in 1868 began selling drugs. He made a fortune, and spent it freely in travel and the education of his children. He was
president of the German bank—later the German National bank—of Denver,
which position he resigned to go abroad. Louis D. Reithmann was also a
Swiss, although not of the same family. Brought up in Ohio, he lived afterward near Indianapolis, and removed to Council Bluffs in 1856, whence he
came to Colorado in 1858. He mined until 1865, went to Salt Lake, and
thence to Montana, where he opened a bakery in company with Frank Hogert,
but three years afterward returned to Colorado and engaged in dairy farming,
and later in the grocery trade in Denver. Henry Reitz, a German by birth,
learned the trade of a baker in London, after which he came to the U S.,
working as a painter for a time. On arriving in Colorado, he sold his ox-
team, and with the money, opened a bakery, making $3,500 in a few months,

But I will not further anticipate. D. C. Oakes having obtained possession of a journal kept by W. Green Russell, who returned with him late in the autumn to the states, published the same with a way-bill, under the title of *Pike's Peak Guide and Journal;* and although it was printed in the little town of Pacific City in Mills county, Iowa, it was widely circulated with similar publications, causing a large emigration to set out for the mountains as soon as the grass began to start in the spring, and even before. On the white covers of thousands of wagons was inscribed " Pike's Peak," often with the addition of some jocose legend;[26] this conspicuous landmark, in the absence of an official name for this region, standing for all the country from which this mountain was visible.

In April 1859 there were ten or twelve hundred persons encamped at Auraria and Denver, the advance of that army stretching across the great plains from the Missouri river in different lines, but principally up the Platte valley. Among the first to arrive was D. C. Oakes, with a saw-mill, which he placed on

after which he went to mining, and accumulated a comfortable fortune by that means, and by painting. Edmund A. Willoughby, son of Gen. Franklin Willoughby, was born in Groton, N. Y., Jan. 6, 1836, and removed in 1857 to Omaha, Neb. In 1858 he joined a party for Pike's peak, which arrived Oct. 27th at Cherry creek, where he associated himself with M. A. Avery in contracting and building, erecting, among other structures, Denver hall, famous in early times. He manufactured the Willoughby brick. He was sheriff of Arapahoe county in 1873, and two years alderman of the 4th ward of Denver. Andrew Sagendorf was born in N. Y., Aug. 26, 1828, and bred a farmer.* In 1856 he removed to Neb., and in 1858 he left Omaha for Pike's peak, and arrived at Cherry creek November 5th, remaining there over winter. In the spring he went prospecting, and with others discovered Spanish bar, where he mined until July. Returning to Auraria he was elected secretary of the town company, which office he held for two years. He was also weighing clerk in the mint at Denver in 1863. In 1866 he was appointed postmaster for Denver, holding the office three years. He subsequently erected the government buildings at the White River Ute agency, and afterward engaged in stock raising in Douglas county. In 1874 he removed to Colorado Springs, and for two years ran the express and transfer line, and finally went into the drug business in this place.

[26] One wagon bore the inscription, 'Pike's Peak or bust!' The disappointed gold seeker returned soon after with his addenda: 'Busted, by Thunder!' emblazoned on his wagon cover. *Elbert's Public Men and Measures,* MS., 2; *Ingersoll's Knocking around the Rockies,* 6; *Sopris' Settlement of Denver,* MS., 1.

Plum creek, twenty miles south of Denver, and which furnished the first lumber for the improvement of that town on the 21st of April.[27] On that same day there arrived from Omaha a newspaper company with a printing press, which was destined to do as much toward building up the town of Denver as the saw-mill, though in a different way. The head of the company was William N. Byers, who, like Oakes, had published a *Guide to Pike's Peak*, which had been extensively sold to the immigrants.[28] It happened that before he arrived at Cherry creek signs of a panic began to appear, and he encountered persons who threatened to have satisfaction of him for having raised expectation by his *Guide* which had not been fulfilled. Oakes was regarded with still greater disfavor, because he had been the first to represent Pike's peak as a mining region, and his name was mentioned with execrations.[29] Henry Allen and William Lari-

[27] The first lumber was purchased by Richard Wooten, who came to Colorado in 1838, and Thomas Pollock, who erected the first frame houses. *Denver Hist.*, 186. Wooten was living in Trinidad in 1882. *Denver Colorado Antelope*, April, 1882. The 2d saw mill was erected by Little, and the 3d by Whittemore. *Sopris' Settlement of Denver*, MS., 12.

[28] Mr Byers had a most important influence in shaping the history of Colorado. I am indebted to him for very valuable material, collected during a tour through the state of Colorado in 1884, in four different manuscript contributions; namely, *History of Colorado*, *The Newspaper Press of Colorado*, *The Sand Creek Affair*, and *The Centennial State*, each filled with the very essence of history. Byers was born in Ohio, Feb. 22, 1831. At the age of 19 he removed to Iowa, and joined a government surveying party for Cal. and Or. in 1851, returning to Washington in 1853, after which he settled at Omaha, then in its infancy. He continued surveying until he came to Colo. In changing his occupation he followed the natural bent of his mind, and made the best use of his talents. He founded the *Rocky Mountain News*, the first newspaper issued in Colorado. The first number appeared April 22d, the day after his arrival, and proceeded by 20 minutes the *Cherry Creek Pioneer*, owned by Jack Merrick of St Joseph, who, being beaten in the race, sold to Thomas Gibson, also of the *News*, and never issued a second number of his paper. This left a clear field for Byers and Gibson, which they improved. George C. Monell of Omaha had an interest in the *News*, but turned back on his way to Denver, and sold it. *Byers' Hist. Colo*, MS.

[29] The following distich was made familiar to thousands on the plains:

'Here lies the body of D. C. Oakes,
    Killed for aiding the Pike's Peak hoax.'

Hill's Tales of Colo Pioneers, 27. His effigy was buried by the wayside, and on a buffalo skull planted at the head was written:

'Here lies the bones of Major Oakes,
    The author of this God damned hoax.'

mer came in for a share of blame also. There was as little reason in this revengeful feeling as there had been in the unbounded credulity which had led them on the first unproved statement of a bookmaker to hasten to place themselves in the front rank of gold-seekers.

But their panic was not groundless. Gold had not yet been found in amount to justify any excitement, although it was the belief of old miners on the ground that it was there. Very few of those who came to mine knew anything of indications, or the methods of mining. They needed to be taught; but until mining had been begun they could learn nothing. Other employments there were none at that early date. The last argument for quitting the country was furnished on the 16th of April, when a man named John Scudder killed another named Bassett in a quarrel. If a course of outlawry was about to commence, they would none of that country; so away they went like senseless steers—senseless in coming or in returning —stampeding down the Platte sixty or seventy strong, swearing they would kill D. C. Oakes and W. N. Byers if peradventure they could lay hands on them.

On foot, unfurnished with transportation or provisions for a journey of such length, the backward moving men kept on. The stories they told of Pike's peak affairs were at least as exaggerated as the representations of the guide-books which they condemned, big lies in their minds seemingly being neccessary to counteract the effect of big lies. And every man they turned back added to the apparent weight of evidence, gaining like a rolling snow-ball. If sixty could turn back sixty, twice sixty could turn back their own number at least, and 240 might be able to influence not only 480, but, by that power which crowds have to create a state of feeling, a much larger number could be made to share in the alarm. Of the 150,000 persons on the plains in the spring and summer of 1859, not less than 50,000 were thus turned back.   This was doubtless the greatest success these sixty men ever achieved ; and their reward was free transportation for themselves, and provisions for the journey.   The return began far up the Platte, and many who had loaded their wagons with merchandise to sell in the mines, or property for their own use, threw it away rather than tax their tired oxen to drag it back five or six hundred miles to the Missouri river.   The route was strewn with goods of every description for hundreds of miles, and of the 100,000 that pushed on to the mountains, less than 40,000 remained there.   Some tarried but a few weeks, and others remained all summer, going home when cold weather approached.

But there was really something back of all this running to and fro, this seemingly wasted effort.   It was slow in appearing, revealing itself little by little in a tantalizing fashion which is sufficient apology for the discontent of those who imagined gold could be picked up like pebbles.   On the 15th of January 1859, gold was discovered in a small affluent of Boulder creek, to which the name of Gold run was given ; and about the end of January a discovery was made in a gulch filled with fallen timber, on the south Boulder, and called Deadwood diggings.[30]   In the spring J. D. Scott discovered a gold-bearing quartz vein, and named it after himself, the Scott, and the place Gold hill.   Out of these discoveries grew the town of Boulder

On the 6th of May a party of Chicago men, headed by George Jackson, a California miner, made a rich discovery on a branch of Clear creek.   The diggings took the name of Chicago bar, or Jackson diggings, and soon overflowed with anxious miners, many of

[30] Compare *Moore's Early Days in Denver*, MS.; *Sopris' Settlement of Denver*, MS.; *Byers' Hist. Colorado*, MS.; *Bradford's Hist. Colorado*, MS.; and *Hollister's Mines of Colorado.*

whom were compelled to look further for want of room. A short distance above the mouth of Fall river and Chicago bar was Spanish bar, so called because there were evidences of former mining at that place; in the vicinity were Fall river and Grass Valley mining camps. But the principal camp on this part of Clear creek was opposite Jackson diggings, and became the foundation of the town of Idaho Springs, which began to take shape the following year. On the 10th another party, led by John H. Gregory, a Georgian,[31] made a discovery just over the

[31] Gregory was a lazy fellow from Gordon county, Georgia, and drove a government team from Leavenworth to Fort Laramie in 1858, intending to go to Fraser river, but being detained at Laramie by want of means had drifted off to Clear creek, and with some others had encamped at a point between Denver and Golden, and called the place Arapahoe. It is said by Hollister, in his *Mines of Colorado*, 63, that he prospected in January, and found the color in the north fork of Clear creek; and that being out of provisions he was forced to return to camp. It does not appear that he made any further effort for several months. He was finally 'grub staked' (furnished with provisions for an interest in his success) by David K. Wall, and induced to lead a party, consisting of Wilkes De Frees, his brother, and Kendall, to the mountains and the stream where he had seen the color. The party set out in April, proceeding from Arapahoe up the north forth of Vasquez or Clear creek, climbing many successive ridges, and floundering through snow banks, until they came to the mouth of a gulch near the head of the creek, and consequently well up in the mountains. Here Gregory suggested that it would be well to dig and look for float gold. While the other men dug he looked on. They obtained a fair prospect, and went on excavating. Then said Gregory to Wilkes De Frees, who had grub staked him, 'Bring your shovel, and come with me.' They went about 300 feet further up the side of the gulch, when Gregory pointed to the ground and said, 'Here is a good looking spot; stick your shovel in there, Wilk.' De Frees obeyed, turning over 'a few shovelfuls of earth. 'Give me some in the pan,' said Gregory again, and De Frees filled the pan half full of dirt, which the Georgian proceeded to wash at the little stream running through a gulch close at hand. The product of that half pan of dirt was half an ounce of gold ! Gregory went back for another panful, with the same result. Claims were immediately staked off. The effect of his extraordinary fortune crazed the weak brain of poor Gregory. All through the night sleep deserted him, and his companions heard his self-communings. He sold his discovery claim, under the impression that he could easily find another as good. The price he obtained, $22,-000, was a fortune to him. At length, in 1861-2, he disappeared from a hotel in Illinois, and was never seen again. The man to whom Gregory sold his mine was Edward W. Henderson. He was born in Austinburg, Ohio, Nov. 29, 1818, and bred a farmer, receiving a common school education. In 1844 he removed to Iowa, and from there he went to Pike's peak, where he arrived in April 1859. After prospecting for a few weeks, he went to Gregory gulch on the 16th of May, and on the 29th, in company with Amos Gridley, he purchased the Gregory claims, paying for them out of the proceeds of the mine. It was a fortunate venture, although he lost some of the money he made in other ones. He erected a quartz mill in 1861, where the Eureka foundry later stood, in company with D. A. January, Ely R. Lackland, and Judge Lackland, in which was a loss. He afterward purchased a

mountains west of Jackson bar, on the north fork of
Clear creek, the richest ever found in Colorado, and
one of the richest in the world. These discoveries
arrested the backward flow of immigration to some
extent. Not less than 30,000 persons hastened after
Jackson when they heard of Chicago bar, and when
Gregory point was made known they threw themselves in there pell mell, each striving to be first.

But the Gregory party had taken the precaution
before giving their discovery publicity to admit their
friends and organize a district, with rules and regulations by which all future claimants should be governed.[32] Comparatively few of those who came found
ground to work;[33] for which reason much discontent
was exhibited, and a mass meeting was called to change
the laws of the district.[34] The new-comers were
unable to cope with the more experienced miners, and
were surprised to find that the committee appointed
by themselves to revise the laws made no material
change in them. They had failed to perceive that
the pioneers were mingling with the assemblage in
every part, nominating their men on the committee.
Not knowing the nominees, the malcontents voted

mill at Gregory point in company with Gridley, but lost in this transaction
also. He finally consolidated his claims with four others, and sold out to a
New York company, his share of the price obtained being $100,000, In 1873
he was appointed receiver of the U. S. land office at Central City. *Clear Creek
and Boulder Val. Hist.*, 454-5.

[32] The mining laws adopted were nearly identical with those of California,
defining the boundaries of the district; forbidding the taking of more than
one claim of a kind, except by purchase properly attested; fixing the extent
of a mountain claim at 100 feet on the lode and 50 feet in width; and of a
gulch or creek claim at 100 feet along the creek or gulch, and extending from
bank to bank; limiting the time of holding without working to 10 days; giving the discoverer a 'discovery claim,' in addition to his working claim, which
he could work or not as he chose; dividing the water of a stream equally between miners, etc. Disputes were to be settled by arbitration. On the 9th
of July another meeting was held, at which it was resolved to elect by ballot
a president of the district, a recorder of claims, and a sheriff. Richard
Sopris was chosen president, C. A. Roberts recorder, and Charles Peck
sheriff. A committee was also appointed to codify the laws of the district.
Hollister's Mines of Colo, 77-9.

[33] Bates and Taschuer hired Gregory at a high price to prospect for them,
and together they found the celebrated Bates lode. *Colo Gazetteer*, 174.

[34] Byers, who was present at this meeting, describes it as looking like a
'flock of blackbirds,' so thickly were the sides of the gulch covered with
men. *Hist. Colo*, MS. 34.

them into office, and accepted their report because they had done so, with a suspicion that they had been outwitted.

Prospecting continued in the mountains, a number of discoveries being made on the headwaters of north Clear creek, Boulder, south Clear creek, and the Platte. Early in June W. Green Russell commenced mining on a tributary of north Clear creek, a little south of, but parallel with, the Gregory claims, in a ravine which took the name of Russell gulch. Six men in one week took out seventy-six ounces of gold, worth from sixteen to eighteen dollars to the ounce.[35] Something over 200 men were at work in Nevada and Illinois gulches and Missouri flat, tributaries of Gregory and Russell gulches, who were producing an average of $9,000 a week. In the latter part of September there were about 900 men at work in Russell gulch, taking out an average of $35,000 a week. Water becoming scarce, ditches were constructed to bring it from Fall river to Russell and Gregory gulches, which cost the miners $100,000. The districts discovered in 1859 in what were later Clear creek and Gilpin counties were, besides Gregory, Russell, Spanish bar, and Jackson, Nevada district, Lake gulch, Griffith, Illinois Central, Enterprise, Central, Eureka, and Virginia. The discoveries in these districts were numerous enough to employ many,[36] but by no means all who sought for claims.

[35] William Green Russell remained in Colorado until 1862, and made considerable money. On his way east he was arrested for a confederate at Santa Fé, but he was released and returned to Colorado, where he remained until 1875, when he removed to the Cherokee country, his wife being a woman of that nation, and died a few years afterward. *Bradford's Hist. Colo*, MS., 4; *Sopris' Settlement of Denver*, MS., 2.

[36] I give herewith the names of mines and their discoverers in 1859: In Gilpin county, the Alger, by William Alger; American Flag; Barrett, by Wesley Barrett; Burroughs, Benjamin Burroughs; Briggs, Briggs Brothers; Butler, James D. Wood; Connelly and Beverly, Connelly and Beverly; Dean-Castro, Dean and Castro; Gaston, James Gaston; Gunnell, Harry Gunnell; Hill House, Payne & Co.; Ingles, Webster & Co.; Indiana, Thomas Brothers; Jennings, Thomas Jennings; Kansas, James Madison; Kentucky, Jones and Hardesty; Miller, A. Miller; Mack, W. Mack; Missouri, Roderick Dhu, Stevens and Hall; Smith, A. A. Smith; Snow, James Snow; Tarryall; Topeka, Joseph Hurst; Tucker, John Nichols; Virginia, J. Oxley; Whiting,

A rumor of discovery, and they swarmed at that
place, alighting like locusts upon a field which could
not furnish ground for one in a thousand of those who
came. Finding themselves too late, they swarmed
again at some other spot, which they abandoned in a
similar manner.

Out of this ceaseless activity grew worthy results.
From Araphoe[37] at the mouth of Table mountain
cañon, where they had gathered during the winter,

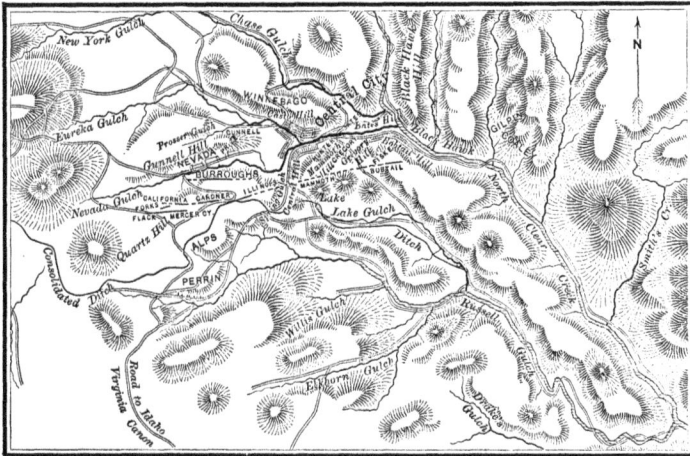

MINES OF GILPIN COUNTY.

Whiting & Co.; Wood, Robert Wood; Leavenworth, Harsh Brothers; California, Hutchinson; French F. Terndull; St Louis. In Clear creek county
the Griffith, George F. Griffith, and the Virginia. These were discoveries
which proved to be real lodes, called at first 'mountain diggings' to distinguish them from the gulch and bar diggings; but these were not all. There
seems to have been a good uniform yield, but never an extraordinary production as in some parts of Idaho and Montana. Hollister, in *Mines of Colo*,
66-7, gives the yield of the decomposed quartz in these mountains diggings
as follows: the highest day's income from the Gregory, working it with a
sluice, was $495, and the lowest $21. Zeigler, Spain, & Co. cleaned up in
three weeks on the Gregory $2,400. De Frees & Co., cleaned up $2,080 in 12
days with one sluice. Kehler, Patton, & Fletcher averaged with 5 hands
$100 a day on the Bates lode. From $125 to $450 a day were obtained from
single sluices, working four men; and so on.

[37] Arapahoe was staked off by George B. Allen. It contained in 1859
nearly 100 houses, but was soon after deserted and converted into farms.
Clear Creek and Boulder Val. Hist., 547. Allen became a resident of a farm
near Golden. He was born in Albany, N. Y., May 17, 1825. In 1846 he
removed to Akron, Ohio, and subsequently to Defiance, where he remained

went the founders of Golden,[38] Golden Gate, Mount Vernon, Central City, and Nevada,[39] all on the affluents of Clear creek. Golden Town company was formed in the spring of 1859, and was an afterthought of its organizers, who were encamped at the Gate of the Mountains, or the mouth of the cañon of Clear creek. The trail to the mines crossed the creek here,[40] and the water being high, J. M. Ferrell constructed first a foot-bridge and then a toll-bridge for teams, and improved the road, making his bridge a good piece of property, as well as the first of its kind in Colorado. Many persons gathered there, attracted by the natural beauties of the scenery, or encamped preparatory to entering the mountains, suggesting thereby a town, when a company was formed, consisting of D. Wall, J. M. Ferrell. J, C. Kirby, J. C. Bowles, Mrs Williams, W. A. H. Loveland, H. J. Carter, Ensign Smith, William Davidson, F. W. Beebee, E. L. Berthoud, Stanton, Clark, and Garrison. They called themselves the Boston company; and having selected two sections of land laid out half a section in lots and blocks, the remainder not being surveyed until the following year. A saw-mill and

five years. Having lost a stock of goods by fire he engaged in brokerage and then in buying and selling stock. In 1857 he removed to Doniphan, Kansas, but on account of failing health determined to cross the plains. After laying out Auraria and Arapahoe, he became interested in quartz and lumber mills. He moved his saw mill across the mountain into California Gulch in 1861, and 'blew the first whistle across the range.' In 1864 he took 160 acres of land on Clear creek where he made himself a home.

[38] The first settlers of Golden were W. A. H. Loveland, John M. Ferrell, Fox Deifenderf, P. B. Cheney, Dr Hardy, George Jackson, Charles M. Ferrell, John F. Kirby, T. P. Boyd, William Pollard, James McDonald, George West, Mark Blunt, Charles Remington, E. B. Smith, J. C. Bowles, Daniel McCleary, I. B. Fitzpatrick, and W. J. McKay.

[39] J. M. Beverly built the first cabin in Nevada, and was elected recorder of the district in the autumn, besides being sheriff and justice of the peace. During the winter he located Beverly's discovery on the Burroughs lode. In 1862 he erected a quartz mill in Nevada gulch. He returned to Chicago in 1868 and was married there; but in the great fire of 1871 he lost all his accumulations and began the study of the law. After being admitted to the bar he revisited Colorado, where he located and purchased a number of mines, which were profitably worked. Beverly was born in Culpepper county, Virginia, in 1843.

[40] It is mentioned by several writers that Horace Greeley visited the mines this year; and it is related that he attempted to swim his mule across Clear creek, and would have been drowned but for assistance rendered him.

shingle-mill in the pineries furnished material for building, which went on rapidly, the town having seven or eight hundred inhabitants before winter.[41]

Golden Gate, two miles north of Golden, where the Denver and Gregory road entered the mountains, was a flourishing settlement. At the mouth of Left Hand creek was a town, later abandoned, called Davenport in 1859. Mountain City at Gregory point was laid out early in May, the first house being started on the 22d by Richard Sopris, who, with J. H. Gest, was one of the Mammoth quartz mining company, which owned thirty claims on that lode. A near neighbor to Mountain City on the south was a miner's camp called Black Hawk, and adjoining it on the north, in Kendall gulch,[42] was Central City, so named by W. N. Byers, its first inhabitant[43] after its founders, Harrison Gray Otis, Nathaniel Albertson, and John Armor.[44] Central finally absorbed the other two

[41] *Helm's Gate of the Mountains*, MS., 1; *Early Records*, MS., 4. *The Rocky Mountain Gold Reporter and Mountain City Herald*, of Aug. 6, 1859, says that Golden at that date, when it had been surveyed but one month, had 50 houses, 1,930 men, and 70 women. Most of these must have been transient, if indeed that might not be said of all. Helm says the first garden he knew of in Colorado was at Golden. This of course applies to the mining population.

[42] Named after Kendall in Gregory's company. In seems the honors were divided by naming the gulch after Kendall and the hill or point after Gregory.

[43] *Sopris' Settlement of Denver*, MS., 7; *Bradford's Hist. Colo*, MS., 4.

[44] Thomas Gibson of the *Rocky Mountain News* had a newspaper office at Central city in July 1859, and published the *Rocky Mountain Gold Reporter* on the press purchased of Jack Merrick, a cap size lever machine. It had a brief existence of five months, when it was discontinued, and the press sold to the Boston company of Golden, whose managers established the *Western Mountaineer*, which a few months later was enlarged and printed on a new press. Among its editors in the winter of 1859–60 where A. D. Richardson and Thomas W. Knox, both of whom afterward achieved national reputations as newspaper correspondents. While the press was in Central City it occupied part of a double log house owned by George Aux, author of *Mining in Colorado and Montana*, MS., in my collection. Aux was born in Marryat, Pa, in 1837. At the age of 14 years he removed to Cleveland, Ohio. Five years afterward he went to Kansas, and May 1850 to Pike's peak. He went to Gregory point, or Mountain city, where he remained until he enlisted in Gilpin's reg. of volunteers raised to keep the territory in the union. In 1864 he went to Montana, with his wife and infant, in an ox wagon, but soon returned and engaged in farming and stock raising in Douglas county. His manuscript is an account of early settlements and military matters chiefly. Benjamin P. Haman erected and kept the first hotel in Central City. Haman was born in Vt and immigrated from Iowa. He married Rachel Berry in 1847. Hugh A. Campbell opened the first stock of goods in Mountain City

places. On the headwaters of Clear creek George F. Criffith laid out a town and called it after himself, Georgetown. It did not grow much that season, nor for several seasons thereafter, but its importance was demonstrated after the discovery of silver mines a few years later.

A part of the population spread across the range, and located Breckenridge on a tributary of Blue river, in what is now Summit county, where several hundred miners were soon congregated. Others penetrated the South park, and a miner named W. J. Holman discovered on a branch of the Platte the Pound diggings,[45] which had a great reputation, the name signifying, as some thought, that a pound of gold a day was their average-production—an opulence which nature does not often bestow upon diggings anywhere. So magnanimous were the first locators in the prospect of sudden riches that they gave the place and the creek on which the placers were situated the inviting name of Tarryall. So many tarried, and such was the squabbling over claims that a portion of the population determined to seek for mines elsewhere, and to their delight soon discovered them. But the first party of eight men which left Tarryall was killed by the Indians, except one, while passing through a ravine, which took from this circumstance the name of Dead Men's gulch.[46]

It was decided that there should be no cause for dissension in the new district, but that even-handed

in a brush tent, and was the first to place a sign above his place of business with the new name of Central City upon it, and to have his letters addressed to Central City, by which means the P. O. department was brought at last to recognize the change. He built the Atchison house in Denver in the winter of 1859. He discovered the Cincinnati lode on Casto hill, and became the owner of 40 acres of Placer mines on Quartz hill, besides other mining property. He was born in Adams county, Pa, and married Mattie W. Whitsitt, of Centreville, Ohio.

[45] Named after Daniel Pound. The amount actually taken out by the Mountain Union company in one week, with 4 men, was $420. Holman, with 5 men, took out $686 in the same time. Bowers & Co. took out in one week $969, with 3 men—57 ounces worth $17.

[46] W. N. Byers, in *Out West*, Oct. 1873; *Dead Men's Gulch and Other Sketches*, MS., 1.

justice should rule the camp, and to emphasize this determination it was named Fair Play.[47] Eight miles north-west of Fair Play a discovery was made by a mountaineer, whose characteristic dress of tanned skins gave him the descriptive appellation of Buckskin Joe, and the Buckskin Joe mines next attracted the unsatisfied. This camp became the town of Alma. Hamilton and Jefferson followed in South park the same season, the latter becoming a town of several thousand inhabitants in the first few years.[48]

[47] *Sopris Settlement of Denver*, MS., 8. There are several stories to account for this name, all of them far fetched and inaccurate.

[48] Before proceeding further with the history of settlement, I will record the names of some of the pioneers of this part of Colorado in 1859. Joseph M. Brown, born in Maryland in 1832, was with General Walker in Nicaragua in 1855. He returned, drifted west, and became a farmer and stock-raiser. Samuel W. Brown, born near Baltimore Dec. 23, 1829, removed to New York in 1844, became a cabinet-maker, served in the Mexican war, going from these battle-fields to Cal., and afterward to Chicago. He followed Walker to Nicaragua, and furnished supplies to the army for one year. In 1857 he married a daughter of John Perry, at Olathe, Iowa. On coming to Colorado he secured 500 acres and went to farming. Thomas Donelson, a native of Ohio, was born June 20, 1824, and bred a farmer. After several removes westward he came to Colorado, where, after one season of mining, he brought out his family and settled on the Platte, 17 miles below Denver. Henry Crow, born in Wis., bred a merchant, came to Colorado in 1859, and after mining for a season returned to Iowa for his family, and located at Central City. He served in the Indian war of 1864, after which he removed to Georgetown. Selling his mines at that place he settled in Denver and organized the City national bank in 1870; but in 1876 withdrew from the presidency of that institution and returned to Georgetown to engage in mining. Charles G. Chever was born at Salem, Mass., Sept. 13, 1827, went to Cal. in 1849, where he resided 10 years in the mines, and then removed to Colorado. In 1861 he was elected clerk and recorder of Arapahoe county. He has ever since been in the real estate business. S. B. Morrison, born in Oneida Castle, N. Y., May 2, 1831, removed to Jefferson, Wis., at the age of 10 years, and in 1859 came to Colorado, where he turned his attention to farming and stock-raising, 3 miles north of Denver. He also erected some quartz-mills in Gilpin and Park counties. John H. Morrison graduated from Rush Medical college, Chicago, and after coming to Colorado he resided first on a farm and then in Denver, where he died July 21, 1876. Jasper P. Sears was born in Ohio, in 1838, and educated at Delaware, after which he removed to St Paul, Minnesota, where he traded with the Sioux. In Sept. 1858, he started for Pike's peak with a stock of merchandise, but did not arrive for a year afterward, owing to sickness and Indian hostilities. In company with C. A. Cook he opened a store at the corner of 15th and Larimer streets, Denver. After 4 years of prosperous trade they opened a banking-house. In 1869 Sears became a government contractor, and dealer in real estate, and made a fortune. Thomas Skerritt, born in Ireland, in 1828, immigrated in 1848 to the U. S. and Canada. In 1855 he married Mary K. Skerritt, who was one of the first women to go to Central City, and accompanied her husband across the mountains to Breckenridge. In the autumn of 1859 he took a land claim on the Platte river, but all his improvements were swept away by the flood of 1864. What remained of the land itself was purchased by

Peter Magnus for the site of the Harvest Queen Mill, and Skerritt settled upon another claim 6 miles from Denver, where he cultivated 200 acres.

Edward C. Sumner, a native of La Fayette, Ind., joined the rush to Pike's peak, and found permanent employment in the Denver post-office. Alfred H. Miles, born in Cleveland, Ohio, Sept. 4, 1820, set out with his family for Cal. in 1859, but stopped in Colo and selected a farm on Clear creek, 9 miles from Denver. He remained there for 7 years, when he moved to Cherry creek and finally to Denver. He has been one of the most successful farmers of Colorado. Isaac E. McBroom a native of Ind., born April 22, 1830, removed to St Joseph, Missouri, at an early age, and in 1850 to Iowa. He came to Colo with the first mining immigration, and settled on a farm near Denver. John Milheim, baker and steel polisher, a native of Switzerland, born in 1835, came to the U. S. in 1849, and from there to Pike's peak. Just before leaving Omaha, he was married to Miss Reithmann, whose brothers also became citizens of Denver, and with whom he opened the first bakery there, which laid the foundation of his fortune. James W. Richards, a native of Ohio, worked on a farm in Ill., and thence went to the Colo mines. In 1865 he established a fast freight line between Denver and Central City, remaining in the business 7 years, when he went into a flour and grain trade He shipped the first car-load of grain over the Kansas Pacific railroad to Denver, and established the first line of transfer wagons in the city, upon which he, with W. J. Kinsey, had a patent. Peter Magnus, born in Sweden, in 1824, bred a farmer, came to the U. S. in 1852, and in 1859 to Colo, and selecting a farming claim brought out his family. The flood of 1864 took his improvements, and grasshoppers in 1873-4-5, nearly destroyed his crops, yet he prospered. He received all the medals at the agricultural exhibition of Colorado in 1870. He was county commissioner for Arapahoe in 1867-9. Mason M. Seavy, born in Maine in 1839, removed to Ill., and thence started with other gold-seekers for Pike's peak in 1859, but turned back at Fort Kearny, and did not reach the mountains until the following year, when he settled in Golden and went into the grocery trade, doing well until he lost a large and valuable train by the Arapahoes, which compelled him to suspend business. He began a second time in Central City, but failed again, owing to commercial complications. In 1872 he settled in Denver, and again prosecuted the grocery business, this time with better success. Daniel J. Fulton, a native of Va, removed to Ohio in 1836, and a few years later to Iowa. In 1849 crossed the plains to Cal. where he mined for 3 years, returned to the states, and in 1859 came to Colo. After mining for a year, and trying his fortunes in Idaho, he settled upon a farm on the Platte, 16 miles below Denver. George W. Hazzard was born at Elk Grove, Wis., Dec. 7, 1837, came to Denver in 1859, and went to the mines of Gregory point and Missouri flats, where, with his brother, he took out gold enough to start in farming 16 miles from Denver. John W. Iliff, a native of Ohio, born in 1831, bred a farmer, and educated at Delaware college, came to Colorado in 1859 with a small train of provisions, purchased with a few hundred dollars which his father gave him, and selling out invested in a small herd of cattle. He followed up the cattle business for 18 years, mastering all its details, and making a large fortune. He owned 200,000 acres of pasture lands, took government contracts, and shipped cattle to eastern markets at the rate of 13,000 a year. He died February 9, 1878. Libeus Barney, a native of Vt, crossed the plains in the first coach of the Denver and Pike's peak passenger line. After mining, with a brother, he tried housebuilding, and erected the hall in which the first provisional legislature met. Farming was next attempted, but a grocery store in Denver was the final resort after these ventures, and in that he did well.

Caleb S. Burdsal, from Ohio, mined near Golden in 1859, and in 1864 was appointed surgeon of the 3d Colo reg. Since then he has practised medicine in Denver. He discovered and named Soda lakes, near Morrison. Joseph W. Bowles, born in Rockford, N. C., came to Denver in 1858. He located a mine on Quartz hill, in the Nevada district, on Clear creek, where he worked for three years on an extension of the Burroughs' lode. He was twice elected sheriff for the district under the miners' organization. In 1862 he purchased a rancho on the Platte, 10 miles above Denver, near the present village of Littleton. George W. Drake, born in Ohio, came to Colo in 1859, and opened a hotel on the old Gregory road 7 miles from Black Hawk, at Cold Spring rancho, in partnership with Homer Medbury, of Ohio. In 1863, he became agent for Gibson's pony express between Denver and the mountain towns. In 1864 he set up a store in Black Hawk, and in 1870 joined the colony at Greeley, which he helped to build up. Three years later he settled in Denver, where he purchased a marble-yard in 1874. Charles Eyser, a native of Holstein, Germany, born in 1822, came to Colo in 1859, opened a provision store in the mines, but returned to Denver in 1863, where he kept a boarding-house, which in 1869 was washed away by a flood. After that he settled at farming. E. W. Cobb, born in Boston, was sent to Cal. as the first agent of Adams' Express co. After two years he went to Australia, returning to Boston in 1857, then to Denver, where he sold groceries for two years, then carried on the Elephant corral a year or so, and after that mined for a few years, until in 1869 he was appointed chief of the mineral dept of the sur.-gen. office. John W. Cline, a native of Canada, mined during the summer of 1859 in Russell gulch and at Breckenridge, but in the autumn took a piece of land 7 miles north of Denver, where he made himself a home. Samuel Brautner, born in Md, came to Cal. in 1852, and finally to Colo, where he engaged in mining and farming. His oldest child is said to be the first white girl born in Colo, but I have shown that white children were born here before the gold discoveries. George L. Henderson, born in 1836, in 1859 came to Central City, and in 1860 to California gulch. He was the first postmaster at Leadville, which camp was thus named at his suggestion.

CHAPTER IV.

PROGRESS OF SETTLEMENT.

1859–1860.

THE ARKANSAS VALLEY—ROAD INTO SOUTH PARK—EL PASO CLAIM CLUB —COLORADO CITY COMPANY—IRRIGATION—THE FIGHTING FARMERS OF FONTAINE CITY—CAÑON CITY—CLEAR CREEK—PUEBLO—CALIFORNIA GULCH—PIONEERS IN THE SEVERAL LOCALITIES—ORO CITY—LEADVILLE —FRYING PAN GULCH—ROAD-MAKING—MINING DEVELOPMENTS— FREIGHTING—MAIL FACILITIES—PONY EXPRESS—STAGE COMPANIES.

WHILE the valleys and head waters of the Platte and its tributaries were being actively explored by one part of the immigration, another part began to occupy the Arkansas valley. A portion of the Lawrence party of 1858 had wintered five miles above Denver, where afterward was Younker's rancho. They contemplated making a town there, and erected a few houses; but before spring they became restless, and some returned to the Arkansas valley, with the design of going back to Kansas. This party of about a dozen persons, among whom were Charles Gilmore, Julian Smith, George A. Bute, and Anthony Bott, crossed the ridge between the Platte and Arkansas rivers when the snow on the summit was three feet deep; but on coming to the spot overlooking the southern slope, and seeing a sunny valley below, they changed their purpose, and selected a site for a town in the delightful region of the Fontaine-qui-Bouille, which they called El Dorado.

On hearing what had been done, others of the original company who had located land claims on the Fontaine-qui-Bouille the previous autumn, some of which covered the new town site, came over from the

(337)

Platte to dispute for possession of the ground.   The quarrel ran high, but a compromise was effected by admitting the land claimants into the town company, all joining in the erection of a large log house as the nucleus of their future city.[1]

This being done, Bute, with two others of the El Dorado company, and Tucker, a squatter on Fontaine-qui-Bouille, with two associates, making a party of six, set out to search for a route into the South park, where they believed gold existed. Following the Indian trail westward to Soda springs, where the Lawrence company had located the town of El Paso[2] the previous autumn, the explorers encamped for two days to admire and enjoy the natural charms of the place, after which they proceeded as far on their way as the Petrified stumps; but falling short of provisions, returned and loaded a wagon with supplies. This wagon they took into the park, its wheels being the first to print the sod in this beautiful mountain basin.   Gold, as I have shown, was discovered in the park during the summer,[3] the mines drawing away

---

[1] El Paso Co., etc., MS., 6.

[2] There was at this time a log cabin at these springs, which had been erected by Richard Wooten, as evidence that he claimed the site before the El Paso town was projected. Sometime in 1859 Wooten sold his claim to R. E. Whitsitt & Co., for $500. A year or two later, Whitsitt's partner sold his interest to the Tappan Brothers from Boston. They bought about the same time 480 acres on the west side of Monument creek, which was known as the Boston tract, and was only put into market as an addition to Colorado springs in 1874. Whitsitt and Tappan lost their right to the springs by abandonment, and they were jumped by one Slaughter, son of a methodist minister from Illinois, who erected a frame house on the claim. He in turn abandoned it, and it was again taken by Thompson Girter, who secured the sulphur springs in South park. He made some improvements and sold to Col Chivington for $1,500, and he to his son-in-law, Pollock, who made a transfer of the property to some other person as security for a debt, this person selling the springs for $1,500.   George Crater of Denver subsequently organized a company which purchased the property, paying $10,000 for it, and afterward sold the 80 acres on which are the soda springs for $26,000 to the company which finally founded the present town of Colorado Springs, of which further mention will be made in the proper place. El Paso County, etc., MS., 9–11. It has been stated that H. A. W. Tabor built the first house at Colorado Springs in the winter of 1859; that he came back to Denver in the following year, and endeavored to organize a company to go down and lay off a town, but failed. The statement is erroneous, but that Tabor was at some time about this date interested in the place is perhaps true.

[3] A writer in the Colorado Springs Gazette of May 23, 1874, ascribes the discovery of gold at Fair Play to this party. The discovery was made in

all the settlers at El Dorado City, which was abandoned. The richness of the South park diggings, however, caused the revival of the town in the autumn under a new name. It had been observed by certain enterprising persons that the pass of the Fontaine-qui-Bouille seemed to offer the most practical wagon route for the immigration to these mines, thousands of persons travelling through it during the summer, a succession of delightful park-like valleys furnishing a natural and easy road into the main park. A company was formed at Denver and Auraria consisting of L. J. Winchester, Lewis N. Tappan, Anthony Bott, George A. Bute, Melancthon S. Beech, Julian Smith, H. M. Fosdick, D. A. Cheever, R. E. Whitsitt, S. W. Wagoner, W. P. McClure, P. McCarty, A. D. Richardson, T. H. Warren, C. W. Persall, A. B. Wade, George W. Putnam, John S. Price, John T. Parkinson, G. N. Woodward, Charles F. Blake, E. P. Stout, Clark and Willis, Mr Cable, and Higgins and Cobb, with two or three others, with the object of founding a city on the deserted site of El Dorado. The president of the company was Winchester, and the secretary Tappan.

One of the peculiar phases of squatter sovereignty in Colorado in 1859 was an organization known as El Paso Claim club,[4] shadowing forth the provisional government. A meeting having been called in the Arkansas valley to deliberate upon the best method to be pursued in holding land in the absence of law and land-offices, El Paso Claim club was the result. The limits over which the club had jurisdiction, and the powers and duties of its officers, were defined; a president and secretary were chosen, and provision made for the selection of jurors to decide upon cases under arbitration. A book of records was kept,[5] and

Aug. by miners from Tarryall; but there were other parties in the park at the time, who joined in working the ground if not in the discovery.

[4] Fowler, *Around Colorado*, MS., 3, 6; Helm, *Gate of the Mountains*, MS., 4.

[5] The names of A. D. Richardson, D. A. and C. B. Chever, Samuel Tappan, William Larimer, S. W. Wagoner, and other prominent men may be

on its pages was recorded the declaration of the Colorado City company's claim of 1,280 acres, signed by
the secretary of the club, H. J. Burghardt, and dated
December 20, 1859. The following summer there
were three hundred houses in the town, and lots were
selling at four hundred dollars.[6] It was a short-lived
prosperity. The breaking out of the civil war, and
other causes, forced travel away from the Arkansas
valley to the Platte route, and built up Denver at
the expense of Colorado City, which lost its hold
upon the car of progress, and was left behind in the
race.[7]

It will be remembered that Robert Middleton and
family, and a few others of the Lawrence company of
1858, wintered at or near Pueblo, where they were
joined by others in 1859, who had arrived early in
that year. A number of these persons, rightfully
judging that when corn was worth from five to fifteen
cents a pound, farming was as profitable as mining,
and much less laborious, determined to put in crops
in the rich Arkansas bottoms. Accordingly they
constructed a ditch which conducted the water of the
Fontaine-qui-Bouille over their fields, and planted
corn.[8] When the corn had reached a good height,
and waved temptingly in the wind and sun, a company of disgusted prospectors, returning to Missouri,
encamped near the settlement, which was called Fontaine City, and foraged their lean and hungry cattle
on the glistening green blades and juicy stalks. The

seen. Houses were erected on the Fontaine-qui-Bouille by R. B. Willis, H.
S. Clark, John Bley, Hubbard Talcott, William Campbell, the last three of
whom opened farms in 1860. *Arkansas Val. Hist.*, 420.

[6] The first store in Colorado City was owned by Gerrish and Cobb, in
charge of William Garvin, the original claimant of the Garden of the Gods.
John George, who still resides in the old town, opened the first saloon. Tappan & Co. put up the first frame house in 1860, which was still standing in
1874. It was occupied as the county court-house before the removal of the
county seat to Colorado springs. *El Paso County, etc.*, MS., 19.

[7] *Tabor's Cabin Life in Colo*, MS., 1–2; *Howbert's Indian Troubles*, MS., 2.

[8] The first farmers in this region, other than the fur-traders, were Robert
Middleton, George Peck, Charles D. Peck, Josiah F. Smith, Otto Winneka,
Frank Doris, George Lebaum, William H. Green, and William Kroenig.
Arkansas Val. Hist., 766.

ranchmen remonstrated, but the Missourians outnumbered them. The settlers then demanded pay, which was refused, and whenever opportunity came drove the cattle into the field, where they were kept and guarded as indemnity for the loss of their corn. Then followed a struggle on the part of the Missourians to recover their teams; but the settlers had entrenched themselves, and prepared to fight. In the battle which ensued some of the Missourians were killed, and some on both sides were wounded. The victory, however, was with the farmers, who received at last payment of damages, and restored the cattle to their owners. The Missourians were glad to get away, having apparently no further use for the fighting farmers of Fontaine City.[9]

In October a town was laid off at the mouth of the Arkansas river pass of the mountains, called Cañon City.[10] Its founders were Josiah F. Smith, Stephen S. Smith, William H. Young, Robert Bearcaw, Charles D. Peck, and William Kroenig. They erected a single log house on the level ground above the hot springs, which were found here, as well as at the pass of the Fontaine-qui-Bouille; and Robert Middleton and wife went to reside in it, this being the actual first family of Cañon City. The following year the house was taken as a blacksmith shop by A. Rudd.

In the spring of 1860 the town site was jumped by a company from Denver, which magnanimously retained some of the former claimants. They relocated the town, making it embrace 1,280 acres, and in April it was surveyed into lots and blocks. The new company consisted of William Kroenig, E. Williams, W. H. Young, A. Mayhood, J. B. Doyle, A. Thomas, H. Green, J. D. Ramage, Harry Youngblood, W. W.

[9] The first store in Fontaine City was opened by Cooper and Wing. Some of the first settlers after the Lawrence party were S. S. Smith, W. H. Young, Matthew Steel, O. H. P. Baxter, George M. Chilcott, John W. Shaw, Mark G. Bradford, George A. Hinsdale, Francisco, and Howard.

[10] *Rudd's Early Affairs*, MS., 1–9; *Fowler's Around Colorado*, MS., 1–8; *A Woman's Experience*, MS., 3–8; *Helm's Gate of the Mountains*, MS., 12; *Prescott's Through Cañon de Shea*, MS., 2–3.

Ramage, J. Graham, M. T. Green, Alvord and Company, St. Vrain and Easterday, and Buel and Boyd, surveyors. Having jumped a town site claim themselves, they organized a claim club for their protection, in which those taking up agricultural lands joined.[11] Coal creek, in the coal region, was, in 1885,

[11] The first grist-mill in Frémont county was erected by Lewis Conley in 1860 on Beaver creek, and was washed away in 1862. No other was built till 1866 or 1867, 4 miles east of Cañon City. In 1872 a grist-mill was erected in the town. The first saw-mill was built the same year by J. B. Cooper, J. C. Moore, Harkins, and A. Chandler. on Sand creek, above the soda springs. As a premium they were presented with an original share in the town of Cañon City. R. R. Kirkpatrick ran a shingle-machine in connection with the mill. The first merchants were Dold & Co., whose stock was presided over by Wolfe Londoner; Doyle & Co., represented by Solomon brothers; C. W. Ketchum and brother; Stevens & Curtis; Majors & Russell, who built a stone store 100 feet in length; R. O. Olds, J. A. Draper, James Gormly, James Ketchum, G. D. Jenks, Paul brothers, Harrison & Macon, and D. P. Wilson. These were all in business in Cañon City in 1860, before the decline of its early prospects. G. D. Jenks also opened the first hotel. Custer and Swisher kept the first meat-market, and E. B. Sutherland the first bakery. W. C. Catlin established the first brick-yard about 1872, to employ the prisoners in the penitentiary. The first newspaper was the *Cañon City Times*, issued in Sept. 1860 by Millett, since of Kansas City. The first postmaster was M. G. Pratt. In 1870 there were but two post-offices in the county. The first district court was held at Cañon City in the spring of 1863 by B. F. Hall, who held but one term before resigning. He found that men who had conducted people's courts were hard to awe into respect for imported judges. The discoverer in 1862 of the oil springs 6 miles from Cañon City was Gabriel Bowen. He sold them to A. M. Cassidy, who manufactured in 1862-5, and shipped to other parts of the country 300,000 gallons of superior quality of illuminating and lubricating oil. Since that time prospecting has been going on to find flowing wells. Some of the first settlers in Frémont county, outside of Cañon City, were George and Al. Toof, John Pierce, Hiram Morey, John Callen, John McClure, and Foster, on Beaver creek; J. Witcher, T. Virden, William Irwin, Ambrose Flournoy, and Robert Pope, on Ute creek; B. M. Adams, M. D. Swisher, Ebenezer Johnson, Sylvester H. Dairs, James Murphy, Jesse Rader, and Mills M. Craig, in Oil Creek valley; Philip A. McCumber, John Smith, James A. McCandless, Ira Chatfield, Stephen Frazier, Gid. B. Frazier, Jesse Frazier, B. F. Smith, John Locke, Jacob R. Reisser, and William H. May, in the vicinity of Florence; James Smith, Bruce, and Henry Burnett, on Hardscrabble creek.

I have said that the town site of Cañon City was jumped in the spring of 1860. The company remained in possession till 1864, when all abandoned it, and sought newer fields of enterprise in the mining camps. Three families only remained in the town. Not long afterward the government surveyed the township and the town site, whereupon it was preëmpted by Benjamin Griffin, W. C. Catlin, Jothan A. Draper, Augustus Macon, and A. Rudd, who deeded to the owners of improvements the lots on which they were placed, and proceeded to set affairs again in motion. These men belonged to a company of 20 families, which migrated from Iowa that year, and who were known as the resurrectionists, because they brought back life to Cañon City. They were Thomas Macon, who, while a member of the legislature of 1867-8, secured for his town the location of the penitentiary; Mrs Ann Harrison, Mrs George, John Wilson, Joseph Macon, Fletcher, Augustus Sartor,

next to Cañon City in size, having a population of five hundred.

The first farm located in what is now Frémont county was by J. N. Haguis, on the 1st of January,

Zach. Irwin, and others with their families. Anson Rudd was one of the three original settlers who would not forsake the place of his choice. He was first sheriff, county commissioner two terms, provost-marshal, oil inspector, postmaster, clerk of the people's court, candidate for lieut-gov., and blacksmith for the county. He was one of the locators of the roads to Wet Mountain valley, to which he guided the German colony; of the road to the upper Arkansas region, and to Currant creek and South park; was for several years president of the Cañon City Ditch company, and was the first warden of the penitentiary after the admission of the state, as well as one of the commissioners to locate it. The first child born was a son of M. D. Swisher, who died in infancy. W. C. Catlin was also of the original settlers, as was J. A. Draper, who was second postmaster, and county treasurer, collecting the first taxes ever gathered in the county. He gave the ground on which the penitentiary was placed. When he sold a tract to the Central Colorado Improvement company it was with the intention of reserving for the use of the public the soda springs; but through some inadvertance in the deed he failed to do so. Other early Cañonites were William H. Green, captain of the 1st Colorado regiment; Folsom, who also enlisted, and was crippled for life; Piatt, W. R. Fowler, author of *Around Colorado*, MS.; J. Reid, Benjamin F. Griffin, S. D. Webster, county surveyor, judge, and member of the legislature; Frank Bengley, who, although a Canadian, enlisted in the union army; Albert Walthers, first keeper of the penitentiary; S. H. Boyd, hotel-keeper; H. W. Saunders, W. H. McClure, who built the McClure house and ruined himself by the help of the D. & R. G. railroad company; B. Murray, who kept the house, and S. W. Humphrey. The first church organized in Cañon City was in 1860-1, by Johnson of Kansas, a methodist, with about ten members. None of these were left when the Iowa colony arrived, and George Murray again organized a church, with 45 members, who purchased a stone building and fitted it up for worship. In 1865 the missionary baptists formed a church, with B. M. Adams pastor, and 18 members, who in 1869 built a small church edifice. In 1867 the Cumberland presbyterians organized under their elders, B. F. Moore, Stephen Frazier, and J. Blanchard. In 1872 the presbyterians were organized by Shelden Jackson, J. K. Brewster being ruling elder, and soon built a small but pleasant church. In 1874 or 1875 the renowned episcopal bishop, Randall, organized that church, which after a few years erected a brick edifice.

The public schools of Cañon City were somewhat late in securing a proper building, which was not erected until 1880. It was of stone, fine, and commodious. The board that secured the bonds for its erection consisted of Charles E. Waldo president, Mrs M. M. Sheets secretary, John Wilson treasurer. The fire department was organized in Jan. 1879, consisting of the Relief Hook and Ladder company No. 1, of 20 members. The following year H. A. Reynolds Hose company of 13 members was added to the department. Mount Moriah lodge No. 15 of masons was instituted in Nov. 1867, under a dispensation of Henry M. Teller, M. W. G. Master of Colorado, and chartered Oct. 7, 1868. In 1881 there were 72 members. Cañon City lodge No. 7 of odd fellows was instituted Nov. 10, 1868, the first lodge south of the divide. It had in 1881 46 members. Grand Cañon Encampment No. 18, July 29, 1881. The united workmen organized Royal George Lodge, No. 7, June 25, 1881, with 24 members.

Cañon City was incorporated April 1, 1872. In 1879 a board of trade was organized. which greatly assisted the city government in purifying morals by forcing out of town certain disreputable characters, a function which, if un-

1860. It was recorded by B. H. Bolin, and was taken previous to the organization of the claim club, whose constitution was dated March 13, 1860.[12] The pretensions of Cañon City to become the metropolis of the future state were founded similarly to those of Colorado City, and were rendered nugatory by the same causes. The first company surveyed a road to the Tarryall mines, setting up mile posts the whole distance of eighty miles. A large part of the immigration of 1860 took this route to the mines, and Cañon City enjoyed for a year or two a prosperous growth; and there, for the time, it ended.[13]

In the winter of 1859–60 the American town of Pueblo was laid off, on the site of the abandoned Pueblo of Mexican times, by a company composed of

usual for such a board, proved beneficial. In Dec. of that year a joint stock company was organized, with a capital of $50,000, to construct water works, consisting of James Clelland, James H. Peabody, George R. Shaeffer, Ira Mulock, August Heckscher, Wilbur K. Johnson, David Caird, and O. G. Stanley. On July 9, 1881, was laid the corner stone of the court house, a handsome edifice, the county commissioners managing the business being Edwin Tobach, Louis Muehlbach, and Joseph J. Phelps; also of the masonic temple, another fine structure—both of brick. In 1881 there were 25 stores in Cañon City, well stocked, some carrying a trade of over $300,000 annually, besides shops of all kinds.

[12] This claim was taken on the north side of the Arkansas river, on a creek whose name is not given. Two brothers named Costans took claims on the south side, 7 miles below Cañon City. On the record they were described as 'situated in Mexico.' The names of M. V. B. Coffin and B. F. Allen occur among the inhabitants of Cañon City precinct in 1860.

[13] Towns and settlements of Fremont county, besides those mentioned, are Badger, Barnard Creek, Carlisle Springs, Clelland, Coal Junction, Copper Gulch, Cotopaxi, Fairy, Fidler, Florence, Galena, Galena Basin, Glendale, Grape Creek Junction, Greenwood, Hayden, Hayden Creek, Haydenville, Hillsdale, Howards, Juniper, Labran, Lake, Marsh, Mining Camp, New Chicago, Oak Creek, Parkdale, Park Station, Pleasant Valley, Rockvale, Salesburgh, Spike Buck, Texas, Texas Creek, Titusville, Tomichi, Twelve Mile Bridge, Vallie, Webster, Williamsburgh, and Yorkville. Among the contributors to this part of my work are Eugene Weston, W. A. Helm, and Anson S. Rudd. Weston was born in Maine in 1805, and came to Colorado in 1860, and to Cañon City the same year, where I found him in 1884. He is the author of The Colorado Mines, MS., treating of placers and early transportation. Helm was born in Pa in 1831. After migrating to several of the western states, he came to Colorado in 1860, and in 1861 settled in Cañon City with his family. On the 'resurrection' of that town he opened a hotel. He is the author of The Gate of the Mountain, MS., well filled with reminiscences. Rudd, who furnished Early Affairs in Cañon City, MS., and whose account forms the basis of early history here, was born in Erie co., Pa, in 1819, and after learning the printer's trade visited Kansas, Mexico, and California, coming to Colorado in 1860, and settling at Cañon City. How he acted his part as pioneer, I have said.

Belt, Catterson, Cyrus Warren, Ed. Cozzens, J. Wright,[14] Albert Bearcaw, W. H. Green, and others. It was surveyed by Buell and Boyd, who laid it out on a broad scale, and the former name was retained. It did not at first, however, extend over the bottom land in front of the town subsequent additions having been made by other companies and railroad corporations.[15]

[14] *Stone's Gen. View*, MS., 19. Wright built the first house in Pueblo, on the corner of Front street and Santa Fé avenue. Dr Catterson's cabin was on Second street, near the avenue. The first family in Pueblo was that of Aaron Sims, and the second that of Josiah F. Smith. Jack Allen opened a small grocery and drinking saloon. A stock of other goods was opened in a store on Santa Fé avenue, over which Dr Catterson presided, and the town was launched upon the sea of commerce. Emory Young, son of W. H. Young, was the first male child born in Pueblo, and Hattie Smith the first girl. *Rice's Politics in Pueblo*, MS., 1; *Rudd's Early Affairs in Cañon City*, MS.; *Weston's Colorado Mines*, MS.; *Helm's Gate of the Mountains*, MS.

[15] Of the pioneers of Arkansas valley the following mention may be made in this place; Harry Youngblood came out with Robert Middleton, and went under an assumed name from some connection he was alleged to have had with the death of Joseph Smith, the founder of Mormonism. George W. Hepburn, a native of N. Y., in 1855 went to Omaha, where he owned an interest first in the *Nebraskian*, and then in the *Times*. In 1867 he settled in Pueblo, where he started, in 1871, a newspaper called *The People*. Charles Nachtrieb, a German, brought a small stock of goods to Colorado in 1859. Jesse Frazer, from Mo., settled in the spring of 1860 on the Arkansas, 8 miles below Cañon City, and was the first to turn a furrow in that region, which he did with a forked cottonwood limb. Reuben J. Frazier, a native of Ind., started a farm in the upper Arkansas valley in the spring of 1860.

There are many more pioneers, known and unknown, of 1859. Of those of whom something is on record, not elsewhere mentioned, are the following: Lewis W. Berry, a capt. in the Mexican war, was born in N. Y., mined at Central City, and finally settled at Idaho Springs. Corbit Bacon, born in N. Y., erected a plank house with a shake roof in Denver in the winter of 1858–9, and went to Central City in the spring. John W. Edwards, a Welshman, resided at Idaho springs. Then there were Thomas Cooper, an Englishman, miner; David D. Strock of Ohio, miner. Anthony Tucker, from Pa, set up a saw mill engine for Bentley and Bayard of Central City—the first steam mill in Colorado; Andrew H. Spickerman, from N. Y., stock raiser on Turkey creek. D. D. McIlvoy, from Ky, farmer and miner; Frank J. Wood, from Chico, opened the first drug store in Georgetown; William M. Allen, of New Brunswick, farmer; Joseph S. Beaman, from Germany, brewer, Central City; Reuben C. Wells, from Ill., purchased the Golden Paper mill, the first establishment of the kind in the state; Jay Sternberg, from N. Y., erected the Boulder City Flouring mills in 1872; Hiram Buck, from Ohio, farmer; August Burk, a Swede, opened a bakery in Denver in 1859; William Arbuthnot from Pa, farmer; Norman R. Howard, from Ill., farmer; Robert Niver, a native of N. Y., farmer; Henry B. Ludlow, from Ohio, farmer; Thomas J. Jones, born in Ill., merchant; John Reese. from Pa, farmer; L. A. Williams, from Vt, erected a steam saw mill at Denver; George C. Griffin, born in Ct, farmer; Edwin Lobach, born in Pa, freighter and farmer; Henry Burnett, from Mass, farmer; Francis R. Ford, from Maine, miner and farmer; B. F. Sahaffer, from Pa. carpenter; Robert L. Lambert,

Late in the autumn a party of prospectors consisting of C. F. Wilson, Rafferty, Stevens, Abram Lee, Currier, Slater, and two others, crossed the range on the west of South park, and discovered good diggings in a gulch on the headwaters of the Arkansas, river, which they named California,[16] and which attracted thousands to that locality[17] in the spring following. The first house erected in the new mines was on the present site of Leadville, and the place was called Oro City. The post-office, which was established at this place, being removed in 1871 two and a half miles up the gulch, the name followed it, and Oro City left its first location open for subsequent development by other town locators. California gulch was thickly populated for six miles,[18] and had two unimportant towns besides Oro; namely, Malta and

freighter and stage owner; Aaron Ripley, from Ohio farmer; Emmett Nuckolls, a native of Va, stock dealer, N. C. Hickman, born in Mo., miner; David Clark, born in Ill., stock raiser; Rufus Shute, a native of N. Y., cattle raiser; J W. Lester, born in Pa, miner. George Rockafellow, was a capt. in the 6th Mich. cavalry during the war, and served afterward under Gen. Conner in the Powder river expedition against the Indians.

[16] Three men in three months took out $60,000. *Weston's Colo Mines*, MS., 2.

[17] Among the first was H. A. W. Tabor, a man of remarkable enterprise and ability, whose biography is given elsewhere in this volume. If not one of the actual discoverers, he has contributed more than any single individual to the prosperity of the Leadville district. In 1860, when first he removed to its site, it contained only a single log cabin. Before the close of the following year its population exceeded 10,000, and the place was acknowledged as the mining centre of Colorado. When the placers had long been exhausted, and the huge bowlders that obstructed their working were found to contain the richest kind of carbonate ores, we again find him at the front, and as a Denver journal remarks, 'not only Leadville, but the whole state of Colorado, is under obligations of gratitude to Mr Tabor for his unflagging faith in the Leadville mines.'

[18] Says Wolfe Londoner, in his *Colorado Mining Camps*, MS., 7. 'California gulch, in 1860 and 1861, had a population of something over 10,000, and was the great camp of Colorado. It was strung all along the gulch, which was something over 5 miles long. . . There were a great many tents in the road and on the side of the ridge, and the wagons were backed up, the people living in them. Some were used as hotels. They had their grub under the wagons, piled their dishes there, and the man of the house and his wife would sleep in the wagon. Their boarders took their meals off tables made of rough boards. . . . Gamblers had tables strung along the wayside to take in the cheerful but unwary miner. The game that took the most was three-card monte.' Indeed, one mining camp differed little from another in this respect. See also *Chipley's Towns*, MS., 2; *Rand's Guide to Colo*, 30; *Bayle's Politics and Mining*, MS., 3.

Slabtown. Twenty miles below, on the Arkansas river, the town of Granite was started not long after, rich mines being at this place, which were first discovered by H. A. W. Tabor, in the spring of 1860. They required quicksilver in separating the gold from the black sand, and were afterward owned by Bailey and Gaff of Cincinnati.[19]

During the summer of 1860 gold was discovered in Frying Pan gulch, at the base of Mount Massive, opposite the mouth of California gulch, by C. F. Wilson, the diggings receiving their name from the circumstance of a frying pan being used to pan out the first metal. These mines did not prove of much value until 1863, when the name was changed to Colorado gulch. Chalk creek mines were also discovered this season by Stephen B. Kellogg and others. A pretended discovery was made in 1860 in the San Juan country by one Baker, which drew 1,000 persons to that region, who found no gold, although it was there, as subsequent exploration and development proved.

Some improvements were made in 1859 in the matter of roads and mining ditches. There was a road from Denver into the mountains via Golden Gate, and another via Bradford; also one into South park, via Mount Vernon and Bergen's rancho, under construction. Three others were surveyed, the St Vrain, Golden, and Colorado wagon road, and the roads into South park via Cañon and Colorado cities. A mining ditch eleven miles long was constructed at Missouri flats by a company of which W. Green Russell was president. Boulder, South Boulder, and Four Mile creeks were diverted from their channels for some distance.

[19] Some of the pioneers on the head waters of the Arkansas were the following: Samuel Arbuthnot, from Pa; David C. Dargin, from Me; Robert Berry, from Ohio; Charles F. Wilson, from Ky; Charles L. Hall, from N. Y.; John Riling, from Ohio; George W. Huston, from Pa; and Philo N. Weston, from N. Y.

Those who returned to the states carried reports sufficiently confirmed by the gold they exhibited to re-arouse the gold fever, causing an immigration the following summer equal to, if not exceeding, that of 1859.[20] The settlements already founded were greatly enlarged, and new ones made, both in the mining and agricultural districts.[21] Over the 600 miles of road from the Missouri to the mountains, a stream of material wealth rolled, which was expected to flow back again in a stream of gold dust a few months later. Contrary to the usual practice of the eastern journals, the *New York Tribune* contributed to the furore for emigration to the mines by advertising Colorado climate and scenery in terms of lavish praise, its editor-in-chief, Horace Greeley, and others of its staff having visited the mountains in 1859, at which time Greeley

[20] *Sopris' Settlement of Denver*, MS., 3. By the middle of July an arastra was running at the mouth of Gregory gulch, owned by Lehmer, Laughlin, and Peck, which was the pioneer quartz mill in Colorado. In September Prosser, Conklin, and co. had a small steam stamp mill in operation. The following month there were five arastras running on north Clear creek, and two small wooden stamp mills, all operated by water power. Another steam, mill, belonging to Coleman, Le Fevre, and co., started up the same month-but broke down, and took a month for repairs. When it started again, however, running on Gunnell quartz, it produced 1,442 pennyweights of gold in seven days, the rock being taken out at a depth of fifty-six feet. At the depth of seventy-six feet, fifteen tons of rock yielded $1,700. A rude three-stamp quartz mill, owned by T. J. Graham, was in operation at Gold hill during the summer, and a large mill, run by water, was erected there in the autumn. Where no mills had been erected, miners were busy getting out ore for those that were expected to be built the coming spring. As winter approached, many, under the impression that mining in the cold season would be impracticable, returned to their former homes to spend the interval in more comfortable quarters, and prepare for future enterprises; but many there were who stayed by their claims in the mountains, fortifying themselves against the expected cold by banking up the earth around their cabins, and filling them with a store of provisions sufficient to outlast the anticipated snow blockade, which never came. Some mining was carried on throughout the entire season, even in the mountains, and there was almost uninterrupted travel, to the surprise and delight of the imperfectly sheltered inhabitants of the different towns.

[21] At the close of 1860 there were 71 steam quartz mills in the Clear creek region running 609 stamps, of an average weight of 416 pounds; and 38 water mills, with 230 stamps, weighing 352 pounds, besides 50 arastras, the total power employed being equal to 960 horse power. In the Boulder region there were four steam mills, five water mills, and 29 arastras, equalling 150 horse power. South park and California gulch had also a number of mills and arastras in 1860. *Collins' Rocky Mountain Gold Region*, 51-3. This is an emigrant's guide, containing tables of distances, maps, and a business directory, with information concerning mining and a miner's outfit.

extended his visit to Nevada and California, Fortunately for the prosperity of Colorado at this period. there was nothing to interrupt the influx of people or property. The freight trains of Russell and Majors dragged their winding length along the Arkansas or Smoky hill route day after day, bringing cargoes of goods, which were stored at their depots and sold to retail merchants on their own account,[22] or carrying the goods of others. Many thousand wagons stretched in a continuous line along the Platte also, from its mouth to its source.[23] Prices were necessarily high, and likewise high because everybody who had anything to sell desired to become rich out of it without loss of time. Mail facilities were introduced, and more quickly than could have been anticipated correspondence with the east became established.[24] On the 4th of March, 1860, Kehler and Montgomery started a line of coaches from Denver to the mining

[22] *Helm's Gate of the Mountains*, MS., 2; *Aux' Mining in Colo*, MS., 6–7.

[23] According to Davis, *Hist. Colo*, MS., there were between 8,000 and 10,000 men of the freighting class, mostly drivers, in Colorado, whom he describes as 'turbulent fellows, spending most of their leisure and all of their money in saloons.'

[24] Besides the many who travelled with conveyances of their own, there were some who took passage with transportation companies, of which Russell and Majors, of St Joseph, were the chief firm. This company organized a line of stages in the spring of 1859, the first coach for Denver leaving Leavenworth March 9th, carrying the mail. They called themselves the Leavenworth and Pike's Peak Express company, and charged an extra postage of 25 cents on a letter, having post offices of their own at Auraria and other towns. The postmaster at Leavenworth was directed to deliver all mail matter for Pike's peak to the express company so long as they would carry it without expense to the government. Nelson Sargent was superintendent of this company. He resigned in the autumn. In the winter of 1859–60 a charter was obtained from the Kansas legislature incorporating the Central Overland California and Pike's Peak Express company, which was a reorganization of the former company, the principal men in it being William H. Russell, John S. Jones, William B. Waddell, Luther R. Smoot, Alexander Majors, and J. B. Simpson. The route pursued by the express companies in 1859 was via the Smoky hill fork of the Kansas river, on the line adopted by the Kansas Pacific railroad. I have already given the history of the California and Salt Lake mail in my *Nevada*. Chorpening owned the line in conjunction with Holladay. In the winter of 1859–60 the fertile brains of W. H. Russell and B. F. Ficklen, president and superintendent of the C. O. and P. P. Express co., conceived a plan of rapid communication with the Pacific coast and intermediate points by means of the pony express, and having prepared the stations, started out their first pony, April 3, 1860, from St Joseph. The route connected with the mail near Atchison, passing through Troy and Marysville to Fort Kearny, keeping on the south side of the Platte

camps.   In May, Sowers and company established a
line, and in June the Western Stage company another,
all together being insufficient to carry the increasing
crowd of passengers.   To this point of progress had
the Pike's peak region arrived in its second year of
growth.

to Julesburg, where it sent a branch to Denver, crossing to the north side of
the Platte, and continuing to Salt Lake, via Scott Bluff, Fort Laramie, and
Fort Bridger.   From Salt Lake it followed the route by Ruby valley and
Carson to Sacramento, California.   The success of this enterprise caused the
transfer of the C. O. and P. P's stages and freight wagons to this route; and
the successful operations of this company on the central route is said by its
friends to have led to its adoption by the first overland railroad.   It demonstrated that it could be travelled in winter, which had hitherto been doubted;
but it was the attitude of the southern states, more than anything, which
caused the central route to be adopted.   These causes together, in the summer of 1861, caused the transfer of the overland mail from the southern or
Butterfield route to the Platte route.   In that year, also, the Overland Mail
co. purchased the interest of Chorpening in the western half of the overland
route.   Later in the year the C. O. and P. P. Express company and pony
express were sold to Ben Holladay, the western half being retained by the
Overland Mail, under the management of Fred Cook, Jacob King, H. S.
Rumfield, general agent and superintendent.   Holladay afterward secured
mail contracts through the north-west.

CHAPTER V.

ORGANIZATION OF GOVERNMENT.

1858–1861.

BLEEDING KANSAS—REPRESENTATIVE FROM ARAPAHOE COUNTY—PROVIS-
IONAL GOVERNMENT—TERRITORY OR STATE OF JEFFERSON—ELECTIONS
AND CONVENTIONS—GOVERNOR STEELE—DIVERS GOVERNMENTS—POPU-
LAR TRIBUNALS—THE TURKEY WAR—SQUATTERS—THE NAME COLO-
RADO—TERRITORIAL ORGANIZATION—GILPIN, GOVERNOR—BOUNDARIES
—CONDITION OF THE COUNTRY—SEAL—MINT—LEGISLATIVE PROCEED-
INGS—GILPIN'S MILITARY OPERATIONS—THE COLORADO REGIMENTS IN
THE CIVIL WAR.

WHILE gold was the spirit of the mountain miner's
dreams, there was a desperate political struggle going
on in Kansas between the advocates of free soil and
slave soil. There were alternating territorial legislatures and state legislatures, and it was a question
under which form of government the people were
living. If Kansas were a territory it extended to the
summit of the Rocky range, and embraced the Pike's
peak country. If it were a state, its western boundary did not reach within three degrees of the historic
mountain.

The little handful of Americans gathered at Auraria in the autumn of 1858, with that facility for
politics which distinguishes our people, took into consideration these questions as affecting their future, and
proceeded in a characteristic manner to meet the difficulty. A mass meeting was held to organize a county,
to be named Arapahoe, after one of the plains tribes
of Indians, with the county seat at Auraria; and an
informal election was held for a representative from
this county to proceed to the capital of Kansas and

procure the sanction of the legislature to its establishment, the representative chosen being A. J. Smith. He was not admitted to the Kansas legislative body, but was successful in his mission, Governor Denver, without waiting for the action of the legislature, appointing county commissioners, who proceeded at once to the performance of their duties.[1] The county being divided into twenty-three precincts or districts,

[1] I find that all the writers who mention this subject speak of Arapahoe county as having been actually established, which was not the case. Another error is apparent, the date of Smith's election being given as Nov. 6th in *Hollister's Mines of Colorado*, 18; *Colorado Gazetteer*, 1870, 24; and *Corbett's Directory of Mines*, 38; while in the *History of Denver*, 631, the commissioners appointed by Gov. Denver are represented as arriving Nov. 12th, 6 days after the election. Probably Smith was sent on his errand some time in advance of Graham, whose mission was an afterthought. Denver, comprehending the situation of the miners 600 miles from law, with no chance of an organization by the legislature for several months, simply commissioned H. P. A. Smith probate judge, and appointed for county commissioners E. W. Wynkoop, Hickory Rogers, and Joseph L. McCubbin—see *Clear Creek and Boulder Val. Hist.*, 468—persons about to start for the mines. There was no other organization than this informal one of Arapahoe county, Kansas. The legislature Feb. 7, 1859, passed an act creating 5 counties; namely, Montana, in which Denver was situated, El Paso, Oro, Broderick, and Fremont out of the mountain region where gold might be found. Montana county began on the 40th parallel, 20 miles east of the 105th meridian, and embraced the territory south to within 20 miles of the 39th parallel, and west to the summit of the Rocky mountains. Oro county lay in an oblong shape east of Montana, and also El Paso, which was south of Montana. Broderick county lay south of Oro and El Paso; and Fremont took in the South park and all the territory west of Broderick and El Paso to the summits of the Rocky mountains. The commissioners appointed were J. H. Tarney, William H. Prentice, and A. D. Richardson for Montana county; D. Newcomb, William J. King, and George McGee for Oro county; Simon C. Gephart, W. Walters, and Charles Nichols for Broderick; T. C. Dixon, A. G. Patrick, and T. L. Whitney for Fremont; and William H. Green, G. W. Allison, and William O. Donnell for El Paso. The commissioners were required to establish the county seats, and to offer for sale by public notice 200 lots in each of these towns, the proceeds of which should be applied to liquidating the expenses of location, any excess over expenses to be paid into the county treasury. They were also required to call an election for county officers at as early a day as practicable, the officers elected, in view of the distance from the capital, being authorized to qualify and proceed to the discharge of their duties before being commissioned. The county commissioners were to be paid $5 per day and expenses for their whole term of 9 months, but the money was to come from the sale of the lots before mentioned, from which arrangement it may be inferred that not more than one, if any, could have received full payment. *Kansas Laws*, 1859, 57–60. Whether on this account or some other it does not appear that these counties were organized; but at the election of March 28, 1859, the following officers of Arapahoe county, having no legal existence, were chosen: probate judge S. W. Wagoner, sheriff D. D. Cook, treasurer John L. Hiffner, register of deeds J. S. Lowrie, prosecuting attorney Marshall Cook, auditor W. W. Hooper, assessor Ross Hutchins, coroner C. M. Steinberger, supervisors L. J. Winchester, H. Rogers, R. S. Wooten, clerk of supervisors Levi Ferguson. *Byers' Hist. Colo*, MS., 49.

sheriff and other officers were chosen for the time from among the population of the county.

On reflection, and in view of the peculiar situation of Kansas, the politicians of Auraria conceived the idea of a separate government under the name of the Territory of Jefferson, and on the 6th of November elected Hiram J. Graham and Albert Steinberger delegates to proceed to Washington with a petition to effect this object. Graham was from New York, but had lived in Illinois and was one of the projectors of Pacific City, Iowa, from which place he went to the Pike's peak country. He was a man of excellent traits and fair ability, but not likely to carry out so extraordinary a scheme as that on which he was bent, of persuading congress to erect a territory in the Rocky mountains to oblige a few hundred persons who did not yet know of any gold diggings of much value, whatever their faith that they should find them. Graham gained nothing by his delegateship but an enlarged experience of the ways of congressmen and the machinery of government. Steinberger was a young man, and dropped out of the delegation at Omaha. He was afterward king of a group of islands in the Pacific, but was deposed by a British man-of-war.

During the winter the isolated community of Arapahoe county governed itself without friction, by the observance of some simple regulations, and the authority of their chosen magistrates; but on the 28th of March, 1860, an election was held, under the laws of Kansas, for the choosing of county officers. There were 774 votes polled, the population having increased at least 500 since the last election. Continuing to increase rapidly, a public meeting was held on the 11th of April at Auraria, which resolved that the different precints should be requested to appoint delegates to meet in convention on the 15th, to take into consideration the propriety of organizing a state or territory; and a central committee was appointed, one of whose duties was the designation of as many new precincts as the spreading population required.

On the 7th of May an address was issued by the committee, appointing an election on the first Monday in June, to choose delegates to a convention to draft a constitution for the state of Jefferson. The election was held, but in most precincts by acclamation only, no returns ever being made. Fifty delegates met in June, in Wooten's hall, Denver, representing thirteen precincts. W. N. Byers was chosen temporary chairman; but on the permanent organization of the convention, S. W. Wagoner was made president, Henry Allen, E. P. Stout, R. Sopris, Levi Ferguson, and C. B. Patterson vice-presidents, Thomas Gibson and J. J. Shanley clerks.

After a two days' session, in which the chief business transacted was the appointment of committees to draft a constitution, it adjourned to meet again on the first Monday in August, the long interval being taken to observe the course of events. A. F. Garrison was chosen president. A committee was appointed by the convention to form new precincts, so that when that body reassembled there were present 167 delegates, representing forty-six precincts.

The convention was now about equally divided in favor of and against a state constitution, and discussion ran high. Three sets of resolutions were offered, one by H. P. A. Smith, providing that the convention should dissolve, and memorialize congress for a territorial organization; another by Beverly D. Williams, providing for a committee to report to the convention on the expediency of forming a constitution, or memorializing congress; and a third by S. W. Beall, in favor of forming a constitution. The resolutions of Smith and Beall were finally withdrawn, and Williams' resolution adopted. A committee was appointed, a majority of whose members reported in favor of a constitution.[2]

[2] *Extracts from Early Records*, MS., 4–6. Among those engaged in early

The convention remained in session one week, the constitution of the state of Jefferson being formed, with limits similar to the present state of Colorado. It was submitted to the people on the first Monday in September, with the alternative, in case of its rejection, that an election should be held in October to choose a delegate to congress, who should endeavor to have the gold regions set off in a territory to be called Jefferson. The constitution was rejected by a vote of 2,007 to 649, demonstrating by the lightness of the vote that gold, and not politics, absorbed the public mind.

And yet there was a party which found time to press the scheme of a provisional government, and which called a mass meeting at Auraria on the 24th of September to consider the subject. An address to the people was prepared, requesting them at the October election to vote for delegates who should meet a little later for the purpose of forming an independent government.[3]

The election took place on the 5th of October, when, owing to the return to the states of a large part of the population, and the indifference of those who remained, only about 8,000 votes were polled. Beverly D. Williams was chosen delegate to congress, and Richard Sopris representative from Arapahoe county to the legislature of Kansas. As on the previous attempt to secure a hearing in congress, Williams accomplished nothing more than to impress the government with the pertinacity of this far off and ambitious political bantling, variously known as Pike's peak, Arapahoe, county, and Jefferson territory. Sopris was given a seat in the Kansas legislature, Governor Denver hav-

government affairs were: E. H. N. Patterson, delegate from Left Hand creek, born in Va, and was at one time formerly editor of the *Placer Times*, of Sacramento, in California early days, and again of the Georgetown *Miner* 10 years afterward; Charles C. Post, miner and lawyer from Missouri gulch; George M. Chilcott, and I. J. Pollock.

[3] The leaders in this movement were Frank De La Mar, S. W. Wagoner, B. D. Williams, G. M. Willing, A. Sagendorf, H. P. A. Smith, Henry Allen, and M. C. Fisher. *Byers' Hist. Colo*, MS., 55.

ing issued a proclamation to the voters of Arapahoe county to elect a representative—although no such county was known to that body.[4]

According to the plans arranged by the provisional government or territorial party, the election of their delegates took place, and on the 10th of October the convention met at Auraria, when eighty-six were found to be present. They adopted a constitution and proceeded to district the mining region, providing for a legislature consisting of eight councilmen, and twenty-one representatives. An election was ordered for the 24th, to choose a governor, secretary, members of the legislature, and other territorial officers, which was done with one unimportant exception, the vote standing about 1,800 to 300. R. W. Steele was elected governor of the territory of Jefferson, and Lucian W. Bliss secretary. Steele's message was creditable, and so was the action of the legislature, which met on the 7th of November and lasted forty days, during which many general and special laws were passed. Among the latter was a charter for the city of Denver. Nine counties were organized, for which probate judges were appointed by the governor, to hold until the first county elections in January 1860.[5] A tax of one dollar per capita was levied to defray expenses; and the assembly adjourned to the 23d of January.

[4] In Sopris, *Settlement of Denver*, MS., 13, he says that he obtained a charter for a ditch to bring the water of the Platte into Denver, which was perpetual, the city of Denver owning it; that he also obtained charters for roads, banking, insurance, and telegraph companies, and much necessary legislation of like character.

[5] The other officers of the provisional government were: C. R. Bissell, auditor; R. L. Wooten, treasurer; Samuel McLean, attorney-general; Oscar B. Totten, clerk of sup. court; A. J. Allison, chief justice; S. J. Johnson and L. W. Borton, associate justices; Hickory Rogers, marshal; H. H. McAfee, supt of public instruction. The members of the council from the 8 council districts were N. G. Wyatt, Henry Allen, Eli Carter, Mark A. Moore, J. M. Wood, James Emmerson, W. D. Arnett, D. Shafer, in the order in which they are named. The members of the lower house were John C. Moore, W. P. McClure, W. M. Slaughter, M. D. Hickman, D. K. Wall, Miles Patton, J. S. Stone, J. N. Hallock, J. S. Allen, A. J. Edwards, A. McFadden, Edwin James, T. S. Golden, J. A. Gray, Z. Jackson, S. B. Kellogg, William Davidson, C. C. Post, Asa Smith, C. P. Hall.

The supporters of the Kansas government who had sent their representative to the capital of that territory, refused to pay a tax to support the provisional government, in a remonstrance signed by six or seven hundred miners. The men of Gregory district, which the new government had erected into Mountain county, held an election on the 3d of January 1860, and rejected the county organization by a vote of 395 to 95. On the other hand, Arapahoe county, as created by the provisional legislature, acknowledged the new government, and held its election according to the law by which it was established.

On the 2d of January, a mass meeting was held at Denver, at which a memorial was adopted, addressed to the president, asking for a territorial organization, and S. W. Beall was delegated to carry it to Washington, but no notice was taken of the petition. The assembly met again on the 23d, pursuant to adjournment, and completed a civil and criminal code, which was observed and enforced in some parts of the " Territory of Jefferson," while in others the miners' courts held sway, and the Kansas government was least observed of any.[6]

The miners had invented a system of regulations, and were satisfied with them, and inclined to reject innovations. Each district had its president or judge, recorder, and sheriff, elected by ballot,[7] the rules laid down for their governance being simple and expeditious. Claim clubs, for the protection of agricultural or town site claims, with similar regulations, served the purpose of legal statutes, the expounding of which was too often accompanied by aggravating delays and ruinous costs. There was little anxiety therefore for change, except among professional politicians and their friends. But the people being generally order loving

[6] In the autumn of 1860 Edward M. McCook was elected to the Kansas legislature, but secured no benefits, and probably no pay. *Corbett's Dir. of Mines,* 42.

[7] Jack Keeler was elected sheriff of Arapahoe district in 1860, and his deputy was William Z. Cozens.

and law abiding, obeyed without question either form
of government, whose officers happened to be established in their midst, which obedience averted any
injurious collision of authorities. Occasionally a
change of venue was taken from one government to
the other, when the litigants suffered by having heavy
costs to pay. And occasionally crimes were committed, which demanded a strong and recognized government for their punishment. In the absence of that,
the people defended themselves as those of California
and each of the new mining territories had done, by
committees which dispensed a rude and vigorous
justice without appeal.[8] They acted spontaneously
and openly, and were known as the people's courts,
electing their judges and marshal as required, and
taking no notice of any but felonious offences. In
some parts of the country they became, from the neces-
sities of the case, vigilance committees, and dealt
with horse and cattle thieves. The penalties inflicted
were in accordance with the crime, and might be
either hanging, whipping, or banishment. Of the
first three homicides, one escaped, one was tried before
Judge H. P. A. Smith and hanged, and the third was
tried before Judge Hyatt and acquitted.

Denver being the principal town had most need of
the people's courts. In the latter part of January
the unruly element became alarmingly conspicuous.
Among the disturbances occasioned by this portion
of the population was what was known as the Turkey
war. It originated in the plundering by them of a
party of hunters from the southern part of the territory with a great number of wild turkeys for sale.
A committee was organized to punish the thieves;
but it was found that they had many defenders, and it
was with difficulty that a bloody conflict was avoided.

---

[8] Previous to April 1860 there were two duels in Denver. In one of them
J. S. Stone, a member of the provisional legislature, was killed by L. W.
Bliss, secretary and acting governor of Jefferson territory, who at a public
dinner made an offensive remark in allusion to Stone, which called out the
challenge.

The next excitement was over the jumping of town lots by squatters who had settled on the outskirts of Denver, and claimed the land under the agricultural preëmption law. Several times deadly weapons were discharged in altercations over town property, though no lives were sacrificed. This led to the organization of a claim club at Denver, the members being bound to defend the town company against squatters, several of whom were banished. In July a still more threatening affair warned the people to be on their

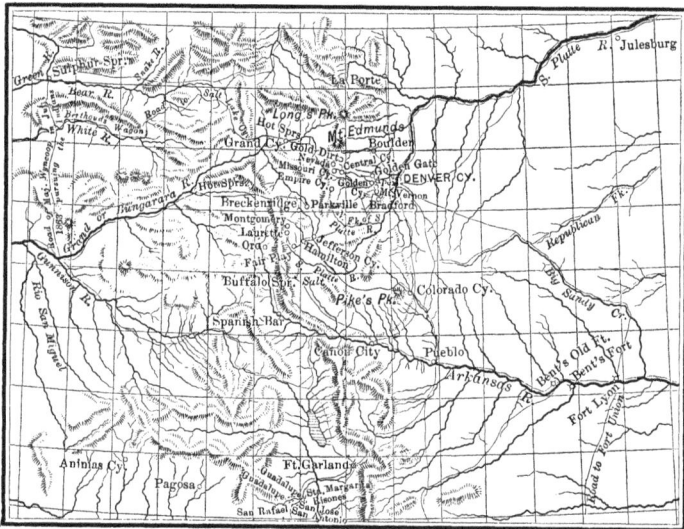

COLORADO IN 1863.

guard. The office of the *Rocky Mountain News* was attacked by a desperate man named Carl Wood, because the paper had condemned the killing of a negro named Starks by a confederate, Charles Harrison, and Byers narrowly escaped being killed. Wood was taken, tried, and banished by the decree of Judge H. P. Bennett.

So determined were the people that justice should be done that Sheriff Middaugh pursued and brought back from Leavenworth for trial James Gordon, who had, without provocation, killed Jacob Gantz in July. He was prosecuted by Bennett, before a judge appointed for the occasion, defended by able lawyers, pronounced guilty by a jury of twelve responsible citizens, and hanged. Four other homicide⁼ were tried and acquitted, and three tried and hanged between March and September. Several horse thieves were also punished and banished. It could not be said that there was no law and no government, but rather that government was triple-headed in these mining regions.

At the second annual election of the provisional government, October 22d, its officers were elected by a vote so insignificant as hardly to deserve the name of an election. The legislature, however, met in November, and held its second session, unnoticed by the people, its doings never being published. It would hardly have survived to a third session had it not been supplanted as it was by a government erected by congress.⁹

That the effort to firmly establish a provisional government was well meant and patriotic I do not doubt. Its failure depended partly upon one of the causes of its creation, the conflicting claims of five several territories, whose boundaries were included in the Pike's peak region; namly the eastern part of Utah, the northern part of New Mexico, and the western parts

⁹ Robert W. Steele, governor of the provisional territory of Jefferson, was an energetic, sanguine man, tall, angular, rather rough, but possessing good common sense and honesty. He was born in Ohio in 1820; removed in 1846 to Iowa, where he studied law; and to Omaha in 1855, where he was a member of the legislature of 1858–9. Then he went to Denver and to Central City, where he was president of the Consolidated Ditch Co. He was governor until June 1861, when the duly appointed officers of Colorado territory arrived. He settled his family at Golden, but removed to Empire in 1862, and afterward to Georgetown. In 1864 he was one of the party which discovered the Argentine district and Belmont lode—the first paying silver deposit in Colorado. This mine was named after August Belmont of New York, and brought $100,000. It was later called the Johnson.

Theodore P. Boyd, justice sup. ct prov. govt, was from Pa; in 1849 came to Cal., and finally to Golden, where he erected the third house. In the winter of 1859–60 he located farms for himself and sons on Clear creek, 7 miles east of Golden.

of Kansas, Nebraska, and Dakota.[10] Had every man in the mines been willing to yield allegiance to the independent government, these other governments were likely to interfere, and probably would have done so, had time been given or complaint been made. There were other reasons, in the instability of the population and the avoidance of the cost of a government. There was nothing in the public acts of the officers or legislators of "Jefferson territory" which was not intended for the public good. They were a portion of the same people who, in their people's courts, settled all matters of law and justice as efficiently as it could have been done anywhere.[11]

[10] That part of Kansas which lay west of the east boundary of New Mexico was confined to the territory between the 38th and 40th parallels. St Vrain and Boulder creek mines, and many farms, were therefore out of this jurisdiction. Breckenridge was in Utah, and California gulch was on debatable ground.

[11] The first people's court at Cañon City was organized by Wilbur F. Stone, who drafted a code for the government of that community. Stone was born at Litchfield, Conn., in 1833, but removed to western New York at the age of 6 years, and later to Mich., Ind., and Iowa. He was educated at Asbury university, and the state university of Indiana, where he graduated from the law department. Settling at Evansville, he practised his profession and edited the *Daily Inquirer*. For a short time he resided at Omaha, editing the *Nebraskian*, but came to Colorado in the spring of 1860. He was a member of the Colorado legislature from Park county in 1862, and again in 1864-5. In 1866 he returned to Ind., and married Minnie Sadler, after which he settled at Pueblo until 1877, when he was elected to the bench of the supreme court. From 1862 to 1866 he was assistant U. S. atty for Colorado. In 1868 he was appointed by the gov. 1st dist atty of the 3d judicial dist of Colo. In 1868 he gave a portion of his time to editing the *Pueblo Chieftain*, the only newspaper south of the divide at that time; and afterward wrote for the *People's Newspaper*, and other journals until 1874. He aided largely in building up Pueblo during a 12 years' residence, and was one of those who secured the completion of the Atchison, Topeka, and Santa Fé railroad to that place. He was a member of the state constitutional convention, and judge of the supreme court. He had ever at command a vast fund of information, which during my researches in Colorado in 1884 were generously placed at my disposal, and which kindness resulted in valuable manuscript contributions to history, entitled *General View of Colorado* and *Land Grants*.

Another high authority on early government matters is *Hallett's Courts, Law, and Litigation*, MS. Moses Hallett was born in Daviess county, Ill., in 1834, and resided there, with the exception of a few years spent away from home in acquiring an education, and in the study of the law in Chicago, until the spring of 1860, when he came to Colorado. He settled at Denver, and after a trial of mining entered upon the practice of his profession. He served two terms in the territorial council. In 1866 he was appointed chief justice of the territory, which position he held for 10 years, after which he was appointed judge for the U. S. dist. of Colorado. Tall and dark complexioned, with an intellectual face and affable manners, he enjoyed the

So many petitions had gone forth for a territorial organizatian by congress that a bill to provide for the

friendship and admiration of the best men. Hallett explains even more fully than Stone the peculiarities, merits, and eccentricities of the people's and miner's courts. He tells us there were arbitrary executions every year, down to 1877. In that year a man name Musgrove, the leader of a gang of horse thieves, was hanged off the end of Larimer street bridge, in open day, without concealment of any sort. The people seldom interfered with the administration of the laws. One instance is, however, given of a territorial judge, who was on his way to Golden to make some order affecting a railroad company, being taken from a train, carried off, and kept 24 hours in durance to prevent the order being made. *Courts, Law, and Litigation*, MS., 6–7.

Wolfe Londoner, in a manuscript on *Vigilance Committees in Colorado*, giving an account of 'all the judgments of capital punishment, and all the executions of the people's courts in Denver,' is a valuable authority. He explains that there were other trials by the same kind of courts, but no other sentences or punishments. The first murder was committed by John Stofel, son-in-law of a German named Beincroff. Stofel killed one of his young brothers-in-law, on Vasquez fork or Clear creek, April 7, 1859. He was suspected, arrested, examined before H. P. A. Smith, admitted his guilt, and, as there was no prison in the country, it was determined to hang him. The examination was held in the second building below what is now Holladay street, east side of Ferry, now 11th street. The execution took place at the corner of Holladay and 10th streets, where Stofel was hanged on a tree; by Noisy Tom, executioner for the occasion. On the 12th of March, 1860, William West was shot by Moses Young, on the west side of Cherry creek, near Larimer street bridge. Young was tried next day, found guilty, a scaffold erected on the spot where the murder was committed, and the day after the trial and conviction he was hanged. On the 12th of June, 1860, Jacob Roeder and family passed through Denver en route for South park, in company with Marcus Gredler and others. Roeder and Gredler quarrelled, and Roeder was killed and buried by Gredler in revenge. The murderer was arrested, and on compulsion showed the grave of his victim. He was tried, sentenced, and hanged the next day, on a scaffold at the foot of the bluff where Curtis street enters Cherry creek bottom on the east side. On the 20th of June two freighters quarrelled, and, on the road near Denver, Hadley stabbed Card so that he died. Hadley was brought back on the 22d, a court organized under a clump of cottonwood trees which stood on 16th street, opposite the Planter's house, this being the only court held in the open air. He was sentenced to be hanged on the 25th, but escaped from his jailers. On the 20th of July, 1860, occurred the murder of Jacob Gantz, by J. A. Gordon, of which I have given an account. Gordon was executed at the same place as Gredler. On the 30th of Nov., 1860, Thomas R. Freeman was killed by Patrick Waters. Freeman lived alone, 2 miles below Denver, and was one of the few who attempted farming that year, raising vegetables for market. Waters was a hanger-on of better men, and accompanied Freeman down the Platte to buy hay, murdering him for his money, near Fort Lupton. The body being discovered, Welters was arrested in Neb., tried at Denver, and executed on a gallows at the farther end of 15th street bridge. The prosecution in this case made the first presentment in writing, as follows: 'The people of the Pike's peak gold region *versus* Patrick Waters. The people of the Pike's peak gold region, assembled at the city of Denver the 19th day of Dec., 1860, do find and present that on the 30th of Nov., A. D. 1860, at the said Pike's peak gold region, one Patrick Waters did make a felonious assault on one Thomas R. Freeman, then and there being, and him, the said Thomas R. Freeman, with premeditated malice, did murder and slay, contrary to all the laws of God and man.

erection of a new territory was at length introduced,[12] which passed both houses and became a law February 28, 1861. The name of Colorado was given to it at the suggestion of the man selected for its first governor.[13] The boundaries of Colorado, as described in the organic act, included all the territory between the thirty-seventh and forty-first parallels of north latitude, and the twenty-fifth and thirty-second meridians of west longitude, forming an oblong square containing 104,500 square miles, or 66,880,000 acres of land, with the usual proviso, that nothing contained in the act should be construed to impair the rights of the Indians while they remained unextinguished by treaty, or prevent the government from again dividing the territory at pleasure, the act in all respects resembling other organic acts establishing temporary governments. The territorial officers commissioned by the president were William Gilpin governor, Lewis Ledpard Weld secretary, Benjamin F. Hall chief justice, S. Newton Pettis and Charles Lee Armor associate justices, Copeland Townsend marshal, James D. Dalliba attorney-general, and F. M. Case surveyor-general. They arrived May 29th, and were cordially welcomed, even by the unpaid officers of the provisional government, whose functions ceased with the appearance of the presidential appointees.

Governor Gilpin was a man capable of inspiring enthusiasm upon occasions. He visited all the principal settlements[14] as rapidly as possible, making him-

---

[12] *U. S. Sen. Doc.*, 15, 36th cong. 1st sess.; *U. S. Sen. Jour.*, 839, 281, 36th cong. 1st sess.; *Cong. Globe*, 1859-60, 1502; *Id.*, 1860-1, 639-45, 728-9, 763-4, 1205-6; *Id.*, v.; *Id.*, xvii.; *Id.*, xxi.

[13] *Gilpin's Pioneer of 1842*, MS., 8. 'Some,' says Gilpin, 'wanted it called Jefferson, some Arcadia. . . . I said the people have to a great extent named the states after the great rivers of the country . . . and the great feature of that country is the great Colorado river. . . "Ah," said he (Wilson of Mass.), "that is it;" and he named it Colorado.'

[14] I learn from *U. S. H. Ex. Doc.*, v., no. 56, 37th cong. 2d sess., and the *History of Gunnison County*, MS., by Sylvester Richardson, that Gilpin, with the assistance of old mountaineers, made a map of the territory in 1861, which was found to correspond remarkably with the subsequent surveys. Richardson was a native of Catskill, N. Y., and a man of cultivated mind, as well as an able mechanic. He came to Colorado in 1860, and resided 12 years

self acquainted with the condition and wants of the territory, and everywhere was received with festivity and favor.[15]   On the 8th of July he took the oath of office, and, the census being completed,[16] proceeded on the 10th to assign the judges to their districts, that the supreme court might be immediately organized.[17] On the 11th he issued a proclamation declaring the territory to be one congressional district, which was divided into nine council and thirteen representative districts, in which was ordered the election of delegate to congress and members of the legislative assembly to take place on the 19th of August.

In the matter of dates Colorado's history has been

in Denver. In 1873 he helped to explore the Gunnison country, and the following year organized a colony to settle it, of which the history will be given hereafter.

[15] William Gilpin was born Oct. 4, 1822, on the battlefield of Brandywine, and appointed to the military academy of West Point in 1836. Upon completing his studies he was commissioned lieut in the 2d dragoons, and fought in the Seminole war under Gen. Jessup, and accompanied Frémont's expedition of 1843 to Fort Vancouver. Gilpin was designed by his maker for a man of mark. Full six feet in height, of a slight frame and nervous temperament, with a fine head and expressive eyes, rather military bearing and French gestures, he was enthusiastic, while his shrewdness and courtesy were sometimes overshadowed by his generalizations. Said one of his friends to me, 'There never was a man like him, and there never will be another; for 20 minutes or so he can talk as closely to the point as any man, but after that he begins to generalize.' On the breaking out of the Mexican war, Gilpin, being again in Mo., was chosen major of the first regiment of Missouri cavalry, and moved south along the great central plateau with his force until he made a junction with the main army in Mexico. In 1847, the Indians of the plains having confederated to cut off immigration westward and to make war on the frontier settlements, Gilpin, by direction of the president, led a force of 1,200 cavalry, infantry, and artillery against them to open up communication. This expedition did not leave Leavenworth until Oct., the troops wintering at Pike peak and fighting the Indians the following summer. *Gilpin's Pioneer of 1842*, MS.; *Pitkin's Political Views*, MS.; *Bradford's Hist. Colorado*, MS.; *Elbert's Public Men and Measures*, MS.

[16] The census showed a population of 25,329, four-fifths of which were men. *Corbett's Legis. Manual*, 57. The count did not really show the whole number of inhabitants, many being prospecting in the mountains. *Rocky Mountain News*, July 17, 1861.

[17] Byers says in his *Centennial State*, MS., 10, that a proclamation was issued on the 23d of July appointing a term of the sup. ct on the first Monday in Sept. following, to be held at Denver. He also says that the first grand jury impanelled in Colo was upon the 4th of Sept., 1861, at Denver, and consisted of Nelson Sargent, foreman, Charles A. Wright, John W. Smith, Alexander M. Smith, John L. Bogg, John G. Vauter, William D. Davis, John B. Ashland, Jonathan U. Price, Milton E. Clark, Warren Hussey, J. F. Gordine, James M. Iddings, Milton M. Delano, Edward H. Hart, P. H. Smith, Andrew Sargendorf, and John M. Clark. See also *Rocky Mountain News*, Sept. 4, 1861.

marked by periods of national importance. It was
the business depression of 1857–8 and the Kansas
troubles which inspired so many with a willingness
to seek new homes and fortunes farther west. The
territory was organized just previous to and while the
civil war was impending; and lastly the state was admitted on the 100th anniversary of our independence.
It is with the coincidence of the territorial organization and the sudden and great strain put upon the
government that I am chiefly impressed; in connection with which must be considered the manner in
which the affairs of the new commonwealth were
managed. Gilpin, although appointed governor by
President Lincoln, was without instructions and without money. Washington was threatened; there were
a dozen cabinet meetings a day; and when the ap-
pointee begged for writttten orders he was told there
was no time to attend to such matters, but to go and
do as well as he knew how and the bills would be
paid. His verbal instructions, taken in the vestibule
of the white house, or in the portico, conferred broad
powers. He was to see that the new territory was
kept in the union. If soldiers were needed, he was
to call them out and command them.[18] He was loyal,
he was a soldier, he would be quick to see the need
of an appeal to arms; but was he a statesman, and
might he not be too quick to discern a danger?
These were questions the cabinet had no time to ask.

The period elapsing between the arrival of the executive and the August election was made use of to
ascertain the political bias of the majority, the population being almost evenly divided between those
who would support the government and those whose
sympathies were on the side of the confederates. This
equality warned the republicans to make haste slowly,
and to adopt a liberal and conservative platform, lest
the loyal part of the democracy should be driven to
encourage disloyalty. A convention was held at

[18] *Gilpin's Pioneer of 1842*, MS., 5–6.

Golden City on the 1st of July for the purpose of nominating a delegate to congress, Hiram P. Bennett being chosen from among eleven candidates.[19] On the 24th a 'union convention' was held by the democrats for the same purpose, which nominated B. D. Williams. The newspaper press was divided, and issued campaign sheets, as might be expected, but were guarded in their utterances.[20]

Williams was beaten by the republican candidate, on election, by 3,801 votes, the total number of votes cast being 9,597.[21]

The legislature, which was also chiefly republican, met at Denver, and held its first session of sixty days, beginning on the 9th of September, adopting and enacting a full code of laws, civil and criminal. The original acts of the legislature recognized the legality of the miners' courts, confirmed their decisions, and provided for the transfer of their cases to the regular courts, thus avoiding all conflict over previous judgments.[22] The adoption of the Illinois practice

[19] Amos Steck was president of this convention, and L. N. Tappan secretary. *Byers' Centennial State*, MS., 8.

[20] The *Rocky Mountain News*, though loyal, opposed drawing party lines too strictly. The publishers issued a second journal, the *Miner's Record*, at Tarryall, during the campaign, which did good work in preserving the loyalty of the people and determining the result of the election. The *Denver Mountaineer*, owned by Moore and Coleman, was a disunion journal, and was bought by Byers and Daily, and silenced in the spring of 1861. *Byers' Newspaper Press of Colorado*, MS., 13.

[21] Hiram P. Bennett was born in Mo. in 1826, and removed to Nebraska, where he was elected to the first territorial legislature in 1854. In 1859 he removed to Denver, where he practised his profession, being associated with Moses Hallett, and distinguishing himself by his successful prosecution of criminals. He served two terms in congress, obtaining the branch mint for Denver, with other benefits to the territory. He resumed his law practice in 1869, but was appointed postmaster soon after, which office he held until 1874. He was a member of the first state legislature from Arapahoe co.

[22] The members of the council representing their districts in the following order were Hiram J. Graham, Amos Steck, C. W. Mather, H. F. Parker, A. U. Colby, Samuel M. Robbins, E. A. Arnold, R. B. Willis, and John M. Francisco. *Colo. Jour. Council*, 1861, 3. Members of the lower house, in the order of their districts, were Charles F. Holly, E. S. Wilhite, Edwin Scudder, William A. Rankin, J. B. Chaffee, J. H. Noteware, Daniel Witter, George F. Crocker, Daniel Steel, Corydon P. Hall, Victor Garcia, Jesus Barela, and George M. Chilcott. *Colo. Jour. House*, 1861, 3, 19. E. A. Arnold of Lake co. was chosen president of the council, S. L. Baker, sec., David A. Cheever asst sec., E. W. Kingsbury sergeant-at-arms. Charles F. Holly of Boulder co. was elected speaker of the house of reps, F. H. Page chief clerk, E. P. Elmer sergeant-at-arms. *Corbett's Legis Manual*, 212.

code was another wise act, giving the territorial courts a system of practice which had been ably expounded by the supreme court of that state. No subsequent legislation was had upon this subject while the territorial form of government was in existence.

The territory was divided into counties [23] and judicial districts,[24] the election of county officers provided for, and a complete organization effected. The capital of the territory was located at Colorado City, and commissioners appointed to select the actual site within the surveyed limits of that town, the commission to perform its duty within a month after the adjournment of the legislature.[25] The location was chosen with the view of making the capital central to the future state. That it was subsequently abandoned was because it was found to be inconvenient. It was fixed at Golden City [26] in 1862, where it remained

[23] The following counties were organized, with county seats temporarily located, as follows: Costilla, county seat at San Miguel; Guadalupe, county seat at the town of Guadalupe (the name of this county was changed to Conejos the same session); Huerfano, county seat at Autubee; Pueblo, county seat at the town of Pueblo; Fremont, county seat at Cañon City; El Paso, county seat at Colorado City; Douglas, county seat at Frankstown; Arapahoe, county seat at Denver; Weld, named after the secretary of territory, county seat at St Vrain; Larimer, named after George William Larimer, county seat at La Porte; Boulder, county seat at the town of Boulder; Jefferson, county seat at Golden City; Clear Creek, county seat at Idaho; Gilpin, named after the governor, county seat at Central City; Park, county seat at Tarryall; Lake, county seat at Oro City; Summit, county seat at Parkville. *Colo Gen. Laws*, 1861, 52–7.

[24] The territory was divided into three judicial districts, the counties of Larimer, Weld, Arapahoe, Boulder, Douglas, and El Paso constituting the 1st, to which Chief Justice Hall was assigned; Jefferson, Clear Creek, Gilpin, Park, and Summit the 2d district, to which Judge Armor was assigned; Lake, Fremont, Pueblo, Huerfano, Conejos, and Costilla, the 3d district, to which was assigned Judge Pettis. *Gen. Laws Colo*, 1861, 395–6.

[25] The committee consisted of S. L. Baker, E. B. Cozzens, and M. Holt.

[26] There were certain rivalries to be considered, as is always the case; but the chief aim seemed to be to prevent Denver having the capital, that town being accused of a desire to secure everything; therefore, at the next session, the legislature, being dissatisfied with Colorado City as a place of meeting, having to camp out and do their own cooking, adjourned to Denver, and removed the capital once more, this time to Golden City. Says Stone, 'The southern men were opposed to adjourning to Denver, and they went away and hid in the woods, and the sergeant-at-arms couldn't find them. Finally we sent men out with flags of truce to bring them in, and getting them together in Mother Maggart's hotel, under pretense of compromising the matter, locked the doors on them, finished the vote, and got the adjournment to Denver.' *Land Grants in Colo*, MS., 11.

until 1868, when it was taken back to Denver; but the feeling in the southern counties being strong against this point, and Pueblo being prevented from getting it in 1872 only by bribery, the constitutional convention provided that the vote of the whole people should be taken five years after the adoption of the constitution, the place receiving the greater number of votes to be declared the permanent capital. The vote was taken in 1881, and Denver, which had been growing in influence, received the majority of votes,

SEAL.

thus ending, to the chagrin of the southern counties, the long struggle for that division of power which will only come with the development of the resources of the south.

The seal adopted for the territory was an heraldic shield, bearing in chief, or on the upper portion of the same, upon a red ground, three snow capped mountains, above surrounding clouds; upon the lower part of the shield, upon a golden ground, a miner's badge, being the same badge prescribed by the regular heraldic rules; as a crest above the shield the eye of God, being golden rays proceeding from the lines of a triangle; below the crest, and above the shield, as a scroll, the Roman fasces, bearing on a band of red, white, and blue, the words Union and Constitution; below the whole, the motto Nil Sine Numine; the whole to be surrounded by the words Sigillum Territorii Coloradensis, and the figures 1861. This design was adopted by the state in 1876.

The message of Governor Gilpin to the legislature contained much good advice, with many original ideas. He recommended a thorough organization by counties, townships, districts, and precincts, and advised a system of "social police" laws for the protection of property, enforcement of contract, taxation, roads, education, and charities; but particularly he desired them to recognize the importance of the judiciary and military departments of the government, which constituted "the bulwark of their liberties." Acting somewhat upon the suggestions made, and also on their own good sense, the first legislature of Colorado, as I have said, did some excellent work in establishing good government, both civil and military. Among their acts was a joint resolution expressing sympathy with the government, and pledging support. Another resolution indorsed the acts of the governor which had reference to preserving the loyal attitude of the territory. Joint memorials asked for the establishment of a branch mint at Denver,[27] for a mail route along the upper portion of the Platte river, from which the mail had been withdrawn by the opening of a cut-off, for a daily mail between Denver and Mountain City (Central City), which, it was alleged, distributed more mail than any office in the territory. An act was passed increasing the rep-

[27] The amount of gold coined at the U. S. mint from Colorado mines in 1859 was $622,000; in 1860 it was $2,091,000. Large amounts were in circulation without coinage, and a certain amount was used in manufactures. On this showing the Coloradans thought themselves entitled to a mint. *Colo Gen. Laws*, 1861, 513.

resentation in the legislative body to thirteen councilmen and twenty-six representatives, the whole number allowed by the organic act, and congress was asked
to increase the per diem from three to six dollars,
which it did not do until 1867. By the act increasing the membership, it was provided that these additional legislators should be chosen at the general election in December 1861, and another session of the
legislature held, commencing on the first Monday in
June 1862, but that thereafter the territorial legislature should meet on the first Monday in February of
each year. The adjournment took place on the 8th
of November.[28]

Meanwhile Governor Gilpin, relying upon the informal permission given him to do whatever he
thought right and proper for the good of Colorado
and the preservation of the government, had exceeded the powers ordinarily invested in a territorial
executive. Believing that the exigencies of the
times required the raising of a regiment, he proceeded
to raise and send it into the field.[29]

[28] The additional councilmen elected for the 2d session were H. R. Hunt,
William A. H. Loveland, N. J. Bond. J. B. Woodson, and Henry Altman.
The additional representatives were Joseph Kenyon, D. C. Oakes, C. G. Hans-
come, William M. Slaughter, H. B. Hayes, J. W. Hamilton, Wilbur F. Stone,
John Fosher, M. S. Beach, José Raphael Martine, José Francisco Gallejos,
and D. Powell. Of the council E. A. Arnold was president, S. L. Baker
chief clerk, D. A. Cheever asst clerk, E. W. Kingsbury sergeant-at-arms.
Of the house, Charles F. Holly was speaker, P. H. Page chief clerk, E. P.
Elmer sergeant-at-arms. *Corbett, Legis. Manual*, 212–14.

[29] Owing to the presence in the territory of a large number of southern
men, he felt the importance of avoiding a conflict, and the necessity of proceeding secretly to the accomplishment of his purpose in order not to pro-
voke opposition from those who, while not openly disloyal, had confederate
proclivities. Two infantry companies were first raised, of picked men, armed
with weapons quietly purchased wherever they could be found. Lead was
obtained from a Colorado mine, and three loads of gunpowder from Topeka,
through the friendship of John Burke. Having now the nucleus of a regiment, a call was made for eight more companies, which were rapidly formed,
and promptly furnished by the governor, who paid the Denver merchants
for supplies by drafts on the treasury, which he had authority for drawing
in the fully given word of the president and secretary of war. But that it
was a fortunate forecast in the executive became apparent when it was discovered, after the call had been made, that the disloyal part of the population was proceeding with equal caution to gather a force to plunder the banks
and business houses of Denver and escape into Texas, there to join the confederate army. At the head of this conspiracy was McKee, a Texan ranger.
He was arrested with about forty of his followers, and confined in jail. The

southerners had their rendezvous about forty miles from Cherry creek, near Russellville, where the first Colorado infantry was sent to capture the remainder. Some prisoners were taken, but about one hundred escaped and went into camp near Fort Wise, on the Arkansas river, where they captured a government train, but were overtaken and forty-one brought back to Denver, where they were a source of infinite vexation, nobody knowing what to do with them, while they had to be guarded and fed at considerable expense.

The 1st Colorado regiment was composed of good material in the main. The regiment was organized as follows: J. P. Slough colonel, S. F. Tappan lieut-col, J. M. Chivington major; captains, E. W. Wynkoop, S. M. Logan, Richard Sopris, Jacob Downing, S. J. Anthony, S. H. Cook, J. W. Hambleton, George L. Sanborn, Charles Malie, C. P. Marion. It was presented with a handsome silk flag by the women of Denver. *Rocky Mountain News*, Aug. 21, 1861. But it contained a certain proportion of undisciplined, strong, and restless men, who had volunteered in the hope of being called upon to go to the front. Their presence in Colorado at this time was a standing menace to confederate sympathizers; but it was not the kind of service which they desired; enforced idleness soon bred a mutinous spirit, and discipline became difficult to maintain, the presence of the regiment in Denver requiring an extra police force to preserve the property of citizens from the nightly prowling of squads of mischievous or drunken soldiers. In November they were removed to Camp Weld, two miles from Denver, where they continued to fret at their bondage and threaten desertion. Two companies were sent to Fort Wise, afterward Fort Lyon, where they were no better pleased. This post, which was in part Bent's new fort, was built by Sedgwick's command of 350 U. S. troops in the winter of 1860-1, after a summer campaign among the Indians. The quarters were of stone laid up in mud, with dirt roofs and floors. Bent's portion was used as a commissary. The post was commanded by Lieut Warner, of the regular army, who regarded the manners of the volunteers with great disfavor, a view which was entirely reciprocated.

In Feb. Major-general Hunter, in command of the department at Fort Leavenworth, yielded to the represeutations of the officers of the Colorado 1st, that unless the men were put into the field they would desert in the spring. Chivington says that it was his influence that procured the change. *First Colorado Regiment*, MS., 3-4. An occasion was opportunely furnished of making them useful by the advance on New Mexico of 4,000 Texan troops, under Gen. H. H. Sibley, and permission was granted Slough to take his regiment south to the relief of the threatened territory. On arriving at Fort Wise orders were received to hasten to the assistance of Gen. Canby, who was being overpowered, the Texans having taken forts Bliss and Fillmore, fought Canby at Valverde, and driven him back to Fort Craig. They were preparing to march on Fort Union, the principal depot of supplies in New Mexico. The Colo troops hastened forward through the Raton pass, and after a brief rest made a forced march of 64 miles in 24 hours the baggage being left at Red river, and the wagons used to relieve the men in squads to prevent their giving out. By great exertion the regiment reached Fort Union on the 13th, where were 400 men, under Col Paul of New Mexico. There were at this time two independent Colorado companies in New Mexico, which had been formed by the governor's permission in the southern counties, and sent to Fort Garland. The captains were James H. Ford and Theodore H. Dodd, a nephew of Gov. Todd of Ohio. These two companies became the nucleus of the 2d Colorado regiment.

The day following the arrival of Slough at Fort Union news was received from Canby of the capture of a large train of supplies, and that Sibley was at Santa Fé with recruits pouring in. Upon this information the Coloradans determined to march on Santa Fé. On the 22d the army set out, consisting of the 1st Colorado, two light batteries, one of the independent companies under Capt. Ford, and two companies of the 5th infantry, in all about 1,300 men, commanded by Col Slough. One company was mounted for scouting purposes, and divided into detachments, under captains Howland of the regular army and Ford. On the night of the 24th the scouts captured a picket guard, and learned that a force of 800 Texans were advancing on Santa Fé. Preparations were at once made to intercept them. Maj. Chivington was ordered to make a night march from Bernal springs, to encamp by day, and to march again by night to Santa Fé, spike the enemy's guns, and do as much as possible to cripple him. All the mounted men in the command, and two companies of foot troops, were detailed, amounting to 400 men. On the first night out, at the Pecos river, Lieut-col Tappan surprised and captured a party of confederate scouts, who were sent to Slough's camp. Chivington continued his march by daylight (there was not a man in the regiment, from the col down, who knew how to obey oders), and met the advanced guard of the enemy a little after noon, which surrendered.

He was now in the Apache cañon, a pass of the mountains ten miles long, between hills from 1,000 to 2,000 feet high, and proceeding at a leisurely pace, when the picket came running back, informing Chivington that he was confronted with a column of double his strength and furnished with artillery, while his batteries were with Slough in the rear. Cannonading was begun, and Chivington deployed his foot as skirmishers on the sides of the mountains out of range of the battery, and held the horse, under Captain Howland of the regular army, as a reserve, under cover, with orders to charge when they saw the enemy in retreat. But when he did retreat Howland failed to charge. His troops parted either way and filed to the rear in confusion. Fortunately for the fame of the 1st Colorado he was not of it. Another troop under Cook awaited orders with the shells whistling and screaming over them. The skirmishers soon made the position of the Texans in the road untenable, and they retired to a better one a mile below, concealing their infantry in the rocks, and posting their howitzers to command the road. Chivington followed cautiously until within an eighth of a mile of the battery, when he halted to get the infantry and horse together, except Cook's, deploying them right and left to outflank the new confederate position. In these movements Chivington, who had hitherto been a man of peace, a methodist preacher in fact, behaved well. He was a native of Ohio, born in 1821, migrated to Ill. in 1848, where he entered the conference of the M. E. church, being transferred to the Mo. conference, and in 1855 to Omaha, Neb. While in Mo. he was a missionary to the Wyandottes. In 1860 he came to Denver as presiding elder of the Rocky mountain district. Of a commanding presence, and in full regimental dress, he was a conspicuous figure as he galloped through the rain of bullets. Further retreat of the Texans was the signal to Cook, who came forward with his 99 horsemen. The road was unfavorable for cavalry, but the charge was successful, resulting in a large number of killed, wounded, and prisoners. On the other hand, the Texans fought bravely and inflicted severe injury. A storm of lead poured down on the enemy from their infantry, but the Colorado regiment was posted above them, and soon drove them down the hillside into the road and to flight. The loss in the battle of Apache cañon was five killed, thirteen wounded, and three missing on the union side. The Texans had sixteen killed, forty wounded, and seventy-five taken prisoners. At sunset Chivington fell back to Pigeon rancho—Pigeon being the name given to a Frenchman named Vallé who owned it—where the wounded were attended to and the dead buried. The prisoners, including seven commissioned officers, were sent to Fort Union under guard of Ford's company of dragoons, and the command fell back to a former camp at Coslasky's for water.

On the 28th, two days after the battle, Col Slough came up with the reserve from Bernal springs, and Chivington was again sent forward across the mountain, with six companies of infantry, to harass the enemy's rear, and a company of dragoons was ordered to scout toward Galisteo. The remainder of the 1st regiment, two batteries, and two small companies of regular cavalry, numbering altogether 600, also moved forward on the road to Santa Fé, not doubting that their passage would be disputed. While halting at

Pigeon's rancho the pickets came in with the information that the Texans were advancing in force, less than half a mile away. Quickly the bugles sounded, the men fell in line, and had gone but a few hundred yards when the firing began.

Had the Texans been aware how greatly they outnumbered the union troops, instead of defeat, they would have prevailed. As it was, after a day's fighting, they called for time to bury their dead. The following day they asked to have the armistice extended to 36 hours. At this moment an order arrived from Canby to stop fighting, and return to Fort Union. The Coloradans were astounded. Canby had so far been driven by the enemy. The loss on the Texan side, in the two battles, was 281 killed, 200 wounded, and 100 prisoners, a total of 581. On the union side 49 were killed, 64 wounded, and 21 captured, a total of 134. Col Slough, on returning to Fort Union, tendered his resignation, being offended, it was said, by Canby's order. The troops were allowed three day's of rest, when information came that Canby had left Fort Craig on the 1st of April, and was having a running fight on the Rio Grande with Sibley's army in retreat to Texas. Orders to march south to divert the enemy's attention, or assist in driving him out of the country were received. On the 6th, the regiment, now commanded by Tappan, set out again on the same road it had lately marched over. Canby and Col Paul were found at a small village at the head of Carnuel pass, endeavoring to make a junction with Slough, while the Texans were at Albuquerque, whither they had fallen back on a feint from Canby looking like an attack. Slough's resignation being accepted, Canby promoted Chivington to the colonelcy over Tappan, who waived his rank in Chivington's favor, and Gilpin approved. On the 14th of April the united commands moved down the pass, and the Rio Grande valley to a point eighteen miles below Albuquerque, and one mile from Peralta, where Sibley was encamped, the Texan army in ignorance of the approach of Canby. Chivington desired the privilege of attacking with the Colorado regiment alone, but was restrained by his superior. The Colorado troops reposed on their arms, in the hope of being called to surprise the confederates, but no such order came. The bugles sounded on the morning of the 15th, within hearing of Sibley's brass band, and the now superior union forces proceeded openly to the conflict. The battle began in the morning by the capture of a train coming from Albuquerque. After breakfast Peralta was attacked; but Canby having to fight in the open field, while Sibley was sheltered by the walls of the town, the fighting was of the mildest ever seen. At two o'clock a high wind having arisen, and the air being filled with sand, Canby withdrew to camp. That afternoon and night Sibley crossed the river, and proceeded down on the west side.

Much dissatisfaction was felt by the Colorado troops concerning the general's failure to attack Peralta. On the 16th, Canby entered Peralta, and marched leisurely down the river on a line parallel with Sibley, but unable to cross until the 20th, at Linitar, when it was learned that the Texans had buried their artillery except two pieces, burned their wagons, and were going through the mountains by Cook springs to Mesilla. Canby then proceeded to Fort Craig, Chivington going into camp at Valverde, a battle-field where a company of the 2d Colorado, before mentioned as being in New Mexico with Canby, had distinguished itself for bravery, losing forty per cent of its number in a vain effort to save the lost battle of the 21st of February. Here the 1st regiment remained inactive until August, waiting for orders and pay, after which it was sent to Fort Union. In July Chivington obtained leave to proceed to Washington, to endeavor to have his regiment transferred to a field of active service, and Col Howe of the 3d U. S. cavalry was placed temporarily in command. He succeeded in securing an order converting the regiment into the 1st Colorado cavalry, with headquarters at Denver. In midwinter it was concentrated at Colorado City, mounted, when it proceeded to Denver, and was received with enthusiasm by the citizens.

The history of the 2d Colorado regiment has less connection with the political history of the state. The first two companies were recruited under the order of Gilpin. They were marched to Fort Garland, and mustered into the service of the U. S. in Dec. 1862. They experienced great hardships in crossing mountains to New Mexico, not to mention the fighting at the battle of Valverde. In Feb. 1862 Col J. H. Leavenworth was authorized by the secretary of war to raise six companies of volunteer infantry in Colorado, which with these two, and two others of a later organization, were to constitute the 2d Colorado regiment. T. H. Dodd was appointed lieut-col. The captains of the new companies were J. Nelson Smith, L. D. Rowell, Reuben Howard, George West, E. D. Boyd, and S. W. Wagoner. In Aug. the regiment was ordered to Fort Lyon, where it remained until April 1863, when six companies were marched to Fort Leavenworth. In June Leavenworth was placed in command of all the troops on the Santa Fé road, with headquarters at Fort Larned. The Indians and the confederates together gave him plenty of employment. On the 2d of July occurred the battle of Cabin creek, with a loss to the enemy of about forty killed and wounded. On the 16th they were joined at Fort Gibson by Gen. Blunt commanding the district of Colorado and western Kansas, and their united force numbering 1,400 met the confederate force of 6,000, under Gen. Cooper, at Honey springs, attacked it and in a battle of two hours routed it, with a loss of 400 killed, wounded, and missing. To prevent his stores falling into Blunt's hands, Cooper burned them. The loss on the union side in this engagement was 14 killed and 30 wounded. From July to October, Leavenworth was in command at Fort Larned. In the latter month he was dismissed the service on account of having enlisted a company, without authority, to act as artillerymen, but the order was subsequently revoked and his record cleared. Dodd succeeded him in command of the reg. During the same month the 2d and 3d Colorado inf. reg. were consolidated into the 2d Colorado volunteer cav. All detachments were ordered to Missouri, and thence sent east. Ford, who had been major of the 2d inf. was promoted to the command of the 2d cav., Dodd being lieut-col. Curtis, Smith, and Pritchard were made majors of three battalions. Ford was appointed to command subdistrict No. 4 of central Mo., with the Colorado vol. cav., the Mo. militia, and a reg. of inf. The reg. consisted of twelve companies, and numbered 1,240 men. It remained in service until 1865, fighting guerrillas chiefly, but taking an energetic part in the destruction of Price's army. In Dec. the regiment was concentrated at Fort Riley, refitted, and put on a footing as winter scouts to protect the road as far west as Fort Lyon. The following spring Ford was promoted to be a brig. gen. by brevet, and took command of the district. In April, May and June 1865, a force of 5,500 men, and two batteries was distributed in this district, prepared for a summer campaign against the Indians south of the Arkansas river. When everything was ready the interior department interfered, and arrested the movement. Irritated at this policy, Ford resigned, and General Sanborn took the command. Again, as he made ready to chastise the hostile Indians, the campaign was broken up by the same interference. In Sept. the reg. was mustered out at Fort Leavenworth. It had done faithful service, and lost about 70 men killed and many more wounded.

The 3d Colorado volunteer infantry was raised in 1862 by Gov. Evans. By the 1st of Feb. 1863, the first battalion was mustered in, Curtis commanding. James H. Ford was made colonel, and James L. Pritchard major. The captains were R. R. Harbour, E. W. Kingsbury, E. P. Elmer, G. W. Morton, Thomas Moses, Jr. In March they set out for the States via the Platte route, reaching Fort Leavenworth on the 23d of April. They shared the hardships of border warfare with the 2d regiment, to which they were finally joined.

Besides the presence of confederate sympathizers, the territory was visited in the summer of 1863 by a small band of Mexican guerrilas, who spread terror through the South park by emulating the sanguinary deeds of the traditional Mexican banditti. The bloody Espinosas they were called. Much mystery surrounded their actions and their motives, since it was not for gain that they committed their crimes. They are supposed to have been out-laws from Chihuahua, and that they were brothers or cousins. One was a large, iron-framed man, with a villainous countenance, the second a smaller man, with nothing marked in his appearance. There was also a third, a mere boy. On their journey to Colorado they killed a merchant of Santa Fé, and a soldier at Conejos. During three weeks in the vicinity of Cañon City they killed 9 men, William Bruce of Hardscrabble creek being the first victim; then Harkins on Fontaine creek; and Alderman at his farm, on the road from Colorado City to South park. Then fell Shoup, a brother of George L. Shoup, Binckley, Carter, Lehman, and others. A company was raised in Califor-nia gulch, by John McCannon, which followed and traced them to a camp on the head waters of Oil creek, in El Paso co., where the larger man was killed by Joseph Lamb. The other Espinosa escaped to New Mexico. He wrote a letter in Spanish to Gov. Evans, stating that he had killed 22 men, and for that reason demanded the restitution of his property captured by the volun-teers. He was finally killed, together with a nephew, by Tom Tobins of Costilla co. *Hollister's Miners of Colorado*, 302–3; *Brickley and Hartwell South-ern Colo*, 29–30; *Baskin's Arkansas Vol. Hist.*, 575–6; *Fowler's Woman's Experience*, MS., 1–2; *Hill's Tales of Colorado Pioneers*, 290–2; *Overland Monthly*, v. 526; *Folsom Telegraph*, Oct. 28, 1871; *El Paso County, etc.*, MS., 30–40. In the spring of 1864 James Reynolds, a pioneer of Colorado, turned guerilla, and picking up a company of 22 confederate deserters in Texas invaded Colorado. On the way they captured a train, which furnished them ample subsistence, arms, and ammunition, $5,000 in drafts, and a larger sum in money. They quarreled over the spoils, and separated, 13 turning back. The other half secreted their plunder, and proceeded to the South park, the former home of Reynolds, capturing a stage coach going from Buckskin Joe to Denver, and robbing the mail. They continued to infest the road for a few days longer, seeming to invite observation, as if they gloried in their valiant deeds of theft and outrage. But they were soon pursued by parties of citizens, and finally overtaken by a squad of volunteers from the mines in Summit co., under Jack Sparks on the north fork of the Platte. Reynolds was wounded and one man killed, named Singleterry. In the flight of the band, one Holliman was captured, who turned state's evidence. Five others were caught by parties lying in waiting on the Cañon City road. They were brought before a military commission, and ordered to Fort Lyon, but attempting to escape, were fired on and all killed.

CHAPTER VI.

POLITICAL AFFAIRS.

1861–1886

GILPIN'S HEROIC SUCCESSES—SUPERSEDED BY JOHN EVANS—WELD AND
ELBERT—LEGISLATIVE ACTION—COINAGE—BENNETT—FAILURE TO ES-
TABLISH STATE GOVERNMENT—FURTHER EFFORTS AND FINAL SUCCESS
—CURRENT TERRITORIAL AFFAIRS—ORGANIC LAW—GOVERNOR CUM-
MINGS—BRADFORD—CHILCOTT—HUNT, MCCOOK, AND ELBERT—GOV-
ERNOR ROUTT—CHAFFEE—POSTAL ROUTES—PATTERSON, BOONE, AND
BROMWELL—THE JUDICIARY—POLITICS UNDER STATE ORGANIZATION
—TELLER—POPULATION AND LANDS—GOVERNORS PITKIN, GRANT, AND
EATON—SENATORS HILL AND BOWEN.

GOVERNOR GILPIN'S confident measures for the preservation of peace and loyalty in the territory, with
the boldness of his demands on the treasury, brought
him into trouble. An audacious temperament is often
the best possession of a man in emergencies. If any
one refused to accept his drafts[1] they were told, " It
is simply a question of whether you will take this
evidence of indebtedness, or give up your goods without any such evidence ; for the articles we need we
must and will have." Several hundred thousand dollars of the governor's orders[2] were on the market, and,
as at first they were not recognized by the government,

[1] A copy of one of these orders is preserved in *Extracts from Early
Records*, MS., which is copied from the archives of the Historical Society of
Colorado, and runs thus: ' Executive Department, Colorado Territory, Denver, Sept. 18, 1861. At sight pay to the order of Mrs Julia A. Ford thirty
dollars, value received, and charge the same to the account of William Gilpin, Governor of Colorado Territory. To the Secretary of the United States
Treasury, Washington, D. C., Number 220.'

[2] The whole appropriation for the expenses of Colorado for the fiscal year
ending June 30, 1862, was $32,000. *U. S. H. Ex. Doc.*, no. i. 44, 37th cong.
2d sess.; *Cong. Globe*, 1860–1, ap. 340. The direct tax levied on the territory
by congress for the same period was $22,905. *Laws Rel. Direct Tax*, 37th
cong. 1st and 2d sess., 8.

financial distress followed, and a strong faction clamored for Gilpin's removal. The record made by the 1st regiment justified his acts so far as to secure the payment of his drafts, but in the meantime much dissatisfaction existed. Those who could not afford to hold, sold them at a loss to speculators; and, though ultimately redeemed, the losers were naturally disaffected, and labored for the removal of the author of their misfortunes.[3] He was succeeded in office April 19, 1862, by John Evans of Evanston, Illinois, who served the people acceptably for more than three years.[4] Secretary Weld, an able young man, but of irregular habits, was removed to make way for Samuel H. Elbert, son-in-law of Evans. Weld died early; but Gilpin lived to see his acts justified.[5] United States Marshal Townsend was removed in June 1862, and A. S. Hunt appointed in his place.

It will be remembered that the first legislature adjourned, to meet again with the full complement of councilmen and representatives allowed by the organic act in June. But it was discovered that a blunder had been committed, as the two sessions would fall within the same fiscal year, while two appropriations would not; and, by permission of congress,[6] another adjournment was made to the 7th of July, when the assembly met at Colorado City, where, as I have

[3] *Byers' Hist. Colo*, MS., 17, 23, 26; *Elbert's Public Men and Measures*, MS., 4-5; *Gilpin's Pioneer of 1842*, MS.

[4] John Evans was of Quaker parents, born in Ohio in 1814. He studied medicine, and practised in Ill. and Ind. He was elected to the chair of the Rush medical college, then organizing in Chicago, and became one of the editors of the *Northwestern Medical and Surgical Journal*, besides being chairman of the committee on public schools of Chicago. He donated $25,000 for the endowment of a chair of mental and moral philosophy in the Northwestern university, the trustees naming the university town in his honor. and electing him president of the board. As a railroad projector and keen politician he was long conspicuous. His daughter Josephine married his secretary, S. H. Elbert, in 1865. Dying soon after, her father erected a chapel in Evans' Addition to Denver to her memory. *Routt, Terr. and State*, MS., 5; *Pitkin's Political Views*, MS., 9-10; *Elbert, Public Men and Measures*, MS., 7.

[5] Weld was a Connecticut man. He went east, and was appointed lieut.-col in a colored regiment, and died of fever in the south during the war. *Elbert, Public Men and Measures*, MS., 1.

[6] *Acts and Res.*, 351, 37, 2.

already stated, it remained in session but four days before returning to more comfortable quarters in Denver. Besides revising and perfecting the work of the first session, the legislature asked congress to increase the jurisdiction of the probate courts, and that the laws be printed in Spanish, for the benefit of the Mexican population. The postmaster-general was requested to provide for a tri-weekly mail from the east, and from Denver to Boulder City; the Union Pacific Railroad and Telegraph company was asked to locate its road through Colorado, and to select one of its board of directors from among its citizens, Evans being recommended. The secretary of the treasury was urged to put a United States mint in operation at an early day, by purchasing the private mint in Denver,[7] which prayer was granted; and the secretary of the interior was solicited to treat with the Indians for lands, chiefly mineral, to which their title had not been extinguished. A joint resolution was passed relating to the Colorado volunteers, commending them to the favorable notice of the president. The election law provided that the general election for delegate for congress, members of the council and assembly, and county officers, should be held on the first Tuesday in September; but as the appropriation for 1862–3 would be exhausted by the July session of 1862, the election of a legislature before 1863 was by joint resolution postponed to that year.

[7] According to the memorial, a private mint had been in successful operation for more than two years when the petition was made. Byers relates that the private banking-house of Clark, Gruber, and Co., Denver, began coining $5, $10, and $20 gold pieces July 20, 1860; and Parsons and Co. also coined some at Hamilton at a later period. The $10's coined at Denver by Clark, Gruber, and Co. were 17 grains heavier than the coin of the U. S. mint *Centennial State*, MS., 1. The bill establishing a branch mint in Denver appropriated $75,000, and was approved April 21, 1862. *Cong. Globe*, 1861–2, ap. 349. In March 1863 a resolution was passed to purchase the lots and assaying house or houses of Clark, Gruber, and Co. The chamber of commerce of Denver, on May 8, 1861, adopted the following rates for gold dust as a circulating medium: Blue river gold, $20 per ounce; French gulch, Humbug gulch, Fairplay gulch, Nigger gulch, and McNulty gulch, $17 per ounce; California gulch, $16 per ounce. Central City adopted the rate of $17 per ounce for Clear creek gold dust, and $15 per ounce for Russell gulch dust. Best retorted gold, $15 per ounce; common retorted and dirty gold,

In July the democratic party attempted to organize, holding a convention on the 10th, but did not become possessed of any power or coherency until after the close of the civil war. At the September election of 1862, Hiram P. Bennett was again chosen delegate to congress, the *News* summing up his services during one session as follows: A mail service and new post routes; post-offices throughout the settled portion of the territory; a land district and removal of the surveyor-general from Utah to Denver;[8] appropriations for surveys; military posts; a branch mint at Denver; payment of the Gilpin war debts;[9] besides laboring for the passage of the Union Pacific railroad bill, and bills for various wagon-roads. With such a record his reëlection was assured,[10] and he resumed his seat, to retain it in the thirty-eighth congress. The amendments made to the organic act by congress in 1863, referring to the judiciary system, gave the justices' courts jurisdiction in matters of controversy involving not more than three hundred dollars, and the probate courts jurisdiction in cases where the sum claimed did not exceed two thousand dollars; besides which the probate courts were given chancery as well as common law jurisdiction, with authority to redress all wrongs against the laws of the territory affecting persons or property. The same act modified the power of the governor, made absolute as to the approval of laws by the organic act, the amendment

$12 per ounce. Before the establishment of these rates the price of all gold dust had been uniform at $18.   Fraudulent gold dust and gold bricks were manufactured by counterfeiters in 1861. The bricks had one corner made of genuine metal, from which the sellers cut a chip which they offered for assay. One banker bought $20,000 worth of these counterfeit bricks.

[8] *Cong. Clobe*, 1861–2, ap. 345. Colorado was consolidated with Idaho and Nevada in 1863–4.

[9] The actual amount of the Gilpin drafts was $306,000, added to which was about $100,000 of debts where the drafts had been refused. Congress assumed the whole amount early in 1862. *Rocky Mountain News*, March 20, 1862.

[10] There were three candidates in the field: Bennett representing the Douglas democracy, indifferent to the fate of the negro, but true to the union; Gilpin, supported by the abolitionists, and J. M. Francisco, Breckenridge democrat.

permitting the legislature to pass an act by a two thirds vote over the governor's veto.[11]

On the 2d of November, 1861, a convention was held in Denver to memorialize congress for a homestead law for the protection of squatters on the public domain, and the same rights allowed to the settlers of Oregon, including holding their claims as bounded by lines drawn by themselves instead of the government survey. To this proposition no answer was returned. But in June 1862 the right of preëmption was extended to the territory, with the appointment of a register and receiver, and the repeal of the graduation act.[12]

There had been from the first a party in Colorado, though not constituting a majority, which desired a state government. The promoters of state organization in early territorial times are usually ambitious men, desirous of place and power, and Colorado offers no exception to the rule. In compliance with the demands of this portion of the electors of the territory, an effort was made at the third session of the thirty-seventh congress, 1862-3, to have an enabling act passed allowing Colorado to form a constitution, which was defeated. But in March 1864, by representing the population to be between fifty and sixty thousand,

---

[11] *Cong. Globe*, 1862-3, ap. 200; *Corbett's Legis. Manual*, 51-4; *Acts and Res.*, 88, 37, 3; *S. Jour.*, 471, 487, 37, 3.

[12] 'An act to graduate and reduce the price of the public lands to actual settlers and cultivators.' An act approved in May constituted Colorado and Utah one surveying district, with the office of the sur-gen. at Denver. The appropriations for surveys was $10,000. No special land laws were enacted in favor of Colorado. The status of land titles was exceedingly simple, after the extinguishment of Indian rights, except in a few cases of Mexican grants; a Mexican.grant, like Indian territory, being of such indefinite dimensions as to invite a contest of wits, if not of weapons, in the settlement. *Hallet's Courts, Laws, and Litigation*, MS., 7-8. In 1873-4 a disturbance arose in Lake co. over the possession of some government land near the present site of Buena Vista. Elijah Gibbs was attacked by a mob calling themselves vigilants, and killed in self-defence one of their number, George Barrington. At another time he killed a man named Coon who belonged to an attacking party and had to escape, the friends of the men who were killed taking up the quarrel, which was carried on for several years, and in which 7 or 8 persons were killed, including Judge Dyer of Granite City, who was assassinated while trying one of the cases which grew out of it. *Byers' Centennial State*, MS., 32-3.

or double what it really was, and by other devices, congress was induced to pass an enabling act, permitting the delegates elected by the people to meet on the first Monday in July to form a constitution, to be submitted to the people at an election to be held on the second Tuesday in October. The campaign was a stirring one, several newspapers being devoted to manufacturing a favorable public opinion; but the people, knowing there was an empty treasury, and not being desirous of replenishing it to the requirements of a state government, decided that it was inexpedient, and voted against it.[13]

There was yet another reason why many rejected the constitution. The organic act of the territory, formed ere yet the civil war had burned its bill of rights so terribly into the conscience of the nation, provided that the right to vote at the first election should be extended to "every free white male citizen of the United States, including those recognized as citizens by the treaties of 1848 and 1853 with Mexico." The first legislature, in an act regulating elections, decreed that only citizens of the United States, persons of foreign birth who had declared their intention to become citizens, and persons of Indian blood who had been declared by treaty to be citizens, should be deemed qualified voters. On the 11th of March, 1864, this act was amended so as more plainly to exclude "a negro or mulatto," and the constitution perpetuated all the territorial laws.

[13] The framers of this rejected constitution were W. A. H. Loveland, president of the convention, Samuel E. Browne, John Q. Charles, J. Bright Smith, James M. Cavanaugh, Richard Sopris, Joseph M. Brown, George T. Clark, John A. Koontz, D. H. Goodwin, A. C. Hunt, Charles A. Cook, G. W. Miller, David H. Nichols, P. M. Hinman, D. Pound, A. Lumry, W. E. Sisty, J. T. Herrick, Robert White, C. B. Patterson, John Locke, D. P. Wilson, Ed S. Perrin, Wm E. Darby, B. C. Waterman, Rodney French, A. J. Van Deren, H. F. Powell, F. H. Judd, C. W. Mather, B. F. Lake, George E. Randolph, W. S. Rockwell, O. J. Hollister, W. R. Gorsline, T. Whitcomb, G. B. Backus, T. C. Bergen, T. P. Boyd, H. H. DeMary, N. F. Cheeseman, C. Nachtrieb, H. Anderson, John McCannon, Thos Keys, W. J. Curtice, Alex. Hatch, A. DuBois, H. Henson, J. D. Parmelee, G. W. Lechner, H. B. Haskell, John T. Lynch, G. W. Coffin, J. E. Washburn, F. Merrill, J. L. Pritchard, G. W. Hawkins, C. C. Hawley, B. F. Pine, W. G. Reid. *Corbett, Legis. Manual,* 225-6.

Though beaten, the state government party was not disheartened. A convention was called in 1865, in which eleven counties were represented out of seventeen; a constitution was submitted to the people, which, without any law to sanction it, was adopted—another illustration of the vox populi vox dei saw. Gilpin was elected governor. The legislature assembled and made choice of two senators, John Evans and Jerome B. Chaffee, who proceeded to Washington to urge the admission of Colorado under the constitution to which a majority of those who voted on the question had assented, if not a majority of all the voters in the territory. Nor did they urge their wishes in vain. Congress again consented to admit the state of Colorado to the union, as Governor Cummings affirmed, in the face of the principles for which the nation had been contending during four years of war, and in the face of their own legislation at the same session ;[14] for the constitution still excluded persons of negro blood from participating in the elections, an example of the power which flaunts itself in the lobby of the national capital, though acting in this instance in the right direction as against that most monstrous of American absurdities, African voting. But President Johnson vetoed the bill.[15] A similar bill was vetoed again in 1867-8, which failed by only one vote in the senate from being passed over his head. The matter was revived periodically for ten years. On the 3d of March, 1875, an enabling act was passed, authorizing the electors to vote, in July 1876, upon a constitution, to be formed in convention to be held at Denver before that time   The period

[14] H. Jour., 1865-6, 622, 657, 668, 672. On the 1st of Feb. 1865, Delegate Bennett had headed a written resolution of the territorial delegates, approving the proposition to amend the federal constitution forever prohibiting slavery in the U. S. Cong. Globe, 1864-5, 596.

[15] Byers' Centennial State, MS., 31. Elbert says that the ostensible reason for vetoing the bill was that the population was insufficient, but the real reason was that the two senators, Evans and Chaffee, would not pledge themselves to vote against Johnson's impeachment. Pub. Men and Measures, MS., 10-11. The reason which Johnson gave was that the proceedings were irregular. Cong. Globe, 1865-6, 210.

was ripe for its acceptance; the political sea was calm; there was nothing in the new instrument at variance with the amendments to the federal constitution, and both congress and the people of the commonwealth were satisfied that Colorado was entitled to become a sovereign state,[16] with boundaries as ample as in its territorial days.[17]

The constitution-makers of Colorado were, by this time, skilled artificers.[18] It was a noble document, with those errors only which the course of events develops.[19] An attempt was made for universal suffrage by introducing a clause making it obligatory upon the first legislature to pass a law conferring the elective franchise upon women, which was, however, to be submitted to a vote of the male citizens at the first election thereafter.

To return to the regular march of events under the territorial régime. Bennett's delegateship terminated with the thirty-eighth session of congress. With the exception of having secured the payment of the Gilpin drafts, and an appropriation for a branch mint, which was really no more than a United States assay-office,

[16] The vote stood 15,443 for, to 4,039 against acceptance. *Corbett, Legis. Manual,* 119.

[17] A joint resolution of the legislature of 1864 protests against the reduction of territorial limits in accordance with the endeavors of the delegate from New Mexico in congress, and instructs the Colorado delegate to be especially watchful and oppose all such attempts. *Gen. Laws Colo,* 1864, 256.

[18] Their names were J. C. Wilson president, H. P. H. Bromwell, Casamiro Barela, George Boyles, W. E. Beck, Byron L. Carr, William H. Cushman, W. M. Clark, A. D. Cooper, H. R. Crosby, Robert Douglas, L. C. Ellsworth, C. P. Elder, F. J. Elbert, W. B. Felton, J. M. Garcia, Daniel Hurd, John S. Hough, Lafayette Head, William H. James, William R. Kennedy, William L. Lee, Alvin Marsh, William H. Meyer, S. J. Plumb, George E. Pease, Robert A. Quillan, A. K. Yount, Wilbur F. Stone, W. C. Stover, H. C. Thatcher, Agapeta Vigil, W. W. Webster, G. G. White, E. T. Wells, P. P. Wilcox, J. S. Wheeler, J. W. Widderfield, Lewis C. Rockwell. Secretaries, W. W. Coulson, Herbert Stanley, and H. A. Terpenning. *Corbett, Legis. Manual,* 116-17.

[19] See Pitkin, in *Political Views,* MS., 13. Only one article of the constitution could be amended at any one session, the sessions being biennial. One foolish provision in the constitution was the publication of the laws in Spanish and German. It would seem that the foreigners we import to govern us might at least learn our language. Sessions were limited to forty days, and every bill was to be read three times before each house for the benefit of stupid members.

nothing had been done for Colorado beyond what the
actual wants of the people demanded.[20]   Bennett was
succeeded by Allen A. Bradford, who in 1862 was
appointed associate justice in place of Pettis, serving
in the second judicial district until elected to represent
the territory in the thirty-ninth congress.[21] He labored
for the passage of a homestead law, for a mineral-land
law, for increased pay for the supreme judges, and
members of the legislature, and for payment of the
mounted militia employed in opening communication
through the Indian country in 1864, of which I shall
speak hereafter.   At the close of this congress the
salaries of the judges were raised to $2,500.[22] Previ-
ously, and by the efforts of the Montana delegate
chiefly, an act was passed appropriating the net proceeds of the internal revenue of 1866–8 to the erection
of penitentiaries in seven several territories, including
Colorado.   At the beginning of the fortieth congress
an act amending the organic law of Colorado made
the sessions of the legislative assembly biennial, the
election for four years for councilmen, and two years
for assemblymen, and the pay six instead of three
dollars per diem.[23]

[20] The appropriation for 1863, including $5,000 for a territorial prison, and
$2,500 for a territorial library, aggregated $69,960.   The appropriations for
1864–5 amounted to $54,700.   This was exclusive of post-routes, which were
of general use.   The routes established in 1863–4 were from Denver to East
Bannack, in Idaho; from Denver via Poncha pass and Conejos to Santa Fé;
from Denver to Bijou basin; and from Golden City via Ralston creek, and
Boulder city to Burlington.   A wagon road was in process of construction
in 1863–4 from the headwaters of Clear creek, through Middle park, and the
valleys of Bear, Uintah, and Timpanogas river to Provo in Utah.
[21] A. A. Bradford was born in Maine in 1815, went to Mo. in 1841, studied
law and was made judge.   In 1855 he removed to Nebraska, where he was
a member of the legislative council in 1856–8, and came in 1859 to Central,
settling finally at Pueblo.   He was a man of many experiences, some of
which I was fortunate enough to secure in a manuscript.
[22] The organic act gave the governor $1,500 with $1,000 more as supt of
Ind. aff., and gave the judges $1,800.
[23] The appropriation for 1866 was $43,000 including $15,000 for surveying.   The post-routes secured were from Georgetown to Argentine; from
Gold Dirt to South Boulder; and from Denver via Mt Vernon and Idaho to
Empire City.   The appropriation for 1867 was $47,090.   The post-routes
opened were from Badito to Spanish peaks; Pueblo to Hermosillo; Pueblo to
Carson City, via Rock Cañon Ridge and Frazier settlement to Jamestown;
and from Eureka to Breckenridge via Argentine and Pera,

In October 1865 President Johnson appointed
Alexander Cummings governor of Colorado in place
of Evans. Cummings was famous about 1862 as
founder of the *N. Y. Daily World,* and notorious
afterward for his peculations in a contract with the
war department. The Coloradans disliked him, and
made his administration unpopular by all the ways
known to journalists and politicians, even to requesting the president to remove him. It was not shrewdness or intelligence that he lacked, but the knowledge
of how to inspire confidence by putting them to a
beneficent use. He remained in office about a year and
a half. In November, George M. Chilcott[24] was
elected representative to congress under the state
constitution, which, as I have already stated, the
president refused to recognize, lest congress should
use the two senatorial and one representative vote of
the new state against him in his impeachment trial.
In the following August Chilcott was reëlected, and
took his seat as delegate, after some loss of time
through having his election contested by A. C. Hunt.
He secured the passage of a bill repealing the act
which discriminated against the whole region west of
Kansas and east of California by charging letter postage on printed matter within those boundaries. He
was also fortunate in securing important action concerning certain land-grants, and appropriations for the
public surveys.[25] He was succeeded in 1868 by A. A.

[24] Chilcott was born in Pa, in 1828. moved in 1844 to Iowa, and was elected
sheriff in 1853, and in 1856 to Neb. when he was sent to the legislature. The
wave of migration caught him in 1859, and carried him to Colorado, where
he arrived in May. He was a member of the constitutional convention of
that year at Denver, returning to Omaha to spend the winter. In the autumn
of 1860 he settled in what is now Pueblo co., engaging in farm work for a
livelihood for two years, after which he took a claim for himself 12 miles east
of Pueblo and brought out his family. He was elected to represent this
region at the first two sessions of the territorial legislature, and was appointed
by Pres. Lincoln register of the U. S. land office for the district of Colorado
in 1863, which position he held until he was elected to congress. Republican in politics, Chilcott was an energetic, cheerful worker, with a fine physique, and universally successful in his undertakings.

[25] The appropriations for 1860 were greatly in excess of any before made,
amounting for every purpose, excepting mails and Indian department, to
$183,446.51. *Rocky Mountain News,* Aug. 5, 1868.

Bradford, elected a second time, who introduced bills for grants of land to two railroad companies, for appropriations for public buildings in Colorado, for the settlement of the southern boundary of Colorado, and for increasing the pay of officers of the supreme courts of Colorado and New Mexico.

Meantime, the territory had twice received a new executive, A. C. Hunt being appointed by President Johnson in May 1867, and Edward M. McCook by President Grant in June 1869. Hunt had been United States marshal, was familiar with the physical and social aspect of the territory, and gave an administration satisfactory to the people; but he was removed to make place for a protegé of another president, according to usage.[26] His successor, McCook, lacked nothing in ability. He was charged with peculation in office as superintendent of Indian affairs, and the charges were investigated, leaving the impression on the public mind that a powerful interest had screened him from just punishment.[27] He held the office from June 1869 to March 1873, when Samuel H. Elbert was appointed.[28] A scheme of this governor's was the reclamation of all the lands west of the Missouri river by irrigation. He called a meeting of delegates from the western states and territories, and had fairly set the matter in motion, looking to secure congressional legislation, when he was removed and McCook reappointed. For several months the senate refused to confirm this action, and Elbert continued to administer the government.[29] On the final issue between

[26] Hunt became interested in railroads, was one of the projectors and constructors of the Denver and New Orleans road. He would ride 100 miles a day on horseback, superintending railroad work. He became largely interested in mines in Texas, and railroads in Mexico, but continued his residence in Denver. *Elbert, Public Men and Measures*, MS., 12; *Pitkin's Polit. Views*, MS., 11; *Bradford, Hist. Colo*, MS., 5.

[27] See Salt Lake *Herald*, Aug. 24, 1874; and in Deer Lodge *New Northwest*, Sept. 5, 1874.

[28] Elbert, a native of Ohio, came to Colorado in 1862 as ter. sec. under Evans, after practising law and politics in Iowa and Neb. After his 4 years of secretaryship had expired, he entered into a law partnership with J. Q. Charles, and was elected to the territorial legislature in 1869.

[29] Elbert went east, and John W. Jenkins, territorial secretary, became

federal republicans and territorial republicans the party was divided into factions, and lost the election to the democrats for the first time in the history of the territory. During the excitement of these political squabbles the plans for public improvements on a large scale were abandoned.

McCook's second term extended over little more than one year, the administration deciding that it could not bear a rebuke which came in the form of a democratic majority, even in a territory, and in March 1875 appointed John L. Routt governor of Colorado. Although a stranger in the territory, he soon became known as its friend, and received the highest indorsement his official conduct could have when he went out of office with the territory, to resume it under the state organization in 1876.[30] While these events were in progress the office of delegate had been filled by Jerome B. Chaffee, after Bradford's second term, until the election of a democrat, Thomas M. Patterson, in 1874. Chaffee had been a delegate in every presidential nominating convention since that of the free soil party in 1856, and was the leader of the

acting-governor in his absence. On the return of Elbert, after the confirmation of McCook, Jenkins addressed a letter to him which he signed as 'acting-governor.' Elbert resented this and returned the document indorsed 'not recognized,' signing himself 'governor of Colorado.' A spicy correspondence followed, Jenkins asserting that he had been notified of Elbert's removal, and Elbert that he had never been officially notified, and that he was governor until the arrival of his successor with a commission. Elbert kept his office at his block on Larimer street, and Jenkins his in McCook's block on Blake street. In the same building was the national bank, delegate Chaffee president, who opposed McCook's comfirmation. D. H. Moffat, Jr, cashier and territorial treasurer, was accused of fraud in connection with his office. Such is politics. *N. Y. Times*, July 28, 1874.

[30] John Long Routt was born in Ky in 1826, but removed to Ill., where in due time he was elected sheriff of McLean co. In 1862 he was captain of Company E of the 94th Ill. volunteers, and remained in the service until the autumn of 1865. Being offered the position of chief clerk of the bureau of the 2d asst postmaster-general, he accepted the office in 1869. The following year President Grant appointed him U. S. marshal for the southern district of Ill., and in 1871 to the post of 2d asst postmaster-general, which position he filled until appointed governor of Colorado. A thorough business man, his own and the public affairs intrusted to him have always prospered. In mining operations he acquired a fortune, becoming largely the owner of the Morning Star and Waterloo mines in Leadville. He was short and strongly built, with great power of endurance. *Bradford, Hist. Colo*, MS., 5; *Routt's Territory and State*, MS., 1-9.

republican party in Colorado, a capitalist, and liberal in dispensing money for the uses of his party. Only the split that occurred through the McCook-Elbert imbroglio could have unseated him.[31] On taking his place in congress he began the demand for the admission of Colorado as a state, and persisted in it through both terms. He secured the authorization of a treaty with the Utes for the cession of that portion of their lands in the San Juan country whose mineral wealth had made it coveted by miners. One of his most important measures was advocating a change in the rules of the house of representatives so as to give the territories a representation in the committee on territories, establishing a precedent which greatly increased the influence of delegates. Under this rule he was the first delegate to report a bill directly from a committe to the house. He was the author, and secured the passage, of a bill enlarging the power of territorial legislatures ; and was instrumental in establishing a mining code, besides greatly extending the mail service,[32] and laboring for the interest of pro-

[31] Jerome B. Chaffee was born in Niagara co., N. Y.. in 1825, removing while young to Michigan, and later to Mo., where he engaged in banking. In 1860 he came to Colorado, and in company with Eben Smith erected the Smith and Chaffee stamp-mill, to develope gold lodes near Central City, his success encouraging other miners in that district. He subsequently became principal owner in the Bob-tail Lode and Tunnel company, from which there was from $300,000 to $500,000 annual income. The name is said to have been derived from a bob-tailed ox being used to haul a drag made by stretching a rawhide across a forked stick, for conveying pay-dirt to the gulch for sluicing. Besides this property, Chaffee became interested in nearly a hundred gold and silver lodes in different stages of development. In 1865 he purchased the banking business of Clark & Co., Denver, and established the First National bank, of which he was president until 1880. His political career began with his election to the territorial legislature in 1861, and again in 1863, when he was chosen speaker of the house of representatives. His election as senator under the constitution of 1866, which was vetoed by President Johnson, and the long controversy over it, brought him conspicuously before the people as a man fit to be a leader, and caused his election in 1870 and 1872. *Byers' Hist. Colo*, MS , 21. A daughter of Senator Chaffee married a son of President Grant.

[32] I will make one more mention of the post-routes, to show the gradual extension southward of settlement. Routes were opened from Badito, via Crestone, San Isabel, and Bismarck, to Villa Grove; from Cañon City, via Greenwood, Mace's Hole, and Dotson's to Greenhorn; from Greenwood to Colfax; from Badito, via Gardner, to Colfax; from Trinidad, via San Francisco, to La Trinchera; from Fort Garland to Zapato; from La Loma to Capote; from Colorado Springs to Fairplay; from Colorado Springs via Easton,

jected railroads. Finally, in the last weeks of his term, he effected the passage of an enabling act for Colorado—March 3, 1875—which was amended, however, so as to postpone the date of admission to July 1876.[33] The career of Patterson, begun under the embarrassment of being in a certain sense an accidental rather than a legitimate and voluntary choice of the people, was creditable. The republican party was divided into two factions, one designing to rebuke and the other to sustain the administration. Nor were the democrats altogether harmonious, many being dissatisfied with the nomination of a late-comer in their midst;[34] to show their displeasure they induced a pioneer of note, A. G. Boone, to announce himself an independent candidate,[35] but he withdrew before the election, leaving the field to H. P. H. Bromwell,[36] the administration republican candidate, and Patterson, on whom the anti-administrationists united with the democrats, with the result already indicated.

Before proceeding to the history of the state organization it is due to the territorial judges and other officers to make mention of them individually as far as space will permit. Chief Justice Hall was succeeded in 1863 by Stephen S. Harding. In 1866 President Johnson appointed in his place Moses Hallett, who was twice reappointed to the same position,

to Gomer's Mill; from Pueblo via Huerfano junctions, Baggsville, and Las Animas, to Fort Lyon; from Creswell, via Bergen park, to Junction; from Fort Collins to Livermore.

[33] *H. Jour.*, 43 cong. 2d sess., 577, 632, 644, 679, 43, 2; *Colo Gen. Laws*, 23–7; *Statutes U. S.*, 44 cong. 1st sess., pp. vii.–viii.

[34] Patterson was an arrival of 1872, a native of Ireland, born in 1840. He was elected city attorney by the common council of Denver in the spring, 1874.

[35] Boone was the eldest son of Jesse Boone of Ky, who was the eldest son of the renowned Daniel. While he possessed those half military and wholly brave and generous traits which distinguish the class to which he belonged, he was not trained to the sinuous ways of legislation, and was moreover about 70 years of age.

[36] Bromwell was born in Md, moved early to Ohio, and then to Ill., where he began the practice of the law in 1853, at the same time publishing a newspaper, the *Age of Steam and Fire*. After a political career in Ill. he came to Colorado in 1870, was a member of the territorial council in 1874, of the constitutional convention of 1875, and of the state legislature in 1879. He was a fine scholar and fond of literary pursuits.

and after the admission of the state again appointed
by President Grant to the higher post of United
States district judge, being commended generally by
his fellow-citizens for honor, ability, and personal
qualifications.[37]

The associate justices appointed in territorial times
were, after Bradford, Charles F. Holly and William
H. Gale in 1865; William R. Gorsline and Christian
S. Eyster in 1866; James B. Belford in 1870, reap-
pointed in 1874; Ebenezer T. Wells in 1871; Amherst
W. Stone and Andrew W. Brazee in 1885.[38] The
United States district attorneys appointed after Dalliba were Samuel E. Brown, 1862; George W. Cham-
berlain, 1865; Henry C. Thatcher, 1868; Lewis C.
Rockwell, 1869; H. C. Alleman, 1873, and C. D.
Bradley, 1875. The territorial secretaries after
Elbert were Frank Hall, appointed in 1866, and reappointed in 1869 and 1873,[39] who was often virtually
governor, and conducted the affairs of the executive
office in a worthy manner, presiding over the legislature and defending the territory from Indian hostilities; John W. Jenkins, appointed in 1874; and John
Taffe, appointed in 1875.[40] The history of Colorado

[37] Says Pitkin: ' His record is the most remarkable of any judge in the
state. As a lawyer his character is irreproachable; he is an honest, upright
judge, a man of great learning, and has shaped the law of Colorado.' *Political
Views*, MS., 8; *Colo Pub. Doc.*, Set E.
[38] Brazee was born in N. Y. in 1826. During the civil war he was in the
army, holding successively commissions as lieut, capt., and maj. of the 49th
N. Y. regt. He also filled the office of judge advocate of the 2d division of
the 6th army corps. In 1867 he was appointed brig.-gen. of the N. Y. Nat.
Guards, 32d brigade. In 1871 he was appointed asst U. S. atty for the
northern district of N. Y., which office he resigned to accept the appointment to Colorado.
[39] Frank Hall was born in N. Y., in 1836. In 1860 he came to Colorado,
mining for 2 or 3 years at Spanish bar and Central City. In 1863 he was
associated with O. J. Hollister in the Black Hawk *Mining Journal.* He was
elected to the legislature in 1864. In 1865 he purchased an interest in the
Miner's Register, at Central City, of which he was editor for ten years, when
he removed to Denver and entered the office of the U. S. marshal as chief
deputy. In 1878 he became managing editor of the *Daily Times*, from which
position he retired to open the Great Western Mining Agency with Prof. J.
Alden Smith, state geologist. During his editorial and official career he has
done much to advance the material interests of Colorado.
[40] The territorial treasurers appointed by the executive were George T.
Clark, 1861; Alexander W. Atkins, 1864; A. C. Hunt, 1866; John Wanless,
1866; Columbus Nuckolls, 1867, reappointed 1868; George T. Clark, 1870,

does not afford those scenes of discord among legislators and disrespect of officials which darken the record
of some of the cotemporary territories.[41] Neither

reappointed 1872; David H. Moffat, 1874; and Frederick Z. Salomon, 1876.
Auditors, Milton M. Delano, 1861; Richard E. Whitsitt, 1864, reappointed
in 1866; Hiram J. Graham, 1866; Nathaniel F. Cheeseman, 1868; James B.
Thompson, 1870, reappointed 1874; and Levin C. Charles, 1874, reappointed
1876. Sup'ts public instruction, William J. Curtice, 1861; William S.
Walker, 1863; A. W. Atkins, 1865; John Wanless, 1866; Columbus Nuckolls,
1867 (the last three ex-officio as ter. treasurers); Wilbur C. Lathrop, 1870;
and Horace M. Hale, 1872, reappointed in 1874 and 187f.

[41] The members of the 1st and 2d legislatures have been named heretofore.
The 3d legislature, which met at Golden, Feb. 1, 1864, and adjourned to
Denver on the 4th, consisted of councilmen Charles W. Mather, president;
Amos Widner, Moses Hallett, Richard E. Whitsitt, Robert Berry, A. J. Van
Deren, E. A. Johnson, William A. H. Loveland, Lewis Jones, R. O. Bailey,
J. B. Doyle, C. Dominguez, and H. E. Esterday; representatives Jerome B.
Chaffee, speaker; A. O. Patterson, David A. Chever, J. A. Koontz, John A.
Nye, John H. Eames, David Ripley, James Kelley, Leon D. Judd, John Kipp,
Alvin Marsh, Samuel Mallory, E. F. Holland, J. E. Leeper, M. C. White,
John T. Lynch, Henry Henson, J. B. Stansell, Joel Wood, J. McCannon,
Pablo Ortega, José Victor Garcia, N. W. Welton, B. J. McComas, L. D.
Webster, and A. Z. Sheldon. Sec. of council, C. B. Haynes; asst sec. W.
T. Reynolds; eng. clerk, E. C. Parmelee; enr. clerk, O. B. Brown; sergt-
at-arms, C. A. Bartholomew.
    The 4th legislature, which held its session at Golden, Jan. 2, 1865, was:
council, J. Wentz Wilson, president; Amos Widner, Moses Hallett, Richard
E. Whitsitt, George R. Mitchell, E. K. Baxter, Lewis Jones, William A. H.
Loveland, H. L. Pearson, Robert Berry, Robert B. Willis, C. Dominguez, H.
E. Esterday; representatives, L. H. Hash, speaker; Hiram J. Bredlinger,
Rufus Clark, Baxter B. Stiles, F. M. Case, D. H. Nichols, A. O. Patterson,
Thomas D. Worrall, Benjamin Lake, A. Mansur, C. M. Tyler, E. F. Holland,
B. F. Pine, John T. Lynch, A. Hopkins, Wilbur F. Stone, James Thompson,
C. North, J. G. Ehrhart, Miles M. Craig, O. H. P. Baxter. Sec. of council,
Ozias Millett; asst sec., James O. Allen; enr. clerk, W. B. Felton; eng. clerk,
W. Adams; sergt-at-arms, Marshall Silverthorne. Chief clerk of the house,
C. H. Grover; eng. clerk, N. S. Hurd; enr. clerk, A. D. Cooper; sergt-at-
arms, Henry Gibson.
    The 5th legislature, convening at Golden, Jan. 1, 1866, and adjourning to
Denver on the 4th, was composed as follows: council, Henry C. Leach, presi-
dent. Joseph M. Marshall, John Q. Charles, George R. Mitchell, Ebenezer
Smith, Benjamin Woodbury, William A. H. Loveland, Robert Douglas, George
W. Mann, H. H. DeMary, O. H. P. Baxter, Jesus María Valasquez, George
A. Hinsdale; house of representatives, E. Norris Stearns, speaker; B. F.
Johnson, David Gregory, Louis F. Bartels, James F. Gardner, H. J. Graham,
S. M. Breath, T. C. Bergen, Perley Dodge, Frank Hall, Columbus Nuckolls,
C. M. Grimes, J. W. Watson, David J. Ball, B. R. Colvin, John Fosher, A.
D. Bevan, George W. Norris, Thomas Keys, J. G. Ehrhart, José Gabriel Mar-
tine, M. Mandrigan, Jesus María Barela, Matt. Riddlebarger, William Lock,
John W. Henry. Sec. of council, Charles G. Cox; asst sec., George H. Still-
well; eng. clerk, Benjamin P. Thompson; enr. clerk, N. F. Cheeseman;
sergt-at-arms, Marshall Silverthorne. Chief clerk of house, C. J. McDivitt;
enr. clerk, A. D. Cooper; eng. clerk, A. Hopkins; sergt-at-arms, Charles
Bartholomew.
    The 6th legislature, which convened at Golden Dec. 3, 1866, adjourned to
Jan. 11, 1867. The council was the same as at the previous session, Robert
Douglas president. The house consisted of E. L. Berthoud, speaker; Peter
Winne, C. H. McLaughlin, Edwin Scudder J. E. Force, C. J. Goss, James

did it become notorious by defalcations in office in the
formative period of its territorial existence, a character which the state has sustained.

The admission of Colorado as a state was the signal
for a struggle for political control. Both parties
organized, the republicans at Pueblo on the 23d of

S Doggett, J. E. Parkman, Columbus Nuckolls, E. T. Wells, J. Y. Glendinen,
C. M. Grimes, Charles B. Patterson, R. W. Davis, Ziba Surles, W. W. Web-
ster, Charles L. Hall, F. C. Morse, Julius C. Hughes, Jacob E. Ehrhart, Juan
B. Lobato, S. Valdez, Juan Miguel Vijíl, Matt. Riddlebarger, M. Mills Craig,
W H. Young. Sec. of council, Robert Berry; asst sec. J. A. Miller; enr.
clerk, N. F Cheeseman; eng. clerk, William B. Rines; sergt-at-arms, B. R.
Wall. Chief clerk of house, C. J. McDivitt; asst clerk, W. J. Kram; eng.
clerk, Root; enr. clerk, Grey; sergt-at-arms, E. H. Brown.

The 7th legislature convened at Golden Dec. 2, 1867, and adjourned to
Denver on the 9th. The council consisted of William W. Webster president.
James H Pinkerton, Amos Steck, Charles A. Cook, Hugh Butler, David D.
Belden, J. Wellington Nesmith, William A. H. Loveland, E. Norris Stearns,
Wiliam W. Webster, Julius C. Hughes, B. B. Field, Jesus María Velas-
quez, Francisco Sanchez; the house, of C. H. McLaughlin, speaker, H. Strat-
ton, Baxter B. Stiles, J. E. Wurtzebach, G. W. Miller, H. L. Pearson, F. O.
Sawin, T Haswell, D. M. Richards, S. F. Huddleston, C. R. Bissell, W. M.
Slaughter, J. C. McCoy. J. E. Wharton, Stephen Decatur, J. A. Pierce,
Ansel Bates, W. J. McDougal, J. Gilliland, B. Fowler, J. Lawrence, Pablo
Ortega, Silverio Suaso, Thomas Suaso, Thomas Macon, E. T. Stone. Sec. of
council, Ed C. Parmelee; asst sec., W. J. Kram; eng. clerk, E. R. Harris;
enr. clerk, A. Hopkins; sergt-at-arms, Ziba Surles. Chief clerk of house, C.
J. McDivitt; asst clerk, M. L. Horr; eng clerk, Joseph Sharratt; enr. clerk,
A. Cree; asst enr. clerk, Charles F Leimer; sergt-at-arms, Wells.

The 8th legislature held its entire session at Denver, from Jan. 3, to Feb.
11, 1870. The council was the same as at the previous session, with the
exception that George A. Hinsdale was president, and that Pinkerton's place
was filled by Jesse M. Sherwood, and Belden's by Silas B. Hahn. The house
consisted of George W. Miller speaker, Matthew S. Taylor, Samuel H. Elbert,
H. B. Bearce, C C. Gird, John H. Wells, Allison H. De France, Thomas J.
Graham, Thomas J. Campbell, H. E. Lyon, A. E. Lea, John F. Topping,
John T. Lynch, D. B Myers, George W. Mann, A. D Bevan, C. M Mullen,
J. G. Randall, D. L. Vandiver, J. C. Hall, Manuel Lucero, Clement Trujillo,
William H. Meyer, Felipe Baca, William Sheppard, J. B. Rice Sec. council,
A. O. Patterson; asst sec., George T. Clark; eng. clerk, J. E. Cobb; enr.
olerk, Henry Bell; sergt-at-arms, E. T. Stone. Chief clerk of house, W. M.
Slaughter; asst clerk, A. M. Barnard; eng clerk, A. M. McCrystal; enr.
clerk, John D. McIntyre; sergt-at-arms, W. W. Remine.

The 9th legislature held its session at Denver from Jan. 1 to Feb 9, 1872.
The councilmen were George M. Chilcott president, Joseph E. Bates, Francis
Gallup, William C Stover, Allison H. De France, Nathaniel P Hill, Benja-
min W. Wisebart, Edward C. Parmelee, Madison W. Stewart, J. Marshall
Paul, Jesus María Garcia, Silverio Suaso, José Victor Garcia. The repre-
sentatives were Alvin Marsh speaker, Frederick Steinhauer, Isaac Bachellor,
Clarence P. Elder, John G. Tilley, J. W. Bacon, B. H. Eaton, John D. Pat-
rick, James P. Maxwell, Charles C. Welch, George E. Randolph, John F.
Topping, W. W. Webster, James F. Gardner, Thomas O Boggs, J. M.
Givens, B. F. Crowell, A. D. Cooper, John G. Randall, Casimiro Barela,
Lorenzo A. Abeyta, Mariano Larrogoite, John A. Manzanares, Pedro Raphael
Trujillo, José A. Valasquez, Francisco Sanchez. Sec. of council, Edward L.
Salisbury; asst sec., Chase Withrow; eng clerk, E. H. Starrette; enr. clerk,

August, and the democrats at Manitou on the 29th, with full tickets for state officers. The election was held on the 3d of October, 30,000 votes being polled, the entire republican ticket for the executive and judicial departments being elected, with a republican majority in both houses of the legislature, and a rep-

S. N. Sanders; sergt-at-arms, Robert N. Daniels. Chief clerk of house, James G. Cooper; asst clerk, Joseph L. Boyd; eng clerk, Rollin Morrow; enr. clerk, C. W. Baldwin; sergt-at-arms, Uriah M. Curtis.   A. W. Archibald successfully contested the seat of Abeyta.

The 10th legislature met at Denver Jan. 5, 1874.   In the council were Madison W. Stewart president, H. P. H. Bromwell, R. G. Buckingham, Thomas Sprague, John B. Fitzpatrick, Hugh Butter, H. C. McCammon, William M. Clark, George M. Chilcott, Jarius W. Hall, Daniel L. Taylor, Juan B. Jaquez, Lafayette Head.   In the house, David H. Nichols speaker, Frederick Steinhauer, Alfred Butters, R. S. Little, J. H. K. Uhlhorn, Joseph C. Shattuck, John McCutcheon, Levi Harsh, James P. Maxwell, David H. Nichols, Henry Paul, Bela S. Buell, William J. Buffington, Benjamin F. Napheys, Charles W. Perry, John W. Prowers, Joseph C. Wilson, William Moore, Joseph Hutchinson, William A. Amsbury, Mariano Larragoite, Casimiro Barela, Alexander H. Taylor, J. A. J. Valdez, William H. Meyer, Manuel S. Salazar, Juan Esquibel.   Sec. of council, Foster Nichols; asst sec., D. C. Limberger; enr. clerk, George H. F. Work; sergt-at-arms, George H. Ward.   Chief clerk of house, Joseph T. Boyd; asst clerk, E. P. Drake; eng clerk, J. A. Koontz; sergt-at-arms, O. H. Henry.

The 11th legislature convened Jan. 3, 1876, at Denver.   The council consisted of Adair Wilson president, Bela M. Hughes, Baxter B. Stiles, B. H. Eaton, John C. Hummel, Silas B. Hahn, E. L. Salisbury, Robert S. Morrison, Andrew D. Wilson, James Rice, James Clelland, P. A. McBride, Silverio Suaso; the house, of Alfred Butters speaker, Edmund L. Smith, Edward Pisko, W. B. Mills, Norman H. Meldrum, J. C. McCowan, M. N. Everett, David C. Patterson, George Rand, John C. McShane, Frederick Kruse, William Larned, John H. Yonley, J. M. Nimerick, Frank Bingham, Albinus J. Sheldon; H. O. Rettberg, James Y. Marshall, I. N. Peyton, Donaciano Gurule, Nicauora D. Jarramilla, Mauricio Apadaca, Herman Duhme, Jr, Francisco Sanchez, T. M. Trippe, Reuben J. McNutt.   Sec. of council James T. Smith; asst sec., Frank Fassett; eng clerk, James D. Henry; enr. clerk, William Barchert; sergt-at-arms, J. A. J. Bigler.   Chief clerk of the house, Joseph T. Boyd; asst clerk, C. L. Peyton; eng clerk, James W. Galloway; enr. clerk, W. B. Dickinson; sergt-at-arms, James D. Wood.

The legislature of 1865, which convened at Golden Dec. 12th, under the state constitution framed that year, but vetoed by the president, adjourned to Denver on the 16th, and sine die on the 19th.   The senate was composed of George A. Hinsdale president, Leander M. Black, Charles A. Cook, L. B. McLain, Truman Whitcomb, L. L. Bedell. A. G. Langford, W. A. H. Loveland, James Castello, Adam B. Cooper, F. H. De Mary, John W. Henry, Jesus M. Velazquez, J. L. Casper.   The house of representatives was composed of D. P. Wilson speaker, A. Lumry, Robert L Hatten, G. H. Greenslit, William Garrison, D. G. Peabody, A. Wright, T C. Bergen, David H Nichols, Isaac Whicker, Jason E. Scobey, Stephen Goodall, Lyman W Chase, Charles B. Patterson, B. R. Colvin, James A. Pierce, Aaron Hopkins, George W. Lechmer, Charles L. Hall, Thomas Keys, F. C. Hughes, Pedro Arragon, José Gabriel Martine, Pedro Lobato, Matt. Riddlebarger, George A. Bates. Sec. of the senate, John Walker; asst sec., Edwin H. Brown, sergt-at-arms, H. B. Haskell. Chief clerk of the house, L. H. Shepherd; asst clerk, C. J. McDivitt; sergt-at-arms, Charles Bartholomew, *Corbett, Legis. Manual,* 226-7.

resentative to the forty-fourth congress, while the democrats elected a representative to the forty-fifth congress.[42] John L. Routt was chosen governor, Lafayette Head[43] lieutenant-governor. William G. Clark[44] secretary of state, D. C. Crawford[45] auditor, George C. Corning[46] treasurer, A. J. Sampson[47]

[42] It is not a little singular that, for the second time, Patterson was elected to represent Colorado in congress through a blunder of the dominant party. The territorial secretary had ordered an election for representatives for the 44th congress, to be held on the 3d of Oct., and another election for the 45th congress on the 7th ot Nov. But the people voted for James B. Belford for both congresses on the 3d of Oct thinking to save themselves trouble. On the 7th of Nov., however, the democrats voted, and elected Patterson by almost the entire vote The canvassing board retused to count it, but after a long contest in congress, Patterson gained his seat, and was, as he had been before, a useful representative

[43] Lafayette Head was born in Mo. in 1825, enlisted in the 2d regt, Mo. vol., and fought in the battles of La Canado, Embudo, Taos, and Santa Clara springs. After the peace he settled in New Mexico as a merchant at Abiquiú, and was appointed U S. marshal of the northern district ot that territory for three years. In 1861 he was sheriff of Rio Arriba co. for two years, and was elected to the legislature from that co. in 1863. In 1855 he was commissioned a lieut in Col St Vrain's regt of volunteers, which served 6 months against the Utes and Apaches. The following year he was elected from Taos to the legislature, and was subsequently chosen to fill a vacancy in the council, of which he was president in 1857. He received the appointment of special agent for the Utes and Apaches in 1859, holding the office 9 years. He was elected councilman in the Colorado legislature from Conejos co. in 1874, and delegate to the constitutional convention in 1875. He received 14,191 votes, against 13,093 given to the opposing candidate, Michael Beshoar, for lieut-gov.

[44] William G. Clark was born in Pa, enlisted in 1861 as a private in company F, 28th regt, afterward E of the 47th regt, Pa volunteers. He was captain of his company when he was mustered out in 1865. He came to Colorado in 1866, settling in Clear Creek co., and engaging in mining, soon becoming known, and being elected to be supt of schools, appointed clerk of the district court, elected member of the legislature, appointed brig.-gen. of militia, and elected a member of the constitutional convention. He received at the first state election 14,582 votes, against 12,843 for James T. Smith, democrat.

[45] David C. Crawford was a native of Canada, removed to Mich. and Wis., and in 1860 came to Colorado. He first engaged in mining in Gilpin and Boulder counties, in 1862 in merchandising in Park co., and in 1865 in farming in Jefferson co. He was elected clerk and recorder for the latter county in 1867, and afterward opened a real estate and insurance office, becoming in 1875 proprietor of the Crawford house at Colorado Springs. He married Amanda J Thornton of Golden. His opponent for the office of auditor was J. F. Benedict, whom he beat by 922 votes.

[46] George C. Corning was born in Ohio in 1837, organized the bank of Topeka, Kansas, in 1868, and in 1870 settled in Colorado, where he opened a bank. The republican vote for treasurer stood 14,038 against 13,310 for Thomas M. Field, democrat.

[47] Archibald J Sampson was born in Ohio, and entered the union army in 1861. He was promoted to a captaincy, but at Hatcher's Run, Va, was disabled for life and discharged. He then studied law in the Cleveland law school, beginning to practise in 1866 at Sedalia, Mo., and married the

attorney-general, Joseph C. Shattuck [48] superintendent of public instruction. James B. Belford [49] was elected representative in the forty-fourth and forty-fifth congresses, although his seat in the latter was successfully contested by Thomas M. Patterson, owing to a misapprehension concerning the day of election.

On the 1st of November the General Assembly of the state of Colorado convened at noon. On the 3d, Judge Brazee administered the oath of office to the executive officers. Early in the session two United States senators were chosen—Jerome B. Chaffee and Henry M. Teller [50]—and three presidential electors, Herman Beckurts, W. L. Hadley, and Otto Mears. The assembly did not adjourn until March 20, 1877.

Three judges of the supreme court were elected by the people; namely, Henry C. Thatcher, Samuel H. Elbert, and Ebenezer T. Wells, Thatcher drawing the short term of three years, which made him the first chief justice, [51] Elbert the six years' term and the

daughter of Judge Allen C. Turner of his native town the same year. He declined office in Mo., and the consulate of Palestine, but was presidential elector in 1872. He came to Colorado in 1874, settling at Cañon City in the practice of his profession, until elected attorney-general of the new state, against G. Q. Richmond, by 963 votes.

[48] Joseph C. Shattuck was born in N. H. in 1835, and educated at the Westminster seminary, Vt, and Wesleyan university, Conn., but without completing the course. He married Hattie M. Knight of Marlborough in 1858, and migrated to Mo., where he was a teacher. In 1870 he came to Colorado with the Greeley colony, of which he was vice-president and manager. He was elected to the legislature from Weld co. in 1874. His majority over G. B. Groesbeck, democrat, in 1876, was 1,831.

[49] James B. Belford was born in Pa, and came to Colorado in 1870, having been appointed associate justice of the supreme court, which position he held until the admission of the state.

[50] U. S. Official Register, 1877, 2. Teller drew the long term ending 1883. He was born in N. Y. in 1830, and practised law in Ill. He had been a republican since the organization of the party, and taken part in the campaign of 1860 for Lincoln. In 1861 he came to Colorado, settling at Central City in the practice of his profession, in partnership with H. A. Johnson, and subsequently with his brother, Willard Teller. He was appointed by Gov. Evans maj.-gen. of the territorial militia in 1863. He organized in 1865 the Colorado Central railroad company, of which he was for five years president, and has promoted many business enterprises. In the U. S. senate he distinguished himself, while laboring for Colorado, by his report on the election frauds in southern states, which he, as chairman of a committee, was forced to investigate. He was also chairman of the senate committee on civil service reform.

[51] Henry C. Thatcher was born in Pa in 1842, completed his law studies in the Albany university, from which he graduated in 1866, coming directly

chief justiceship for three years, and Wells the term
for nine years. Wells was a man of fine character
and ability, but resigned soon after election. The bar
of Colorado, in convention, nominated Wilbur F.
Stone to fill the vacancy, a nomination which met the
hearty approval of the public, and which was confirmed at the next general election. Four district
judges were elected for six years; namely, William E.
Beck, Victor A. Elliott, John W. Henry, and Thomas
M. Bowen, in the order in which they are here given.
The attorneys for the four districts were Edward O.
Wolcott, David B. Graham, James M. Waldron, and
Columbus W. Burris. A full set of regents for the
university, trustees of the school of mines, managers
of the penitentiary, trustees of the deaf and mute
institute, and members of the state board of agriculture, were also elected, such was the care of those
having affairs in charge that the state should commence its career in the possession of all its dignities.

The population of Colorado, when admitted, was
135,000, the disproportion of the sexes remarked
upon a decade earlier having in a great degree become adjusted. Its boundaries remained the same.
Its assessed valuation, exclusive of untaxable mining
property, amounted, in real and personal property, to
$44,130,205. Upon this the legislature fixed the
limit of taxation, for all purposes, at twenty-three
mills. In 1879 the state tax had been reduced to one
and a half mills on the dollar, while the local taxes
were correspondingly reduced. There was no funded
debt, and the floating indebtedness was small, owing
to a clause in the constitution prohibiting the state,

to Colorado, and settling at Pueblo. He was appointed, in 1868, U. S. atty
for the district of Colorado, holding the office but little more than a year,
when he resigned. He was an active member of the constitutional convention in 1875, being chairman of several of the most important committees.
In person he was six feet in height, with bright blue eyes, and possessed of
genial manners. 'Thatcher,' says Pitkin, 'made one of the ablest judges
ever on the bench. He declined reëlection. He died at San Francisco, while
on a visit there, at the age of 41, of Bright's disease.' *Political Views*, MS., 8;
Hallett's Courts, Law, and Litigation, MS.

counties, or cities from loaning their credit. These were magnificent measures for a young commonwealth to adopt.

The public lands received through the enabling act were the 500,000 acres granted to all the new states by the law of 1841 ; 50 sections for the erection of public buildings ; 50 sections for a penitentiary ; 72 sections for a state university ; six sections adjacent to twelve salt springs ; the sixteenth and thirty-sixth sections for common school purposes, besides the usual five per centum of the ʼproceeds of the sale of agricultural public lands to be applied to internal improvements. I have shown how this dower of some of the north-western states was wasted. Governor Routt had witnessed the same fraudulent use of the school and other lands in Illinois, Iowa, and Nebraska. The constitution of Colorado made the governor and secretary a board to select the state lands. To their everlasting honor, instead of squandering these lands upon party favorites, they labored to make them produce the highest amount for the purposes for which they were intended. The plan adopted was not to offer the school lands for sale, the chief part being so situated as not to be irrigable, and therefore not worth more than the minimum price of $2.50 an acre, but to lease them for an amount equal to the interest on their present value, and hold them for pasturage, or for any purposes. It was found they brought between $40,000 and $50,000 annual rental. Seventy-eight miles of land along the Republican river was also entered for the state. The legislature then passed a bill authorizing the sale of alternate sections of state land, the purchasers contracting to construct ditches of sufficient capacity to water their land and the state land through which the ditch was carried. By this means also the value of the unsold land was raised in some situations to $30 per acre, and the school lands of Colorado acquired a value of many millions more than they were worth when the state

received them. Wisely the public institutions of the
state, instead of being supported by legislative appropriations offering temptations to jobbing members,
are sustained by a direct tax for the purpose designed.
The result of this care for the public funds is the rapid
accomplishment of those beneficent objects for which
the gifts of the general government were intended or
for which the state is taxed.

The successor of Routt in the executive office was
Frederick W. Pitkin, during whose administration the
Ute war took place, of which I shall speak in
another place. A serious riot in Leadville and another in Denver were the chief events in 1879–80.
In the former instance martial law was proclaimed
in Leadville to bring to reason the miners who had
organized a strike, and suspended every branch of
business. It was expected that the governor's action
would destroy all chance of his reëlection; but such
proved not to be the case. During his first term he
had become a sort of Admirable Crichton to the people,
and if he lost any of his former influence in his second
term, it was through being a candidate for the United
States senatorship and having active rivals in the
race. The lieutenant-governor during his administration was Horace A. W. Tabor,[52] and the secretary
of state N. H. Meldrum.[53] Belford was elected rep-

[52] Tabor was elected lieut-gov. in 1878, and became such for Pitkin's second
term by succession, the vice-governor elect, George B. Robinson, having been
assassinated, and the president of the senate by law succeeding him.

[53] Frederick W. Pitkin was born in Manchester, Conn., in 1837 of an hon-
orable line of ancestry, the Pitkins and Griswolds of Conn., and educated at
the Wesleyan university of Middleton, from which he graduated in 1858. He
studied law at the Albany law school, and after graduating removed to Milwaukee, Wis., in 1860, where he enjoyed a lucrative practice until failing
health compelled him to seek a change of climate. He visited Europe in 1873,
and subsequently Florido without benefit, and in 1874 came to Colorado,
where he has obtained a degree of health which has enabled him to reëngage
in business pursuits. George B. Robinson was assassinated Nov. 27, 1880, a
few weeks after his election, under the following circumstances: Some miners
had taken offence at certain tyrannies practised by the manager of the Robinson consolidated mine in Summit co., aud Robinson had been appealed to
for the removal of the obnoxious manager without effect, he having no power
to remove without the consent of the other trustees. On the evening of the
27th Robinson, with two other men, visited the mine, and was challenged by
the guard, who hearing no answer, discharged his gun. An autopsy, how-

resentative to congress in 1878, by a majority of more than 2,000 over the democratic candidate, Patterson, and twice reëlected, his majority at his last election being 2,737 over the democratic candidate, Wallace. In 1884 George G. Symes was elected representative in congress.

The governor who succeeded Pitkin was James B. Grant, a man of large means, fine ability,[54] educated, methodical, even-tempered, and strong enough to act upon his own convictions. He was the first democrat honored with an election to the executive office.[55] The lieutenant-governor elected with him was William H. Meyers. Grant was succeeded by Benjamin H. Eaton, elected in 1884,[56] a man of strong and quiet character, and acquainted with the history and the requirments of the country. The lieutenant-governor elected with Eaton was P. W. Breene. Na-

ever, revealed a number of wounds from bullets and shots fired from a position in the rear, while the guard swore that he fired upward in such a manner as not to have hit the murdered man. Other testimony confirmed the suspicion of foul play. He came to Colorado in 1877 from Mich., and engaged in wholesale and retail grocery business. He was a man of education and culture, and was worth $2,000,000. *Denver Tribune*, Nov. 28, 1880.

[54] James B. Grant was born in Ala, in 1848. On the breaking out of the civil war, although but 13 years of age, he joined the confederate army, spending several months in the field, after which he went to reside with his uncle, Judge Grant, of Davenport, Iowa, who sent him to the agricultural college of that state, where he spent 6 years, subsequently taking a course at the university of Cornell, and finishing his education by travel and study in a German university.

[55] *Routt's Territory and State*, MS., 6. Grant's opponent, E. L. Campbell, was defeated by political legerdemain, though it was said it was on account of unfitness. He was fairly nominated in the republican convention. Among the candidates for nomination was H. R. Wolcott, asst manager of the Argo Smelting works, of which N. P. Hill was manager. Chaffee was chairman of the republican state committee, and Hill, who was in the U. S. senate, and who had been opposed by Chaffee, wished to defeat his measures and lessen his power, in order to get an enemy out of the way before the next senatorial contest. Hill and Wolcott, with their friends, bolted from the republican party with the object of weakening Chaffee, rather than with regard to the fitness of the candidate for governor. It was fortunate that their antagonism elected so good a man, and unfortunate that the reason they gave for it was prejudicial to the defeated candidate.

[56] Benjamin Harrison Eaton was born in Ohio in 1834, and brought up on a farm. Being ambitious he studied and taught school until the Pike's peak fever carried him to Colorado. He began mining in California gulch, but soon turned his attention to farming, being the first settler near the town of Greeley. He later owned and cultivated 7,000 acres of land, all of which he irrigated. Irrigation in Colorado owes much to him. He was also interested in cattle raising and mining.

thaniel P. Hill was chosen in 1879 to succeed Chaffee in the United States senate.[51] His services to the state during six years in the senate were not unimportant. He secured the removal of the White river and Uncompahgre Utes to Utah, and the opening of the reservation to settlement, which added 12,000,000 acres of land to the wealth of the state. He obtained a land office at Gunnison for the convenience of settlers on these lands; an appropriation of $20,000 to bore artesian wells in the arid regions of the state; the exchange of such sixteenth and thirty-sixth sections of school land as fell in the mineral regions for agricultural land; $300,000 to erect a United States court-house in Denver; improvements in the mining law, enabling miners to make adverse claims before the clerk of the district where they happened to be, instead of in the district where the claim was located, as before, and also enabling them to take the oath of citizenship without the trouble and expense of a journey to some distant point; made Denver a port of delivery, enabling merchants to import direct from foreign countries through the seaports; secured the Hot Spring reservation to settlers; procured authority for the postmaster-general to extend mail facilities in rapidly increasing settlements without waiting for congressional action; and secured on increased rate of fees in certain cases where the old law worked a hardship to witnesses in the United States courts. Nor was his labor given altogether to local affairs, but he combatted the great land stealing corporations, which upon one pretense and another were wheedling congress out of the public domain; he labored for the

[51] *Colo Jour. House*, 1879, 111–12. Hill was born in Orange co., N. Y., in 1832, and brought up on a farm, of which he was left in charge at the age of 16 years. He was the son of an old-time democrat, who had represented his county in the general assembly, and held the office of county judge, and notwithstanding unusual responsibilities for his years, found time to fit himself for college which he entered at the age of 21, at Brown university, Providence, R. I. In 1856 he was made tutor in the chemical department, and in 1860 professor of chemistry, a calling which led directly to his usefulness in and his connection with Colorado, as has already been indicated in the history of mining.

postal telegraph bill, for a tariff on wool, and for a better national financial policy. But nothing more commended him to the people of Colorado than his attitude on the silver question, as the advocate of a bi-metallic currency. Upon this subject he became the peer of senators Stewart and Jones of Nevada, and many republicans desired his reëlection in 1884[58] on this ground. But having in 1882 used some political weapons against a rival, these were turned upon himself at last, cutting him off from a career for which he was well qualified. Henry M. Teller, senator from 1877 to 1883, was appointed to the cabinet when Arthur came to the presidency. To fill the vacancy caused by the resignation of Teller, Governor Pitkin appointed George M. Chilcott, who had been prominently before the legislature in 1879 as candidate with Hill for the senatorship. In the contest for the appointment in 1883 the principal candidates were Routt, Tabor, and Bowen, three millionaires, and each fought hard for the position, but Pitkin chose Chilcott. Pitkin himself was an aspirant, and the political gossips said that a strong pressure was brought to bear upon the governor by the others, they promising that if his choice should fall upon one of them for the appointment they would use their influence with the legislature when it met to have him elected to the senate. Pitkin, however, resisted the combination, which punished him by defeating him when he became openly a candidate. Tabor was elected for the thirty days remaining of the Teller-Chilcott term, and

[58] *Denver Tribune*, Oct. 26, 1884; *Senate Miscel.*, 47th cong. 2d sess., i. no. 8, p. 10. A silver congress was held at Denver in January 1885, to which Belford and Symes were delegates from Colorado. The points laid down in the resolutions were 1st the doctrine of bi-metalism, as embodied in the U. S. laws previous to 1873; 2d that the interests of trade demanded free coinage at the existing standard; 3d a demand that congress should withdraw from circulation $1 and $2 bills; 4th censure of the secretaries of the treasury for unlawful evasions of the provisions of the Bland bill; 5th a demand for amendments to the National bank act, compelling them to keep 15 per cent of their legal reserve in silver; 6th that congress should restore silver to its ancient and rightful equality with gold in respect to coinage, and asking protection for the silver industry.

Thomas M. Bowen of Del Norte for the term from 1883 to 1889.[59] The legislature in 1885 elected Teller to succeed Hill, who had now a strong combination against him. A large amount of money was used in the struggle for place, and the people of Colorado begun to question whether it was well that the capitalists of the state should decide political preferment. The election of 1884, which gave the first democratic president in twenty-four years was strongly republican, the plurality for Blaine being nearly 9,000. The presidential electors chosen were F. C. Goudy of Gunnison, F. F. Obiston of Idaho Springs, and B. F. Crowell of Colorado Springs. Goudy was chosen as the messenger to carry the certificate to Washington. Some amendments were made to the constitution of the state at this election by a majority of nearly 11,000.

Of the justices of the supreme court elected in 1876, only Elbert in 1886 was on the bench. Wells, who drew the nine years' term, resigned after serving one year, and Wilbur F. Stone was elected to fill the vacancy. Elbert, whose term expired in 1882, was elected in 1885 to succeed Stone. He will go out of office in 1897. Thatcher, whose term expired in 1879, was succeeded by William E. Beck. The judge who took the bench at the expiration of Elbert's first term was Joseph C. Helm, who will go out of office in 1891. The supreme judges are not nominated by political parties, but by the bar association, and the character of the Colorado courts has seldom been as-

---

[59] Thomas M. Bowen, born in Iowa in 1835, elected to the lower house of the legislature at the age of 21 years. He served in the union army from 1861 to 1865, first as captain of Neb. volunteers, 1st regiment, afterward as colonel of the 13th Kansas infantry, and lastly as brevet brigadier-general in the army of the frontier, and later in the 7th army corps. After the war he was justice of the supreme court of Arkansas for four years, and accepted the executive appointment for Idaho in 1871, but resigned and returned to Arkansas, where he was defeated for the U. S. senate by S. W. Dorsey. He came to Colorado in 1875, resumed the practise of law, and was elected judge of the 4th judicial district on the admission of the state, and held the office for 4 years. He engaged in large mining enterprises and became wealthy. In 1882 he was elected to the state legislature which made him senator.

sailed. The most serious accusation ever made was against the United States judges in the case of a strike among the employés of the Denver and Rio Grande railroad, in May 1885, under the direction of the knights of labor, some members of which order had been dismissed from the company's service. Arms were carried by a part of the strikers, when persuading their associates to desist from labor, and although no violence was offered, the fact of arms having been shown was considered as sufficient evidence of the intent. The men were arrested, tried for contempt, and imprisoned from three to six months. The charges brought by the knights of labor against the judges were that the receiver of the road was appointed by one of them; that the men arrested were not allowed to call witnesses, unless they paid the expenses, which would be over $160 each, or swore that they were paupers, neither of which could they do. That they had not been tried by a jury; but that in fact the judge had made the complaint, tried, and sentenced them without a hearing, being at the same time concerned in the road, thereby construing the law in the interest of a rich corporation against the constitutional rights of other men. The order made threats of impeachment when congress should meet.

Whether or not there was found sufficient proof to sustain the complaint of the knights of labor in this case, it is evident that the danger which threatens society is the overweening influence of wealth. The temptation to men who have acquired millions, rightfully or wrongfully, in a few years is to consider themselves better than their neighbors, and less regardful of the rights of men. At bribery or any moral or political corruption they do not hesitate. They would constitute themselves a privileged class, and return toward feudalism by surrounding themselves with the largest number of dependents in the form of ill-paid laborers, that being the only form of serfdom at present known under our government. How long they can maintain that position in political economy and ethics will depend upon the nerve of the working classes to resist the tendency; and nowhere is the struggle more apparent than in mining states, not even in manufacturing states, where tender childhood is pressed into the service of the capitalist, and made to earn its daily bread at the sacrifice of its future manhood and womanhood.

It is difficult to determine which class exercises the more baneful influence upon public morals, the low ignorant foreigner, or the unprincipled monied monopolist. But aside from these, Colorado has a larger proportion of men of culture among its men of business and affairs than any of the intra-montane commonwealths; and, in proportion to its population, more college bred men than most of the older states. In its people, its climate, its impressive scenery, natural wealth, and liberal institutions it is altogether a noble state, needing no encomiums from its historian other than the simple narrative of the achievements of its founders.

CHAPTER VII.

INDIAN WARS.

1860–1880.

WHEN the territory of Colorado was organized, its governor and Indian superintendent found there several powerful tribes, with which the government had already had dealings. As early as September 17, 1851, a treaty was made at Fort Laramie with the Ogalalah and Brulé Sioux, and the Arapahoes and Cheyennes, by which the country claimed by them should be included within the following limits; commencing at Red Buttes, on the south side of the north fork of the Platte river, at the crossing of the immigrant road, following this stream to its source in the Rocky mountains, thence along their summits to the head waters of the Arkansas river, down the Arkansas to the crossing of the Santa Fé trail, thence northwesterly to the forks of the Platte, and up the north branch to the place of beginning. It was estimated that the area contained in the Upper Platte agency, as it was called, was 122,500 square miles, while the population did not exceed 5,500, not more than 2,000 of these being warriors. The treaty required them to keep in their own country, to avoid

wars with the neighboring tribes, to refrain from robbing travellers, and for this righteousness they were
to receive annuities, to be distributed at Fort Laramie.
Of the region here designated, the Sioux and one
band of Cheyennes ranged the portion lying north of
the present state of Colorado, while the Cheyennes
and Arapahoes occupied the country next the
Arkansas.

That part of the country south of the Arkansas was
traversed by the Kiowas, Apaches, and Comanches,
with whom a treaty, similar to the Laramie treaty,
had been made in 1853, but with whom the government had now and then occasion to display armed
force, in order to punish or prevent depredations upon
persons and property upon the Santa Fé trail, which
was traversed by the caravans of the Santa Fé
traders, the supply trains en route to the military
posts in New Mexico, the United States mail for
California, and frequent companies of immigrants and
travellers. These Indians also were looked after by
the incumbent of the Platte agency.

That portion of Colorado lying west of the Rocky
mountains was inhabited by the Utes, branches of
which great nation extended to the Sierra Nevada, as
I have shown. In Colorado there were three divisions; two in the southern portion yearly presented
with goods at the New Mexico agencies, but the more
northern tribes were still wild and shy, although
numerous and warlike. The whole number was estimated at 10,000.

It would have required greater diplomacy than the
average superintendent of Indian affairs can command
to adjust the yoke of civilization to the necks of
15,000 free-born American savages without galling.
The task was made more difficult by the animosity
between the Utes of the mountains and the Arapahoes
and Cheyennes of the plains; but in a double degree
by the feeling already engendered by the action of
the military in punishing the plains people for attacks

on travellers.[1] And, while the retaliations of the savages are written in letters of blood, the outrages of the white men upon the Indians must go forever unrecorded. In June 1860 congress appropriated $35,000 for the purpose of making a new treaty with the Cheyennes and Arapahoes, and also with the Kiowas and Comanches, who for three years previous had occupied the country on the south side of the Arkansas, which was crossed by the Santa Fé trail, to the peril of travellers. Commissioner A. B. Greenwood arrived

[1] The history of aboriginal brigandage on the plains has never been written, and only now and then related, in part as a frontier experience, to enliven some traveller's tale. From the authorities in my possession I learn that following the Mexican war certain tribes made an alliance to war on the traffic of the Santa Fé trail. They succeeded in cutting off the connections between the troops in New Mexico and their base of supplies in the United States. In 1847 the southern Utes were pursued into Fremont county by Mexican troops, and, making a stand in the defile of the Arkansas above Cañon City, sustained a heavy loss; hence the name of the gorge, Ute cañon. Londoner relates that 8 out of a party of 9 trappers were murdered by the Utes in California gulch in 1854. *Colorado Mining Camps*, MS., 8. On Christmas day of that year all the inhabitants at the Pueblo, on the Arkansas river, were massacred in a drunken revel by a wandering band of Utes, who had been invited to partake of the hospitalities of the season. *Thomb's Mex. Colo*, MS., 1–3. The authorities differ as to whether there were 17 or 29 of the victims, all of whom were Mexicans. In 1855 I find the troops from Fort Massachusetts, now Fort Garland, pursuing and punishing the Utes of southern Colorado, for their raids into New Mexico. When en route to the Platte agency point of distribution, with annuity goods in 1854, the agent met at the crossing of the Arkansas from 1,200 to 1,590 lodges of Kiowas, Comanches, Osages, Arapahoes, and Cheyennes, being a war party en route to wipe out, as they expressed it, all frontier Indians on the plains. When near the Kansas River they were defeated by 100 Sacs and Foxes, in a three hours' battle. The Mexicans of New Mexico were their chief source of supply, and as long as these could be made to furnish horses, mules, and captives to the United States Indians, with which they carried on a profitable trade among themselves, they were comparatively well-behaved towards travellers on the great western highways; but when New Mexico became a part of the United States, and they were forbidden to rob and kill its people, they quarrelled with those tribes who made and observed treaties, and began robbing and killing anywhere to make up the loss.

In 1855 Agent Thomas S. Twiss, on arriving on the ground, found that the Arapahoes had been charged with killing cattle and sheep to the amount of $15,000, which would stop their annuity for some years. They admitted the thefts, but excused them on the plea of sickness in their band, and famine consequent on not being able to go after buffalo, and submitted cheerfully to the loss of their annuities. A war was going on between the United States troops, under Harney, and the Sioux, which had put an end to Indian trade in buffalo skins, etc,. so that the prospect looked dark for the coming winter. In March 1856, Harney entered into a peace treaty with all the Sioux of the plains, which was intended to restore the former equilibrium in affairs; or, rather, he proposed to improve the condition of the Sioux and other tribes by teaching them agriculture. But before the plan could be carried out a

at Fort Wise—formerly Bent's fort—about the middle of September, but finding only the Arapahoes on
the ground, appointed A. G. Boone special agent to
carry out the intentions of the government, and returned to Washington. In February 1861 Boone
concluded a treaty with the Cheyennes and Arapahoes, by which one third of the area claimed by them
between the South fork of the Platte and Arkansas
rivers was ceded to the United States. Their reser-

collision occurred at Platte bridge, beyond Laramie, where a company of
troops were stationed to protect immigrants to California and Oregon. The
commandant accused the Cheyennes of having stolen some horses which they
had in their possession, and imprisoned them. The savages attempting
escape were fired at and one killed. Later the Cheyennes were attacked by
a body of United States troops, and six killed. They then sued for peace,
which was granted. Nevertheless, some of them continuing hostile, Colonel
E. V. Sumner, with United States troops, in July 1857, destroyed their principal village. Meanwhile the agent coming to Bent's fort with annuity
goods, and desiring to leave them there, Bent refused, but finally rented the
place to the government, fearing to remain.

On the 18th of August Sumner arrived at the fort, when he ordered the
goods distributed to the Arapahoes. In 1859 W. W. Bent was appointed
agent for the upper Arkansas. His extensive acquaintance with the Indian
tribes gave him an influence over them which a stranger could not have had.
In Bent's report for this year he remarks that the Kiowas and Comanches,
being driven out of Texas, had for 2 years appeared in full numbers and for
long periods upon the Arkansas, and were then permanently occupying the
country between the Canadian and Arkansas rivers, with 2,500 warriors; and
that so soon as the troops were withdrawn from Fort Riley, a post erected in
the region of the Arkansas river in 1852, they had assumed a threatening
attitude, for which reason he considered it essential to have two permanent
posts for troops, one at the mouth of Pawnee fork, and one at Big Timbers,
both on the Arkansas, for the protection of travellers upon that route, that
since the gold discovery had become numerous. And this he urged for the
sake of the Indians themselves, who were being gradually advanced upon from
all sides, and who should be brought into subjection and treated with, to the
end that they might be assigned reservations and assisted in learning to support themselves by agriculture and stock-raising. Fort Larned was thereupon established at the mouth of Pawnee fork, and Bent's fort purchased
and converted into an army post, under the name of Fort Wise. This year
the Utes killed J. L. Shank and J. L. Kennedy in the South park, and a
party of 7 unknown men, with 12 horses, in a gulch, to which from this circumstance was given the name of Dead Men's gulch. Byers, in *Dead Men's
Gulch*, MS., 1.

In June 1860 a large number of Arapahoes and Apaches, with a few Sioux,
met at Denver, and organized an expedition against the Utes. They entered
the Ute country midway between Platte cañon and the present town of
Morrison, the Ute village being near where the Platte leaves the South park.
The Arapahoes were repulsed, and returned to Denver with 5 dead and 32
wounded. Another expedition, organized soon after, fled back in confusion,
alarming the white population by representing that the Utes were assembled
in great numbers, prepared to attack them, which, as they were encamped
in the heart of Denver, was certainly not to be desired, but the alarm proved
groundless. Such was the attitude of Indian affairs in Colorado at the period
of its settlement.

vation was bounded westward by a line drawn north and south from the mouth of the Huerfano, in what is now Pueblo county ; but they did not keep upon it. Meanwhile some of the Arapahoes and Cheyennes who had not been present at the treaty of February, made that an excuse for nullifying it; and the Kiowas and Comanches, who had accepted annuities, had committed depredations in 1862 which called for the interference of troops. Further than this, civil war now came on, and the savages were not willing that the civilized men should have all the battling and butchering to themselves.[2]

The only force in the territory during the summer of this year was the 2d Colorado regiment, commanded by Colonel J. H. Leavenworth. The Indians kept the recruits in practice. In August the headquarters of the regiment was removed from Denver to Fort Lyon, as Fort Wise was now called, where in January 1863 they were joined by the 1st Colorado cavalry, under Chivington. In April the 2d regiment was ordered to Fort Leavenworth, and in June to Fort Larned, to protect the Santa Fé road and watch the Texans, with whom they fought the battle of Cabin creek on the 2d of July, inflicting a loss of forty killed and wounded, with but one man killed and twenty wounded on the side of the Coloradans. These troops, with a few hundred others, on the 16th fought another battle in Kansas, in which the confederates lost 400 killed, wounded, and missing, the loss on their side being 14 killed and 30 wounded. Soon after the 2d regiment was ordered away from Colorado, Governor Evans was directed to raise a third, which was marched to the States as soon as organized. The 2d and 3d regiments were consolidated in October 1863, and formed the 2d Colorado cavalry, which was kept continually moving until the spring of 1865.[3]

[2] See *Fowler's Woman's Experience in Colorado*, MS.; *Gilpin's Pioneers of 1842*, MS.; *Howbert's Indian Troubles*, MS.; *Rocky Mountain News*, passim.

[3] *Chivington's First Colorado Regiment*, MS., 13; *Prescott's Through Cañon De Shea*, MS., 4; *Byers' Hist. Colo*, MS., 85; *Evans, Interview*, MS., passim.

The first regiment remaining in Colorado was the
only armed force in the country north of Fort Garland; and, notwithstanding treaties and negotiations
conducted with great care and at a great expense,
there was a general insolence among the treaty Indians which boded no good. In 1864 affairs culminated.
A combination was effected between the several bands
of Sioux and all the plains Indians of Colorado and
south of the Arkansas in Kansas, to attempt the
expulsion or extermination of the white population.
Their first overt act in Colorado was to replenish
their commissary department by taking 175 cattle
frm the herd of Irwin and Jackman, government contractors, who were encamped with their stock in Bijou
basin, forty miles south-east of Denver, in April. A
detachment of the 1st cavalry, under Lieut Ayre,
was sent after them, which recovered only twenty
head, having come up with them when night was
closing in and snow falling, the Indians running off
the stock while the officer in command parleyed with
the chiefs. A soldier who became separated from
the command was wounded, but no fighting occurred.
Being without subsistence, the detachment returned
to Denver. Soon afterward a second expedition of
100 cavalrymen and two howitzers, under Ayre, was
ordered to go as far as Fort Larned, by the head of
the Republican and Smoky Hill forks. When near
the fort they encountered the Cheyennes, who
charged the troops 400 strong. So desperate was
the onslaught that they rushed up to the mouth of
the cannon, falling within reach of the gunners.
Twenty-five or thirty were killed, among them a chief
who had signed the treaty.

In the same month another party of Cheyennes
drove off a herd of horses from Kiowa creek, and
Lieut Clark Dunn from camp Sanborn, near Frémont orchard, pursued them with twenty men. He
found the Indians, about fifty strong, who attacked
when the demand for the return of the horses was

made, and killed and wounded four of the soldiers. The troops returned the fire, but being armed only with revolvers and sabres, inflicted but little loss, and after a chase of several miles returned for fresh horses and guns, the Indians in the meantime escaping. A third depredation similar to the others being committed near the junction of South Platte, a detachment under Major Downing, guided by an Indian trader named Ashcraft, surprised the Indian camp at Cedar cañon, where they had fortified, and killed twenty-five, destroying their village and capturing one hundred horses, one soldier being killed in the fight.

In June all the troops were ordered to the Arkansas, east of Fort Lyon, except one squadron, and Governor Evans applied for permission to call the militia of Colorado into the service of the United States, as the territorial law was defective, and the means of arming and equipping them was wanting, at the same time asking leave to raise a regiment of United States volunteers for one hundred days. This last request was finally granted, but not before the occasion for their services had been greatly augmented by repeated and horrible outrages. About the middle of June, when the last company of the 1st cavalry was encamped on Cherry creek, fifteen miles from Denver, under orders to join the regiment on the Arkansas, messengers arrived in Denver from the settlements on Box Elder creek, from two to twenty miles distant, with information of a general stampede of the stock in that region, and the murder of the Hungate family, consisting of the husband, wife, and two children. This event, which brought the war to the doors of Denver, caused great excitement. The remains of the murdered settlers were brought into town, and exhibited to the angry population. Governor Evans applied to the adjutant of the district to have the troops on Cherry creek sent in pursuit of the savages; orders were despatched to camp Sanborn, eighty miles below, to send after them a detachment, and

General Curtis, commanding the department, was telegraphed to allow the cavalry then en route for Fort Lyon to return, which request was granted, but in the interval of delay the Indians made good their escape. The militia were ordered to organize as home guards. The friendly Indians were placed at camp Collins and Fort Lyon.

In July the agent for the upper Arkansas made a visit to Pawnee fork to meet a large concourse of Cheyennes, Arapahoes, Comanches, Apaches, and Kiowas, with whom he held a council. They all expressed the greatest regard for the white people, and disavowed all knowledge of hostile acts. A short time after this friendly council, according to the assertion of the agent, the Kiowas visited Fort Larned, and, while the war-chief was engaged in conversation with the officer in command, his braves stampeded all the horses, mules, and cattle belonging to the post. A few days afterward the Arapahoes made a raid on the settlers along the river, caused, as the agent asserted, by the commanding officer at Larned firing upon them as they were coming, under a flag of truce, to offer their services to recover the stolen stock. The situation was becoming critical. It was estimated that there was not more than six weeks' supply of food in the territory. Mail communication with the east was cut off; mail-bags containing letters, money drafts, land patents, newspapers, and other miscellaneous matter were cut open and their contents scattered over the prairie. But one station was left standing on the overland mail-route for a distance of 120 miles. The farms were all deserted between Fort Kearny and Julesburg, and for 400 miles the movable property of the company was withdrawn as much as possible, leaving a large amount of grain and provisions, which fell into the hands of the Indians. Trains of merchandise, all that were upon the way for hundreds of miles, were seized, their conductors killed, and the property appropriated.

There was this year a large immigration to the Pacific states, numbering, according to a memorandum kept at Fort Laramie, 19,000 persons who passed that post. From this account it would make probably a total of double that number. Among these, how many fell by the hands of savages will never be known. The Coloradans thought they could count 200 victims for the season, over fifty of whom were their own people. On the 19th of August two Cheyennes gave notice to Elbridge Gerry, Indian trader, living at his station, 67 mile below Denver, in the Platte valley, to remove his stock, as on the 21st they would make a raid along the river, and take whatever property came in their way. They would divide into parties of twenty or more, and strike simultaneously at Fort Lupton, Latham, Junction, and the head of Cherry creek, and also at Pueblo. Their rendezvous was appointed for Point of Rocks, on Beaver creek, 125 miles from Denver. Gerry hastened to Denver, arriving at midnight on the 20th, when orders were immediately issued, placing all the militia and recruits of the one-hundred-days' men, under the control of the district commander, Colonel Chivington. Messages were despatched to the threatened localities, and the force at command divided among them. At the appointed time the Indians stealthily approached the points indicated, but finding them guarded, retired.

For thirty days there had been no mails from the east, letters having to be sent round by sea to San Francisco, and being from four to six weeks on the way. No stages or trains moved in Colorado except under escort. Early in September, the hundred-days' regiment was completed, and dispatched by Colonel Chivington to points on the overland route to open communication; while a portion of the home-guards under H. M. Teller, major-general of the militia, patroled the road between Denver and Julesburg, the 1st cavalry being employed as heretofore, chiefly on the Arkansas. These movements produced two results, the opening of communication with the Missouri, late in October, and the surrender of a small portion of the Cheyennes and Arapahoes, who had hitherto refused to make a permanent treaty with the superintendent of Indian affairs. When the outbreak first occurred, the governor issued a proclamation to the friendly Indians to repair to points which he named, to be taken care of by the agents; the Arapahoes and Cheyennes of the Arkansas to Fort Lyon; the Kiowas and Comanches to Fort Laramie; the Sioux to Fort Laramie; and the Cheyennes and Arapahoes of the upper Platte to Camp Collins. In response to this invitation 175 Arapahoes, under a chief called Friday, took up their residence at Fort Collins, and another band of the same tribe, under chief Left Hand, repaired to Fort Lyons but did not long remain. The agent distrusted them, and they distrusted the agent. It has been asserted, and as strenuously denied, that although apparently friendly, some of them acting as spies to give information of the movements of the hostile Indians, that they were go-betweens for their own people as well.

About the time the hundred days' men took the field, the Cheyennes, who had their principal village on the head waters of Smoky Hill fork, 140 miles north-east from Fort Lyon, sent three messengers to that post to inform Major E. W. Wynkoop of the 1st cavalry that Bent, their former agent, desired them to make peace, and that they were prepared to do so, provided peace should also be concluded with the other plains tribes. They also informed him that they had a number of white captives. Wynkoop, who had just been reënforced by a detachment of infantry from the department of New Mexico, sent by General Carleton in command, deemed it his duty to attempt the release of the prisoners, who were women and children. He left Fort Lyon in charge of the infantry, and marched to the Cheyenne village with 130 mounted men and one battery, finding himself confronted there by from 600 to 800 warriors drawn up in battle array. Making the best display possible of his resources for defence in case of an attack, and putting on a bold front, he obtained a council, at which he urged the Cheyennes to prove their desire for peace by relinquishing the captive women and children. Much hesitation being shown, he left the village and retired one day's march to a strong position, taking with him the three messengers whom he held as hostages, giving the Cheyennes three days in which to determine upon a course of action. At the end of that time the prisoners were delivered up, and several of the chiefs consented to accompany the major to Denver to learn upon what terms peace could be concluded with the Indian department.

Here, however, they met with an unexpected rebuff. It appeared from their own report that the majority of their people were still at war, as well as the Kiowas, Comanches, Apaches, and fourteen different bands of the powerful Sioux nation, including those from Minnesota. A peace made with them would not be binding on the others, as the governor explained to them. He reminded them also of their refusal to meet him in council in the previous autumn, and of their neglect to avail themselves of the protection offered in his proclamation, since which time they had been concerned in the most atrocious crimes, besides destroying a large amount of property. The war was still going on ; and while they might surrender to the military authorities, which he advised them to do, he could not make a treaty with them until peace was restored, they being for the present accountable to the war department.

This opinion was not indorsed by the commissioner of Indian affairs, who could not help believing that very much of the difficulty on the plains might have been avoided if a spirit of conciliation had been exercised by the military and others. What the feeling of the military was at this time appears in a despatch of Major-general S. R. Curtis, commanding the department, to Colonel Chivington, in which he says: "I want no peace until the Indians have suffered more. . . . I fear the agent of the interior department will be ready to make presents too soon. It is better to chastise before giving anything but a little tobacco to talk over. No peace must be made without my directions." Following the advice of Governor Evans, about 400 of the Cheyennes and Arapahoes from the Cheyenne valley surrendered at Fort Lyon to Major Wynkoop, and were rationed at that post. Not long after Major Scott J. Anthony succeeded to the command, and after feeding the Indians for a short time, restored to them a portion of their arms, and ordered them to remove to the region of Sand creek, forty miles distant, where they could hunt, removed from any contact with white people passing along the road.

On the 27th of November Colonel Chivington, with a force of 900 men, attacked this camp, treating it as hostile, and killing 131 persons, men, women, and children, with a loss on his part of 50 killed and wounded. That the attack was premeditated, and intended as a part of the further suffering which General Curtis had said must be inflicted before peace could be made with the hostile Indians, those concerned in it have never denied. But about its moral and political aspect there has been much controversy. A commission was appointed in Washington to investigate the conduct of Chivington, and testimony was taken on both sides. It was called a massacre by the Indian department, and is so called by a large portion of the people of Colorado to this day. Another class would justify Chivington to the fullest extent, a resolution of thanks being passed in his favor by the Colorado legislature.[4]

⁴The facts seem to be that Curtis was urging Chivington to punish the Indians. Winter was coming on, before which it was desirable to strike a

In the spring of 1865 the plains Indians renewed hostilities with all the more fervor that now they had a real grievance, and many persons were killed upon the roads leading from the Missouri westward, and on the Platte; in consequence of which the head of the military department instructed General James H. Ford, commanding the district of the upper Arkansas, to proceed with all his forces against them, and to pay no attention to any peace propositions. But in

blow. It was sufficient excuse, whether true or false, the report that some of the hostile Indians visited the camp of the non-combatants, and shared with them the spoils taken from the white people. It made no difference that these Indians were professedly peaceable, and under the protection of the U. S. flag. Chivington organized an expedition of 650 of Col Shoup's 3d Colorado, or 100-days' men, 175 of the 1st Colorado, and a detachment of New Mexico infantry then at Fort Lyon. He moved secretly and rapidly to the fort, taking care that word should not be carried to the Indian camp. He surprised the camp at sunrise. The Indians, not knowing who they were or what the purpose of an armed force at this hour, sprang to arms, and fired the first shot. The butchery then began, and lasted until 2 o'clock, the Indians being driven up the creek several miles. They fought valiantly, and considering the odds in numbers, killed and wounded about as many as the troops—all of their killing being of fighting men, while the greater part of those killed by the troops were old men, women, and children.

George L. Shoup was colonel of the 3d cav. William L. Allen, farmer and stock-raiser, who came to Colorado in 1859, was one of the 100-days' men. David H. Nichols was captain of a company. He was a member of the legislature of 1864-5, and sheriff of Boulder co. previous to his election to the legislature. He was again sent to the legislature in 1873, and in 1878 was one of the penitentiary commissioners. O. H. P. Baxter of Pueblo was at Sand creek as captain of a company. He was also a member of the legislature the following winter, and a member of the council at the 2 following sessions. He came to Colorado in 1858, and was one of the first locators of the town of Pueblo. Martin Brumbly of Cañon City, who came to Colorado in 1859, was a private at Sand creek. Azor A. Smith, a graduate of Rush medical college, removed to Colorado in 1859, and was appointed surgeon of the 1st Colorado. He has since occupied various public positions, and was elected to the legislature in 1876. In 1878 he was appointed postmaster of Leadville. Irving Howbert, born in Ind. in 1846, and son of William Howbert, the pioneer preacher in southern Colorado, who died in 1871, was in the Sand creek affair. He has furnished me a manuscript on *Indian Troubles in Colorado*. I have drawn from his notes some valuable hints of the early settlement of El Paso and Park counties. *A Woman's Experience in Colorado*, MS., by Mrs W. R. Fowler, also contains incidents of the Indian war, of alarms that were well-founded, and others that were exaggerated by fear. Further authorities are *The Sand Creek Affair*, MS., by Byers; correspondence between Mr Byers and Mrs Jackson in *N. Y. Tribune* of Feb. 5 and 22, and Mar. 3, 1880; *Ind. Aff. Rept*, 1865, app., 515, 527; *Id.*, 1867, app.; Speech of Chivington, in *Hett's Tales of Colorado Pioneers*, 88-92; *McClure's Three Thousand Miles*, 358-95; *Elbert's Public Men and Measures*, MS., 6-7; *Howbert's Indian Troubles*, MS., 8; *Gilpin's Pioneer of 1842*, MS., 8; *Dixon's New America*, 49-51; *Townshend's Ten Thousand Miles*, 142; *Beckwith's Rept*, 44; *Cong. Globe*, 1864-5, 250-6; *Newlin's Proposed Indian Policy; Council Jour. Colo*, 1865, 2; *Gen. Laws Colo*, 1864, 259; and many brief allusions by various writers.

May a committee consisting of United States Senator
J. R. Doolittle, L. F. S. Foster, and L. W. Ross
were, at their own solicitation, appointed to negotiate
with the hostile tribes, and an order was issued to
suspend the campaign against them. The Indians,
however, could not so suddenly be brought to enter-
tain the idea of peace. In the mean time the command of the district of the upper Arkansas was given
to General Sanborn, who, with Leavenworth, agent
for the lower Arkansas, in the course of the summer,
obtained the consent of the Kiowas, Comanches,
Arapahoes, and Cheyennes to meet in council early
in October at Bluff creek, forty miles south of the
Little Arkansas, any commissioners the president
might appoint. At this council treaties were entered
into between these tribes and the United States.
The proposition of Sanborn, as chairman of the commission—Harney, Murphy, Carson,[5] Bent, Leavenworth, and Steele being the other members—was to
make reparation for the injury done the Indians at
Sand creek, by repudiating the action of the Colorado
cavalry, and restoring the property captured or its
equivalent, and giving to each of the chiefs to hold in
his own right 320 acres of land, and to each of the
widows and orphans, made such by that affair, 160
acres, besides allowing them all the money and
annuities forfeited by going to war. The amount
appropriated as indemnity for the Indian losses at
Sand creek was $39,050. A treaty was affected
with the southern bands of Cheyennes and Arapahoes,
and with the Kiowas and Comanches, by which they
consented to allow the president to select a reservation away from contact with white people, a conces-
sion which led to their removal to the Indian Territory, where they have since remained, the govern-

[5] Carson, who figured prominently on the Indian side in the investigation,
died at Boggsville, Colorado, in August 1868. In Nov. his remains, with
those of his wife, were removed to Taos, N. M., where they were honored
with a masonic funeral. *Bozeman Avant Courier*, March 24, 1876. He was a
colonel in the volunteer U. S. service in New Mexico during the civil war,
and was Indian agent before that in N. M.

ment paying them at the rate of $40 per capita, or $112,000 annually, for forty years. A treaty was also effected with the Apaches who were confederated with the Cheyennes and Arapahoes on the same terms.

With the close of the civil war the volunteer regiments were disbanded and the regular army sent to take their place. Notwithstanding the treaties, four infantry and two cavalry companies were stationed at Fort Lyon; two infantry and two cavalry companies at Fort Garland; one cavalry and two infantry companies at Fort Morgan, in Weld county; at other posts in the district of the upper Arkansas twenty-one companies of mixed infantry and cavalry; and in the district of New Mexico thirty-three companies; all these being in the territory formerly roamed over by the treaty Indians. Nor were they suffered to rust in garrison; for between the Sioux and the other plains tribes they were pretty constantly employed. Hostilities were renewed in 1866, and in the winter of that year, as related in my histories of Montana and Wyoming, occurred the defeat of Fettermann's command at Fort Philip Kearny, by the Sioux. In the spring of 1867 a systematic war was begun along the Platte, in which the Cheyennes and Arapahoes were implicated with the Sioux. About the first of September, 1868, Colorado was visited by a party of seventy-five Cheyennes and Arapahoes with passes from forts Larned and Wallace. They went through Colorado City and the Ute Pass, killing a party of Utes, and returning by an unfrequented trail, stampeded and captured a herd of 120 horses. This act being regarded as a declaration of war, the stockade erected in 1864 was hastily repaired, and arms collected for defence. Meanwhile a company of scouts pursued to recover, if possible, the property taken, but were surrounded by the Indians, and only escaped by the arrival of a party from Denver, at whose appearance the Indians fled, their swift horses distancing those of the volunteers. A few days afterwards a war party appeared in the valley of Monument creek, killing three persons, wounding two others, and driving off all the stock they could gather up. North of here they killed four other persons, and burned one residence. This was the last foray of the plains Indians in the Colorado territory. Two years longer war raged upon the plains. Every mile of the Union Pacific and Kansas Pacific railroads was disputed. But with their completion came peace; for against the despotism of steam and electricity there is no power in the Indian to defend himself.

The Utes, occupying the country west of the Rocky mountains, had taken no part in the hostilities thus far recorded, but rejoiced in whatever punishment was inflicted on their hereditary enemies, the Cheyennes and Arapahoes. Of this people there were seven bands loosely confederated, but having each a chief and council. The most powerful of these occupied the north-west portion of Colorado, and have been most commonly known as the White River Utes. Their chief was Nevava. Their territory bordered on that of the Arapahoes and Cheyennes, with whom, whenever they met, courtesies were exchanged in the form of scalps and horses to the victors. South of the White River Utes were the Uncompahgre Utes, whose chief was Ouray; and south of these were the southern Utes, whose chief was Ignacio. These three bands belonged in Colorado. In New Mexico were three bands, known as the Mowaches, Tabaquaches, and Wemiquaches. In Utah, west of the White River Utes, dwelt the Uintah Utes.

In 1861 the Colorado superintendent of Indian affairs sent Lafayette Head, an experienced agent, to reside at Conejos in charge of the Tabaquache Utes, and to distribute presents to other bands, in order to gain their confidence. In 1862 several chiefs, includ-

ing Ouray of the Uncompahgres, were induced to
visit Washington with Agent Head, where they witnessed the movements of troops, the action of artillery, and other impressive demonstrations. But in
1863 the Utes were somewhat troublesome, having
been engaged in several raids, which they said were
against the Sioux, but in which they carried off considerable property of the white people. To counteract the hostile tendency, agents were appointed to the
other bands of Utes, Simeon Whitely being appointed
to the northern agency established in Middle park.
A council was held with the Tabaquaches, who relinquished their claim to the lands the government desired to purchase; namely, the San Luis valley and
mountains, and that portion of the country west of
the Rocky mountains in which settlements had already
been made. From this time there were no serious
troubles between the Colorado Utes and the white
population, although depredations were occasionally
committed by the New Mexico bands in the southern
counties.[6]

A council was held with the Utes in Middle park
in 1866. There was the usual dissatisfaction because
a treaty had been concluded with one band and not
with the others. There was also a very just dissatis-

[6] In 1865 a council was held at Fort Garland to settle the troubles between
the Utes and the Mexican population, and a peace concluded by a mutual
indemnity. In 1867 a chief of one of the New Mexico bands, Kaneache, had
a quarrel with a United States officer, in which threatening language was
used on both sides. A collision was averted by the sagacity of L. B. Maxwell. But Kaneache's heart became bad toward the white race, and he
made a raid upon the cornfields of the Purgatoire valley, claiming the soil
and the crops, which so exasperated the Mexican planters that retaliatory
measures were resorted to. The troops from Fort Stephens, a camp at the
foot of the Spanish peaks, interfered, and met with a slight loss. Kaneache
now took the war-path in earnest, raiding up the Purgatoire, around the
Spanish peaks, over the Cucharas, and up the Huerfano. Couriers were sent
to invite the Tabaquaches and Ouray to join him. Instead of joining him,
however, Ouray placed all his people under the surveillance of Fort Garland,
commanded by Col Carson, and repaired to the Purgatoire to warn the settlers. The enemy was met by a small force of Tabaquaches, under Shawno,
one of their chiefs, whom Carson sent to bring in Kaneache, dead or alive.
The order was obeyed, Kaneache and another hostile leader being captured
and taken to Fort Union. Five white men were killed during the raid, and
much property taken or destroyed. But for the exertions of Ouray, many
more lives would have been lost,

faction on the part of the Tabaquaches on account of
the character of the annuity goods furnished them,
which were disgracefully worthless, rotten, and dis-
gusting, and might reasonably have been made the
ground of revocation of the treaty. In 1868 another
treaty was made with all the Colorado Utes, in which
some of the provisions of the former were confirmed,
but important modifications made. The bounds of
the reserved lands were the southern limit of Colorado on the south, the 107th meridian on the east, the
40th parallel on the north, and the territory of Utah
on the west. The government was pledged to expend
annually for the Utes a sum not to exceed $30,000 in
clothing, blankets, and other articles of utility ; and
$30,000 in provisions until such time as these Indians
should be found capable of self-support. Among
themselves there were certain causes of difference.
The United States had insisted that there should be
a head chief over all the confederate tribes, through
whom business could be transacted without the
tedious council in which they delighted to exhibit
their eloquence and their obstinacy. Nevava had
passed away, and his sons, of whom he had several,
each claimed the inheritance of the chieftainship of
the White River Utes. There were many in this
tribe who would gladly have accepted this distinction
—Antelope, Douglas, Johnson, Colorow, Jack,
Schwitz, and Bennett. But in their stead was
appoined Ouray, of the Uncompahgre band chief over
all, with a salary of $1,000 a year ; and the lesser
chiefs were forced to content themselves with such a
following as their individual qualities could command.
There was much jealousy. The White River Utes
who thought the head chief should have been chosen
from among themselves, began conspiring against
Ouray as early as 1875, and talked openly of killing
him. The neglect of the government in sometimes
failing to deliver the annuities was charged against
the head chief, who was said to be in collusion with

certain white men in depriving them of their goods, a suspicion to which the greater wealth, dignity, and prosperity of Ouray gave some coloring, for Ouray, like Lawyer of the Nez Percés, was far above his contemporaries in shrewdness and intelligence. But the attempts to unseat Ouray amounted to nothing.[7]

The effect of this dissatisfaction was to culminate in disasters more serious and important than the overthrow of the head chief. In 1876 the White River Utes began burning over the country north and east of their reservation, claimed by them, although properly belonging to the Arapahoe lands, which had been purchased. The following year a chief known as Jack made overtures to their traditional foes, the Cheyennes and Arapahoes, with whom he appointed a rendezvous in western Wyoming. Here he found congenial sympathizers, who filled his ears with stories of the excitement and glory of war. The southern Ute agency was at Los Pinos on the Uncompahgre river, a few miles from the present town of Ouray, where the head chief had his residence. The agency of the White River Utes had been removed to the southern bank of that stream. Early in 1879 the venerable N. C. Meeker, first president of the union colony, was appointed to the charge of the White River Utes. He undertook to carry out the designs of the department, by selecting agricultural lands and opening a farm at the new agency, by encouraging the Indians to build log houses, and by opening a school which was taught by his daughter. He found himself opposed from the outset by the Indians, some

[7] Ouray was brought up in part under the influences of the Mexicans, and was made much of afterward by Agent Head. Evans appointed him interpreter at the Conejos agency, paying him $500 a year. He assisted in distributing the sheep and cattle presented to the Utes after the treaty of 1863. Keeping his own, he bought others with his money, and in the course of time was able to employ Mexican herders. He erected a good dwelling, well furnished, near where the town of Ouray is located, where he lived in comfort until his death in 1880. *Evans' Interview*, MS., 13-15; *Dead Men's Gulch*, MS., 1-11; *Ingersoll's Knocking Around the Rockies*, 96-106; *Denver Tribune*, Aug. 28, 1880; *Colorado Mining Camps*, MS., 12-15; *Sturgis' Ute War*, 7-8; *Treaties with Indians*, MS., 11.

of whom pretended that when the sod was once broken, it was no more Ute soil, the real difficulty being that Johnson, a brother-in-law of Ouray, wanted the land selected by Meeker for pasturing his numerous ponies. Several councils were held, and when the excitement was abated, Meeker resumed farming operations, when Johnson assaulted him, forcing the agent out of his own house, and beating him.

Meeker then wrote to the department that if he was to carry out his instructions, he must have troops. Assistance was promised. Orders were issued by the commander of the department, that a troop of colored cavalry from Fort Garland, under Captain Payne, should scout through the parks on the border of the reservation to protect the settlers and prevent arson, and join a command of 160 cavalry and infantry from Fort Fred Steele, under Captain Thornburg, ordered to repair to the reservation. When he was at Bear river, Indian runners brought the news to the agency, and in much excitement required the agent to write to Thornburg not to advance, but to send five officers to compromise the difficulties. Meeker wrote as requested, sending a courier with the letter, which left the matter to Thornburg's judgment. The decision of that officer was to advance, and to reach the agency September 30th, but to quiet the Indians by promising to meet five of the Utes at Milk creek on the evening of the 29th.

On the morning of the 29th, a large number set off with the alleged object of having a hunt, taking their rifles and ammunition. The ordinary affairs were being transacted with less than customary friction, owing to the absence of so many turbulent spirits, when at about one o'clock the lightening fell out of a clear sky. A runner from Milk creek brought the news that a battle was going on between the troops and Indians at that place. This information was not imparted to Meeker, but half an hour after it was received twenty armed Utes of Douglas' band attacked the agency. Twelve men and boys were quickly slaughtered. The agency buildings were robbed and burned. The gray headed philanthropist was dragged about the agency grounds by a log chain about his neck, and with a barrel stave driven down his throat. The women were seized and carried to the tepees of Douglas, Johnson, and Persune, to be subjected to their lusts.

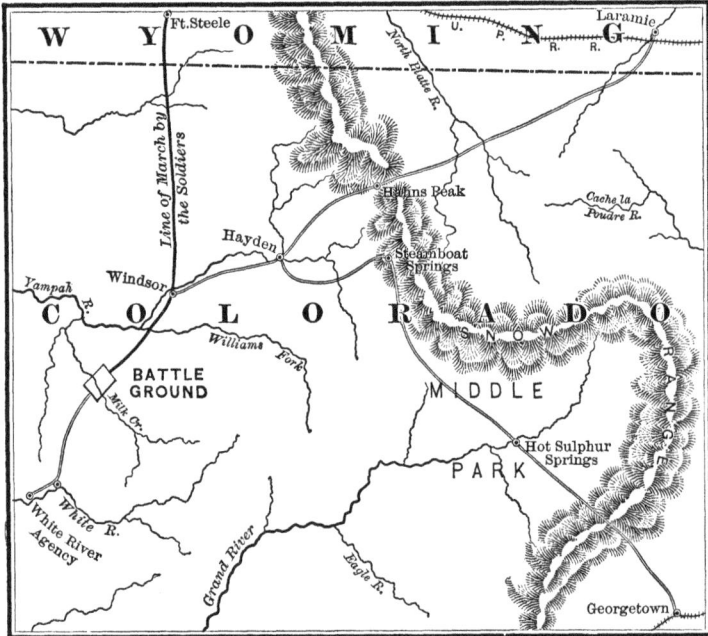

THORNBURG BATTLE GROUND.

At Milk creek were other deplorable scenes. The pretended hunting party had ambushed Thornburg at ten o'clock that morning, in a narrow pass at this place, and separated the troops from the supply train in the rear. Major Thornburg, in attempting to fall back, made a charge on the cordon of Indians, and was killed, with thirteen of his men. The command then devolved on Captain Payne of the 5th cavalry, who reached the train with forty-two wounded, including every officer but one.

Trenches were dug, and breastworks erected out of the wagons and their contents, to which were added the carcasses of horses and mules, and even the bodies of dead soldiers, piled up and covered with earth. In the centre of the entrenchments a pit was dug, to be used as a hospital, where the wounded were placed, the surgeon himself being one of them. The Indians attempted to force the troops out of their intrenchments by setting fire to the tall dry grass and brush in the defile, and nearly suffocating them ; but, although they had no water, they, put out the fire with blankets as it came near, and so conquered that peril. At sundown the Utes came up and were repulsed. That night a scout, named Rankin, stole ont of camp, and, finding a horse, mounted and rode to Rawlins, 160 miles, arriving on the morning of the 1st of October. It was not until the 9th of October that information was received, via the Uncompahgre agency, at Los Pinos, that the women and children were alive, in captivity. Troops were rapidly concentrated for the relief of Payne. Meanwhile, on the third night after the attack, Captain Dodge, with the colored troop before mentioned, succeeded in eluding the Utes, and joined Payne in the entrenchment; but to very little use, as all the horses had been killed but two, and as this troop only added forty more to the loss sustained by the government, their dead bodies being soon added to the fleshy and rotting rampart by which they were surrounded. As the Indians generally withdrew at night, some relief was obtained by dragging away and burying the decaying animals, and carrying water from a spring near at hand. In this manner were passed six days.

Relief came on the 5th of October, when Colonel Merritt arrived, after a forced march of 72 hours, with a force of 550 men. For the appearance of this particular officer the besieged had waited with a confidence which sustained them through one of the most trying ordeals ever experienced by troops. There was a skirmish next day, but the Indians soon retired, and the dead were buried as decently as the circumstances allowed. In the affair of the 29th, 35 Indians were killed. The loss to the white forces was 14 killed and 43 wounded. Thornburg's body was but little mutilated. The Utes had disposed the limbs decently, and placed a photograph of Colorow in one hand, to signify by whom he had come to his death. The officers engaged in this affair, besides Thornburg, were captains J. Scott Payne and Joseph Lawson of the 5th cavalry; Lieutenant J. V. S. Paddock of the 3d cavalry; lieutenants Wolf and Wooley of the 4th infantry, and Lieutenant S. A. Cherry of the 5th cavalry, the sole officer unhurt, and E. B. Grimes. Thornburg was a Tennessean. He enlisted as a private, September 1861, in the 6th Tennessee, serving until August 1863. He rose in five months to be sergeant-major, and in two months more to be lieutenant and adjutant. He subsequently entered West Point academy, graduating in 1867. He was commissioned second lieutenant of 2d artillery, and was stationed at San Francisco, Fortress Monroe, Alcatraz, and Sitka, and was professor of military science at San Diego, California, and subsequently at the East Tennessee university, going thence to Fort Foote, Maryland; and from there to San Antonio, Texas; then to Fort Brown, and to Omaha. He became major of the 4th infantry at Fort Fred. Steele. Merritt reached the agency on the 11th, finding twelve dead and mutilated bodies.[8]

[8] Others not here named were likewise killed. The twelve were N. C. Meeker, E. W, Eskridge, his clerk, a lawyer by profession, and had been a banker; W. H. Post, assistant agent and farmer; E. Price, blacksmith; Frank Dresser, Harry Dresser, Frederick Shepard, George Eaton, W. H. Thompson, E. L. Mansfield, Carl Goldstein, and Julius Moore. N. C. Meeker was born in Euclid, Ohio, in 1815. He was early known as a newspaper and magazine writer. He married the daughter of one Smith, a retired sea-captain, joining a society known as the Trumbull Phalanx, a branch of the

While the command remained at White river, Lieutenant Weir and a scout named Humme were killed
while hunting in the vicinity of the agency, but no
demonstration was made against the Indians.

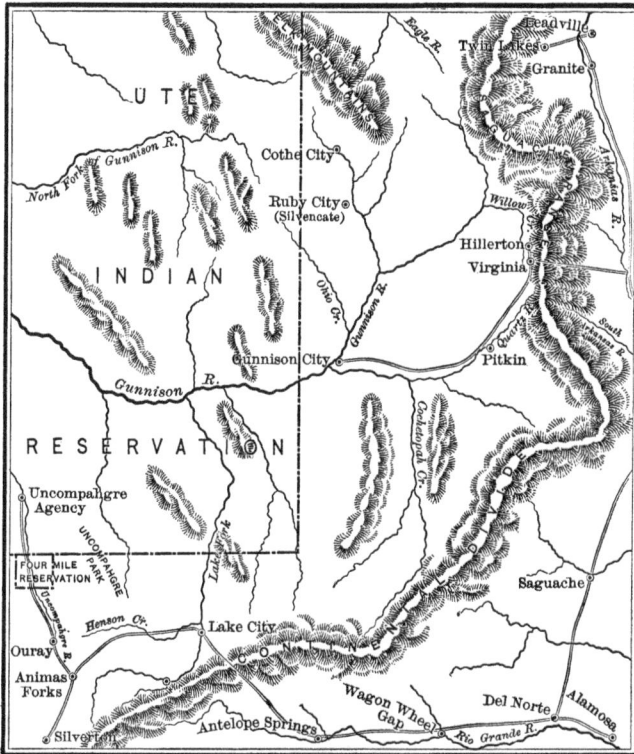

UNCOMPAHGRE AGENCY.

North American Phalanx and Brook Farm Societies. Communism not coming up to his expectations, he returned to Cleveland, and went into a mercantile business in a small way, prospering very well. Then he became war
correspondent of the N. Y. Tribune, and later was on the editorial staff. In
1869, being sent to write up Mormonism, he spent a little time in Colorado,
and was so charmed with the scenery and the climate that he determined to
settle here with his family. In this design he was encouraged by Greeley,
who promised to aid him with the Tribune. Out of this grew the Union colony. How Greeley kept his word the readers of the Tribune remember, and
the flourishing town of Greeley attests, named in acknowledgment of his
services.

The captives were finally given up, owing to the skill of Postal-agent Charles N. Adams and the influence of Ouray. The Indians guilty of the crimes committed at the agency did not present themselves, and finally Adams went on to Washington with Ouray, Jack, and other lesser personages to the number of a dozen. After nearly a fortnight of negotiations there, during which the government insisted upon two points, the relinquishment of the criminals and the removal of the Utes to a reservation outside of Colorado, Jack and three other Utes returned with Adams to this state to attempt once more the capture of Douglas, Johnson, and others under criminal charges. About the middle of February they were so far successful that Douglas and Johnson were among the Indians who accompanied them east, Douglas being left in confinement at Fort Leavenworth.

On the 6th of March a new convention was entered into between the Ute representative in Washington and the agents of the United States. By this arrangement the chiefs agreed to endeavor to effect the surrender of the Indians implicated in the massacre of Meeker and his employés, or, if not able to take them, they promised not to obstruct the government officers in the same effort. They agreed to cede the Ute reservation, except that the southern Utes, or Ignacio's band, were to be settled in severalty on agricultural lands on the La Plata river, and in New Mexico. The Uncompahgres were to settle upon lands on Grand river, near the mouth of the Gunnison, in Colorado and Utah. The White River Utes agreed to settle on lands in severalty on the Uintah reservation in Utah. The severalty bill passed by congress allowed 160 acres of pasture and the same amount of farming land to each head of a family, and 80 acres to each child. The consent, first of congress, and secondly of a majority of the three bands, was to be obtained to this arrangement, when $60,000, or as much more as congress might appropriate, should be distributed among them.   An annuity of $50,000 was also to be paid them, and a support furnished them and their children until they became self-supporting.[9] This schedule was so altered as to require the surrender of the murderers before the White River Utes should receive all their share of the money, and an annuity of $500 each was to be taken out of the Ute annuity to be paid to the widows of the men slain at

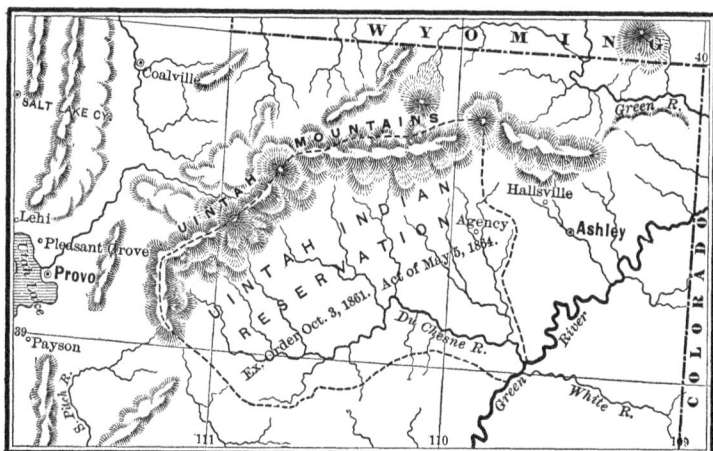

UINTAH RESERVATION.

the agency.   On the other hand, Schurz insisted on an appropriation of $350,000 for different objects beneficial to the Utes, to be expended in surveying

[9] *Denver Tribune*, Mar. 7, 1880.   The history of the progress of the Ute commissions was reported in the *Tribune* from day to day, and from its columns I have drawn most of my statements and some of my conclusions. The account of the massacre, etc., contained in *Baskin's Denver Hist.*, is apparently derived from a similar source.   There is a pamphlet by Thomas Sturgis, *The Ute War of 1879*, Cheyenne, 1879, pp. 26, showing why the Indian bureau should be transferred from the interior department to the military, which also contains a history of the outbreak.   I find partial accounts in *Byers' Centennial State*, MS., 46–52; *U. S. H. Doc.*, 1879–80; *Helena (Mont.) Herald*, Oct., Nov., and Dec., 1879; *Helena Independent*, Oct. 16 and 30, 1879; *Sen. Jour. Colo*, 1881, 42–3; *U. S. Sen. Doc.*, i. 29, 46th cong. 2d sess.; *U. S. H. Doc.*, ix., pt 5, pp. 109–11, 121–5, 46th cong. 2d sess.; *Stockton Independent*, Mar. 17. 1880.

their lots, building houses and mills, buying wagons, harness, cattle, and other property. Back annuities, which by the terms of the treaty of 1868 might be paid in cattle, the Utes insisted should now be paid in cash, and enough added to it to make it $75,000 annually. The bill finally passed with these provisions. Douglas was kept in confinement at Fort Leavenworth for more than a year. His tribe were removed to Utah. Ouray returned to Colorado, where he died in August. Colorow lived to cause further trouble.

HIST. NEV. 31

CHAPTER VIII.

MATERIAL PROGRESS.

1859-1875.

It is time now that I should turn to the consideration of the material development of the country. After the first three or four years of immigration and gold mining, during which $30,000,000 of gold was produced, it began to be realized that the placer diggings were soon to be exhausted, and that quartz mining only could be made remunerative in the future. A more discouraging discovery was that the ores in quartz were refractory, and the proper methods of working them unknown. It was then that many Colorado miners, hearing of Salmon river in what was then Washington territory, migrated in that direction with the same impetuousness with which they had first flown to the rumored El Dorado of the Rocky mountains. Failing to reach there for want of a wagon-road, they, with others from the western states, began prospecting on the headwaters of the Missouri river, and discovered gold. Forthwith the town of Bannack sprang up, then Virginia City, and simultaneously other towns in what was soon Idaho, followed by the rapid population of the still later territory of Montana, Colorado furnishing a large proportion of the first settlers of that region.[1]

Placer, gulch, and bar mining had about come to an end in 1859 in Arapahoe county ; in Clear creek and Boulder counties in 1860; in the parks by 1861; and in Gilpin county by 1863. It revived somewhat afterward in the parks.[2] The richest of the gulch claims had proved to be the croppings of quartz ledges, which were easily worked, the gold near the surface being freed from its matrix by elemental forces operating for ages. Little water at first accumulated in these mines ; simple machinery answered for hoisting the ore, and fuel was cheap. Arastras and stampmills were introduced as early as 1859, as I have before mentioned, and were quite numerous in 1860. But to the surprise of their owners the mills were often found not to save gold enough to pay expenses. D. D. White is said to have thrown a quantity of gold-dust into the battery of his mill in Boulder county that he might be able to declare that he had cleaned up some gold, and not a trace of the gold thus devoted could be found. The first successful mill was the property of Robert and Cary Culver and John Mahoney, and was set up in July 1860 at Gold hill, ten miles from the town of Boulder, to work the ore of the Horsfal mine, discovered[3] in June 1859, and which had already yielded $10,000 by sluicing. Two months later a six-stamp Gates mill belonging to Wemott & Merrill arrived from Chicago, and was set

[1] The following persons were in both Colorado and Montana: W. McKimons, J. Daniothy, E. Nottingham, A. W. Pillsbury, J. Brady, F. Temple, W. Rogers, John Call, John Willhard, Christopher Richter, Nicholas Kessler, W. J. English, G. W. Krattcar, Sargeant Hall, O. W. Jay, Joseph Eveans, Wilson Butt, James M. Cavanaugh, William Arthur Davis, O. Bryam, James Williams, Thomas Foster, John M. Shelton, Charles L. Williams, Benjamin R. Dittes, John Fenn, Thomas Garlick, William Fern, David Alderdice, C. B. Reed, A. E. Grater, Alexander Metzel, Edward D. Alston, J. W. Marshall, Isaac Hall, William Stodden, George L. Shoup.

[2] *Hollister Mines of Colo*, 122–3.

[3] By David Horsfal, M. L. McCaslin, and William Blore. Blore was a native of Otsego co., N. Y., though of German descent, and was born in 1833. He resided in Pa when a child, going to Neb. in 1856, and being one of the Colorado pioneers of 1858. He purchased land and went to farming and stock-raising.

to work upon this lode, the proprietors of the former
mill discarding their own and purchasing an interest
in this.   By this means $600 to $700 per cord—ore
being measured, not weighed, at this time—was saved,
and the Horsfal yielded over $300,000 in the succeed-
ing two years.   Some other mills made good returns
for a time;[4] but, as I have said, at no great depth the
ores generally proved refractory to the treatment to
which, following the methods familiar in California,
they were subjected.   The milling processes practised
on the Comstock enabled the mill men to extract the
metal from a ton of ore at a cost of from five to ten
dollars; consequently low-grade ores could be profitably worked ; but it was found that quicksilver, which
in California and Nevada saved the free gold and carbonates by amalgamation, was wholly indifferent to
the sulphurets and pyrites[5] of Colorado, and that the
ores would have to be treated by some then unknown
method, and at probably a greatly increased cost.
Much money was expended in unprofitable experiment for the whole period between 1864 and 1867,
and many claims were abandoned which have since
been profitably worked.[6]   From $7,500,000 annual

[4] Archibald J. Van Deren of Ky came to Colorado in 1859, and operated
successfully one of the first stamp-mills brought to Colorado at Nevada
gulch.   He was commissioner of Gilpin co. in 1861.   In 1863 he was a member of the legislature.   The John Jay mine was discovered by him.   Ensign
B. Smith, born in N. Y., came to Colorado in 1859 with his family, building
the second house in Golden, which he kept as a hotel.   In 1860 he removed
to Black Hawk and erected a quartz-mill of 6 stamps, which he sold, and
erected another at Buckskin Joe, which ran for half a year, when he abandoned it and returned to hotel-keeping.   He was appointed probate judge in
1862.   In 1863 he built, in connection with his brother and W. A. H. Loveland, the Clear creek wagon-road from Golden to the Golden Gate road-
Perry A. Kline, born in Pa, came in 1859, and mined in the Gregory and
Russell diggings, and in 1860 at California gulch, French gulch, and Buckskin Joe.   In 1861 he was employed in a mill on the Gunnell lode, near Central City, and became superintendent.   He was subsequently superintendent of several different mills, among others the Kansas Consolidated, running 52 stamps.
[5] Pyrites are sulphurets of iron, whereas combinations of sulphur and
other metals are called sulphurets.   Pyrites may have, besides iron, the sulphurets of other metals.
[6] Warren R. Fowler, author of Around Colorado, MS., was born in N. Y.,
and in 1849 came to Cal., and to Central City in 1860, which he helped to
build up.   He has remained, mining and farming in different parts of the
state, finally making his residence at Cañon City.

production the mining output diminished until in 1867 it was but $1,800,000,[7] when men ceased to exhaust their means in worthless "new processes," and returned to their stamp-mills, which wasted from one half to two thirds of the precious metals, and all of the lead and copper contained in the ores, but still afforded a profit. During this period many miners parted with their properties to eastern men, who had advanced money on them, and they were lying idle, which accounted in part for the decrease of gold production in Colorado. Time was required to establish titles and start up the mines under a new régime. Also a large per cent of the unsold mining property was bonded to be sold, in which condition it could not be worked. Gradually the new owners, having command of capital, secured the services of mining experts from Europe, who introduced processes of dressing and smelting ores, which being improved upon by native ingenuity, resulted in a solution of the problem. The yield of the Colorado mines in 1870 rose to $5,000,000, and in 1871 to $6,000,000.

In the meantime the discovery had been made that some of the supposed gold mines were really not gold, but silver; as, for instance, the Seaton mine in Idaho district, which became almost valueless from the small amount of gold contained in the bullion produced by it, the name of Seaton gold being synonymous with a nearly white metal. Comparison of the ore with some from the Comstock mines revealed a resemblance, but the owners were still doubting, because they knew nothing of silver in Colorado, and no competent assayer was at hand to decide the question. In the summer of 1864, however, there was discovered a lode, which, on being tested by experts, was pronounced to be undoubted silver ore. This important revelation changed at once the reputation of such

[7] *Tice's Over the Plains*, 226; *Helena Republican*, Sept. 15, 1866. The *Montana Post* of Apr. 30, 1869, says that Montana produced in 1868, $15,000,-000 in precious metals, against $2,107,235 in Colorado, and that Montana's agricultural product was $5,913,000, against $2,683,840 in Colorado.

mines as the Seaton, which, from being regarded as almost worthless, assumed a great if unknown value. It also stimulated prospecting afresh, and prompted the holders of mines which were lying idle to attend to their development.

It was in 1864 that a company of capitalists of Boston and Providence requested Nathaniel P. Hill, at that time professor of chemistry at Brown university, to visit Colorado, in order to examine a land grant in which they were interested. This examination led to a second visit in 1865, when the mines of Gilpin county were subjected to thorough research, and the attention of the man of science was drawn to the imperfect methods in use for treating ores. After acquainting himself with his subject, Hill paid two visits to Swansea in Wales, taking with him enough of the Colorado ores to make practical tests at the Swansea works, and studying ore-reduction in other parts of Europe. Returning to the United States in the autumn of 1866, he organized the Boston and Colorado Smelting company, with a cash capital of $275,000, and proceeded to erect a furnace at Black Hawk, near Central City. This furnace solved the knotty problem of how to reduce refractory ores, and make abandoned mines of value. For ten years its fires were never out, but other furnaces were added by the company until there were eight, which were always fully employed. In 1878 the company removed its works to Argo, a suburb of Denver, where seven acres were covered by them, and where ore was brought by the railroads, not only from different parts of Colorado, but from New Mexico, Arizona. Utah, and Montana. The company had increased its capital before removal to $800,000, and its products from $300,000 in 1868 to $2,250,000 in 1878. Until he was chosen to the United States senate, Professor Hill devoted his entire energies to the mining development of the country, whose savior, in this direction he became. Not that smelters before 1865–7

had been overlooked, though there might be smelters
and no gold or silver. The first furnace erected was
in September 1861, by Lewis Tappan, who had discovered a lead mine in Quartz valley. Governor Gilpin was in need of bullets for his 1st Colorado cavalry, and did, I am bound to believe, draw his drafts
on the treasury to erect this smelter in order to supply them. These bullets had the reputation of being
poisoned, so few of the wounded recovered, though it
was not the governor who was at fault, but the
smelter, which did not extract the poisonous metals
mixed with the silver in the lead thus obtained.[8] The
second furnace erected was for smelting gold, and
was built at Black Hawk in 1864 by James E. Lyon,
but failed of its purpose, as I have already intimated.

After reduction works were successfully introduced
at Black Hawk, they multiplied in the gold and silver
districts. The mills resumed crushing, those few
mines which produced ore free from sulphur being
generally furnished with apparatus for turning out
bullion, and the majority sending their concentrated
ore to the reduction works.[9] of Colorado, or quite

[8] I find these facts in a manuscript on *Mining and Smelting in Colorado*, by
John Bennett, of Littleton, who was born in Stafford co., Eng., in 1820, and
migrated to America in 1849, landing at N. O., and drifting to Wis., where
he remained working in the lead mines until 1860, when he came to Colorado.
He made the plan of the furnace which furnished lead for Gilpin's regiment.
It was 'built of rock, with a channel chiseled out to receive the lead as it
was melted in the fire, a blacksmith's bellows, a water-wheel, and a small
stream of water to give blast to the furnace.' Bennett assisted Hill in selecting ores to be taken to Europe. *See*, also, *Gilpin's Pioneer of 1842*, MS.

[9] One run only was made. A 'button,' 2½ feet in diameter and six inches
in thickness was the result, which was placed on exhibition at the national
bank, and the works closed, the process proving too costly. Meagher, *Observations*, MS., 2. Meline, *Two Thousand Miles on Horseback*, 66-8, tells all
that I have told here, but in the light of a huge joke, or at least, with little
sympathy for the disappointed smelter-owner.

[10] Cash and Rockwell of Central City, between 1867 and 1870, erected
works near Central City for the reduction of gold ores, which saved 95 to 98
per cent of the precious metal. *Wallingham's Colo Gazetteer*, 230. Besides
Hill's smelter at Black Hawk, there were reductions-works for the treatment
of silver ores at Georgetown in Clear creek co., erected by Garrott and
Buchanan, but sold to Palmer and Nichols: and Stewart's silver-reducing
works, also at Georgetown; Brown Co.'s reduction works at Brownville, 4
miles from Georgetown; Baker's works 8 miles above Georgetown; the
International Co.'s works in east Argentine district; and the Swansea reduction works, 4 miles above Georgetown. At the latter, both gold and silver

often to Omaha or Chicago, where large smelters had
been erected for the purpose of reducing and refining
the ores from Colorado, Montana, and other mining
regions to which railroad transportation was being
extended. The expense of the treatment and handling made a low grade of ores comparatively worthless. In the first place, the mills charged from $20
to $35 per cord [11] for crushing the rock, to which was
added the cost of concentration, reduction, and transportation, in all from $45 to $50. Still, the average
assay of all the silver ores treated was $118, of which
80 per cent was guaranteed to the miner. Some ores
yielded from $350 to $650 per ton, these being sent
to Newark, England, or elsewhere for reduction. [12]

While the territory was passing through this experimental period of its mining history, it had yet other
brawbacks in the operations of swindling companies,
which brought discredit upon the country by cheating
their stockholders, and then unblushingly pricking
the bubble. One fraud of this kind gained more
notoriety than many excellent investments. In other
cases there were really good mines in the hands of
operators, who mercilessly, by a system of assessments
and practices known among miners as freezing out,
excluded all but a favored few from participation in
the benefits of mining property in which they had in
the first instance embarked their small capital. If a
prison is the proper thing for men brave and bold
enough to rob contrary to law, a rope would be about
right for the vile creatures that cheat and steal within
pale of the law. Besides those intentional wrongs,
there were many failures which were the result of

ore were reduced. In Summit co. there were the Sukey Silver Mining Co.'s
reduction works, and the works of the Boston association, which were all
the smelters in operation in 1870. Ruins of experiments were to be seen in
all the mining districts.

[11] A cord measured 128 cubic feet, and weighed from 6 to 10 tons, according to density.

[12] It would be out of place for me to go into details concerning the methods of reducing ores in Colorado. No two smelters used the same processes,
and every process was varied to adapt it to the requirements of the minerals to be separated.

folly in the management of funds, in the erection of expensive but unnecessary buildings, or attempts at the hitherto unheard-of processes to which I have alluded. From the depression of this period I shall show by and by that the mining interest completely emerged, if not all at once, yet before the admission of Colorado into the union. In nine years, ending 1880, the small county of Gilpin produced $18,126,-564 in gold and silver.[13]

Going back to the beginning of this chapter, it was not altogether the failure of placer mining, the ignorance of and subsequent blunders made in quartz mining, with their concomitant ills, of which Colorado had to complain in the years of her infancy In common with, but to a greater comparative extent, the new commnnity suffered like the older ones the burdens and the losses by civil war, which had diverted men and capital, raised prices, depreciated currency, and even swallowed up the means of transportation across the plains. The summer of 1863 was a season of drought, when boats could not ascend the Missouri with freight for points above the mouth of the Kansas river, and goods became scarce. The grass on the plains was burnt up by the sun, so that stock did not thrive; the city of Denver was visited by a fire which destroyed property worth a quarter of a million, and all things conspired to make desolate the hearts of the pilgrims from home and plenty.

Following this exceptional summer was an equally exceptional winter, which began in October and was severely cold. The impoverished cattle on the plains perished by hundreds. Hay and grain brought twenty cents per pound, and fuel advanced a hundred per cent. Trains with supplies and machinery were snowed up en route, and some were lost. Others

[13] Gilpin co. produced $2,240,000 in 1876, which it did not exceed for 9 years except in 1878 and 1880. In the latter year the yield was $2,680,-090,

were a year arriving. While these circumstances made gold more than usually a necessity, mining was interrupted by the cold. The spring brought no relief, the rains descending in floods, driving out of their claims the few miners who had returned to the mountains, and destroying the crops which had not entirely succumbed to the drought. On the 19th of April the waters of Plum and Cherry creeks suddenly rose, and sweeping through Denver, carried destruction and death in their course. A million dollars worth of property, and twenty lives were lost.[14] Similar, though less extensive damage was wrought by the storm in other portions of the territory. Following this sudden flood, was a heavy and continuous rainfall, which, with the melting snow in the mountains. caused a second slower rise, which overflowed the farming lands, and remaining up for a month ruined the crops, the young fruit trees, and in many instances changed the face of the county by deposit-

[14] The storm which caused such devastation in Denver came from the south-east, and was a heavy fall of rain, followed by hail, which dammed the water from the mountains until its weight forced the barriers, filling up the valley, and carrying everything before it. Mixed with the water and hail was the sand which had accumulated in the bed of Cherry creek, giving it additional weight. The flood struck the town at 2 o'clock in the morning, and 12 hours afterward water was still rolling on in massive billows, which rose so high in their frantic course that a man standing on one bank would be momentarily hidden from sight on the other. A cupful of the liquid was found to be half sand. The fall of the creek through the town was 35 feet to the mile; above it was much greater. The city hall stood in the hitherto dry bed of the creek. It was utterly destroyed, and a safe containing the valuables of the city was never seen again. The office of the *Rocky Mountain News* was erected on piling on a little island in the creek bed. It had in it 5 printing presses, one weighing between 2 and 3 tons. All were swept away with the building, and so lost and covered up that they were not discovered for 9 or 10 years, when the heaviest press was found in the middle of Platte river, below the mouth of the creek. A portion of another press—the one Byers brought from Omaha in 1859—was found covered 10 feet deep with earth when the water company excavated for their first works at Denver. Against such power as this nothing could stand—houses, bridges, property of every kind disappeared forever. Five persons asleep in the *News* office were aroused only in time to spring from a window into an eddy formed by drift lodged for the moment against the building, from which they were drawn and rescued just as the office was carried away with all it contained, and the lot on which it stood. The pioneer saw mill of D. C. Oakes was carried away. Byers, besides losing all his town property, had his farm, which was in a bend of Platte river, destroyed by the cutting of a new channel. *Hist. Colo*, MS., 48. Gibson, Arnold, Schlier, Lloyd, Stover, and other farmers were ruined. Reed, Palmer, and Barnes together lost 4,000 sheep, and so on. For a new country it was a great disaster.

ing sand to a considerable depth over it. The roads became impassable for weeks from the thorough saturation of the soil of the plains, and every kind of business was brought to a stand still.

This stagnation in the life giving industries was followed by an uprising among the Indians along the overland route, which added still further to the distress already felt on account of interrupted communication with the east. The situation called for a military force, which was organized about midsummer for ninety days' service, and sent out to open the closed communication with the east, which it effected. An account of these affairs is elsewhere given; I only remark here that Colorado, young and heavily taxed as she was, had already raised two regiments in defence of the government, which were then in the field, and that the 1,200 ninety days' men made the third. Had business been better it might have been more difficult to raise this last; but at all events matters could not mend until the embargo on transportation was raised. The vengeance meted out to the Indians reacted during the following winter, when again all commuuication was cut off for two months, the Platte route desolated for 250 miles, and again the territory raised 300 militiamen to open communication.[15] The dangers and losses to freighters greatly raised the charges on freight, as also the price of every commodity, and the result was that by the time the heavy milling machinery so long delayed was upon the ground the companies owing it had exhausted their treasuries These were the dark days of Colorado; yet never so dark that faith in her was lost by those best acquainted with her resources. Two things they waited for which came not far apart —a knowledge of the true methods of extracting gold and silver from refractory ores, and railroad communication. I might add that confidence in the value

[15] *Bayle's Politics and Mining*, MS., 4; *Evans' Interview*, MS., 16; *Elbert's Pub. Men and Measures*, MS., 9.

of agriculture, which was established after a few years of experimental farming, tended to give permanence to other enterprises. These years of waiting, from 1864 to 1867, were not lost. They proved the stuff of which not the mountains but the men were made. No more did they depend on freight teams to bring to them from the Missouri flour, corn, and potatoes. In a single season, 1866, Colorado became self-supporting; in 1867 she exported food to Montana, and contracted to supply the government posts; and in 1868 made food cheaper than in the States.[16]

I have not yet given the actual history of the discovery of silver in Colorado. An assay made of ore from the Gregory lode in 1859 resulted in showing a yield of $16\frac{3}{4}$ ounces of silver per ton, and $10\frac{1}{2}$ ounces of gold ; the assayer being John Torry of the United States assay-office, New York, a notice of which was published,[17] but does not seem to have attracted much

[16] Says Bowles, in his letters to the *Springfield Republican* in 1868, afterward published in a vol. entitled *The Switzerland of America*, 'At a rough estimate the agricultural wealth of Colorado last year was 1,000,000 bushels of corn, 500,000 of wheat, 500,000 of barley, oats, and vegetables, 50,000 head of cattle, and 75,000 to 100,000 of sheep.' Of the prolific qualities of the new soil he says: 'The irrigated gardens of the upper parts of Denver fairly riot in growth of fat vegetables, while the bottom-lands of the neighboring valleys are at least equally productive without irrigation. Think of cabbages weighing 50 to 60 pounds each! And potatoes from 5 to 6, onions 1 to 2 pounds, and beets 6 to 10.' Byers speaks of watermelons 'piled up on the top of one another,' so abundantly were the vines laden. *Hist. Colo*, MS., 43. Market prices for 1868, before harvest: barley, 3 cents a pound; corn, $3\frac{1}{2}$ to $4\frac{1}{2}$; corn-meal, 5 cents; oats, 3 cents; potatoes, 2 and 3 cents; wheat, $3\frac{3}{4}$ cents; tomatoes, fresh, 3 cents; cabbages, 1 cent; beef 12 to 15 cents; cheese, 20 to 22 cents; butter, 45 cents; flour, 7 to 9 cents; eggs, 50 to 60 cents a dozen. Formerly the simple freight on all these articles had been from 6 to 10 cents a pound. Concerning locations of farming lands at that period there were the Cache-la-Poudre valley on a branch of the Platte in Larimer co., which, besides grain, vegetables, and hay, produced from 15,000 to 20,000 pounds of butter; the Big Thompson valley, in the same country, which produced, besides grain, hay, and vegetables, 7,500 pounds of cheese; the Platte valley, between Denver and the Cache-la-Poudre, which produced, besides a large crop of grains, etc., 23,000 pounds of butter; the same valley, for 20 miles south of Denver, and Bear creek also had considerable cultivated land. In the main valley of the Arkansas about 6,000 acres were under cultivation; on the Fontaine-qui-Bouille, 6,000; on the St Charles, 1,500; in the Huerfano valley, 5,000; all of which comprised about half of the land actually farmed in the territory in 1868.

[17] In the *Rocky Mountain News*, Aug. 20, 1859. See also *Clear Creek and Boulder Val. Hist.*, 278; *King, U. S. Geol. Explor.*, iii. 588–62. I find in *Aux's Mining in Colorado*, MS., 4, that the author claims for himself and A. Miller the first discovery of a silver lode, in July, 1859. They found it near

attention, probably owing to the shifting nature of
the mining population, and the prevailing ignorance
of silver mining. Nevertheless, the Ida mine, near
Empire, in Clear creek county, was recorded as a
silver lode by its discoverer, D. C. Daley, in September 1860. It was assayed by Day of Central, and
found to contain 100 ounces of silver per ton.
Another lode was recorded October 4, 1860, called
the Morning Sun Silver lode. A number of other
locations was made of silver lodes by E. H. F. Patterson and others, and not infrequent mention was
made of these claims in the local prints.[18] They were
found in Gilpin and Clear creek counties, but chiefly
in the latter, about Georgetown. The Seaton mine
was discovered in July 1861, by S. B. Womack and
others, who mined it for gold only. It became one
of the celebrated silver mines of the world. The
existence of silver was not, however, authoritatively
proved until several years later.

In the summer of 1864 Cooley and Short, while
prospecting on Glazier mountain, discovered a lode
which became known as the Cooley, ore from which
being carefully assayed by Frank Dibdin, a metallurgist, and other experts, was pronounced to be beyond
doubt silver. Dibdin indeed seems to have established a fact which the Coloradans were slow to
grasp, that theirs was a silver mining region, with
much better prospects for a solid future than if their
mines had been all gold mines. This was the first
rift in the cloud of dullness which had at this period
settled over the pregnant mountains. The first paying silver lode was the Belmont, later the Johnson.
discovered in September 1864, by R. W. Steel, James
Huff, and Robert Layton. The first accurate assay
of the Belmont gave $827.48 per ton. This inter-

Central City, and called it the Dalles; but thinking it worthless, after
recording, abandoned it. Grasset relocated it, and sold to Tappan Brothers,
who worked it for lead, which was sold to the government and condemmed
as poisonous.

[18] *Rocky Mountain News*, Nov. 2, 1860; *Governor's Mess.*, in *Western
Mountaineer*, Nov. 22, 1860.

ested eastern capitalists. C. S. Stowel erected the first mill in the argentiferous district in which Georgetown is situated, in 1866. For the reduction of the ore an ordinary blast furnace was provided, which failed, after several weeks of trial, to liquefy it so that the metal could be run off. When the owner, and even Dibdin himself, had exhausted their science and ingenuity in the effort, a negro named Lorenzo M. Bowman, from the lead mines in Missouri, offered his services, and, from a practical knowledge of the temperature to be attained, succeeded in smelting the ore. But, as I have before stated, these first efforts were unprofitable, and it was not until about 1868 that there was a marked improvement in quartz mining. Stamp mills, which had been for a time superseded by a variety of experimental structures, began again about this time their continuous crunching and grinding upon the rocky gangue of the precious metals, which has since never ceased, and promises to go on with increasing din forever.

The number of stamp mills running in the autumn of 1868, in Gilpin county, was thirty-eight, with an average of nineteen stamps to a mill,[19] and the bullion shipment was $1,775,477, of which $123,730 was in silver. The number of mines in this county, in which development had begun in 1870, was over 170; of those in which hoisting apparatus was employed on account of depth, about a dozen. Clear creek county had at the time fewer mills, but between 300 and 350 mines, on which some work had been done. Boulder county had about 100 mines, with some improvements, and only two quartz mills. Summit county had no mills, and about 20 mines, not much developed. Lake county had 70 mines in one district, the Red mountain,[20] which assayed well, but were not yet improved to any extent.[21]

[19] *Rocky Mountain News,* Feb. 3, 1869.
[20] This district was discovered about the 1st of August, 1869.
[21] Forty other miscellaneous mines are mentioned, 19 of which were in Gilpin, 14 in Clear creek, two in Park, two in Jefferson, and four in Lake county. See al o *Denver Rocky Mountain Herald,* Aug. 27, 1869.

In another place I have mentioned that in 1860 a prospector named John Baker led an exploring party into that rugged, south-west portion of Colorado, vaguely known as the San Juan country, from which the company returned disappointed. The history of this expedition, on account of subsequent developments, becomes a portion of the history of mining discovery.

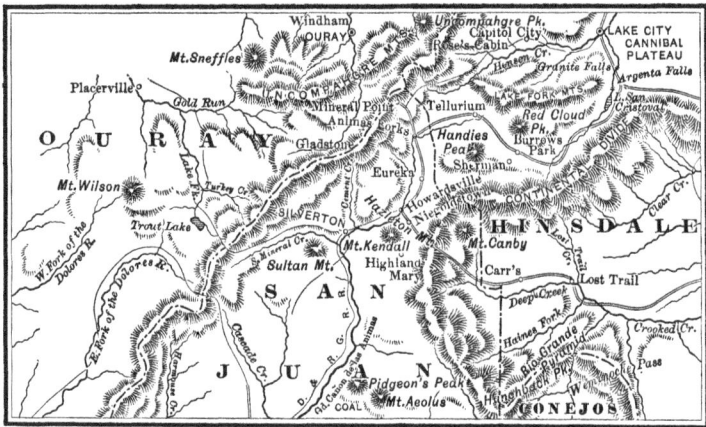

SAN JUAN MINING DISTRICT.

The San Juan country, as now known to the world, includes Las Animas district, situated on the upper waters of the Rio Animas with Baker park as a centre ; Lake district, situated on the Uncompahgre slope ; and Summit district, situated on the eastern or Rio Grande slope of the continental divide. It is the wildest and most inaccessible region in Colorado, if not in North America. The mountain ranges, which are lofty, are broken and deflected from the main Cordillera del Sierra Madre, which bends to the south-west from the foot of South park. Crossing Saguache county it swerves still more to the west, until midway between the meridians 107° and 108° it bifurcates, the main ridge separating the head waters

of the Rio Grande and Rio Animas, and turning eastward forms the so-called San Juan range. The other
ridge continues in a south-west direction, becoming
the Sierra San Miguel and the Sierra La Plata. It
is as if the great spinal column of the continent had
bent upon itself in some spasm of the earth, until the
vertebra overlapped each other, the effect being
unparalleled ruggedness, and sublimity more awful than
beautiful. Here, indeed, is one of the continental
summits, from which flow many rivers, tributaries,
and sources of the Colorado and Rio Grande, in rapid
torrents, frequently interrupted by cataracts of considerable height. In the midst of a wild confusion of
precipitous peaks and sharp ridges are a few small
elevated valleys, or as the early trappers would have
designated them "holes," but which are without much
relevancy denominated parks by modern Coloradans,
after the great parks of the country. Among these
higher valleys is the historical Baker park, a simple
widening of the bottom land of the Rio Animas at
the north end of the cañon, for six or eight miles, to
a width of one mile. Animas park, another widening
of the Animas valley, is thirty or more miles further
down the stream, and consequently at a less altitude,
and being on the south side of the divide has a climate
much warmer than the upper park. The lower valleys of all the tributaries of the Las Animas are small,
but of great fertility. They are the Navajo, Nutria
or Piedra, Florida, Pinos, Plata, and Mancos, all
flowing into the Rio San Juan. The higher portions
of these valleys abound in yellow pine, and spruce, fir,
and aspen are found on some of the slopes in the
vicinity of Baker park. Below the cataracts, the
streams abound in salmon-trout, and game is abundant.
Such are the more prominent features of the San Juan
country as it existed in 1860, and for a dozen years
thereafter.[22]

[22] *San Juan and Other Sketches*, MS., 12–17; *Pitkin's Political Views*, MS.,
4; *Out West*, Dec.–Jan., 1873–4.

Baker was a mountaineer of note. He had heard from the Navajos and other Indians that the royal metal existed in the mysterious upper regions of the Sierra Madre, proof of which was exhibited in ornaments and bullets of gold. More than these pretended revelations no one knew, when Baker determined to prove the truth or falsity of the Arabian tales of the Navajos, who had frequently received bribes to disclose the new Golconda, but evaded making the promised disclosure. Finding at Pueblo a considerable number of prospectors who had passed an unprofitable season in looking for placer mines, and who yet had the courage for new undertakings, Baker raised a company variously stated at from ' a few' to 1,000 and even 5,000, who set out on their crusade as gayly as knights of old, albeit their banners were not silken, and their picks and shovels were not swords. Proceeding into New Mexico, they entered the San Juan valley ; from there, by the way of the Tierra Amarillo and Pagosa,[23] they penetrated the country as far as the headwaters of the Rio de las Animas, where, in anticipation of the future populousness of the country, they laid out a town, calling it Animas City, which was seen longer on the maps than on the ground. Some placer diggings were found along the various streams and in the vicinity of Baker park, but nothing which promised to realize the exaggerated expectations of the discoverers. Small garnets and rubies were also picked up, and indications were believed to be seen of diamonds.[24] The main portion of the company went no further than Animas City, but a few penetrated to the Rio Grande del Norte. Reinforcements with provisions failed to arrive as expected, and the condition of the adventurers became critical. Anxious to avoid the long journey back

[23] Pagosa is the Indian word for hot springs.
[24] D. C. Collier of Central City visited the San Juan country the same season, with others, and offered to stake his reputation as a geologist and journalist on this being the richest and most extensive diamond field in the world. *Out West*, Dec.-Jan. 1873-4.

HIST. NEV. 32

through New Mexico, the company separated into
squads, each of which sought according to its judgment
a shorter way out of the maze of cañons and peaks
than the one by which they came. Many perished
by starvation, cold, and Indians, and those who survived suffered the pangs of death many times over
before they found egress from the imprisoning mountains [25] Baker lived to be a wealthy cattle-owner,
and to organize an expedition to explore the grand
cañon of Colorado. . He was killed at the entrance
to the cañon, with all his party save one, a man in the
prime of life, who reached the outlet after days of
indescribable suffering, with hair bleached like snow,
and both hands and feet blistered, in which condition
and insensible he was finally rescued. He had
devoured his shoes, his leathern belt, and buckskin
pouch. So suffered, and often so died, the vanguard
of civilization on this continent. Before the inexora-
ble laws of nature an heir of centuries of intellectual
growth is no more than the jelly-fish to the sea,
which casts it upon the sands to rot in the sun !

The outcome of the San Juan expedition deterred
further exploration for several years ; and in the meantime mining affairs fluctuated in the older districts, as
I have described. In 1868, by a treaty made with
the Utes, they were allowed the exclusive use of all
that portion of Colorado west of the 107th meridian,·
and south of 40° 15′ north latitude, or, in brief, four
fifths of the whole territory west of the main sierra,
including the San Juan country.

At this period the boundary between New Mexico
and Colorado was not clearly defined, but the mining
district of Moreño, believed to belong to the former,
was coveted by the latter, and the Colorado legislature memorialized congress to annex it to their terri-·
tory, hearing of which the New Mexico legislature,

---

[25] Adam Augustine and David McShane, residing later in Monument valley, were members of this expedition, as were also Charles Jones of Gilpin
co., and Charles Hall of Salt-works, South park.

in February 1868, addressed to that body a counter
memorial. Congress does not appear to have concerned itself much about either, and in the meantime
the boundary line was being surveyed westward from
the north-east corner of New Mexico on the 37th
parallel to the north-west corner, which survey was
reported as completed in 1868–9.[26] It found several

[26] See *Sec. Int. Rept*, 39, 41, 2. This report gives an interesting description
of the route with the various streams and valleys crossed, and mentions the
abandoned cliff-dwellings in the valley of the Rio Mancos. A. D. Wilson of
the Hayden geological survey, while pursuing his labors in the topographical
corps, discovered a stone building 'about the size of the patent-office at
Washington.' It stood upon the banks of the Rio de las Animas, and contained about 500 rooms. A part of the wall left standing indicated a height
of 4 stories. A number of the rooms, fairly preserved, had loop-hole windows
but no doors. They had evidently been entered by ladders, which were
drawn in by the occupants. The floors were of cedar logs, the spaces between
the logs being filled neatly by smaller poles and twigs, covered by a car-
pet of cedar bark. The ends of the timber were hewed and frayed, as if
severed by a dull instrument; in the vicinity were hatchets and saws made
of sandstone slivers, two feet long, worn to a smooth edge. A few hundred
yards from this 'casa grande' was a second large ruin, and between them
rows of small dwellings made of cobble-stones laid in adobe, which on account
of the shape of the stones were in a more advanced state of destruction than
the larger buildings. The ruins of this ancient town were overgrown with
juniper, and piñon, the latter a dwarf, wide-spreading pine, which bears
beneath the scales of its cones together with nutritious nuts. From the size
of the dead and the living trees, and their position on heaps of crumbling
stone, a long time must have elapsed since the buildings fell. The preservation of the wooden parts does not militate against their antiquity. In Asia,
cedar lasts for thousands of years. The cedars of the south-west Colorado
region do not rot even in groves. The winds and whirling sands carve the
dead trees into fantastic forms, drill holes through their trunks, and gradually,
after ages of resistance, wear them away into dust, which is scattered
abroad, atom by atom. Subsequent investigation showed the casas grandes
of Wilson to be on the northern edge of an immense settlement, which once
extended far down into New Mexico, covering several thousand square miles,
and comprising also portions of Colorado, Utah, and Arizona. The most southern ruins exhibit the best architectural designs. The region is remote from
civilization. From Fort Garland, which is west of the Rocky mountains and
east of the Rio Grande del Norte, in latitude 37° 23′ north, longitude 27° 20′
west, the route leads across a trackless desert, where no shrubbery is found
but sage-brush and grease-wood, and no animal life except rattlesnakes,
horned-toads, lizards, and tarantulas. Patches of alkali whiten the sands,
and the sun beats down on all with a blistering heat. The streams coming
from the rocky range flow through deep cañons, often thousands of feet
below the surface—that is, when they flow at all, which they do not all the
year—and springs are of rare occurrence, even in the cañons The country
sought lies in a triangle between the Rio Mancos, La Plata, and Rio San
Juan, and around the triangle is a net-work of ravines crusted with ruins.
The San Juan and La Plata have some width of bottom-lands between their
sides, but the Rio Mancos runs between walls closely approaching each other.
On the rocky terraces of the more open cañons are multitudes of ruins; even
in the wilder and narrower ravines are single houses or groups of two or
three perched on the face of the dizzy cliff, so far above the valley that the
naked eye can distinguish them merely as specks. Above them the rocks

Mexican towns north of the line,[27] and one, La Costilla, directly upon it. Soon after the survey the legislature of New Mexico memorialized congress to have the counties of Costilla and Conejos reannexed to New Mexico upon the ground that Colorado had obtained them "through fraudulent representations," and that the people desired it, which was not the fact.[28] The boundary remained unchanged.[29]

In 1869 Governor Pile of New Mexico, as if to retaliate, and meet covetousness with covetousness, fitted out a company of experienced prospectors to explore the headwaters of the San Juan and the contiguous country, who learned at this time little to encourage effort in that direction. But the following year a party, having pushed their explorations westward to the Rio Animas near Baker park, discovered the Little Giant gold lode, samples of which were sent to New York for assay, and yielded from $900 to $4,000 per ton. Other discoveries followed, chiefly of silver lodes, and Las Animas district was formed in 1871, while the mountains swarmed with prospectors. This being a violation of the treaty of 1868, the Utes and the miners were soon antagonistic, though no open hostilities followed. In 1872 troops were sent into the country to keep out the miners, which action on the part of the government only stimulated the desire of occupancy. A commission

project so that they could not have been approached from above, and there remains no means of reaching them from below, though signs of a trail doubling among the rocks are here and there visible. In the few cases where towers exist they are curved and smoothly rounded. Emma C. Hardarce, in Hayden's *Great West*, 445–56.

[27] Trinidad, with 500 inhabitants, Calaveras, San Louis, Guadalupe, Conejos, San Antonio, and several minor Spanish settlements were found to be north of the line, according to the survey report.

[28] *U. S. H. Misc. Doc.*, 97, 41st cong., 2d sess.; *H. Jour.*, 383, 41st cong. 2d sess.

[29] The survey of 1868-9 seems to have been made merely preliminary, and the final boundaries of the state of Colorado were not established for 10 years thereafter. *H. Com. Repts*, 708, 45th cong. 2d sess. There was a bill before congress in 1869 to extend the boundaries of Nevada, Minnesota, and Nebraska, and the territories of Colorado, Montana, and Wyoming, which was referred to the committee on territories and there lost. *U. S. H. Jour.*, 132, 40th cong. 3d sess.; *U. S. Sen. Jour.*, 150, 40th cong. 3d sess.

was also appointed to negotiate the purchase of the mineral lands of the Ute reservation, which, through the machination of interested persons in Wall street, failed of its object. An order was issued in February 1873, at the request of the interior department, requiring all miners, prospectors, and others to quit the reservation before the first of June. So strenuous were the objections to the order that a detachment of troops was ordered to march to San Juan to enforce it, and was half way up the Rio Grande when it was suspended by the president. A commission was again ordered, and a treaty made by which the Utes surrendered a tract of country containing 3,000,-000 acres of territory, which, though unparalleled for roughness,[30] was considered of inestimable value by mining men.

In 1874 more than a thousand lodes were claimed, upon many of which the work required by law was done.[31] In 1875 roads had been opened by which machinery was transported to the Animas district, 11,000 and 12,000 feet above the sea, where it was put in operation before winter. The first mine worked was the Little Giant in Arastra gulch. With this exception, the leading lodes in this district were argentiferous galena, highly impregnated with gray copper, the veins being large and well defined, yielding in the smelter $150 to $2,000 per ton.[32] Blue

[30] Ernest Ingersoll, in *Harper's Magazine*, April 1882. See also Ingersoll's *Crest of the Continent*, 162, 'a record of a summer's ramble in the Rocky Mountains,' and supplementary to *Knocking around the Rockies*, which describes Colorado as seen in 1874, when, attached to the U. S. survey, the author made a tour of the mountains.

[31] The mining laws were generally known and understood, like common law, except in the matter of local rules in different districts. In 1881 R. S. Morrison and Jacob Fillius, lawyers of Denver, published a volume on *Mining Rights*, pp. 336, 12 mo., containing all the Colorado statutes on mining, including the rules adopted under the provisional government, and all successive regulations, with the U. S. laws on the subject. The law to which referencee was had above required a discovery shaft to be 10 feet deep, and $100 worth of work to be performed annually to hold it; or, if $500 worth were done, a patent might be obtained.

[32] The names of some of the earliest mines of note were the Highland Mary, Mountaineer, North Star, Tiger, Thatcher, Chepauqua, Comstock, Pride of the West, Philadelphia, Susquehanna, Pelican, Gray Eagle, Shenandoah, Bull of the Woods, Prospector, McGregor, Aspen, Seymour, Letter

carbonates of lime were found on Sultan mountain, and large deposits of iron ore at its foot.

The Eureka district lay north of Animas, with the town of Eureka, nine miles from Silverton, surrounded by large ore bodies. The Uncompahgre district, the highest in the San Juan country, contained a better class of ores than the lower districts. Lake district, in Hinsdale county, and more accessible than the others, had for its chief town Lake City. Hundreds of mines were located here, its tellurium lodes being the only ones of note in the San Juan region. One hundred and fifty tons of selected ore from the Hotchkiss sold in San Francisco at the rate of $40,000 per ton.[33] Ouray county, which is on the northern skirt of the San Juan country, was found to contain not only silver mines of the highest value, but the gold district of San Miguel. This gold district reveals one of those wonderful pages in the history of the globe which inspire awe, the gravel deposits, 100 to 150 feet above the present San Miguel river, being evidently the bed of some mightier stream, which in a remote past rolled its golden sands toward that buried sea, to which geological facts point a significant finger. The present cost of carrying water to these ancient gravel beds is in itself a fortune, which only the certainty of greater riches would tempt associations of miners to expend.

But it is as a silver region that San Juan became, and will remain, preëminent. Some of the mountains, notably King Solomon in San Juan county, were so seamed with mineral veins of great width that they could be seen for two miles. The most remarkable of the Ouray county lodes was Begole,

G., Empire, Sultana, Hawkeye, Ajax, Mollie Darling, Silver Cord, Althea, Last of the Line, Boss Boy, Crystal, King Hiram, Abiff (gold), Ulysses, Lucky, Eliza, Jane, Silver Wing, Jennie Parker.

[33] Some of the leading lodes in Hinsdale county are the Accidental, American, Hotchkiss, and Melrose in Galena district, yielding from 100 to 600 ounces of bullion per ton, in the concentration works at Lake City; Belle of the East, Belle of the West, Big Casino, Crœsus, Dolly Varden, Gray Copper, and Hidden Treasure. Ocean Wave, Plutarch, Ule, Ute, and Wave of the Ocean are in Galena district.

known as Mineral farm, because the locations upon it cover forty acres, and the veins twelve acres. It was located in 1875, and developed by a company which built reduction works at Ouray, the county seat, in 1887. One vein carried a rich gray copper in a a gangue of quartzite, much of which milled from $400 to $700 per ton, and another in some parts carried a hundred ounces of silver with forty per cent of lead, per ton. The latest discovery in the San Juan region was of carbonates, in the western part of Ouray county, on Dolores river, where the mining town of Rico was located in one of the inclined valleys near the top of the globe. Almost every kind of ore was found in this district, not often in regular veins, but in irregular deposits, lead and dry ores occurring in contiguous claims. Also coal, bituminous and anthracite, limestone, bog and magnetic iron, fire-clay, building-stone, and wood for charcoal, from which it is evident nature designed this for a centre of reduction works and founderies. A branch of the Denver and Rio Grande railway was constructed to Silverton, one to Antelope springs, one to Lake City, and one to Ouray. The region which I have briefly described under the general name of San Juan comprises the counties of La Plata, Hinsdale, San Juan, Ouray, and Dolores, created in the order in which they are here named, out of the territory purchased from the Utes in 1873.

CHAPTER IX.

FURTHER DEVELOPMENT.

1875-1886.

THE San Juan region was only fairly started on the road to development when a fresh fever seized the Coloradans and drew many to an older field, but where discovery made it seem new. California gulch, as the reader knows, was discovered early, and had yielded in the first five years over $3,000,000. After that its productiveness lessened, dropping annually, until in 1876 the diggings yielded but $20,000.[1] During sixteen years the miners had been accustomed to move out of their way with difficulty certain heavy boulders which neither they nor scientific geologists had recognized as of any value. No one for all this time had thought to question whence they came.

Among those who had long followed placer mining in California gulch was W. H. Stevens, who in 1876 discovered a supposed lead mine on a hill on the south side of California gulch, a mile and a half above the present site of Leadville. This is known as the Rock mine, and adjoining it is the Dome mine, also owned

---

[1] A gold lode, the Printer Boy, was discovered in 1868, which drew prospectors for a season, who soon abandoned further search.

by Stevens and his partner, Leiter.[2] From the Rock mine Stevens took samples of ore, which being assayed by A. B. Wood yielded from twenty to forty ounces of silver to the ton. It now became apparent what was the nature of the boulders which had so troubled the miners while sluicing in the placer diggings.[3] Further exploration revealed richer ore, and carbonate of lead similar to that of White Pine district, Nevada, was found to exist over a number of eminences surrounding the mining camp of Oro. These hills, before unmarked, now took names of the mines first located upon them, or of their discoverers. The Carbonate mine, discovered by Hallock and Cooper, gave its name to Carbonate hill; the Iron mine to Iron hill; Long and Derry mine to Long and Derry hill; Yankee mine to Yankee hill; Breece mine to Breece hill; Fryer hill being named after one of the discoverers, Borden and Fryer. These hills were the seat of so many different groups of mines,[4] some loca-

[2] *Leadville, Colorado, the most Wonderful Mining Camp in the World, etc.*, Colorado Springs, 1879, is the name of a pamphlet written concerning the discovery. Soon after the first location there were discovered north from the Rock the Adelaide, Camp Bird (by Long and Derry), Pine (by the Gallagher brothers), and Iron. In Strayhorse gulch the Wolfstone was located the same year, these being, according to the authority above quoted, all the important discoveries of 1876. The Iron mine paid its owners in the first two years $200,000 above expenses, which were $57,500. The Silver Wave mine adjoined the Iron. Maurice Hays, and brother, and Durham are mentioned among the original locators. *Belmont Nev. Courier*, Oct. 21, 1876.

[3] This statement is premature as to time, for although silver was known to exist in the lead ore in the beginning, the nature of the composition was not at once understood. Carbonate of lead is the silver base in nearly all the ores, which, however, vary in the different groups.

[4] The *Leadville Democrat* of Dec. 31, 1881, gives the principal mines of these various groups as follows: On Fryer hill, the Robert E. Lee, Chrysolite, Matchless, Little Chief, Dunkin, Amie, Little Pittsburg, Climax, Carboniferous; and among the less known, the Little Sliver, American, Forepaugh, Bangkok, and others. On Carbonate hill were the Evening Star, Morning Star, Glass-Pendery, Cloutarf, Yankee Doodle, Ætna, Carbonate, Maid of Erin, Henrietta, Wolf Tone, and Vanderbilt. On Iron hill, the Iron Silver, Smuggler, Tuscon, Lime, Cleora, Silver Cord, Silver Wave, Rubie, Adelaide, Frenchman, and Belgium. On Yankee hill the principal was the property of the Denver City company. On Breece hill the Breece, Iron, Highland Chief, Miner Boy, Colorado Prince, Black Prince, Highland Mary, and others, On Long and Derry hill, the Long and Derry, Hoosier Girl, Belcher, Preston. Hawkins. In California gulch, the Last Rose of Summer, Columbia, A. Y., Gilt Edge, La Plata, Rock, Dome, Stone, and Leopard. In Iowa Gulch, to the south, were the Florence, First National, Kaiser, Brian Boru. On Bald Mountain, at the head of California gulch, the Green Mountain

tions, however, being made in gulches which subsequently proved to be rich in veins of carbonate. The oxide of iron imparted to one group of ores a red color, chromate of iron gave another group a yellow hue, while the predominance of silica and lead in others imparted a gray color. Chloride of silver permeated all the ores, and horn silver was found in all the prominent mines. What were termed the hard carbonates were those in which silica was predominant, with iron for a base, preventing disintegration as in the before mentioned boulders. The soft carbonates had a base of lead. The normal position of the lodes appeared to have been in contact or horizontal veins, sometimes called blanket veins, with limestone as the contact, iron above the ore, and trachyte as the cap, the latter being covered from ten to a hundred feet with drift. The veins dipped slightly to the east, and varied in thickness from a mere line to a chamber of ore from ten to forty feet in height, giving evidence of disturbance bewildering to the prospector. The ores in almost all cases were easily smelted without roasting.

Such in brief was the character of the new mines to which thousands hurried in 1877 and 1878. In June 1877 the first building was erected in Leadville,

mine, while 'scattered along the whole length of the gulch were numerous other mines and prospects in various stages of development.' In Evans' gulch were the Ocean, Seneca, and Little Ellen. Six miles from Leadville, across the Arkansas river, were Frying Pan and Colo gulches, with the Sundown, Defiance, Venture, Gertrude, Golden Curry in the former, and the Silver Moon, Little Mystic, and others in the latter. West, in Half-moon and Little Half-moon gulches, were the Susquehanna, Harding, Billy Wilson, and Iron Duke. Lackawana gulch and Twin lakes are mentioned as rich districts. In the latter were the Eagle Nest, Boaz, Gordon, Bengal Tiger, M. R., Pounder, Australia, and others. In Hayden and Echo cañons were the Black Diamond, Black Crook, Nabob, Copperopolis, Garfield, Ross, Sweepstakes, Fisher, Antelope, Dexter, and Mountain Quaie. North of Leadville were Mosquito, Buckskin, and Pennsylvania gulches, in which were the London and New York, Sunny South, Bonanza Queen, Bonanza King, Grace, St Louis, Steele, Stonewall, Fannie Barrett, Silver Leaf, and 'a large number of rich claims.' Northwest of Leadville was Tennessee park, where were El Capitan, Plattsburg Junior, Sylvanite, and other rich claims. South of Leadville, in Georgia and Thompson gulches, were the Coon valley and Mishawaka. In a new district, the Holy Cross, on French mountain, 150 mines were located, 'nearly all of which are in pay mineral.'

which soon grew so as to absorb the mining camp of
Oro, where Tabor was keeping a store and post-office,
in a resident population of about fifty persons.[5] The
effect on Tabor's fortunes was magical. The Little
Pittsburg, in which he was third owner, proved
exceedingly rich. Soon after it was opened he, with
one partner, was able to pay $90,000 cash for the
interest of the other owner.[6] A month later the second partner was brought off for $265,000, and Tabor
became associated with Senator Chaffee in the ownership of the mine. In an incredibly short time, not
only Tabor, but many others, could lay claim to be of
America's privileged order—millionaires.[7] Nor can

[5] So says Tabor in a brief MS., *Early Days*, devoted to Leadville history.
Mrs Tabor, in *Cabin Life in Colorado*, MS., relates how by mutual labor and
hardship in the mines they acquired $7,000 in money, after which they set
up a store and boarding-house, with a post-office and express office, the care
of all falling on her, while her husband looked after a contract for furnishing
railroad ties to the Atchison and Santa Fé railway, in which he made nothing,
not even wages. They were still keeping their little trading-post in Oro
when the Carbonate mines were discovered, Tabor 'grub-staked,' as the
miners' phrase is, Rische and Hook, two prospectors who discovered the Little
Pittsburg, on Fryer hill, in April 1878, and in Oct. bought and sold his hundreds of thousands worth of mining property for cash.

[6] Rische, who with Tabor bought out Hook, was a Prussian, born in Min-
den, in 1833, and immigrating to America in 1852, worked at shoemaking in
St Louis. He served in our civil war, coming to Colorado in 1868, and work-
ing at his trade in Fairplay. He retired from the ownership of the Little
Pittsburg with $310,000, and afterward owned in the Nevada, Hard Cash,
Last Chance, Little Rische, Wall street, and Willie mines. *Leadville in Your
Pocket*, 176-7; *Leadville Dem.*, Jan. 1881.

[7] Among the men who profited by the discovery of the carbonate mines
was J. Y. Marshall, born in Pa, and came to Colo in 1873, settling at Fairplay. He was elected to the legislature in 1875, and removed to Leadville
in 1878. He was elected judge of the district court in 1881, serving two
years. He was the first president of the Robert E. Lee mine, not far from
the Little Pittsburg, which proved very valuable, and made its owners rich.

J. J. Du Bois, born in N. Y., came to Colorado in 1877, locating the same
year in California gulch, and prospecting for mines. The time of his arrival
was fortunate. In August he had an interest in four claims, and in Dec.
staked out the Little Eaton, 'in snow waist deep,' the mine being afterward
sold for $1,200,000. Du Bois was elected mayor of Leadville in 1884.

Charles J. Rowell, a native of Vt, located himself in 1880 at Leadville, in
a law partnership with A. S. Weston. In May 1882 he was made business
manager of Tabor's property, of which he had control for 18 months, resuming
his law practice late in 1883. He became owner, with Tabor and Weston, of
the Santa Eduviges, in Chihuahua, and also owner of valuable mining property in Montana.

Lyman Robison, born in Ohio, came to Colorado in 1878, and, with a partner, located the Col Sellers mine at Leadville, which produced in 4 years
$400,000, and was then valued at over $1,000,000. He was one of the incorporators of the South Park Land and Cattle co. in 1881, with a capital of

it be denied that in some instances their liberality and public spirit were as princely as their fortunes.[8]

$750,000, and in 1885 was vice-president. His residence in Cañon City cost $50,000. He married in 1866 Mary A. Roodnight of Chicago.

Peter W. Breene, from Ireland, located himself in 1874 at Leadville, where he became part owner in the Crown Point, Pinnacle, and Big Chief mines, besides having other mining interests. He was elected to the lower house of the general assembly in 1882, and lieut.-gov. in 1884. He married Mary L. McCarthy, principal of a public school at Leadville, in May 1884.

John D. Morrissey, born in N. Y., came to Colorado in 1872, settling at Georgetown, working at mining until 1878, when he removed to Leadville, and became interested in the Crown Point and Pinnacle mines, which, though slow in developing, finally made him wealthy. Crown Point yielded, in Sept. 1883, $20,000 per month, and was afterward still richer.

Samuel Adams, born in Canada in 1850, removed to New York city in 1866, and to Colorado in 1880. Soon after arriving he purchased half of the Brooklyn mine, at Leadville, for $50,000 cash. In 1881 he bought other mining interests, and organized the Adams Mining company, with 150,000 shares at $10 per share. In 3 years the company took out $425,000, paying $220,000 in dividends, leaving $50,000 in the treasury after paying all expenses, besides having $600,000 worth of ore in sight in 1885

John T. Elkins, from Mo., joined Price's army in 1861, and surrendered to Gen. Canby in 1865, going to Nebraska afterward; then to New Mexico, where he was a freighter and miner until 1878, when he came to Leadville. He obtained interests in the Leadville Consolidated, Boreal, Small Hopes, and Annie, selling the Annie in 1881 for $750,000, $500,000 of which he invested in Kansas City real estate. He was elected state senator in 1884.

F. De Maineville and W. H. Brisbane were partners in Wilmington, Del., from 1871 to 1876, when they removed to Cheyenne, Wy., where they kept a hotel until 1879, in which year they came to Leadville, investing what capital they could command in mining property. In 1882 they erected the De Maineville block, at a cost of $16,000 for the land, and $25,000 for the building; and secured a large amount of real estate in Leadville.

Luther M. Goddard, born in Wayne co., N. Y., in 1837, was in 1864 engaged in freighting across the plains between Leavenworth and Denver. In 1878 he came to reside in Colorado, and began the practice of law at Leadville that year, investing some money in the Pendery mine, which in 1879 proved rich, when he sold five sixths of it for $200,000. He afterward acquired an interest in Crown Point and Silver Cross, the former at Robinson, in Summit co., and the latter in Chaffee co., both of which proved valuable properties. He was elected judge of the district court of the 5th judicial district in 1882 for a term of 6 years.

[8] Horace A. W. Tabor was born in Vt in 1830. At the age of 19 years he removed to Mass., where he remained until he came to Colorado in 1859, and had his share of the rough work of erecting a new state. He had resided in Kansas, and been a member of the Topeka legislature. He was the first to realize any large amount from the mines at Leadville, and thereafter kept in the lead. In 1881 he owned the following mines wholly or in part: the Matchless, Scooper, Dunkin, Chrysolite, Union, Emma, Denver City, Henrietta, Maid of Erin, Empire, Hibernia, New Discovery, May Queen, besides mining property in Mexico, and 6 claims in the San Juan country. He erected the Tabor opera-house, costing $850,000, and built the bank of Leadville for a safe deposit. He was first in the organization of a fire department, presenting the hose company with their outfit; caused the construction of waterworks, the incorporation of a gas company in which he was principal owner, and which expended $75,000; organized the Tabor Milling company for crushing dry ores, investing $100,000; and equipped the Tabor light cavalry, 50 men, at a cost of $10,000, besides donating $10,000 annually to schools and

On the 1st of August 1877, there were six buildings on the site of the present town of Leadville,[9] and by the end of the year 300 inhabitants. But until smelters on the ground should test the various ores there could be no certainty of riches sufficient to cause a great influx of population. The town organization was perfected in January 1878. About the same time the first smelter was completed by the St Louis Smelting and Refining company, Weise superintendent, which received its ore through the sampling-works of A. R. Meyer & Co.[10] During eleven months ending November 30, 1878, 1,080 tons of bullion were produced from 3,330 tons of ore. Only one furnace, with a capacity of fifteen tons daily, was employed until late in the season when the capacity was doubled. By the end of the year four other smelters of various capacity were in operation.[11] The smelters

churches, and giving freely in private charities. The Tabor block in Denver cost, with the land, $200,000; the Windsor hotel was owned chiefly by him; his private residence cost $40,000; and his interest in the First National bank amounted to nearly half the shares.

[9] At a meeting on the 14th of Jan., 1878, at which 18 citizens were present in Gilbert's wagon-shop, where Robinson's block now stands, at the corner of Chestnut and Pine streets, steps were taken to organize the town, and give it a name. It was suggested to call it Harrison, after the owner of the first smelter; and Agassiz, after the great naturalist; and Carbonateville, after its ores; but Leadville, proposed by J. C. Cramer, was finally adopted. The town then had 70 houses and tents. On the 26th the governor issued a proclamation for an election of town officers Feb. 2d. H. A. W. Tabor was chosen mayor, C. Mater, Wm Nye, and J. C. Cramer trustees, and C. E. Anderson clerk and recorder. *Kent's Leadville in Your Pocket*, 32–3.

[10] Meyer & Co. purchased the first ore in 1876, and shipped 300 tons to St Louis by ox-teams, which did not pay for the expense of transportation and reducing; but as the grade increased by development, 50 tons shipped in the spring of 1877 proved very well worth the handling. Meyer & Co. established the first sampling works in 1877; Burdell and Witherell in Nov. 1877; Eddy & James in July 1878. *Loomis' Leadville*, 19–20.

[11] The works of J. B. Grant commenced running on the 1st of October. 1,643 tons of ore purchased averaged 84 ounces of silver to the ton; and 305 tons averaged 325 ounces. On the 9th of Oct. the Adelaide company commenced smelting. During 11 days in blast before the 1st of Dec., 90 tons of bullion were produced from 240 tons of ore. The Malta smelting works, J. B. Dickson & Co., started up on the 12th of October. By the 1st of Dec., they had smelted 1,081 tons of ore, and produced 181 tons of bullion, valued at $38,538. The average number of ounces of silver to the ton of ore was 47; to the ton of bullion, 170. On the 28th of Oct. the smelter of Burdell & Witherell began operations, and 970 tons of ore were turned into 210 tons of bullion worth $85,000. These were all low grade. The high grade ores were reduced elsewhere at first. In 1879 A. Eilers erected a smelter at Leadville, which he ran for two years. Eilers was born in Germany in 1839, and edu-

settled the question of the value of the Leadville mines, and the growth of the town in 1879 was phenomenal, even for a mining country. In the first four months of the year the increase of population was 1,000 a month ; after that it ran up to 3,000 a month ; about the last of the year there were 35,000 residents. Real estate was held at high figures, and lot jumping was practised, as in early times at Denver. A hotel with accommodations for 500 guests, several lesser ones, a church and a theatre were erected during the summer, besides private dwellings and mining improvements, which required 1,000,000 feet of lumber per week.

This activity was joyful madness. Men seemed to tread on air, so elated with hope were they, and not only with hope but with realization. In 1879 Leadville was created a city of the second class, with an efficient police and fire department, water and gasworks under construction, telegraphic communication, a local railroad company organized, hospital accommodations, and other concomitants of modern civilization It had a post-office requiring ten clerks, with a money-order department issuing orders at the rate of $355,911 per year, and cancelling stamps at the rate of over $32,000 annually. In 1879 the Denver and South park railway was within thirty miles of Leadville, and at the same time the Denver and Rio Grande road was extending a branch to Leadville, where it arrrived in August 1880.[12]

cated at the mining school of Clausthal and university of Gottingen. At the age of 20 years he graduated, and immigrated to the U. S., being employed by mining engineers in New York for several years. In 1869 he was appointed deputy U. S. mining statistician, which position he held until 1876. He then migrated to Salt Lake, where he erected the second Germania smelter in 1877-8. He then came to Colorado, and erected a smelter at Leadville, which he sold, and went to Europe in 1881, where he spent two years. On returning to Colorado he organized the Colorado Smelting company in Pueblo, where a furnace was started up in Aug. 1883, the works in 1886 having 4 furnaces, with a capacity of 200 tons daily, and employing 125 men.

[12] George W. Cook, born in Bradford, Ind., in 1850, was appointed superintendent and general agent of the Leadville division of the Denver and Rio Grande road, upon its completion. Cook ran away from home at 12 years of age to enlist as a drummer-boy, and was mustered out in Jan. 1866. That he

The business of Leadville demanded banks almost at once, and in May 1878, the first in Leadville was established under the name of Lake County bank. Soon afterward it organized as the First National bank with a cash capital of $60,000. The exchange for 1879 amounted to $10,000,000.[13] In October the

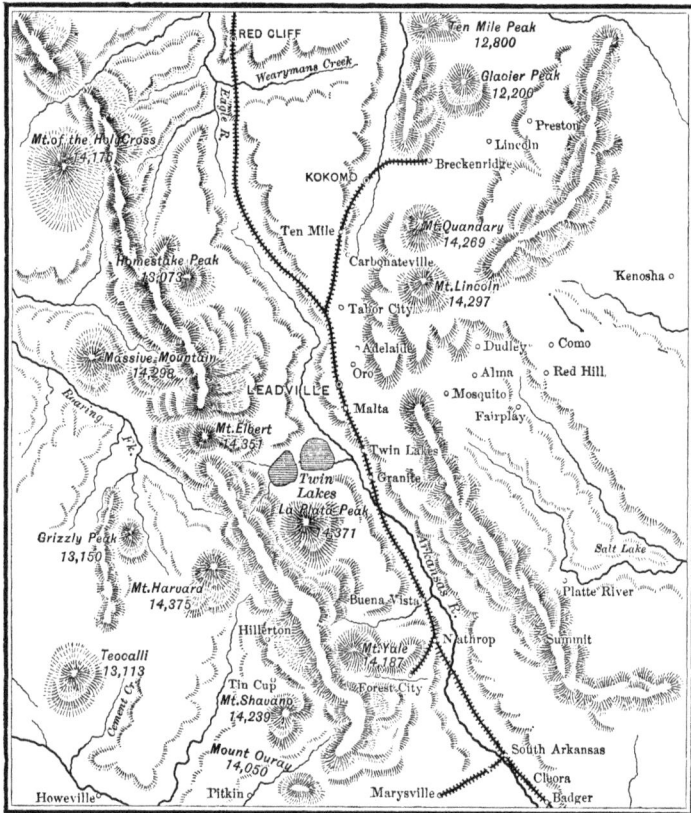

LEADVILLE AND VICINITY.

drummed through the war to fall on his feet in Leadville was a rare manifestation of the favor of the fickle goddess.

[13] The officers and stockholders were F. A. Revnolds, pres.; Nelson Hallock, vice-pres.; John W. Zollars, cashier; A. L. Ordean, asst cashier; August R. Meyer, J B. Grant, J. S. Raynolds, Charles Mater, J. C. Cramer, Charles I. Thompson, Peter Finerty, E. D. Long, J. H. Clemer, Charles T. Limberg, Rufus Shute.

bank of Leadville was opened with a capital of about a million dollars, and drew $11,500,000 [14] exchange during 1879. Others soon followed and in 1880 there were five, since which another has been opened.[15] Newspapers, schools, and churches enjoyed the benefits of abundant money. All this prosperity was the result of mining, and it would be superfluous to go into further details concerning individual mines or miners. It is sufficient before proceeding with the history of discovery to state in evidence of the permanance of the Leadville mines that the average output of mineral from them for the first half of 1885 was 10,000 tons per day.

It could not be expected that a community with a growth so marvellous, and founded upon mineral wealth should have no other or more dramatic incidents in its career than comes from rapid growth. The richer the country, as a rule, the more poisonous the parasites which it attracts to fester in the body politic; hence vigilance committees and midnight hangings had to have their day in Leadville.[16] Two

[14] H. A. W. Tabor, pres.; N. M. Tabor, vice-pres.; George R. Fisher, cashier. The Miners' Exchange bank, James H. B. McFerran, pres.; and George W. Trimble, cashier; and the Miners' and Mechanic's bank were the next in order in 1879. In April 1880, the City bank of Leadville was incorporated with a capital stock of $50,000. J. Warren Faxon, president; C. C, Howell, vice-president; and John Kerr, cashier. At the close of 1880 the organization was surrendered, and a private bank opened, C. C. Howell & Co. proprietors. *Leadville Democrat*, Dec. 31, 1881. In August 1883 the Carbonate bank was opened. John L. McNeil, the first cashier, and subsequently president, was born in Tioga co., N. Y., in 1849, and came to Colorado in 1870. He was employed as chief clerk of the office of the Denver Pacific R. R. for a few months, when he took a position as teller in the Colorado National bank, and held it until 1876, during which year a bank was opened at Del Norte, of which he was chosen manager. In 1880 this bank was moved to Alamosa, where it became the First National bank of that place. At the request of citizens of Leadville, McNeil, as above, organized the Carbonate bank.

[15] *Loomis' Leadville; Leadville Chronicle Annual,* 1881.

[16] At the first meeting of the town board T. H. Harrison was appointed marshal, T. J. Campbell police magistrate, and A. K. Updegraff town attorney. Harrison was soon driven out of town by the lawless element. At the second election in April George O'Connor was chosen marshal, and four policemen assigned to support his authority. Suspecting one of them of complicity with the 'roughs,' he was about to remove him from the force when he was killed by him, only 18 days after assuming the office. The ruffian's name was James Bloodsworth, who escaped arrest. At a special meeting of the board next morning, Martin Duggan was appointed marshal, and accepted the office. Almost immediately he received written notice that he would be

men named Frodshem and Stewart were taken from the sheriff and hanged November 20, 1879 ; following which the criminal and vicious class, to the number of several hundred, organized and threatened to retaliate by killing some of the supposed vigilants, and burning the newspaper offices. A few days of intense excitement followed, the city being patrolled nightly by the Wolf Tone guards and Tabor light cavalry. The action of the committee was approved by the majority of responsible citizens, who regarded it as necessary under the provocation given by the men who were hanged. This sentiment, together with the firmness of the militia, finally awed the vengeful would be rioters, and the city was restored to order.[17]

In the latter part of May following, however, another kind of mob violence was threatened, the men employed in several mines being upon a strike. The disturbances increased gradually for several weeks, all business being brought to a stand, and some of the most vicious of the idlers, who were glad of the opportunity to harrass better men, inciting the discontented miners to a riot. On the 12th of June, owing to threats, all the places of business in the city were closed, and a procession of citizens paraded, in the hope of impressing the strikers with their solid force. A proclamation was read in front of the opera house, signed by the Citizens' Executive Committee of One Hundred, declaring that men who desired to

killed unless he should leave town within 24 hours. Duggan made no sign that he had received the warning, but took precautions against seizure. Within a few days a murder was committed at a saloon by a negro, and the police had taken the wretch to jail, when the outlaw organization attempted his release. Duggan faced the mob with a revolver in each hand, and made them understand that he had the nerve to shoot any bold enough to interfere with the execution of the laws, and they retired. Duggan served his term, declining reëlection, P. A. Kelly being his successor. But Kelly was intimidated, and the city council telegraphed for Duggan, then in Mich., to return and take the marshalship. He complied, and served out Kelly's term, but refused reëlection. He remained in Leadville, however engaged in mining. Duggan was born in Ireland, migrating to the U. S. at the age of 6 years, and living in N. Y. until 16 years old, when he went to Kansas, and from Leavenworth to Colorado, where he engaged in mining and freighting.

[17] See *Denver Tribune*, Nov. 22 and 23, 1879.

HIST. NEV. 33

return to work at former wages [18] would be protected. A motion being made to adopt this as a resolution, the strikers, about 1,500 in number, shouted No! and assailed the citizens with threats and opprobrious epithets. An attempt was then made by the militia companies to clear the streets,[19] which only increased the confusion, and the belligerent attitude of the strikers. Hoping to preserve order by a show of law, the sheriff, L. R. Tucker, arrested the military commander, and disarmed the companies; but just at that time a supply of arms arriving from Denver, under escort, the mob made a movement to seize them, and were met with presented carbines. A partial peace was restored at nightfall, although the strikers still held out, and the Citizens' Executive Committee of One Hundred remained in session, and the fire companies in readiness during the night. A number of telegrams were sent to Governor Pitkin asking that martial law should be declared, and an officer ordered to Leadville to muster into service the militia, which had disbanded on being disarmed. The governor replied by instructing the sheriff to summon to his aid every law abiding citizen,[20] and promised to consider the question of martial law. Other telegrams followed the first, and about midnight a petition, headed by the sheriff, and signed by all the principal property owners in the city, was despatched to the executive, still urging martial law,[21] which was thereupon proclaimed, and Major-general David J. Cook ordered to

[18] Miners received from $3 to $4 per day. *Kent's Leadville in Your Pocket,* 150. The cost of living was high, but diminishing as the railroads approached.

[19] The Wolfe Tone guards was the oldest militia organization in Leadville, dating from July 12, 1879. It numbered 80 privates, and 18 commissioned and non-commissioned officers; John Murphy, capt. The Tabor Light cavalry organized August 2d, and mustered 64 men; Cecil C. Morgan capt. There was a 3d company, the Carbonate rifles, 44 men, W. P. Minor capt., ready to act as required.

[20] The law gave the sheriff this authority. *Gen. Laws Colo,* 1877, 237; and *Laws of 1879,* 135. In case of violence he might call out the military, or the aid of citizens.

[21] *Pitkin's Political Views,* MS., 1; *Boettcher, Flush Times,* MS., 2–4; *Denver Tribune,* June 15, 1880; *Colo Sen. Jour.,* 1881, 40–1.

Leadville to take command of the militia, and muster in as much force as he should find necessary. In the interim, pending his arrival, William H. Jones of Leadville was commissioned a brigadier-general, to take the command and perform the duties of his position. Provost-marshal J. L. Pritchard forbade the assembling of groups of people upon the street, or in public halls, and ordered all saloons and places of business closed by ten o'clock in the evening. On the night of the 14th General Cook arrived, and found the excitement in part allayed, and some of the miners returning to their work. Also that W. A. H. Loveland, managing editor of the *Democrat*, a paper which sided with the strikers, had been deposed, and Clark, one of the editors of the *Crisis*,[22] published to stir up disorder, had absconded. Notwithstanding the serious nature of the disturbances, no lives were lost. On the 22d of June the order of the 13th was revoked, and civil authority reinstated, the miners having returned to their work. Besides the loss to Leadville of half a summer's labor and profit, the state was taxed $19,506 for the expenses of the militia. For a time these incidents clouded the reputation, as they retarded the progress, of Leadville; but the

[22] The first paper established in Leadville was the *Reveille*, by R. S. Allen, in 1878. The printing-office was a log house on Elm street, below Chestnut. Being a prospector by nature, Allen had pioneered journalism in several new mining camps. He published the *Register* at Central in early times, and the *Sentinel* at Fairplay somewhat later; and, when carbonates were discovered, appeared in Leadville, where for a year and a half he published the *Reveille*, and then suspended, and went his way. The second newspaper in Leadville was the *Eclipse*, a daily democratic journal, established in 1878, and suspended in 1879. On the 29th of June, 1879, appeared the daily *Chronicle*, owned by Carlyle C. Davis, John Arkins, and James M. Burnell. Their printing-office was one of the first buildings on Chestnut street, a one-story frame structure 20 by 30 feet. None of the trio had any means which was not in their business, and used the office for a lodging-house. The first issue was a small sheet of 5 columns. Its success from the start was so great that it was twice enlarged in 3 months. In May Burnell sold to the other partners. In Dec. they purchased a 4-horse-power steam engine, with a press capacity of 1,800 an hour. In April 1880 Arkins sold to Davis, who conducted the business alone, publishing a 6-column daily, quarto size, and a 9-column weekly, an able, instructive, and illustrated paper. *The Democrat*, and the *Herald*, a little later in starting, are also able papers, of which mention is made in another place.

advent of railroads in August, and the continued discoveries of rich ore bodies. soon restored the balance.[23]

Such natural wealth on the east side of the continental divide was sure to inspire the desire of search
upon the occidental slope. But all that country, as
I have already stated, was left in reserve for the Utes.
The first attempt of miners to occupy the Ute country was in 1861, when a party of prospectors all perished at the hands of the Indians in Washington
gulch, since known as Dead Men's gulch, on the
head of Rock creek, a branch of Roaring fork of
Grand river. A few men who were undeterred by
the massacre of the first party, or who had forced

[23] It will be instructive to mention the smelters in and about Leadville at
the close of 1879, with their output. Little Chief, S. Tyson supt, started
Aug. 5, 1879, with one furnace—silver and lead, with a trace of gold—total
value of bullion, $212,775.88. Ohio and Missouri, J M. Rockwood supt,
started July 16, 1879; one furnace; total value, $154,817.89. Cummings &
Finn, Frederick H. Williams supt, started July 25, 1879; three furnaces;
total value, $323,039.24. Gage-Hagaman, G. W. Bryan metallurgist, started
May 23, 1879, one furnace; total value, $160,454.84. Raymond, Sherman,
and McKay, started June 26, 1879; one furnace; total value, $143,837.20.
Elgin Mining and Smelting company, started June 24, 1879; one furnace;
total value, $425,251.20. Harrison Reduction works, started Oct. 1878;
three furnaces; total value, $1,018,164.24. J. B. Grant & Co. smelter, Grant
manager, started Sept. 23, 1878; eight furnaces; total value, $2,397,474.48.
Leadville Smelting co., started May 15, 1879; one furnace; total value,
$199,177.80. La Plata Mining and Smelting co., started Nov. 2, 1878; four
furnaces; total value, $1,969,636.24. American Mining and Smelting co.,
O. H. Hahn supt, started June 5, 1879; two furnaces; total value, $223,837.36.
Billing & Eiler's Utah smelter, Fritz Wolf supt, started May 14, 1879; two
furnaces; total value, $1,022,670.16. California Smelting co., started Sept.
1879; two furnaces; total value, $76,870. J. D. Dickson & Co. Lizzie fur-
naces, started June 1879; two furnaces; total value, $785,010.40. J. B. Steen
& Co, Malta Smelting works, started June 1878; one furnace; total value,
$62,560.76. Adelaide Smelting works, started 1878; one furnace; total
value, $75 252.96. To sum up, 34 furnaces in less than a year, reducing
210,341,719 pounds of ore, produced 37,727,797 pounds of bullion, containing
6,913,408 ounces of silver, valued at $7,743,116.86, and 818.8 ounces of gold,
valued at $16,376.37, and $1,496,437.64 worth of lead, =$9,250,928.85.
Besides the ore smelted in the local works, there was sent away to be reduced
$2,751,879.76 worth of ore, to be reduced in foreign smelters, and $30,000 in
gold from the gold mines, making the product for the period above given
$12,022,808.61. *Leadville Carbonate Chronicle*, Jan. 3, 1880. The outlay was
of course enormous to produce this result, but it could never be so great for
any other year for these companies, and the amount of ore to be smelted
must increase with time and facilities. Supposing the supply to be practically unlimited, as it seems, mining becomes in Colorado a permanent industry on a grand scale. The product of Lake co., in gold, silver, and lead,
up to 1882, was $56,945,117.69.

themselves in at about the same time, found gold in Union park, Taylor park, German flats, and Tincup flats, but none were able to hold their ground against the Indians except a company in Union park, which erected fortifications, and mined in the intervals of hunting and skirmishing. They seem to have conquered a peace, for this limited region continued to be occupied for twenty years.[24] Very little was known of the country. Old mountaineers had traversed it. Frémont had crossed its northern portion by the White river branch of the Colorado in 1844. Gunnison had explored it by the Grand river branch, the southern fork of which was named after him by Governor Gilpin. Expeditions under Macomb and Ives had traversed the south-west corner, following the old Spanish trail from Santa Fé to Salt Lake. Ives explored the lower Colorado in 1857–8 to a point eighty miles below Grand cañon, where he organized a land expedition and explored the plateaux traversed by it. This expedition approached from the west, and did not extend to the Gunnison country. Baker's party penetrated it to the Grand cañon of the Colorado, where they were killed by the Indians, as I have already related. In 1869 Major J. W. Powell explored the Grand cañon with an efficient company and outfit, adding much to the interest already felt in the country.[25] He had been preceded in the Gunni-

[24] See *Richardson's History of the Gunnison Country*, MS., or an account of its exploration and settlement. Sylvester Richardson was born in Albany, N. Y. Migrating first to Sheboygan, Wis., he followed architecture and boat-building, with music-teaching. In 1860 he came to Colorado, where he practised medicine 22 years. In 1861 he went into cattle-raising, but the Indian war of 1864 ruined his business. He afterward settled in the Gunnison country.

[25] In the summer of 1867 Powell visited the Colorado mountains with a party of amateur naturalists, during which expedition he explored the cañon on Grand river below Hot Sulphur springs, and also the Cedar cañon, by which Grand river leaves Middle park. His curiosity thus stimulated, he determined upon further explorations. In 1868 he organized another expedition, which spent the summer among the mountains, and encamped for the winter 120 miles above the mouth of White river. During the winter, which was a mild one, excursions were made southward to the Grand, down White to Green river, north to Bear river, and around the Uintah mountains. Gradually these exploring excursions had become geological and scientific,

son country in 1866 by Benjamin Graham, who, in 1870, conducted a second expedition,[26] which spent the summer in prospecting the west slope of the Elk mountains, where they discovered many galena lodes, carrying cerussite in limestone formation, and a coal vein on Rock creek. A log fort was erected, and prospecting continued, but the Utes in 1874 burned the fort and drove out the prospectors, who lost all their property except their arms, and were compelled to make their way home, 100 miles, on foot, subsisting by shooting game. In this instance the Utes proved themselves able astronomers, as the 107th meridian, their eastern boundary, agreed to the year before, lay a few miles east of the Rock creek camp. In 1874 Hayden's scientific and exploring expedition passed the summer in the Gunnison country, but to these the Indians made no objection, knowing they were transient visitors, but not, perhaps, being aware that the knowledge which they gathered would send them more prospectors,[27] although, as it happened, the

and were carried on under the patronage of the government. The better to carry out his project of exploring the Colorado cañons, Powell had 4 boats built in Chicago, as strong as could be made, and transported by rail to the point where the U. P. R. R. crosses Green river. On the 24th of May the fleet left Green River city, in Wyoming, provisioned for 10 months, and supplied with scientific instruments, arms, ammunition, and tools, and two of them decked. The boats were named and manned as follows: *Emma Dean*, J. W. Powell, J. C. Sumner, and William H. Dunn; *Kitty Clyde's Sister*, W. H. Powell and G. Y. Bradley; *No Name*, O. G. Howland, Seneca Howland, and Frank Goodman; *Maid of the Cañon*, W. R. Hawkins and Andrew Hall. A summer of extraordinary travel and magnificent discovery followed, in which the object was accomplished, the examination of the grand cañon of the Colorado, besides which there were several others—Contract cañon, 41 miles long, with walls from 1,300 to 2,700 feet in height: Glen cañon, 149 miles long, with walls from 200 to 1,600 feet in altitude; Marble cañon, 65½ miles long, 200 feet deep at its head, and 3,500 feet deep at its lower end; Grand cañon, 217½ miles in length, and from 3,000 to 6,000 feet in depth. *Powell's Explor. Colo River*, 5, 79–102.

[26] This party consisted of R. A. Kirker, William Gant, Samuel McMillen, Louis Brant, James Brennan, and C. M. Defabauch. See Fossett's *Colorado*, a descriptive, historical, and statistical work of 592 pages, 8 mo, with maps and illustrations: New York, 1880; the most complete of the many books about the centennial state. Kirker was a resident of Park county, and active in exploring the mountains, particularly the Park range. A. Thornton was a prospector in this region about this time.

[27] I have several times had occasion to refer to Hayden's researches in the course of this work. The reports of Hayden, Endlich, Peale, Gannett, and Holmes were of great service in making known to the world the mineral

first who came and stayed were of a date at least contemporaneous with the government explorations just recorded.

In 1872 a party of prospectors returning from the San Juan country, where they were unwelcome, passed up the Gunnison river, and examining the old diggings on Rock creek, discovered a number of silver lodes in the vicinity.[28] A company was raised in Denver the following spring to visit the alleged discovery, among whom were John Parsons, Lewis Wait, and Thomas Croider. They went and returned by the old Washington gulch pass, via Red mountain, Twin lakes, Buckskin Joe, and Fairplay, bringing a

wealth of western Colorado. See Hayden's *U. S. Geol. and Geog. Survey of Colorado and Adjacent Territory*, 1874, p. 515, Washington, 1876. In Hayden's letter to the secretary of the interior, which serves as a preface, he names the assistants with him in Colorado as follows: first division crossing the mountains by the Berthoud pass, explored in 1861 by Berthoud while looking for an overland mail route by the way of Denver, consisted of A. R. Marvine geologist, S. B. Ladd topographer, Louis Chauvenet asst topographer, M. L. Ward and W. S. Holman meteorologists, E. A. Barber botanist, W. W. Williams asst, 2 packers, cook, and hunter. The second division consisted of Henry Gannett topographer, Fred Owens asst topographer, A. C. Peale geologist, Frank Kellogg, asst, Arch. R. Balloch asst, 2 packers and a cook; field, the Grand river. Third division consisted of A. D. Wilson topographer, F. Rhoda asst, F. M. Endlich geologist, Gallup meteorologist; field, the San Juan country. With Hayden were G. B. Chittenden topographer, W. H. Holmes geologist, W. H. Jackson photographer, Anthony asst, Ernest Ingersoll naturalist, Frank Smart asst, 2 packers and a cook.

The geographical surveys west of the 100th meridian, conducted by George M. Wheeler of the corps of engineers for several successive years, were of unusual interest. He had under his orders a party of engineer officers, and accompanying him a number of specialists. John J. Stevenson, geologist, in 1878 examined the coal-measures at the east base of the Rocky mountains, particularly from Trinidad south to Santa Fé. The reports down to 1884, which have been published, show a vast area of research for all the several branches of the survey, but they are for the most part too labored and technical for the general reader. There are few Hugh Millers in geology, and until there are more, that science will remain a dense and tasteless topic which should glow and sparkle with suggestion and meaning to the commonest understanding. A little in these reports concerning the effect of certain rock formations on the aspect of a country, its soils, rivers, and vegetable productions, both before and after it comes under improvement, would prove an attractive feature in geological works. The paleontology of Colorado is remarkable and interesting, as shown in the *Bulletins of the U. S. Geological and Geographical Survey of the Territories, Second Series, No. 1*, containing descriptions of fossil fishes and mammalia. This subject, combined with an intelligent study of the rocks, and the interest attaching to the relics of a long-past semi-civilization in Colorado, should furnish a fascinating field of observation to the ordinary mind as well as to the specialist.

[28] The names of some of this company were Douglas McLaughlin, James Brennan, and George Green (colored).

report so satisfactory that an expedition was immediately organized to return and explore the whole Gunnison country. It consisted of thirty men with eight wagons and a pack-train, which proceeded to cross the mountains by the South park, Poncho, and Cochetopa passes. The geologist of the expedition was Sylvester Richardson, the metallurgist Richard Cook, and the botanist Parsons, the recognized leader. On arriving at the Indian agency of Los Pinos, they were forbidden by the assembled Utes, numbering 1,500, to continue their journey. But upon holding a council, and taking the sense of the meeting by vote, it was found that there was an equal division, when the head chief, Ouray, gave his voice in favor of allowing the party to proceed

The company proceeded to the junction of Tomichi creek and Gunnison river, where they met a couple of white herders in charge of the government cattle belonging to the agency, and who conducted the wagons to a ford of the river. On the site of Gunnison City Richardson took an astronomical observation, and being satisfied that they were on the east side of the 107th meridian, determined to there found a town, and occupy the beautiful valley of the Gunnison. After several more days of toilsome road-building and travel, the expedition arrived at the head of Rock creek, and at once erected a small smelter, near where the town of Scofield was subsequently located. In two months a sufficient test had been made, and the company returned to winter at Denver, the wagon-train by the same route by which they came, and the pack-train by the Washington gulch trail.

Arrived at home, Richardson made his report to persons interested, residing in Chicago, Quincy, and Denver, which being favorable, furnaces and machinery were purchased, and all things placed in readiness to commence mining in Gunnison county as soon as spring should open. Before spring arrived a panic had occurred in business circles, which put an end to the schemes of the Parsons company. But Richardson, remembering the beauties of Gunnison valley, and being resolved to locate himself there, called a meeting at Denver, and proceeded to organize a joint stock company for the purposes of settlement. About the 1st of March the company was incorporated, with

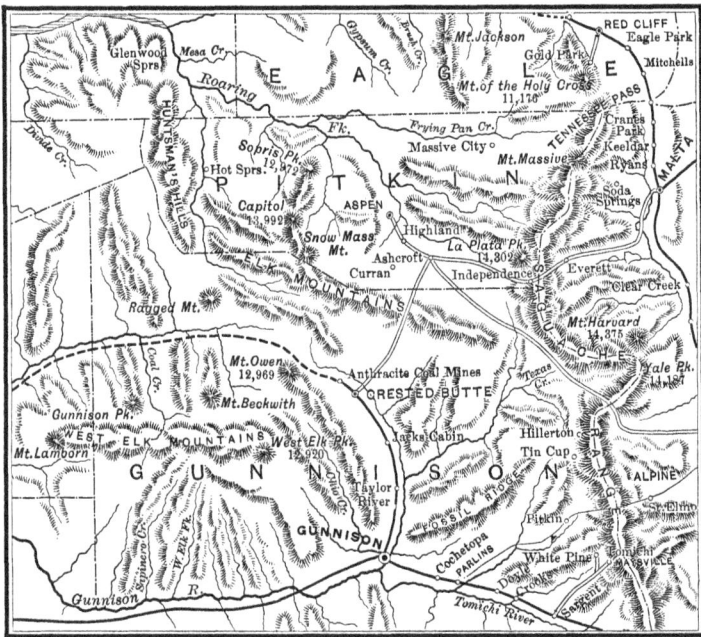

GUNNISON MINING REGION.

Richardson president, George Storm vice-president, Charles A. Beale secretary, and a board of directors consisting of these persons and J. B. Outcalt, John Spradling, George W. Hughes, and Doctor Knowles. The colony arrived at Gunnison river April 21, 1874. The land was surveyed into quarter sections; each colonist drew 160 acres by lot, and a town was laid off on Richardson's portion, and named Gunnison, after Captain Gunnison, who first surveyed this valley.

In the autumn dissensions arose in the company, some members of which abandoned their interests and went prospecting to the north. Alll returned to Denver to winter, and of the thirty original members only three resumed their occupancy in 1875, namely Richardson, and John and William Outcalt. Gradually settlers, especially cattle-owners, came to remain. In 1876 a new town company was formed, which took possession of the present site of Gunnison, outside of Richardson's claim. But this company also quarreled and dissolved. In 1879 there were two rival organizations—the East and West Gunnison town companies. The Denver and Rio Grande railway was being pushed westward with a purpose to develop the country, and the west Gunnison town company by liberal donations of land secured the station and car-shops.

In March 1879 the legislature established the county of Gunnison, and attached it to Lake for representative and judicial purposes. Its boundaries commenced on the summit of the Saguache [29] range, between the headwaters of the Arkansas and Colorado, where the south line of Lake county crossed the divide, extending along the said summit to the north line of Lake county, thence west to the west boundary of the state, and south to the north line of Ouray county, this being the north boundary of the San Juan purchase, thence east to the west line of Saguache county, following the boundary of this county to Saguache range, and north along its summit to the south-west corner of Lake county, embracing more than 10,000 square miles. [30] Settlement and discovery progressed slowly. In 1877 the Jennings brothers located a mine of bituminous coal at Crested Butte mountain, and the following year How-

[29] An Indian word, pronounced sí-watch, meaning blue stream. *Richardson's Hist. Gunnison Country*, MS., 15.

[30] *Gen. Laws Colo*, 1879, 213–16; *Fossett's Colorado*, 565. Pitkin county was taken from the north-east corner of Gunnison and Montrose, Delta and Mesa from the western portion.

ard F. Smith purchased some coal interests and started the village of Crested Butte. The existence of coal of a good quality was of itself a reason for extending railroads in this direction.[31] But prospectors from Lake county, the overflow of Leadville, began pouring into the Gunnison country early in 1879—so early, indeed, that they had to tunnel the snow in one of the passes of the mountains. Rich discoveries in gold and silver were made, and the usual sanguine expectation was aroused.

The first important discovery of silver was of the Forest Queen, in the summer of 1879. The history is simple and romantic. A Maryland man, W. A. Fisher, who had driven an ox-team across half the continent, became fastened in the mire of the mountains and was helped out by a spectator, O. P. Mace, whereupon Fisher gratefully promised him a half-interest in the first mine he should find. A few days later Mace was informed of the discovery of the Forest Queen lode, half of which he received from Fisher under the name of Ruby camp, and which he almost immediately sold for $100,000.[32] The village of Ruby a few miles west of Crested Butte became a dependency of the mine. Other discoveries, and other incipient towns followed; namely, Aspen, Gothic, Schofield, Elko, Bellevue, Irwin, Pitkin, Virginia, Tin Cup, Ohio City, Hillerton, Massive, and Highland. But in the midst of hope and promise the brightest, a thunderbolt fell. The Utes, viewing the gradual, but sure encroachments upon their reserved territory, turned in their rage and slaughtered, not the intrud-

---

[31] A well-known mineralogist is reported to have said that while a pound of Penn anthracite will make 25 pounds of steam, a pound of this bituminous coal will make 23 pounds; but while one pound of eastern anthracite is burning, two pounds of this will burn. Therefore, while the pound of Penn anthracite is making 25 pounds of steam, this coal will generate 46 pounds. *Ingersoll's Crest of the Continent*, 257.

[32] *Graybeard's Colorado*, 82. 'Graybeard' is John F. Graff, and his book series of letters to the *Philadelphia Press*, being notes of a journey to Denver and back, in the autumn and winter of 1881-2, p. 90, 1882. It is a superficial but pleasantly written view of the country, gathered chiefly from conversations with men.

ers, they were too many and strong, but their best
friend, the philanthropist Meeker, and his family, at
the agency, as I have related. This outbreak was an
interruption, but not a long one. The rush to the
Gunnison country in 1880 was greater than ever
before, being a repetition of the Leadville excitement.
A region was explored fifty by a hundred miles in
extent. The mineral formation while similar to that
of California gulch was less of the carbonate character, and consequently more difficult of reduction,
sometimes requiring roasting. Yet, as the mines were
frequent and rich, the Gunnison country, on account
of its extent, was regarded as the great treasury of
the state. In July 1881 the Denver and Rio Grande
railway was extended to Gunnison city, and in the
latter part of November to Crested Butte. Before
this, however, smelters and mills had been erected.
Such marvels of progress were seldom witnessed as
this mining and railroading progress in the heart of
the mountains; nor could it have been possible, no
matter how great the skill, without the native wealth
to sustain the outlay.[33]

[33] Some facts with regard to Gunnison mines are here given. The formation of the mineral bearing country is generally porphyry, quartzite, and
limestone, or decomposed granite. Among the noteworthy lodes near Pitkin
are the Fairview, Silver Islet, Silver Age, Terrible, Old Dominion, Green
Mountain Group, Silver Queen, Silver King, Western Hemisphere, Black
Cloud, Merrimac, and Silver Point. The Fairview averaged in the early period
of its development, 160 ounces of silver per ton, with 38 per cent of lead; and
a large amount carried 450 of silver per ton. Silver Islet samples of dressed
ore averaged 450 ounces, undressed, 275, with 25 per cent of copper. It
belonged to C. C. Puffer, who sold it for $30,000 before much work had been
done on it. Gov. Routt bought the Red Jacket, a 4-foot vein, for $20,000.
Near Ohio City were the Ohio, Dodson, Grand View, Ontario, Gold Point,
Humboldt, Tornado, Parole, Camp, and Gold Link. Free milling quartz and
gold were found near the surface, changing to silver below. Near Hillerton
the Prince mine, on Gold Hill, showed five feet of carbonates, carrying silver
272 ounces to the ton, and traces of gold. The Royal Oak Mining company
of New York owned mines in this section. Tin Cup, Silver Cup, Gold Cup,
Golden Queen, Hirbie Lee, Allentown, Anna, Dedricka, Mayflower, Red Lion,
Thompson, Little Anna, and Big Galena, were among the prominent mines
about Tin Cup. The Golden Queen was one of the few true fissure veins,
assaying $60 per ton, mostly in gold, and showing cube galena. The Tin Cup,
Gold Cup, and Silver Cup were on one lode or deposit, being carbonates,
in limestone, worked by the Bald Mountain co., and paying well in silver.
Highland Mining district on Roaring fork and Castle creek contained a belt
of limestone 18 miles long by 3 miles in width, between these streams in which

I have now given the principal history of silver and gold mining in Colorado for the first twenty years, from 1859-60 to 1879–80. A detailed account of all the minor discoveries would be more tedious than interesting. In the following chapters a summing of results, brought down as nearly to 1886 as amid transition so rapid it will be possible to do, will conclude the history of this portion of the state.[34]

an immense amount of mineral was found. The Monarch lode cropped out of the earth 20 feet in height and 25 feet in thickness, averaging 60 ounces of silver to the ton. The Smuggler, Spar, Cphir, and Richmond yielded handsomely—the Ophir $500 per ton, the Richmond, owned by Stevens and Leiter, from $70 to $100 per ton. The Smuggler, the oldest location near Aspen City, carried from 70 to 100 ounces of silver per ton. The ore of the spar was heavy baryta, with masses of copper and chlorides yielding richly. The Silver Bill lode showed native silver, and milled 94 ounces per ton. The Little Russell milled $300 per ton. Massive City is in the centre of a carbonate belt. Ruby was regarded as the point of convergence of three mineral belts, and the richest of all the districts. Among its notable mines were the Forest Queen, Lead Chief, Bullion King, Independence, Monto Cristo, Ruby Chief, Little Minnie, Silver Hill Crystal, Zume, Justice, Bobtail, Hopewell, Pickwick, Fourth of July, Eureka, and Old Missouri. The ore of the first 7 named yielded from $200 to $2,000 per ton. The Good Enough Smelting co. erected in 1880 a chlorodizing and amalgamating mill, the machinery of which filled 25 railway cars. W. H. Webb, J. R. T. Lindley, S. L. Townsend, and M. B. C. Wright were owners in this plank. The Fireside, Ruby, Equator, Morning Star, Dictator, Capitol, Hunkidori, and Hub are in this district. The first location, the Ruby Chief, was made by James Brennan. It carried ruby mineral. The Forest Queen in 1879 shipped 24 tons of picked ore to Pueblo and Denver that yielded $10,800. Crested Butte had a smelter in 1879 though there are no silver mines in its immediate vicinity. Gothic district, 7 miles north of Crested Butte, is located on Copper creek and East river. Its business center is Gothic City at the foot of the Gothic mountain. Among the noted mines are Independent, Silver Spence, Rensselaer, Vermont, Jenny Lind, Keno, Wolverine, Triumph, and Silver Queen, which carries 350 ounces of silver per ton of gray copper. Goodwin & Co. own the mine. The Silver Spence has a vein of galena, antimonial silver, native and ruby silver and sulphurets, from 4 to 20 inches in thickness. The Evening Star lode, on the same creek, is of fine-grained galena ore intermixed with white feldspar. There were four smelters in the Gothic district in 1880, within a radius of ten miles. On Rock creek were also many argentiferous veins and a smelter. The Silver Reef, three feet wide, was purchased by T. Foley of Leadville and E. B. Craven of Cañon City. Discoveries had been made the same year on Grizzly creek, 30 miles within the Indian reservation.

[34] Some of the authorities consulted for this chapter and not previously noted, are: *New Colorado and the Santa Fé Trail*, by A. A. Hayes, Jr, which, while it touches on the subjects herein contained, is chiefly a humorous view of unfamiliar scenes, and of little value as an authority. *The Footprints of Time, and a Complete Analysis of our American System of Government*, p. 738, by Charles Bancroft, Root publisher, Burlington, Iowa, 1877, is as its name implies a compendium of facts relating to our govermental system, and contains a brief outline of the history of each state and territory. A useful book of reference. *Summering in Colorado* is a volume of 158 pages published at Denver in 1874, by Richards & Co., with the design of attracting tourists to the grand and romantic scenery of the Rocky mountains. It is descriptive, with

a few photographic views, and a table of altitudes and distances. *Colorado and Homes in the New West*, by E. P. Tenney, president of Colorado college, p. 118, Boston, 1880, is probably intended to advertise the college; at the same time it gives a pleasant impression of Colorado as a whole, and is a readable book on a plane above comicality, at which it is fashionable to strain in modern travels. *Two Thousand Miles on Horseback*, by James F. Meline, p. 317, New York, 1867, is the narrative of a journey to Santa Fé and back in 1866, but contains more than the ordinary amount of information to be found in such books, and for the date at which it was published was interesting, while much that it contains is still of value. Meline was a contributor to the *Catholic World*, in which the above narrative first appeared. He died at Brooklyn, Aug. 14, 1873, aged 60 years. The *Mines of Colorado*, by Ovando J. Hollister, editor and proprietor of the *Colorado Mining Journal*, is a volume of 450 pages, devoted to a brief historical sketch of the discovery of the mines previous to 1867, with a description of the different districts as they then existed, for which reason it deals more with gold than silver mining. It is sufficiently practical and scientific together to be intelligible to the general reader.

The Colorado Mining Directory and Mining Laws, 1883, p. 908, contains a description of every developed mine in the state at the date, arranged by counties, with the statutes on mining, an admirable authority for its purpose. *On the Plains and among the Peaks, or how Mrs Maxwell Made her Natural History Collection*, by Mary Dartt, Philadelphia, 1879, furnishes little that is available for the historian, but is in a measure authoritative as to the fauna of the country. Mrs Maxwell's collection of Colorado mammals and birds was exhibited in Washington in 1876–77, and received much praise. *Hist. Colorado*, MS., by Carlyle C. Davis, Leadville, treats of the history of the *Chronicle*, and other newspapers of Leadville, the early history of the town, and its present prosperity and peculiarities. Davis was born at Glen Falls, N. Y., in 1846, and came to Colorado in Oct. 1878, as one of the proprietors of the *Chronicle*, which became a leading journal in the state. *Towns about Leadville*, MS., by James N. Chipley, gives a brief account of the rise of the mining towns in Lake co., and the history of leading mines. The Robert E. Lee mine took out in one day, according to Chipley, $118,000, and many days $50,000. Chipley was a native of Mo., born in 1854, and came to Denver in 1873; thence to Leadville in 1878. *The Flush Times in Colorado*, MS., by Charles Boettcher, Leadville, is a narrative of the author's migrations, and incidentally a history of the places where he has tarried for certain periods; at Cheyenne, in Wyoming, Greeley, Boulder, and Leadville, in Colorado. Boettcher was born in Germany in 1852, immigrating to the U. S. in 1867, and to Wyoming in 1868, whence he came to Colorado in 1871, and to Leadville in 1878. *Smelting in Colorado*, MS., by Franz Fohr, contains some loose statements concerning smelting; as, for instance, that at Denver, Pueblo, Cañon City, and Leadville, such works exist; and that the output of Leadville alone, not including outlying camps, was in 1884, 1,000 tons of bullion daily. *Progress in Colorado*, MS., by Charles I. Thompson, who had charge of the St Louis smelting works, and the Leadville Improvement company's property, gives a history of the troubles of the latter corporation with squatters, as well as many items of general information. Thompson was born at Newburg, N. Y., in 1836, removed to Ohio in his childhood, to Kansas City in 1865, and to Leadville in 1878. *Business in Leadville*, MS., by Charles Mater, is a view of early mining, supplemented by the crowning fact that Leadville Iron and Silver Consolidated mines have yielded $30,000,000 annually ever since 1879, with many more general items of interest. Mater was born in Germany in 1835, and came to the U. S. in 1853, migrating to Colorado in 1869. *Notes on Colorado*, by William Gilpin, pp. 52, is a pamphlet descriptive and geological, issued in 1870. *Milwaukee Monthly Magazine*, June 1872, 203–10, descriptive. *San Juan and Other Sketches*, MS., is a compilation of historical articles, made for this work. *The Mines of Colorado*, by Samuel D. Silver, MS. deals with early times in California gulch, and the subsequent discoveries. Silver was born in Fort Wayne in 1840, and came to Colorado in 1872. *Karl's All the Year Round in the Recesses of the Rocky Mountains*, pp. 20, descriptive, illustrated.

Journalism in Colorado has always ranked high, many of the weekly and daily publications being of an order to do credit to cities much older than Denver. On the 23d of April, 1859, two newspapers were issued at Denver, then Auraria, the *Rocky Mountain News* and the *Cherry Creek Pioneer*. The latter was issued by John Merrick, on a cap-size lever press, and suspended after the first number. The *News*, which was owned by William N. Byers and Thomas Gibson, continued to appear weekly. In July 1859, Gibson sold to John L. Dailey, and he in 1870 to Byers, who conducted the business alone for 8 years, when he sold to K. G. Cooper and associates, who in two months sold to William A. H. Loveland and John Arkins, or the News Printing co. In politics the *News* was republican until it came under late management. The *Rocky Mountain Gold Reporter* was started in July 1859, at Central City, by Thomas Gibson, who published it about three months, when he returned to Nebraska. The press he used was that brought out by Merrick, and after his departure it was taken to Golden City, where it served the Boston co. to print the *Western Mountaineer*, which flourished for one year under the conduct of George West, the material and press being sold in Dec. 1860 to Mat. Riddlebarger, who took it to Cañon City. Early in the spring of 1860 H. E. Rounds and Edward Bliss came from Chicago with a newspaper outfit, which Byers & Dailey managed to consolidate with the *News*. In the mean time Gibson had returned to Denver with another press, and on the 1st of May, 1860, began the issue daily and weekly of the *Rocky Mountain Herald*, the first daily in the territory. The *News* soon followed with a daily edition, and also published the *Bulletin*, for circulation among immigrants, which was discontinued in a few months. The *News* and *Herald* were active rivals. Both maintained pony-express lines to the principal mining camps, delivering the daily in 3 or 4 hours—25 cents a copy, $24 a year. But this was not all the extra outlay required. There being no U. S. mail for nearly two years, the mails from the east came by express, at 10c. a newspaper and 25c. a letter, which, with the heavy freight and express charges on material, made newspaper publication not so profitable as it seemed. As soon as the telegraph was completed to Fort Kearny, the rival papers began taking despatches forwarded by express daily, and, when the news was important, by pony, at a heavy cost. After the destruction of the *News* office, in 1864, Byers & Dailey purchased the *Herald* to continue business. The publication of the *Herald* was resumed, in 1868, by O. J. Goldrick. Late in 1860 a third daily was started at Denver, called the *Mountaineer*, by Moore and Coleman. It was strongly confederate in sentiment, and was bought out and silenced by Byers & Dailey in the spring of 1861. During this year there were two ephemeral publications at Central City, the most notable of which was the *Mining Life*, by L. M. Amala, a native of the Sandwich islands. The little press which had done duty in Central and Golden was used in the winter of 1860–1 in starting the pioneer paper of southern Colorado, namely, the *Cañon City Times*, owned by H. S. Millett and Riddlebarger before mentioned. It ran but a few months, disappearing with the population, and following it into South park, where already there had been a paper, called the *Miners' Record*, started by Byers & Dailey, in July 1861, at Tarryall, which was discontinued after the political campaign of that year was over, in which it played an important part. During the summer a sheet called the *Colorado City Journal* was published in Colorado City, but printed in Denver, on the *Commonwealth* press, and partly made up from that paper. It was also a republican paper, edited by B. F. Crowell, and was discontinued when the campaign ended. In the spring of 1862 there was a newspaper published at Buckskin Joe, on the *Times* press, brought from Cañon City, which, like its predecessors, soon succumbed to changes in population and business. On the 26th of July, 1862, Alfred Thompson established the *Miners' Register* at Central City, a tri-weekly, printed on a Washington hand-press, and type brought from Glenwood, Iowa. David C. Collier soon became associated with the *Register* as editor, and was of eminent service to the territory in upholding the government during the rebellion. In April 1863 Collier, in company with Hugh Glenn and George A. Wells, purchased the paper. In May it was enlarged to a 24-column sheet, and in August was issued as a daily. In Sept. Glenn sold out to Collier & Wells, and in Nov. the *Register* appeared in new type, and commenced the regular publication of telegraphic news. The telegraph was completed at this interesting period of the war, and extras were issued as often as any important news was received. When the carriers appeared a shout was raised, and everyone hastened into the streets to learn and discuss the news. At the quartz-mills the sight of an extra-carrier was the signal to blow the whistles for leaving work until the despatches were read to the anxious men. Wells sold his interest in the paper to Frank Hall in Oct. 1865, the firm being now Collier & Hall. In July 1868 the name was changed to *Central City Register*. In 1873 Collier disposed of his interest to W. W. Whipple, Hall being editor. This partnership was not of long duration; Hall became sole proprietor, and on June 1, 1877, the whole establishment passed into the hands of James A. Smith and D. Marlow, who conducted it for 7 months, when they took in H. M. Rhodes as partner and editor. About this time, Feb. 1878, another paper, named *The Evening Call*, was started in Central, under the management of G. M. Laird and D. Marlow. In May this firm purchased the *Register*, consolidating it with the *Call*, under the name of *Register-Call*, and issuing a daily and weekly edition, John S. Dormer editor-in-chief, and J. P Waterman mining reporter. Throughout all its changes the *Register* has remained republican. In 1863 a paper was started at Black Hawk, called the *Colorado Miner*, by W. Train Muyr, which became during the year the *Black Hawk Journal*, with Hollister & Blakesley publishers, and afterward Hollister & Hall. In 1866 this establishment was moved to Central, and published as the *Times*, by Henry Garbanati and O. J. Goldrick. In politics it was democratic. Early in 1868 Thomas J. Campbell purchased it, and, changing the name to *Colorado Herald*, published a daily and weekly. In the latter part of 1870 it was sold to Frank Fossett, who managed it until it suspended altogether, in 1873. In Jan. 1866 the *Valmont Bulletin* was started on the same pioneer press which had made the circuit of Central, Golden, Cañon City, Tarryall, and Buckskin Joe, and been returned to its owners in Denver. The proprietors of the *Bulletin* were W H. Allen and D. G. Scouten. In April 1877 it was removed to Boulder, and published as the *Valley News*, by W. C. Chamberlain, for 1½ years. In the autumn of 1868 it became the *Boulder County Pioneer*, J. E. Wharton editor. Soon after the stockholders leased it to Robert H. Tilney, who changed the name to *The Boulder County News*. In 1870 the *News* passed into the hands of D. A. Robinson and D. G. Scouten. In May 1871 it was sold to Henry M. Cort. who sold it again, in Aug., to Wynkoop & Scouten; and before the year was out, Scouten and Joseph P. McIntosh owned it. In 1872 Wynkoop alone owned it. In 1874 it was sold to Amos Bixby and Eugene Wilder, who enlarged it to an 8-column journal. In 1878 Bixby sold his interest to William G. Shedd, proprietor of the *Sunshine Courier*, and the two papers were united, under the name of *News and Courier*, Shedd & Wilder proprietors, Thomas H. Evarts editor, assisted in 1879 by P. A. Leonard, and Charles Tucker. It was still a leading newspaper in 1886. The pioneer press, on which the *News* was started, was afterward taken to New Mexico, and used in issuing the first paper at Elizabethtown. The *Sunshine Courier* was started by J. B. Bruner and J. W. Cairns in May 1875. Cairns sold in 1877 to Hawkins; and in the same year Hawkins sold to William G. Shedd, who in 1878 purchased the whole, and removed it to Boulder, where it was consolidated with the *News*. In 1866 George West, who had been captain in the 2d Colorado volunteer infantry, returned to Golden, and established *The Transcript*, a democratic journal, still in existence in 1886, and with one exception the oldest established paper in Colorado. West was a printer by trade, and had owned, with others, a stereotype foundery in Boston before coming to Golden in 1859 with the Boston company. As a newspaper man he was always successful. The *Denver Tribune* was established in 1867 by H. Beckurts, and became one of the great dailies of the city, issuing also a weekly, and being in politics republican. On the 1st of May, 1868, the Georgetown *Colorado Miner* was first issued, by E. J. Wharton and A. W. Barnard. E. H. N. Patterson, who wrote over the signature of 'Sniktau,' was for a long time connected with this paper. He died in 1880. W. B. Vickers, another journalist, died the same year. The character of the *Miner* was always well sustained. On June 1, 1868, Pueblo was presented with the first issue of its first local newspaper, the *Colorado Chieftain*, by M. Beshoar and Samuel McBride, proprietors, and George A. Hinsdale and Wilbur F. Stone, editors. The paper was well printed and edited-At one time Beshoar was sole owner, and at another McBride owned the establishment. McBride finally sold to John J. Lambert, who continued to publish it. George S. Adams and E. G. Stroud were employed upon its editorial columns after Hinsdale and Stone. In 1872 a daily edition was issued, with C. J. Reed as editor. After Reed came A. P. George, R. M. Stevenson, C. Conover, G. Shober, and G. G. Withers. The second newspaper of Pueblo was published in 1871 by a stock company, with George A. Hinsdale editor. It was democratic in politics. About the same time the Caribou *Post* was published, Collier & Hall proprietors, and A. Bixby editor. The Greeley *Tribune* was first published in 1870 by N. C. Meeker; and the Greeley *Sun* in 1872, by H. A. French. Both were weekly. The *Golden Eagle*, John Sewell proprietor, a republican paper, was started 1871, and the following year merged in the *Golden Globe*, both of Golden City. In July 1871 the *Longmont Sentinel*, the first newspaper in this colony, was published by Lowe and Hall. It changed proprietors and name the following year, and became the *Longmont Press*, E. F. Beckwith editor and publisher, and F. C. Beckwith associate editor. F. C. Beckwith was born in N. H. in 1840. He received a good public school education, and came to Colorado at the age of 19 years. He mined and farmed, and was active in founding the town of Burlington, situated one half mile from the site of Longmont, which superseded it, and which he was instrumental in establishing at that place. The Denver *Daily* and *Weekly Times* was established in 1872 by Roger S. Woodbury; politics, republican. The Boulder *Rocky Mountain Eagle*, started in 1873 by William Morris, was sold to Wangelin & Tilney, who changed it to the *Colorado Banner*, a weekly. In 1880 Tilney became sole owner. In 1876 the Black Hawk *Post*, a democratic journal, was established by William McLaughlin and W. W. Sullivan. The latter sold his interest to James R. Oliver, and McLaughlin soon after died. It subsequently was owned by Oliver and Brandgust. In the same year the *Democrat* was started at Pueblo by A. Y. Hall. It was founded with the material used a year or two earlier to start the *Republican*, by J. M. Murphy, which was sold. Hall brothers were proprietors of the *Democrat* for a time, when they sold it to another Missourian, named Royal, who changed the name to the *Daily News*. In 1877 the Longmont Printing company issued the *Post*, edited by W. L. Condit. It was changed after a short time to the *Valley Home and Farm*, and managed by W. E. Pabor in the interest of agriculture, until it passed into the hands of a company, and was renamed the Longmont *Ledger*. On the 24th of May, 1877, the Georgetown *Courier* was first issued, J. S. Randall being proprietor and Samuel Cushan editor. The first newspaper at Del Norte, *The Prospector*, was issued in 1874 by Nicholas Lambert, brother of J. J. Lambert, who founded the Pueblo *Chieftain*. In 1875 M. R. Moore became proprietor. The *Cactus* and the *Democrat* appeared later at Del Norte, but were discontinued. The Silverton *Miner* was started in 1875 by John R. Curry of Iowa. M. R. Moore was editor in 1876. In 1875, also, the *Silver World* was first published at Lake City by H. M. Woods, who sold it in 1877 to H. C. Olney. Moore was editor in 1877-78. Woods started another paper in 1877 at Lake City, the *Crescent*, which ran only one year. The *Times* was the first paper in Ouray, founded by Ripley Brothers in 1877. The same year the *San Juan Sentinel* was started and discontinued. In 1879 the Ouray *Solid Muldoon* was established by David F. Day. It is the property of the Muldoon Publishing company. The same year the Cleora *Journal* was started by Dr S. C. McKeaney, but only ran 3 months. The *Mining Register* of Lake City was started in 1880 by J. F. Downey. The Salida *Mountain Mail* was founded by M. R. Moore in 1880, and sold in 1883 to W. W. Wallace. A great number of newspapers, corresponding to the growth of new towns or the resurrection of old ones, started up about this time. In 1880 the Telluride *Journal* was first issued. In the same year the Buena Vista *Miner* started, E. D. Hunt proprietor, who removed it to Maysville, and sold to J. S. Painter, the paper being discontinued in 1882. In 1881 the Maysville *Mining Ledger* commenced publication, J. H. Nomaker proprietor. The office was removed to Salida, and destroyed by fire in 1882. Mrs C. W. Romney established the first paper in Durango in 1880, soon after which the Durango *Herald* was published by Marsh Brothers. Tompkins Brothers issued a paper for a short time at Nathorp in 1880, which was suspended. About the same time the Dolores *News* was published by Frank Hartman; and the *Mountaineer*, at St Elmo, by Howard Russell; the *True Fissure*, at Alpine, which soon suspended; the *Chaffee County Times*, at Buena Vista, by P. A. Leonard; and the Buena Vista *Herald*, by A. R. Kennedy, who sold it in 1884 to A. R. Crawson. The Buena Vista *Democrat* was issued in 1882 by J. A. Cheeley, who transferred it to W. R. Logan. The Poncho Springs *Herald*, started by Tompkins Brothers in 1881, was discontinued in 1882. In 1882 the Salida *Sentinel* appeared, Petton & Brown owners. It was consolidated with the *Mountain Mail* in 1883. In that year the Salida *News* was published by W. B. McKinney. The Silverton *Democrat* was issned first in 1882. On the 18th of Feb., 1880, the *Boulder County Herald* was established, by Otto H. Wangelin. On the 17th of April it issued the first daily published in Boulder. The Denver *Republican*, a daily and weekly, was founded in 1879 by the Republican company. Later it was consolidated with the *Tribune* as the *Tribune-Republican*. A number of other journals belong to Denver—the *Colorado Journal*, a weekly, founded in 1872 by W. Witteborg; the *Colorado Farmer*, a weekly, founded in 1873 by J. S. Stanger; the *Presbyterian*, a monthly, founded in 1871 by S. Jackson; *The Financial Era*, a weekly, started in 1878 by F. C. Messenger & Co.; the *Colorado Post*, a weekly, issued by the *News* Printing company in 1879; *The Colorado Antelope*, a monthly journal devoted to 'woman's political equality and individuality,' published by Mrs C. M. Churchill, started in 1882; *Real Estate and Mining Review*, first published in 1873 by T. E. Picott; *Denver Opinion*, *Inter-Ocean*, *Great West*, and *Vidette*. A paper called the *Evans Journal* was started at Evans in 1871 by James Torrens, and one at Sterling at a later period. The Castle Rock *News Letter* was published in 1875 by C. E. Parkinson, and the Castle Rock *Journal* was issued about 1880. The Fort Collins *Express* was the first paper in Larimer county, and was founded by J. S. McClelland in 1873. The Fort Collins *Courier* was founded by Watrous and Pelton in 1878. W. E. Pabor started the *Colorado Grange*, an agricutural monthly journal, in 1876, at Longmont. The *Mentor* was issued at Monument in 1878 by A. T. Blachley. The Colorado Springs *Gazette* was established in 1873 by the Gazette Publishing Company. In the same year the *Mountaineer* was started by a printing company at the same place; and in 1875 the *Deaf and Mute Index*, by H. M. Harbert. More recent publications at Colorado Springs are the *State Republic* and the *Evening Times*. Pueblo and South Pueblo have added to the early El Paso county journals the *Banner*, by A. J. Patrick; the *Evening Star*, a daily, by Lacey & Westcott; *Saturday Opinion*, by J. A. Wayland; *Commercial Standard*, and *Colorado Methodist*. Bent county published first the *Leader*, in 1873, at West Las Animas, C. W. Bowman proprietor, and the *Tribune* at La Junta more recently. Custer county's first newspaper was the Rosita *Index*, started in 1875; and succeeded by the *Sierra Journal* at the same place; the Silver Cliff *Tribune;* the *Miner*, a daily and weekly, issued in 1878 by W. L. Stevens, and the *Prospector*, a daily, owned by McKinney and Lacey. Fremont county has the Cañon City *Record*, founded in 1875 by H. T. Blake; Cañon City *Mercury;* the Cañon City *Democrat;* the Cold Creek *Enterprise*, and *Cold Creek Hawkeye*. Las Animas county was first represented in 1875 by the Trinidad *Enterprise*, daily and weekly, by J. M. Rice, 1878, and by the *Review*, *Advertiser, and News*, the latter a daily and weekly, started by Henry Sturgis in 1878, all at Trinidad. Huerfano county had the La Veta *Quill*, and a newspaper at Walsenburg. Saguache county has the Saguache *Chronicle*, founded by W. B. Felton in 1874, the Saguache *Advance*, and the Bonanza *Enterprise*. La Plata county is represented by the *Southwest* at Animas City, started by Engly & Reid in 1879, and by the *Herald* and *Democrat* at Durango. Conejos county had the Alamosa *News*, started by M. Curtiss in 1878, the *Independent*, started the same year by Hamm & Finley, the *Gazette*, and later the *Democrat*. San Juan county added the Silverton *Herald*, and *Democrat*, established in 1882, to its Pioneer *Miner*. Hinsdale county had a second paper at Lake City, the *Mining Register*. Dolores county had but one journal, the Rico *News*. Ouray county gained the *Red Mountain Review*. Mesa county had the Grand Junction *News*, and Grand Junction *Democrat;* Montrose county the *Messenger*, and one other paper. Delta county had a paper of its own. In Pitkin county were the Aspen *Times* and *Sun*. Gunnison's first newspaper was the *Gunnison News*, started in April 1880. It was followed in May by the *Review*, both weekly journals. Soon the *News* suspended, but late in 1881 another weekly, the *Press*, was started. In the spring of 1882 the *Review* issued a daily, and soon the two papers consolidated and issued the daily *Review-Press*, Aug. 1st. The *News* was revived in the spring of 1882 as the *News-Democrat*. The *Mining Journal*, started in the autumn, suspended in 4 months. *The Sun*, started in the autumn of 1883, survived 10 months. The county still had left 7 newspapers, besides those in Gunnison City; namely, the *Elk Mountain Pilot*, at Irwin, established in 1880; the *Crested Butte Gazette*, established in 1880; *Pitkin Independent*, 1880; Pitkin *Mining News*, 1882; Tomichi, *Herald*, 1882; Tin Cup *Miner*, 1880; Tin Cup *Banner*, 1880, suspended in 1882; the *White Pine Cone*, 1883; and Gothic *Record*. In Summit co. were the *Breckenridge Leader*, *Breckenridge Journal*, and Dillon *Enterprise*. Park county published the Fair Play *Flume*, the Alma *Bulletin*, and the Como *Headlight;* Grand county, the Grand Lake *Enterprise*; Clear Creek county, in addition to its papers already named, the *Silver Flume* at Georgetown, and at Idaho Springs the *Advance*, the *Iris*, and *Gazette*. Boulder added to the *News-Courier* the *Herald*, a daily and weekly. Lake county, rich in journalism, had at Leadville the *Eclipse*, started by G. F. Wanless in 1878; the *Reveille*, founded by R. S. Allen the same year, daily and weekly; the *Leadville Chronicle*, a daily, founded Jan. 29, 1879, by Davis, Arkins, and Burnell; the *Herald*, a daily, started by R. G. Dill in Oct. 1879; the *Democrat*, a daily, founded Jan. 1, 1880, by a stock company. In Oct. 1883 C. C. Davis purchased the *Democrat*, and changed its politics, but not its name. The *Times*, an evening daily, was started in 1881 by a stock company. Four successive weeklies under the same name—the *Monday Morning News*—have come into existence, to perish at the end of a few weeks, except the last. The *Mining Index* also had a brief existence. The *Leaflet* also belonged to the ephemeral class of publications. The journals in existence in 1886 were the *Chronicle*, *Herald*, and *Democrat*, all republican in politics, although Lake county is democratic. The typographical, pictorial, and editorial features of these journals are worthy of notice. The *Chronicle-Annual* for Jan. 1882 is a complete representation of Leadville and the mining industry, and also the scenic attractions of the county, with historical and biographical sketches, presented in 42 quarto pages, in a handsome paper cover. The *Weekly Democrat* for Jan. 1, 1881, contains 20 six-column pages of matter concerning the mines of Lake county, with historical and other matter, and numerous wood-cuts illustrative of the wonderful growth of the then 4-year old city. The *Rocky Mountain News Illustrated Almanac*, 1882, is a highly creditable publication, containing, besides much information, illustrations of the natural history of the state, well executed. The Denver journals, and the numerous well-printed pamphlets on all sorts of subjects, exhibit the progress of the art preservative in Colorado.

In connection with the newspaper history of the country, L. R. Freeman should be mentioned. In 1850 he took the first printing press that crossed the Missouri river above St Louis to Fort Kearney, on the Platte. With the advance of the Pacific railroad, he pursued his way westward, publishing his paper, *The Frontier Index*, at Kearney, North Platte, Julesburg, Laramie, Bear River, and Ogden. In 1885 he was at Yakima, in Washington, working his way to Puget sound. No other newspaper in the United States has so varied a history as the *Index*.

Among the authorities drawn upon for the above history of Colorado journalism are *Pitkin's Political Views*, MS., and a dictation from Roger W. Woodbury of the *Denver Daily Times*. Woodbury was born in N. H. in 1834, and came to Colorado in 1866. After a few months in the mines he resumed his trade of compositor on the *Denver Tribune*, but was soon made local editor, and then managing editor and part owner. He sold his interest in 1871, and the following year established the *Daily Times*. He had $20,-000 when he started, but retained the sole ownership, and performed all the editorial work until 1883, when he sold it for $42,500. He was appointed brig.-gen. of the state militia in 1882, and served one term, and was president of the Denver chamber of commerce. *Byers' Newspaper Press of Colorado*, MS., is an invaluable authority from 1859 down. *Good Times in Gunnison*, MS., by A. B. Johnson, furnishes the history of flush times and early newspapers in that country. Johnson was born in Iowa in 1856, and graduated from Simpson university in 1880. He was principal of a graded school in Seward, Neb., for a year, and then came to Colorado. He was for a few months editor of the *Castle Rock Journal*, when he removed to Gunnison City to take charge of the *Daily Review Press* in the autumn of 1882. *M. R. Moore's Press and People of Colorado*, MS., is another excellent authority on newspaper matters, the author having been connected with half a dozen journals in the south and southwest portion of the state. Moore was born in Indiana in 1858, and came to Colorado in 1875. He belongs to the San Juan country. James F. Meagher, in his *Observations*, MS., on Colorado, also furnishes some newspaper information. He came to Colorado from New York city, where he was born in 1841, and drove a six-yoke team of oxen up the Platte in 1864. After residing in different parts of the state he settled in Salida.

Among other manuscript authorities is *Carlyle C. Davis' History of Colorado*. Davis was born at Glenn's Falls, N. Y., in 1846, and did not come to Colorado until 1878, since which time he has been connected with journalism in Leadville. *El Paso County, as It has been and Is*, MS., contains a selection of extracts from different journals on this subject, and incidentally on newspapers. *Byers' Centennial State*, MS., 40, has some information on the founding of county papers. So has *Eaton's Gunnison Yesterday and To-day*, MS., 6, and *Horn's Scientific Tour*, MS., 5. Different publications treating of journalism, to which reference has been made, are *Farrel's Colorado, the Rocky Mountain Gem*, 66, a pamphlet published in 1868 in Chicago by Ned. E. Farrell, containing an epitome of the territorial physical history and resources, good for the period: *Ingersoll's Knocking around the Rockies*, 10-11; *Pabor's Colo as an Agricultural State*, 783-7; *Balch's Mines and Miners*, 355; *Fossett's Colorado*, 158-9; *Denver Tribune*, July 15, 1880; *U. S. H. Misc. Doc.*, 47th cong. 2d sess., xiii. pt 8, pp. 209, 170-194; *Pettengill's Newspaper Directory*, 183-4; *Corbett's Legis. Manual*, 39-43.

CHAPTER X.

AGRICULTURE AND STOCK RAISING.

1861–1886.

Land Surveys—Analyses of Soils—Altitudes—Irrigation—Importance of the Subject—Convention—Laws and Regulations—A Most Perfect System—Ditching—Greeley and the Union Colony—Land-Investment, Canal, and Irrigating Companies—Grain-growing Districts—Products—Horticultural and Agricultural Societies —Granges—Failure of Coöperative Commerce—State Board of Agriculture — Agricultutal College — Stock-raising — Native Grasses—Incorporated Cattle Companies—Sheep and Horses.

Turning from metals and mines to the agricultural and other interests of Colorado, we will find fresh congratulations to offer the occupants of this favored land. I have already briefly touched upon the fact that in this portion of the elevated regions of the mid-continent, as in other portions which were wont to be represented by travellers as desert countries, experiment proved that moisture only was required to mantle the bare earth with bloom. Wherever that was present, or could be introduced by artificial means, farming was likely to prove remunerative. The survey of the public lands began in 1861,[1] the work being carried on first in the Platte valley, where the lands along the Cache-la-Poudre, Big Thompson, Little Thompson, St Vrain, Boulder, Ralston, Clear

[1] The first surveyor-general of Colorado was Francis M. Case, who was appointed soon after the establishment of the district of Colorado, April 5, 1861. The salary at that time was $3,000 a year; under the act of June 15, 1880, it was reduced to $2,500. *Balch's Mines, Miners, etc.*, 569; *Byers' Centennial State*, MS., 27; *U. S. Sen. Jour.*, 400, 37, 2; *U. S. Sen. Doc.*, i. no. 1, 616, 464–5, 37, 2. The office of the sur-gen. was opened June 17, 1861, the standard meridian passing through Pueblo, and about 18 miles east of Denver, and the base line being on the 40th parallel.

creek, Bear creek, and Cherry creek branches was
nearly all taken up in 1862, as well as that on the
Fontaine-qui-Bouille[2] branch of the Arkansas. The
first three years' experience taught the farmers to
depend upon artificial irrigation alone, for which
reason claims were nearly all bounded on one side by
a stream coming down from the highlands extending
some distance upon their margins to furnish the facilities for filling the necessary ditches with water. The
surveyor-general in 1866 estimated the quantity of
land under cultivation to be 100,000 acres, and that one
half the population of 35,000 were engaged directly
or directly in agricultural pursuits. He also estimated the area of arable land to be equal to 4,000,-
000 acres, and remarked that the immigration of
permanent well-to-do settlers kept the farming interest up to the wants of the population.[3] Of the condition of the farming interest at this period I have
spoken previously, stating that in 1866, for the first
time, the agricultural productions began to exceed
the wants of the population of Colorado, and to offer
a surplus in the markets of Montana, and at the government posts. In 1867 the surveyor-general, referring to his predecessor's views, gives it as his opinion
that there were 10,000,000 acres of cultivable land in
the territory,[4] showing how the idea grew of the
agricultural capabilities of the mountain region out of

[2] The report of the sur-gen. for 1862 speaks of the Huerfano and Arkansas
rivers as having the most extensive grain growing farms east of the mountains. On the Rio Grande also, and its tributaries, was a large population,
mostly Mexican, engaged in agricutural and pastoral pursuits. *U. S. H. Ex.
Doc.*, ii. no. i., p. 112, 37, 3. According to *Balch's Mines and Miners*, 570, a
local land-office was established at Golden City June 2, 1862, which was
removed to Denver; one at Denver Sept. 12, 1864; one at Fairplay Oct. 29,
1867, removed to Leadville July 1879; one at Central City Dec. 27, 1867; one
at Pueblo May 27, 1870; one at Del Norte June 20, 1874; and one at Lake
City May 5, 1877. According to *DeCoursey's Glenwood*, MS., 2, a land-office
was established at Glenwood in 1884. Durango has also a local land-office.
These several offices are made necessary by the patenting of mining claims
since the act of July 1866.

[3] Rept of John Pierce, in *U. S. Mess. and Doc.*, Int. Dept, 1866-7, 2, 39,
371.

[4] W. H. Lessig, in *Rept Sec. Int.*, 1867-8, iii. 40, 2. In the following year
he stated the 'common product' of wheat to be from 40 to 60 bushels per
acre.

which Colorado was created. The report of the land department in 1870 estimated the agricultural productions of Colorado at $3,500,000, while the bullion product was put down at $4,000,000. An abstract made in 1882 shows that in the ten previous years 2,501,318.35 acres had been purchased for cash or located with warrants,[5] besides the occupation of a large unknown quantity of unpurchased public lands by herdsmen.

The soil of Colorado varies with position. Its distinctive characteristics are the large proportion of potash, the form in which the phosphates exist, being easily soluble in a weak acid; the low percentage of organic matter and the high proportion of nitrogen contained in the organic matter ; the large proportion of lime, and the generally readily available form of all the constituents.[6] Climate is governed by altitude, and there are infinite modifications.[7] In the

[5] *U. S. H. Ex. Doc.*, xix. no. 72, p. 146, 47, 2.

[6] Upland clay loam contains: Volatile matter, 1.31; matter soluble in strong acid, 5 33; insoluble, 93.36. Adobe soil, volatile, 2.49; soluble matter, 11.40; insoluble, 86.11. Platte valley soil, volatile matter, 10.10; soluble, 2.58; insoluble, 87.32. Sandy clay loam, volatile matter, 4.23; soluble, 3.98; insoluble, 92.28. The volatile matter contains nitrogen; the soluble lime, magnesia, potash, iron-oxide, alumnia, carbon, phosphoric, acid, sulphuric acid, nitric acid, carbonic acid, chlorine, soda, etc. *Colorado Soils*, by T. Jamieson, Aberdeen, Scotland.

[7] William E. Pabor, associate editor of the *Colorado Farmer*, who has published a little book on *Colorado as an Agricultural State*, quotes from a statement concerning the soils of Utah, that they are not likely to be very different from those of Colorado, and then gives them in the following proportions: Black loam, 7,200, Sandy loam 3,800, loam and gravel 8,250, loam and clay 3,500, loam and alkali 1,200, clay and gravel 5,000, clay and plaster 3,500, alkali, iron, and sand 2,500, sand, alkali, and volcanic ash 1,000. p. 40. But this proportion is applicable only to the improved lands, and not to the whole area. The altitude of towns and cities in feet is as follows: Álamosa., 7,492; Alma, 10,254; Animas City, 6,622; Baker Mine, 11,956; Bakerville, 9,753; Black Hawk, 7,875; Boulder, 5,536; Breckenridge, 9,674; Cañon, 5,287; Caribou, 9,905; Central, 8,300; Colorado Springs, 6,023; Conejos, 7,880; Del Norte, 7,750; Denver, 5,197; El Moro, 5,886; Empire, 8,583; Evans, 4,745; Fairplay, 9,964; Fall River, 7,719; Fort Collins, 4,815; Fort Garland. 7,945; Fort Lupton, 5,027; Fort Lyon, 3,725; Frisco, 9,500; Georgetown, 8,514; Gold Hill, 8,463; Golden, 5,687; Granite, 8,883; Greeley, 4,779; Grenada, 3,434; Gunnison, 7,743; Hamilton, 9,743; Hermosillo, 4,723; Hot Sulphur Springs, 7,725; Howardville, 9,527; Idaho Springs, 7,512; Jamestown, 7,123; Jefferson, 9,862; Kit Carson, 4,307; Kokomo, 10,200; La Junta, 4,137; Lake City, 8,550; Las Animas, 3,952; Leadville, 10,247; Longmont, 4,957; Los Pinos, 9,065; Manitou, 6,297; Marshall, 5,578; Montezuma, 10,295; Nederland, 8,263; Nevadaville, 8,800; Oro, 10,704; Ouray, 7,640; Pagosa Springs, 7,108; Present Help Mine, on Mt Lincoln, 14,000; Platteville,

valley of the Platte the soil is identical with that of the river-bottoms of the Missouri, while the uplands have a rich, warm, sandy loam. The southern valleys are more sandy, and, of course, warmer at the same elevation than the northern. The river-bottoms yield bountiful crops without irrigation, and the uplands even more abundantly with it. In a general sense agriculture in Colorado depends upon a judicious use of water supplied to the thirsty earth by artificial means; and of irrigation I will give some account in this place. As early as 1861 the legislature passed an act providing for the free use of the water of any stream on the margin of a land claim; or if not situated upon any stream, for the right of way of a ditch through the land lying between it and the nearest water. The ditch should not be larger than necessary, nor should there be any waste of water;[8] and where the stream was not large enough to supply the continuous wants of the entire country dependent upon it, a justice of the peace should appoint commissioners to apportion the water equitably, to settle disputes, and assess damages where they were shown to occur. The right to use a water-wheel or other machinery for raising water to a required level was granted by law, and other privileges and restrictions enacted.[9] This law was amended from time to time as a knowledge of the wants of the agriculturalists suggested, and in 1872 irrigating ditches were exempted from taxation. In 1876 a

5,690; North Pueblo, 4,713; South Pueblo, 4,676; Quartz Hill, 9,300; Rollinsville, 8,323; Rosita, 8,500; Saguache, 7,723; Saint John, 10,807; Salt Works in South Park, 8,917; Silverton, 9,400; Steven's Mine, 11,943; Terrible Mine, 9,243; Trinidad, 6,032; Uncompahgre Agency, 6,400; White River Agency, 6,491. From this list it will be seen that only two towns are under 4,000 feet in altitude; 9 are over 4,000; 7 are over 5,000; 6 are over 6,000; 12 are over 7,000; 11 are over 8,000; 8 are over 9,000; 7 are over 10,000; 2 are over 11,000, and 1, 14,000. *Fossett's Colorado*, 14–15. It is needless to remark that only mining towns exist at an altitude above 7,500 feet.

[8] Meline remarks in 1866, in *Two Thousand Miles on Horseback*, 88, that the ditches were dug too deep, at too great an incline, creating a current which washed out and deepened the water-way, and that there was consequently a waste of water. Probably experience taught the owners to avoid these errors.

[9] *Session Laws*, 1861, 67–9.

law was placed on the statute book forbidding any person in the summer season to run through an irrigating canal any greater quantity of water than absolutely needful for domestic purposes, the watering of stock, and moistening his land.[10] Other matters, such as priority of right and association for purposes of irrigation, came up and were discussed and settled by statutes from time to time, the importance of the equal distribution of water growing more and more apparent. And not only as relating to lands usually regarded as cultivable, but as applied to a large extent of country known as arid lands, which down to a recent period had been looked upon as worthless.

This subject had engaged the attention of thinking men in Colorado, who believed that the whole or much of the great wastes in the several states and territories west of the Missouri not sufficiently watered by rainfall might be redeemed by an interstate system of irrigation, and for the purpose of discussing and bringing the subject before the people a convention of trans-Missouri states was held at Denver October 15, 1873,[11] at which was agitated the question of the interest of the general government in assisting to recover from sterility so great a portion of the public domain. Little resulted from the convention, except the enlargement of men's ideas in the direction of scientific agriculture.[12]

In 1879 the department of agriculture appointed a commissioner, J. Brisbin Walker, to visit Colorado to take observations of the country preliminary to making a practical test of the value of artesian wells in furnishing water for irrigation.[13] Government, how-

[10] *Colo Gen. Laws*, 1877, 518; *Dow's Tour in America*, 103-14.

[11] The convention was addressed by Gov. Elbert, through whose efforts chiefly it was brought together. See *Speech of Elbert before the Convention of Trans-Missouri States*, 4-8.

[12] *Report on the Problems of Irrigation*, by William Ham Hall, state engineer of California, dealing with the social, political, and legal questions; the physical, practical, and technical obstacles to be overcome, with the construction, operation, and maintenance of irrigation works, is a most important publication exhaustive of a subject still comparatively novel in the United States.

[13] *Denver Tribune*, Nov. 13 and 22, 1879.

ever, has been anticipated in the application of acquired information by enterprising companies, which are rapidly redeeming arid lands, and filling their coffers at the same time.

The first canals were constructed in Weld county, one at Greeley by the Union colony,[14] and another at Evans, both taking water from the south Platte, and conducting it for six or eight miles among farms.

In 1877 English capitalists organized the Colorado Mortgage and Investment company, which, among other things, became interested in irrigation, organizing a subordinate branch at Fort Collins under the name of Larimer and Weld Irrigation company, which purchased water rights, and as much land as could be obtained, and constructed a canal over fifty miles in length. This proved a profitable investment. Water rights were sold for $2, and later for $1.50, an acre ; and the land, obtained at government or railroad prices, brought from $13 to $15 per acre, with a perpetual water right. The High Line Irrigating

---

[14] This canal, Hayden remarks, has too great a fall, the current being so strong that it is with difficulty forded by teams. The Union colony was organized in New York on the 23d of Dec. 1869, with 59 members, to which many others were soon added. It was a direct outgrowth of the advertising which the *N. Y. Tribune* gave Colorado. Horace Greeley was its prime mover and treasurer, and one of its most active agents was N. C. Meeker, also of the *Tribune*. It sent out a locating committee, consisting of Meeker, H. T. West, and R. A. Cameron, who, after looking over the ground, determined upon the present site of Greeley, in Weld county. They purchased 12,000 acres from the Denver Pacific Railway co. and others, and made arrangements for the purchase of 60,000 acres of government and 50,000 acres railroad land within three years, at from $3 to $4 per acre, by paying interest from the date of contract. Charters were obtained for irrigating-canals covering the entire area. A town was laid off at the delta formed by the Cache-la-Poudre and Platte rivers, on the line of the Denver Pacific R. R., and subdivided into 520 business lots, 25 x 190 feet in size; 673 residence lots, ranging from 50 by 190 to 200 by 190; and 277 lots reserved for public buildings, schools, churches, etc. The adjacent lands were divided into plats of from 5 to 120 acres, according to the distance from the town centre, and each member allowed to select one, under his certificate of membership. A public square of 10 acres was reserved in the middle of the town, artificial lakes constructed, trees planted, and by June 1870 water was flowing through all the principal streets from a canal fed by the river. In 1871 the colony contained 350 buildings of all descriptions, 17 stores, 3 lumber-yards, 3 blacksmith and wagon shops, a newspaper office, and livery-stable. The colony was not coöperative, beyond a general irrigating, fencing, and public-buildings fund or funds. *Byers' Centennial State*, MS., 39–40; *Saunders' Through the Light Continent*, 51–3, London, 1879, 8vo, 409 p.

canal of the Platte Land company, another foreign
organization's work, is a still longer and larger canal
to irrigate the high plains east, south-east, and north-
east of Denver, by making a wide detour, in some
places constructing tunnels, and in others flumes. The
cost in 1884 had reached two and a half million dollars. It is thirty-six feet wide on the bottom, and
seven feet deep for the first thirty miles, after which
it gradually narrows and shallows. It is intended to
water 300 square miles of territory. The Northern
Colorado Irrigation company, which, at an enormous
outlay, constructed eighty miles of a main line of
canal, and as much more of lateral branches, completed its work in 1883 ; and immediately commenced
another seventy miles in length and sixty feet in
width at the bottom, extending from about Pueblo to
La Junta, in the neighboring county of Bent, and
taking water from the Arkansas river. Still another
corporation is the San Luis Park Irrigating company
of New England capitalists whose canals will irrigate
500,000 acres.[15] The Larimer and Weld company
are also constructing a dam on the north Poudre,
which will supply water to land a thousand feet higher
than the valley of the stream. Obviously so extensive a system of irrigation, involving such expendi-
ture, and affecting so many rights and interests, must
become the subject of even more careful legislation
in the future than in the past.[16]

The undulations of the plains in Colorado make
irrigation and cultivation easy. The water supplied
at the upper side of the land is caused to flow gently
from a trench or furrow, in which frequent breaks are

[15] It is estimated that 65,000 gallons annually are required to properly
irrigate one acre. *Descriptive America*, May 1884, p. 6. It is also ascertained
that land which has once been thoroughly soaked, except where very porous
and gravelly, requires less water than at first, and often becomes so wet as
to require drainage.

[16] I find in *Dow's Tour in America*, Melbourne, 1884, p. 113, some suggestions on this subject. He remarks that, 'For want of such laws the progress
of irrigation in California is seriously impeded.' Dow's book is a sensible
record of observations on the agriculture and resources of the U. S., neither
fulsome nor grudging. He was a special commissioner of the *Australasian*

made in the lower rim, slowly moistening the surface
of a field, which in two or three days is ready for the
plough. Cereals require to be watered only once or
twice in a season. Much has been said about the
amount of irrigable land in Colorado, which has been
estimated from 1,250,000 to 3,000,000 acres, of which
in 1882 only about 100,000 acres were in use.[17]   In
1889 it was estimated that there were at least 6,000
miles of main irrigating canals, with lateral branches
of much greater length.

The principal grain-producing counties of Colorado
at the present are five, Arapahoe, Boulder, Jefferson,
Larimer, and Weld, although with the progress of
canals it is not safe to claim priority for any. Doubtless by the time my pages are in print some of the
southern counties will have become powerful rivals of
the northern belt. But as I prefer to keep to the
records of the state agriculturists for statements here
given, what is unknown is left to conjecture. The
five counties here mentioned produced in 1881, 980,-
000 bushels of wheat, and 66,000 bushels of corn. In
1882 four of the same counties produced 1,158,820
bushels of wheat, and 186,000 bushes of corn. The
crops of barley, oats, potatoes, hay, alfalfa, and vegetables were in proportion. The value of the yield of
five counties in 1881 was $1,771,750; of four counties
in 1882 it was $3,047,750. The increase is without
question due to the greater facilities for irrigation,
which in 1883 had more than doubled the cultivable
area of 1882.[18]   The total value of all the crops of the
state in 1882 was $8,947,500.

[17] Pabor, in *Colorado as an Agricultural State*, 58, after 12 years of personal observation, publishes answers to the question, Is Colorado an agricultural state? in the affirmative, describing the various farming localities, and
giving facts regarding the culture of grains, fruits, and vegetables, with an
account of irrigation, its expense to the individual, etc.
[18] I have the *Agricultural Statistics of the State of Colorado*, pp. 16, for 1883,
before me, a pamphlet issued by the state board of agriculture. From its
tabulated report I gather that the amount of land in the whole state under
irrigation in 1883 was 416,594 acres; the number of acres in pasture, 1,367,-
255; in oats, 33,684 acres, yielding 925,029 bushels; in barley, 6,179 acres,
yielding 112,761 bushels; in rye, 1,628 acres, yielding 20,343 bushels; in corn,

The natural fruits of a country cannot be relied upon as indications of what the land will produce under cultivation. Colorado presented to the first explorers only a worthless thorn-apple; a rare but pleasant flavored plum; small, acid gooseberries, of little value; a cherry which was rather palatable; currants of black, yellow, and red varieties; with raspberries, strawberries, and whortleberries in great abundance Apples, pears, peaches, and grapes were raised in the gardens of the Mexican inhabitants of San Luis park before the settlement by Americans from the United States These fruits first appeared among the farmers on the Arkansas Strawberries began to be cultivated in 1865. The following year they brought $3 per quart. About the same time apples, pears, and peaches were being raised from seed in the Platte valley, and grew thriftily at first, but died afterwards because their roots had penetrated below the soil to gravel and sand. Small fruits were then set out, and flourished [19] where the soil was moist at certain seasons of the year. Experience showed that where trees were irrigated in the autumn they were able to resist winter killing, which was caused not by cold, but by the drying up of the wood by the sunshine of the winter season. Upon making this discovery, about 1873, fruit trees began again to be planted, since which time there has been a steady improvement in horticulture.[20] Among the first horticulturalists were Joseph Wolff of Boulder, whose first orchard of three hundred trees was killed; J W. Parker of the Cache-la-Poudre valley, J. S. Flory of St Vrain valley, Anson Rudd, and W. A. Helm of

21,763 acres, yielding 356,478 bushels; in buckwheat, 7, yielding 154 bushels; in wheat, 67,342 acres, yielding 1,419,443 bushels. A few acres of sorghum were grown in 1873 in Boulder, Bent, Delta, Fremont, Larimer, Montrose, Pueblo, and Weld counties, aggregating 67 acres, and yielding 2,366 gallons of syrup. *Graybeard's Colorado*, 55–7; *Galveston News*, Dec. 1, 1874, p. 3; *Los Angeles Evening Express*, Aug 4, 1884.

[19] *Hollister's Mines of Colorado*, 424–5; *Denver Mountain Herald*, July 2, 1869.

[20] *Byers' Ceutennial State*, MS., 35.

Cañon City, and Jesse Frazier, ten miles east of Cañon, in the Arkansas valley. The state organized a horticultural society, of which D. S. Grimes was made president, and the legislature of 1883 passed an act to "encourage horticulture and forestry in Colorado, and to establish a state bureau of horticulture,"[21] appropriating $1,000 annually toward its support. The amount of land in orchards in 1882 was given in at 2,500 acres, and the value of the fruit at $1,250,000. An agricultural society was organized in 1863, and in 1864 a charter was obtained from the legislature, with an appropriation of $500 to be expended in prizes, the society assuming the burden of erecting the buildings and purchasing the land for a fair ground.[22] Granges were established in 1874 throughout the agricultural portions of the territory, the movement being for some time a popular one, each grange having its hall for holding meetings. In Denver the granges had a commercial establishment and a flouring mill on the principle of coöperative societies, but they failed for want of cohesiveness.

In 1877 the State Board of Agriculture was established, and at the same session an act was passed to provide for the building and maintenance of the agricultural college of Colorado, the real property of which was vested in the above board, which was given control of the college and farm, and of all appropriations for the support of the institution; the college to be built and maintained by a direct tax of one tenth of one mill on every dollar of real and personal property in the state.[23] The college was located at Fort Collins, in Larimer county, and was opened in 1879. Scholarship was made free with certain limi-

[21] Colo Session Laws, 1883, 210. For statistics I have consulted Pabor's book, Rept of State Geologist, 1881-2, and Rept of the State Board of Agriculture, 1883.

[22] The incorporators were J. B. Doyle, R. Stubbs, S. Cort, Lewis Jones, H. E. Esterday, A. O. Patterson, David Gregory, R. Sopris, W. N. Byers, Thomas Gibson, F. H. Judd, J. H. Eames, Celeden Valdez and V. Wellman. Colo Session Laws, 1864, 221; Sopris' Settlement of Denver, MS., 13.

[23] For the acts governing these boards, see Colo Gen. Laws, 1877, pp. 88-90, 97-106; Colo Session Laws, 1879, 6-7.

tations as to age and previous requirements. Graduation confers the degree of bachelor of science. Institutes are held during the winter at different points for the benefit of farmers in the vicinity, at which valuable papers are read by the faculty, who having experimented on the college farm are able to impart the result of their investigation, to those who have less time, knowledge, and facilities for experimental work.[24]

Reports are annually published by the state board of agriculture, which, with the several agricultural journals of the state, place Colorado upon an equality with the older agricultural communities in point of progressive farming.

Stock raising in Colorado has attained an importance second only to mining, the estimated total value of its cattle, sheep, and other animals in 1884 being $25,090,000. I have given so particular an account of cattle raising as an industry in my *History of Montana* that it is not necessary to repeat it here, the customs and laws to which the keeping of large herds has given rise being substantially the same in both countries. The discovery of the nutritive quality of the grasses of the Platte valley was made as early as 1858, when A. J. Williams, who was among its pioneers, not having any food for his eighteen oxen during the winter, turned them out upon an island in the Platte near old Fort Lupton to take their chances of living, or of dying by starvation. To his surprise, on visiting the island in the spring of 1859, he found them alive, sleek, and fat. But in 1847 St Vrain and Bent had driven several thousand cattle from Texas and New Mexico to the Arkansas valley, and wintered them near Bent's fort. Subsequently Maxwell and others established cattle ranchos on the streams lead-

---

[24] The faculty consisted in 1885 of C. L. Ingersoll, president, prof. logic and pol. economy; A. E. Blount, prof. ag. and botany; Charles F. Davis, B. S., prof. chem. and physics; F. H. Williams, prof. pract. mech. and drawing. *Pabor, Colo as an Agricultural State*, 182.

ing out of the Sierra Mojada, at the foot of the Hua-
jatollas, and on the upper Las Animas. Around
Cañon City stock raising was begun, in a small way,
about 1862-3. Beckwith brought the first large herd
into Wet Mountain valley from Texas in 1872. Two
herds were driven across the divide between the
Arkansas and South Platte before 1866, when Williams, who had not lost sight of the subject, brought
1.500 Mexican cattle into Platte valley, since which
time the importation has never ceased,[25] although for
a number of years the business was conducted on a
small scale, compared with latter investments.[26]

The principal grasses on which cattle fatten are the
gramma and bunch species, the former having a small
seed growing on one side at a right angle to the stalk.

[25] I find this statement in an extract from *Out West*, Sept. 1873, in *The
Discoverer of Pike's Peak*, MS. It agrees with the statement in Williams'
biography, in *Hist. Denver*, 627-9. Sopris mentions as the first importers of
cattle from Texas John W. Allen, and Reed, whose first name seems to have
been Allen. The former died at Denver in 1881, and the latter returned to
Lexington, Mo., in 1876. Thomas W., William, Andrew Wilson, and John
Hitson were among the first to avail themselves of the opportunity offered
to make money by raising cattle. *Settlement of Denver*, MS., 16. Byers mentions J. W. lliff. *Hist. Colo*, MS., 42. Later stock-men were H. S. Holly &
Co., Jones Brothers, Beatty Brothers, Lane & Murray, Towers & Gudgell,
Downen Brothers, H. B. Carter, R. M. Moore, and others.

[26] According to Wolfe Londoner, Texas cattle were imported for beef only,
and fattened on the grass of the plains. *Colorado Mining Camps*, MS., 10.
This dictation consists of fifteen pages of type-writing, equal to 30 pages of
this volume. Londoner was born in New York in 1835, came to Cal. in 1850,
a boy in a sailing vessel, and went to washing dishes for $50 per month.
After a time the auctioneer, Jessell, gave him employment at $150 a month.
Returning home in 1855, he was sent to Dubuque, Ia, to take charge of two
stores owned by his father. When the panic of 1857 came on there was a failure for the Londoners, who removed to St Louis. In the course of events Wolfe
found employment with A. Hanauer, later of Salt Lake, and Dold, who sent
him, in 1860, to Colorado to erect a business-house in Denver, and afterward
in Cañon City, where they put him in charge of $50,000 worth of goods, and
the finest stone building in the territory. The Baker exploring party for San
Juan outfitted at this store. When business declined in Cañon City, Londoner was sent to California gulch, then in the height of its prosperity, and
when that camp was deserted, in 1866. he went to Denver. Being now possessed of means of his own, Londoner engaged in merchandising with his
brother, and made money. until in 1884 his sales amounted to $1,000,000
annually. He was elected county commissioner and chairman of the committee on finance, which devolved upon him the building of the Denver court-
house, which cost $300,000, the land on which it stands being worth $75,000
more. The building and furniture are the pride of Denver, and for the manner in which Londoner discharged his trust, the board, when he left it, 'drew
up a resolution which was good enough to put on my grave when I die,' says
the recipient of the testimonial.

When not irrigated, it is only a few inches high, but grows to two feet in height when furnished with water, and is better feed than any native grass known. This grows near the mountains, buffalo grass on the plains, and bunch grass on the mountain sides. Besides these three there were exhibited at the exposition in Denver, in 1884, over a hundred varieties of native grasses, all having a seed on the side, except the bunch grasses.[27] Cattle so well fed will live a week with nothing to eat, and a snowfall seldom lasts a longer time. Should the snow remain, the cattle stampede to the Arkansas valley; so that, with the advantages of the climate and the sagacity of the animals, the owners sustain few losses. Still, prudence will more and more dictate the saving of hay for winter feeding.

With the growth of the business of cattle-raising there came the formation of incorporated companies, and legislative enactments. Among other laws which concern the branding, herding, protection from disease, and other necessary regulations, is a statute authorizing a commissioner to attend the annual round-ups, and to seize and sell all unbranded cattle for the benefit of the common school fund.[28] A state board of inspectors exists by law. The objectionable feature of the stock business would seem to be the absolute control of immense tracts of country, with the springs and streams, by companies or individuals, as for example, the possession of many thousands of acres of rich bottom land, and forty miles of water front on the Arkansas river, by one man, J. W. Prowers. The Prairie Cattle company have over $3,000,000 invested in cattle, and control many miles of water front, and hundreds of thousands of acres of fenced pasture, in Bent county. In northern Colorado the stock companies are chiefly in Weld and Arapahoe counties; south of the divide they are for

[27] *Stone's General View*, MS., 9–10; *Hollister's Mines of Colorado*, 426-9.
[28] *Roller's Colorado Sketches*, MS., 3; *Farrel's Colo as It is*, 53-5.

the most part in Bent, Las Animas, Elbert, and
Pueblo. There are two stock associations, one at Denver [29] and the other at Pueblo. Each holds an annual
meeting [30] for the discussion of subjects connected
with its interests. [31] The Colorado Cattle company
secured 81,000 acres near Pueblo, under patent from
the government, [32] and individual owners control other
large tracts in this portion of the state, requiring a
separate organization. The whole number of cattle
in Colorado in the spring of 1884 was given at 1,005,-
000. [33] The number of sheep in the state, in May of
that year, was put down at 1,497,000. Shepherding
has made rapid advancement since 1871, about which
time sheep began to be imported in considerable num-

[29] Joseph L. Bailey was an active organizer of the Colorado Cattle-growers'
association, with headquarters at Denver, and for two years its president.
He was from Pa, and arrived at Cherry creek in June 1859. He made some
money working for the Pike's Peak Express co., with which, and with credit,
he started in a meat market, clearing, with his partner, over $30,000 in 18
months. There being no banks in the country, the money was deposited in
the earth under their shop, and was stolen by their book-keeper, leaving
them bankrupt. Bailey then took offices under the Denver city government
as street commissioner and marshal; and was deputy provost-marshal under
Wanless, and deputy U. S. marshal under A. C. Hunt. He was also in the
secret service of the treasury department, to hunt out the counterfeiters
which infested the territory for a time. He was deputy sheriff under Sopris,
Kent, Wilson, and Cook for a number of years, and was twice chosen a
member of the city council. The fire department of Denver owes much to
his exertions during two years while he was chief. He organized the Fire
men's Officers' association, to consult upon matters pertaining to the department. In 1865 he established Bull's Head corral, the rendezvous of the
leading stock men of the western states.

[30] The pres. of the northern association in 1883 was Jacob Scherrer; vice-
pres., J. F. Brown; sec., L. R. Tucker; treas., J. A. Cooper; ex. committee,
R. G. Webster, W. H. H. Cranmer, Joseph W. Bowles, H. H. Metcalf, J.
W. Snyder; state inspection commissioners, J. W. Prowers of Bent co., J. L.
Brush of Weld, Nelson Hallock of Lake, L. R. Tucker of Elbert, and George
W. Thompson, Jr, of La Plata. *Colo Stock Laws*, 3, a compilation according
to act of the legislative assembly of 1883 of all the acts relating to stock, is
a good authority on stock matters.

[31] *Life on a Ranch*, by R. Aldridge, contains an account of cattle-raising
in Colorado, Kansas, and Texas. Hall's *Annual Rept Chamb. Com.* contains
statistics, 133–6. E. P. Tenney's *Colo, and Homes in the New West*, 16–19,
gives a condensed account of the grazing interest; also Hayden, *Great West*,
134–8, and *The Grazing Interest and the Beef Supply*, by A. T. Babbitt, MS.,
11, a dictation from the manager of the Standard Cattle company of Wyoming.

[32] *Helena Independent*, Aug. 14, 1879.

[33] These figures are taken from a list of county productions in *Descriptive
America*, May 4, 1884, p. 26; but a circular on *Live-stock Movement*, issued in
1884, by Wood brothers of Chicago places the production of Colorado at
991,700 cattle, and 1,260,000 sheep.

bers. There was at first active hostility between the owners of neat cattle and the sheep graziers, because the pastures overrun by sheep were practically destroyed for cattle. In the autumn of 1873 the owners of flocks in Huerfano county complained to the governor that parties had been attacked and killed, or their animals scattered, with the avowed purpose of driving this kind of stock out of the country. But the legislature interposed with laws for the protection of all stock-owners equally, and sheep raising is now the third industry in the state, if it is separated from cattle raising on one side, and agriculture on the other. One-year-old lambs average four pounds, ewes five or six, and rams twelve to fifteen pounds of wool. The yearly clip exceeds 7,000,000 pounds, having a value of $1,500,000. The flocks consist mainly of Mexican sheep, improved by the introduction of thoroughbred Merino rams. Money invested in sheep by care and good fortune could be doubled in three years ; but as snow storms and late, cold, spring rains have more power to harm sheep than other stock, some allowance is made, in calculating profits, for these contingencies.[34] Alfalfa ,as it was found to be superior feed for sheep, as well as all kinds of stock, began to be cultivated in the agricultural counties with success, although it was found difficult of introduction without irrigation. Horses were longer in becoming so much objects of the stockmen's care as in Nevada and Montana, requiring, as they do, more attention than cattle, besides being more expensive. In the whole state there were in 1886 about 100,000 horses and mules, and 25,000 other kinds of stock, comprising swine, and cashmere, angora, and common goats.

[34] Pabor, *Colo as an Agricultural State*, 193–201; *Harper's Mag.*, 193–210, Jan. 1880; Denver *Rocky Mountain News*, Nov. 29, 1870; *Colorado Condensed*, 42; *Denver Tribune*, Oct. 10, 1884; *Proceedings 1st Nat. Conv. Cattle-men*, 12–13; *Tenth Census*, vol. 3, 144; *Gunnison Sun*, Jan. 5, 1884.

CHAPTER XI.

Survey—Denver Lands—Municipal Organization—The Question of Capital—Post-office and Assay Office—Railways—Telegraphs—Street Railways—Public Buildings—Schools and Churches—Style of Architecture—Water System and Drainage—Manufactures—Smelters—Chamber of Commerce—Exposition Grounds and Buildings—Banking—Society and Culture—Biography.

Considering the resources of the state to be first mining, second stock-raising, and third agriculture, a brief history of each of the counties will afford an opportunity to speak of manufactures where they occur, and of mineral resources not yet noted.

Arapahoe, first alphabetically, as well as in point of time, had an irregular existence before the organization of the territory of Colorado, as the reader will remember. In 1861 its boundaries were defined by survey, its area being 4,860 square miles in the form of a parallelogram. The first gold discovery was made in the western end of the country, but these placers were soon exhausted and no new ones discovered. The county was treeless and arid except immediately upon the streams, of which it had a good number, and its prospects in 1866, viewed from almost any standpoint, were not flattering. Two things have redeemed Arapahoe from poverty, first the prosperity of Denver as the metropolis, and later the redemption of its arid lands by irrigation, of which I have already spoken   The value of its live stock in 1884 was $1,540,000. Of its agricultural productions in the past there is no record, but that there will be none in the future the increasing area of irrigated land renders improbable.

Denver, the county seat, has had its beginnings narrated. It was incorporated first by the provisional legislature, and organized a city government December 19, 1859, by the election of John C. Moore, mayor. The government was not, however, strong enough to prevent a conflict of lot owners and lot jumpers the following summer, which had nearly terminated in bloodshed, the secretary of the town company, Whitsitt, and others narrowly escaping being shot by the irate squatters. A committee of citizens maintained order until congress, in May 1864, passed an act for their relief, by extending to Denver the operation of the act of May 23, 1844, and authorizing the probate judge of Arapahoe county to enter at the minimum price, in trust for the righful occupants according to their respective interests, section 33, and the west half of section 34, in township 3, south of range 68, west of the 6th principal meridian, reserving only such blocks and lots for government purposes as the commissioner of the general land office should designate.[1] Thus was the question of titles settled. In the meantime there had been a change of government, and Denver was re-incorporated under the laws of the first territorial legislature, November 7, 1861. The first mayor was Charles A. Cook, the first board of alderman H. J. Brendlinger, John A. Nye, L. Mayer, W. W. Barlow, J. E. Vawter, and L. Buttrick. P. P. Wilcox was police magistrate, W. M. Keith city marshal, J. Bright Smith city clerk and attorney, E. D. Boyd city surveyor, George W. Brown treasurer and collector.[2] D. D. Palmer street commissioner, and George E. Thornton chief of police.[3]

---

[1] *Cong. Globe*, 1863–4, app. 168; *U. S. Mess. and Doc.*, 1856–66, 251–2.

[2] Brown resigned in Dec., and Joseph B. Cass was elected.

[3] *The Charter and Ordinances of the City of Denver*, with amendments from 1861 to 1875, compiled by Alfred C. Phelps, Denver, 1878, contains the names

The city authorities had for a few years the same trouble with the outlaw class which every border town of any magnitude has had, in which the ordinary course of justice was sometimes accelerated by the vigilants of society. It suffered by flood and fire, as I have before mentioned[4] in its early history.

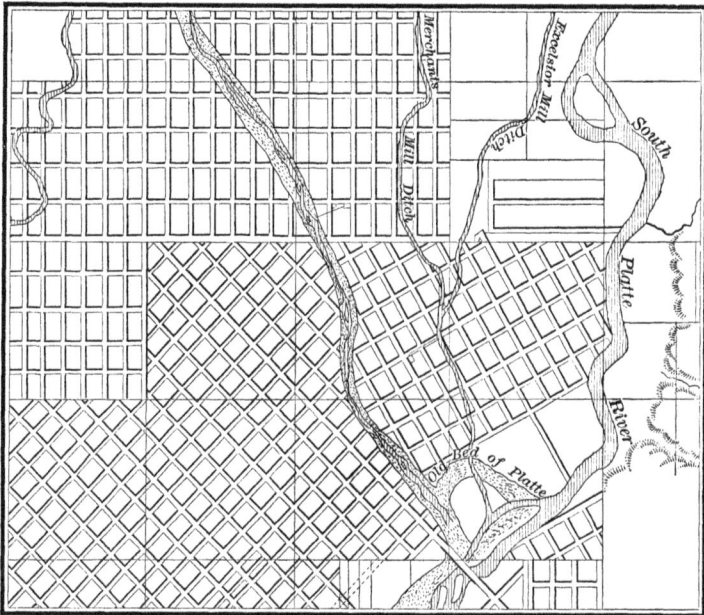

PLAN OF DENVER, 1862.

It was a question with the early settlers of Colorado whether Denver or Cañon City should be the metropolis of the country. All depended upon the route taken by the principal part of the immigration

of the several boards of city officers during that period, for which I have not room. The town site of Denver absorbed Auraria, and touched upon the site of Highland, later North Denver.

[4] The fire broke out April 19, 1863, between 2 and 3 o'clock in the morning. In spite of great exertions, the business portion of the city was almost entirely destroyed in a few hours. Many who lost everything at that time were later among the solid men of Denver; but many more never recovered from the disaster.

and freight. In 1859–60 the Platte and Arkansas routes divided the travel. Denver was south of the travelled route to Utah, Nevada, and California, and was supposed by its rival to be almost hopelessly isolated. But fortune, in collusion with the stage company, settled that matter. The Pike's peak company having removed its line from the Smoky Hill fork of Kansas river, which line terminated at Denver by the route since followed by the Kansas Pacific railway to the Platte route, was itself no longer on the main line, but was forced to accept a branch from Julesburg, where the overland mail crossed the north side of the Platte. The distance saved in the length of the line to San Francisco by adopting the northern route was 600 miles. The men of Denver used their influence to procure a survey of a direct route from their city to Salt Lake, and in 1861 E. L. Berthoud was employed by W. H. Russell and Ben Holladay, interested in transportation, to examine the country west of Denver for such a route. The survey demonstrated that a road could be laid down White river and other streams which would shorten the distance from the Missouri to the Pacific 250 miles. But the Platte or old immigrant route continued to be used until the railroad era succeeded to stage lines, and Denver, although left aside, was still nearer to the trans-continental artery than any other town in Colorado, and with that advantage had to be content.[5]

Denver next secured the mint, which although not a mint, but only a United States assaying office, was

[5] The first postmaster of Auraria was Henry Allen, appointed in the spring of 1859, at which time there was no mail route created, and none was established before the autumn of 1860. Allen soon resigned, and Park W. McClure was appointed, the first who had any office. When the war began he joined the confederacy, and Samuel S. Curtis was appointed; but he also left the place to take a commission in the federal army. His deputy acted as postmaster until the spring of 1864, when William N. Byers was appointed, who held the office 2½ years before resigning. This covers the pioneer period. Byers was appointed again in 1879. Previous to the U. S. appointments the Central Overland California and Pike's Peak Express company, which was the Leavenworth and Pike's Peak Express company under a new name, had postmasters of its own, the first of whom was Amos Steck. *Byers' Hist. Colo*, MS., 27–8.

a power, besides being a temptation, the first embez-
zlement of importance occurring in Denver being
perpetrated by the pay clerk, who absconded with
$37,000, most of which was recovered, together with
the thief. Defalcations had not been frequent in
the history of Colorado, and this one stirred pro-
foundly the moral sense of its people. Denver also
succeeded in retaining the capital, as has been before
stated, against several attempts to locate it elsewhere.
But it has been to the energy with which the public-
spirited men of Denver have labored for the concentration of railroads at this point that the continued
ascendency of this city has been due. Originally,
and when Berthoud surveyed the mail route to Salt
Lake, it was expected that the central line of Pacific
railroad would come to Denver; but its engineers
finding a more feasible route north, finally passed just
within the line of the territory, injuring rather than
benefitting it. This inspired the friends of Colorado,
and particularly the leading men of Denver, with
the purpose of building a branch road to the Union
Pacific at Cheyenne. The Kansas Pacific was slowly
making its way westward, and was likely enough at
that time to come to Pueblo, the most formidable
rival of Denver. Whether to build a road toward
Cheyenne or Pueblo was for a time a moot question.[6]

[6] As early as 1861 a railroad called the Colorado Central was projected to
connect Golden with Denver, and to be extended to the other mining towns,
which road was chartered in 1865. In 1867 a proposition was made by the
Union Pacific to assist in completing a branch road into Colorado, if the
grading should be done by the Coloradans. The first meeting to consider
this proposition, and of building the Colorado Central, was called July 10,
1867, at Denver, and was thinly attended. It was resolved, however, to request the county commissioners to order an election for the purpose of voting
on the proposition to issue bonds for $200,000 in aid of the branch road, and
such an election was ordered for the 6th of August. In the interim it became known that the managers of the Colorado Central were working in the
interest of Golden as the future capital, and designed taking the road on the
north and west side of the Platte instead of first to Denver, a movement in
which they were supported by the mountain towns. On this discovery the
commissioners of Arapahoe county so changed the order of election as to make
the issue of bonds dependent upon the road being constructed on the east side
of the Platte. The vote on this proposition stood 1,160 for to 157 against.
But the Colorado Central company in September declined the conditional
bonds. In November a director of the Kansas Pacific company, James Archer,

While the claims of Colorado were receiving but scant recognition from the transcontinental line, Gen-

visited Denver, and made it known that only by the contribution of $2,000,000 in county bonds could the building of the Kansas Pacific to that point be secured. As this proposal was not to be entertained, it was determined to make another effort to secure connection with the Union Pacific, and to facilitate negotiations a board of trade was organized on the 13th of November. On the following day George Francis Train addressed the board, and steps were taken to organize a railroad company. On the 17th and 18th other meetings were held, and on the latter day the Denver Pacific Railway and Telegraph company was organized, with a capital stock of $2,000,000, and a board of directors. The officers elected on the 19th were B. M. Hughes, president; Luther Kountze, vice-president; D. H. Moffat, Jr, treasurer; W. T. Johnson, secretary; F. M. Case, chief engineer; John Pierce, consulting engineer. In three days $300,000 had been subscribed, and an attempt was made to induce the Colorado Central to accept the county bonds and join forces, but without success. In December the county commissioners issued a call for another special election in Jan. 1868, to vote upon the proposition to issue $500,000 in bonds to aid the railroads, for which the county was to receive the same amount in stock. The vote stood 1,259 in favor of to 47 against the issue of the bonds, and soon after an arrangement was entered into with the Union Pacific by which that company agreed to complete the road whenever it should be ready for the rails. A bill was introduced in congress early in the session of 1867–8 for the usual land grant to the Denver Pacific; but before any action was taken, the Kansas Pacific road agreed to transfer its land grant between Cheyenne and Denver to the Denver Pacific, and the bill was amended to grant a subsidy in bonds to the latter company, and in this form was passed in the senate July 25, 1868. Nothing more binding than a verbal agreement had been passed between the Union and Denver Pacific companies, when in March 1868 Gov. Evans and Surveyor-gen. Pierce, representing the latter, met the directors of the Union Pacific cc. in New York and reduced to writing the terms finally agreed upon, which were, on the part of the Denver company, that the road should be graded and the ties laid; that the Denver Central and Georgetown Railroad company should be organized; and that application should be made for a grant of land to the Denver Pacific road. A line having been decided upon, work was commenced May 18, 1868, in the presence of a concourse of people. At the end of three months the grading had been completed to Evans, half the distance, and in the autumn the road-bed was completed to Cheyenne. But so far the Union Pacific company made no movement toward completing any part of the road, and, indeed, the subsidy bill which had passed the senate had failed in the lower house of congress, all of which delayed progress. On the 3d of March, 1869, however, another bill embodying the important features of the former one was passed, and became a law. The grading and ties being ready, the Union Pacific was called upon to fulfil its contract, which it did not do, owing to financial embarrassment. About this time, the president of the Denver Pacific having died, Evans was elected to fill that position, and he proposed to the Union Pacific to sell the iron to the Denver Pacific, which would complete its own road. The former contract was cancelled, and an arrangement entered into with the Kansas Pacific which took a certain amount of the stock of the Denver Pacific, and proceeded with the completion of the road, which was opened to Denver June 22, 1870, the Georgetown miners contributing the silver spike which was used at the inauguration ceremonies, when, also, the corner-stone of the depot at Denver was laid, with imposing rites, masonic and civic. Thus, after three years of unintermitted effort, Denver established itself as the initial railroad point in Colorado. In August of the same year the Kansas Pacific reached Denver.

The Denver Pacific was not for the first ten years financially remunerative,

eral William J. Palmer, who, while helping to build
the Kansas Pacific, had vainly labored for its extension westward by way of the grand cañon of the Arkansas, conceived the idea of a railway which, running
southward from Denver along the base of the mountains, should penetrate them by branches through
each available cañon and pass, and render tributary
the mineral wealth which they contained. It was
due no less to his foresight in the conception of this
enterprise than to the ability and energy which he
brought to bear on its execution, that the Denver
and Rio Grande railway became the greatest factor
in the development of Colorado, and in many respects
the most notable of North American railroads. From
1871, when construction began, to 1878, 337 miles of
road were built, connecting Denver with Cañon City
and the adjacent coal-fields, with the extensive beds
of coking coal at El Moro, and with the town of Alamosa on the Rio Grande del Norte, to reach which
point was made the then famous crossing of the
Sangre de Cristo range at Veta pass. In the latter
year began the great struggle with the Atchison,
Topeka, and Santa Fé for the possession of the
grand cañon of the Arkansas, a detailed account of
which is elsewhere given. Emerging victorious from
this conflict in 1880, the Denver and Rio Grande entered upon a career of great prosperity, building during the next three years 980 miles of mountain road.[7]

first because it could not be while it had no feeders from the mining towns,
and secondly because in 1877 the Union Pacific company, failing to get control of it, constructed a parallel road running to Golden, and absorbing the
Colorado Central, which had completed its road to Denver, and extended to
Georgetown, with branches to Black Hawk and several other mining towns.
This company also, in 1881, completed a cut-off from Julesburg to Evans on
the Denver Pacific, which subsequently came under its control.

[7] The achievements of the Denver and Rio Grande railway in mountain
climbing and cañon threading entitle it to its appellation of the 'scenic line of
the world.' Five times it crosses the main ranges of the Rocky mountains,
and at the following elevations above the sea: Veta pass, 9,392; Cumbres,
10,115; Tennessee pass, 10,418; Marshall pass, 10.852; and Fremont pass,
11,328 feet. To gain these heights a grade of over 200 feet was necessary for
about 100 miles of the route. A journey over these passes abounds in thrill-
ing interest, while the views may challenge comparison with the most noted
of Alpine prospects. Two of the grandest of Rocky mountain cañons, the

A telegraph line was established from Omaha to Julesburg, on its way across the continent, in 1861,

grand cañon of the Arkansas and the black cañon of the Gunnison, together with a score of lesser ones, are traversed by this wonderful road. An idea of its great general height above the sea may be gained from the fact that about 400 miles, or one fourth of its entire length, lie wholly above 8,000 feet elevation. In 1883, Gen. Palmer resigned the presidency, and was succeeded by Fred. W. Lovejoy. Various troubles, principally complications with the Denver and Rio Grande Western railway and the Colorado Coal and Iron companies, culminated in a receivership in July 1884, W. S. Jackson being appointed receiver. Reorganization was effected in 1886, with Jackson as president. Among other railways directly tributary to Denver I may mention the Denver, South Park, and Pacific, which had its organization in Denver, with Gov. John Evans at its head. It started up Platte cañon, and in 1879-80 had a race for Leadville with the D. & R. G., in which it was beaten, gaining trackage privileges, however, over its rival's line from Buena Vista

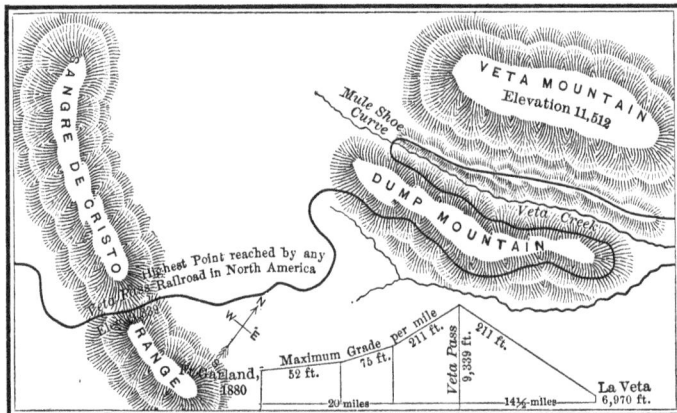

MAP OF THE ALIGNMENT OF THE DENVER AND RIO GRANDE R. R. AROUND DUMP MOUNTAIN.

to the 'Carbonate Camp.' It was soon afterward sold to the Union Pacific, and extended by way of Alpine pass across the snowy range to the Gunnison country, and also through the ten-mile region to Leadville. It comprises about 300 miles of road with steep grades, and abounds in magnificent scenery. The Denver, Utah, and Pacific is another Denver enterprise, and runs to the mouth of the St. Vrain cañon, a distance of 44 miles. The Denver Circle railway was organized November 16, 1880, with W. A. H. Loveland president. The design was to surround the city, and induce settlement in the environs, making it convenient for manufacturers and stockmen to locate their factories and yards upon the line. About five miles of narrow-gauge road were constructed. Of railroads outside of Colorado, yet connected with the interstate lines, the first, after the Kansas Pacific, to extend a long arm to Denver, was the Burlington and Colorado, the extension of the Burlington and Missouri river, itself a part of the great Chicago, Burlington, and Quincy system, by which Denver was first given an unbroken connection with Chicago. The Burlington reached Denver May 28, 1882. The Atchison, Topeka, and Santa Fé had previously been built to Pueblo, from which point it reached Denver over the rails of the D. & R. G. At La Junta its main California line diverged southward, and passing Trinidad climbed Raton pass on the southern border of the state.

by the Pacific company, the contractors being Charles
M. Stebbins and Edward Creighton.   A proposition

William A. H. Loveland, a native of Mass., has been called the founder
of the mountain system of railroads.   He served in the Mexican war, and
was wounded at Chapultepec.   Was in Cal. 5 years, and finally came to
Colorado and settled in Golden.   He obtained the right of way up Clear
Creek cañon for a wagon road, which he built, and which became the germ of
the railroad.   He was also interested in newspapers, having purchased the
Rocky Mountain News of its original owners in 1878, and was afterward interested in the management of the *Leadville Democrat*.

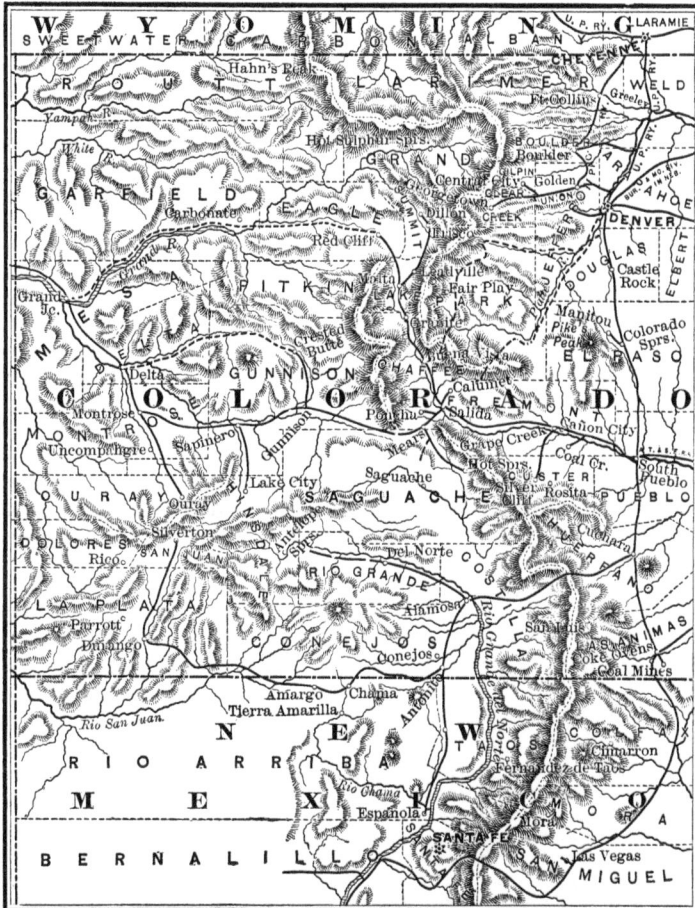

RAILROADS OF COLORADO.

Isaac W. Chatfield was a contractor on the Denver and South Park,
building the principal portion between Denver and Littleton.   He owned
720 acres in the Platte valley, near Littleton, and also engaged in selling
groceries at Leadville in 1879.   He was one of the projectors of the Ten-

was made to the citizens of Denver to construct a branch to that place on certain conditions, which were rejected. An agency was then established for forwarding messages to Julesburg, a distance of 200 miles, by the daily coach, from which point they were forwarded by telegraph, and answers received in the same manner. This arrangement lasted for two years, the business being so important that in the spring of 1863 Creighton made another proposition, which was accepted, and a branch to Denver completed October 1st. A branch line to Central was soon put in operation. The receipts from the Denver office, B. F. Woodward, manager, were not infrequently $5,000 a month, and the first year's net income was more than twice the cost of the line. This line reached Denver from Julesburg by a cut-off to Fort Morgan and via Living springs, which was adopted by the stage-line from the Platte. In 1865 the Pacific Telegraph company was merged in the Western Union company, which extended a line from Denver to Salt Lake, via Fort Collins and Virginia Dale, abandoning the old route via Laramie, making Denver the repeating station for California despatches. In 1866 the United States and Mexico Telegraph company was organized, mainly in Denver, the directors being D. H. Moffat, H. M. Porter, F. Z. Salomon, W. N. Byers, S. H. Elbert, and B. F. Woodward. Porter was president. The line was completed to Santa Fé in 1867, but the intention to continue it to Mexico was frustrated by

mile, Kokomo, and Breckenridge railroad, and contracted for the extension of the Eagle river branch of the Rio Grande, through Tennessee pass. See further, *Leadville Democrat*, Jan. 1, 1881.

For railroad matters I have consulted some chapters in *Hist. Denver*, 248–64; *Hall's Annual Report, Chamb. Com.*, 1884, 13–16; *Descriptive America*, May 1884, 27; *Official Railroad Guide of Colorado; Cong. Globe*, 1871–2, 1400; *Leadville Democrat*, Dec. 31, 1881; *Barneby's Life and Labor in the Far, Far West*, 2–3; *Denver Tribune*, Dec. 12, 1879, and Nov. 18, 1880; *Evans' Interview*, MS., 7; *Colorado Gazetteer*, 1871, 119–24; *Faithful's Three Visits*, 149; *Byers' Hist. Colo.* MS., 22–6; *Leadville Chronicle Annl; Graff's Colo*, 57–62, 66–7, 76–8; *Stone's Land Grants*, MS., 6–7; *Elbert, Public Men and Measures*, MS., 7; *Brickley and Hartwell's Southern Colo*, 61–7; *First Annual Rept Denver Pacific R. R.; Hayden's Great West*, 101; *Denver Rocky Mountain News*, May 20 and Dec. 16, 1868, Jan. 27, 1869, and Jan. 18, 21, and 25, June 22, and Sept. 25, 1870; *Denver Tribune*, Nov. 28, 1879, and April 16 and May 29, 1880; *Report State Geologist*, 1881–2, 1–27.

the disorders in that country. A contract was made
with the Denver Pacific Railway company to extend
the line to Cheyenne the same year, and in 1870 a
controlling interest was sold to the Western Union,
of which Woodward was appointed assistant superintendent. This company soon controlled all the lines
in Colorado.

The first street railway in Denver was completed
in January 1872 by a company incorporated in 1867,[8]
with a charter for thirty-five years. In 1871 a Chicago company, headed by L. C. Ellsworth, purchased
the franchise and began the construction, the Champa
street line being the first section operated, extending
from 27th and Champa to the station of the South
park railroad in west Denver, a distance of two miles.
In 1873 the north Denver branch was completed, 2½
miles. In 1874 the Broadway branch was completed,
1¼ on 16th street and Broadway, and a mile between
23d street and Park avenue. In 1876 1¼ miles additional were opened on Larimer street, from 16th
toward the fair-grounds.

The area of incorporated Denver is 13½ square
miles, but with its several additions it is nearly
twenty-one square miles. Its population is 125,000,
or something more, and it publishes over twenty journals of all kinds. It has 500 miles of irrigating
ditches within city limits, and 300,000 shade trees.
Among its public buildings the city-hall, built of
stone, cost $190,000; the opera-house, of brick and
stone, $850,000; the court-house, of stone, $300,000;
the Union Railway station, $450,000; the episcopal
cathedral, brick, $100,000. The public schools of
Denver are second to none in the world. As a rule,
the teachers are efficient, and in the boards of management there is comparatively little of the ignorance, stupidity, and rascality too often found in such

[8] The incorporators were Amos Steck pres., D. A. Cheever, sec., Moses
Hallett, Wilson Stinson, David J. Martin, Lewis N. Tappan, Edward C.
Strode, Robert M. Clark, Alfred H. Miles, Luther Kountze, Freeman B.
Crocker, Cyrus H. McLaughlin, J. S. Waters, and M. M. DeLanc.

bodies during these latter days of progress and high enlightenment. Twenty-one school-houses cost $700,-000, not one-half of which amount went into the pockets of aldermen, school-directors, or contractors. A course in the high school fits the graduate for entering a college or university.[9] Private and denominational schools find liberal support. Of the latter

[9] O. J. Goldrick was the pioneer of education in Colorado, opening a school in Denver in 1859. He was afterward for several years city editor of the *Rocky Mountain News*, canvasser, and correspondent. From Denver he went to Salt Lake, where he was managing editor of the *Vidette*. The Mormons not liking his paper gave him warning to leave, and he returned to Denver in 1868, where he published a paper until 1882, and where he died. *Byers' Centennial State*, MS., 18. In 1862 private schools were opened by Miss Ring and Miss Indiana Sopris. The school board of dist no. 1, of Arapahoe co., was organized Oct. 23, 1862, Amos Steck pres.; Lewis N. Tappan sec.: Joseph B. Cass treas. *Gove, Education in Denver*, MS., 1-6. Goldrick was elected superintendent of schools for Arapahoe co. in that year, and organized the first public school, for which provision had been made by the legislature, on ground in the rear of West Lindell hotel, A. R. Brown being the principal. He had two assistants and 140 pupils. Previous to 1871 the school fund was applied only to the support of teachers and other current expenses; but in that year a movement was made to acquire school property. Amos Steck had, in 1868, presented the local board with three lots on Arapahoe street. In 1870-71, 5 more lots were purchased in the same block, for which $3,500 was paid. In 1872 bonds were issued for $75,000, payable 10 per cent in 5 years, and 10 per cent annually thereafter, bearing interest at one per cent monthly. In this year the Arapahoe school building was completed. It was built of brick and stone, three stories high, containing 11 school-rooms and one class-room, with a basement fitted up for the residence of the janitor, the whole heated with hot-air furnaces, and well ventilated and lighted. The entire cost was $79,205.47. In 1873-74 the legislature created the city of Denver a special school district. Four of the wards, the 2d, 3d, 4th, and 5th, availed themselves of the privileges of the act. From 1872 to 1874 the Arapahoe building and some rooms in the methodist academy (discontinued) served for school purposes; but it was found necessary then to erect another building, which was placed on Stout street, and cost $24,089.19, containing 8 rooms. Previous to the opening of this school, F. C. Garbutt had been superintendent, with a corps of 17 teachers. He was succeeded in 1874 by Aaron Gove, a man of high attainments and remarkable educational and executive ability, who employed 25 teachers, and who established the 9th, or first high-school grade, to which 108 pupils were admitted. Three more grades completed the course in the high school, and prepared the graduate for college. The first class graduated in 1877. H. I. Hale, one of the class, passed a highly creditable examination on entering West Point as a cadet. In 1875 the schools had again become so crowded that relief was obtained by renting, and the same year 16 lots were purchased on Broadway, on which the third large building of brick and stone was erected at a cost of $28,645. But so rapid was the increase of growth in the population of Denver about this time, that in 1876 it became necessary to rent rooms for four new schools. Addition was yearly made to these accommodations until 1879, when 10 lots were purchased in the eastern part of the city, and an elegant stone building, costing $28,000 erected thereon. The Broadway school was also enlarged, and the Arapahoe school relieved by renting; the number of pupils in all the public schools having reached 2,700.

there are several, the principal of which belong to the catholics, episcopalians, and methodists. The university of Denver, an outgrowth of the Colorado seminary, established by the methodists in 1864, is conducted under the auspices of that church, though as a non-sectarian institution. In character and scholarship it compares favorably with eastern colleges. There are fifty-four religious societies[11] in Denver, many of them owning elegant and valuable church property.

[10] Byers, *Centennial State*, MS., 30-1; *University of Denver.*

[11] The first recorded religious services in Denver took place in 1859, when a methodist preacher, named Hammond, began holding services in an unfinished building on Larimer street, between 15th and 16th streets. In Jan. 1860 the venerable J. H. Kehler, an episcopalian minister, held services in Goldrick's school-house, on McGaa (later Holladay) street. Afterward a room was secured in Ruter's block, and an episcopalian church organized. About the same time a southern methodist church was organized by a preacher named Bradford, and a small brick church erected at the corner of Arapahoe and 14th streets. This was the first church edifice erected in Denver, and was sold to the episcopalians in 1861, when Bradford and many of his congregation went to the assistance of the southern confederacy. That year the missionary bishop, Talbot, of the episcopalians, visited Denver, and before he would dedicate the church required it to be free of debt; $500 was raised and the church dedicated. On the 15th of Dec., 1861, A. S. Billingsley organized the First Presbyterian church of Denver, under instructions from the board of domestic missions, old school, which held its services at International hall, on Ferry street, in west Denver, then known as Auraria. Of the 18 members, 11 were women. In April 1862 Billingsley left, and A. R. Day succeeded him in November, who seems to have been an active missionary, for he soon secured the donation of a lot from Maj. John S. Fillmore, paymaster U. S. A., on 15th street, between Arapahoe and Lawrence. Liberal contributions were made by citizens, and the mission board gave $600, so that in 1863 an edifice of brick was begun, 37x65 feet, ground area, which was completed in 1865, when Day resigned, and J. B. McClure of Ill. became pastor after several months, during which the pulpit was vacant. He preached two years, when again the church was left without a pastor until 1868, when A. Y. Moore of Ind. succeeded, but not being supported by the mission board, resigned the same year. The church then negotiated with the new school board to be taken in charge and connected with the presbytery of Chicago, a call being extended to E. P. Wells to preach to them. On the 20th of Nov., 1868, the church was incorporated, and on the 28th Wells was installed pastor, who remained in charge 6 years. In 1871 the church became self-supporting, and in 1874 adopted the name of Central Presbyterian Church. By this time the membership had outgrown the edifice, and in May 1875 property was purchased at the corner of Champa and 18th streets for the site of a new church. The corner-stone was laid Jan. 6, 1876, and the building so far completed as to be occupied in 1878. During this period, Wells having resigned in 1875, Willis Lord was pastor for one year, when ill health compelled his resignation, and Dr Reed officiated until Dec. 1878, when his death occurred. The edifice for which they labored cost $50,000, and had a membership of between 400 and 500. The 17th street presbyterian church was founded by that portion of the parent church which maintained its connection with the old-school board, and solicited the ministrations of their former pastor, Day, who continued with them until April 1869, when he went to preach at Boulder.

The material for substantial building being convenient, the prevailing style of domestic architecture is good, not a few private residences costing from $20,000 to $100,000, and a less number from $45,000

He was succeeded by C. M. Campbell, who preached until April 1870, in which year the Colorado presbytery was organized. In Feb. of that year the name was changed to Westminster church, which it did not long retain before resuming its former one. In July 1870 W. Y. Brown became pastor, and in 1872, after several years of meeting in rented rooms and other churches, an edifice of brick, in the Gothic style of architecture, with windows of stained glass, presented by eastern sunday-schools, and capable of seating 300 persons, was completed and dedicated March 10th. The cost of this church was $12,200. In 1873 Brown was succeeded in the pastorate by R. T. Sample, who, in 1874, withdrew, and was followed by C. H. Hawley, who, in 1876, gave way to I. W. Monfort, and he, in 1877, to J. H. Kerr.

The Dutch Reformed church began with the organization in 1871 of a society of persons of this belief, who held meetings every Sunday. In the autumn they purchased two lots on the corner of Lawrence and 23d streets for $800. In the following April a church organization was effected by Florain Spalti, Casper Gugolz, John U. Gabathuler, and William Nordloh. The Ohio synod was called upon to extend its aid, and sent J. A. Keller to report upon the prospect. On his representation the board of missions sent F. Hatzmetz to preach. A church edifice was commenced, when Hatzmetz returned to Ohio, and Keller replaced him, the church being completed in 1874. It was constructed of brick and stone, and cost $5,300. The membership of this church was small in proportion to English-speaking congregations.

The first methodist preaching, as stated above, was by the 'church south.' It had no regular organization until July 16, 1871, when A. A. Morrison became its pastor. A lot was purchased on Arapahoe street, and a church erected. Morrison was succeeded in 1872 by W. H. Warren; in 1873 by E. M. Mann; in 1874 by W. C. Hearn; in 1875 by W. G. Miller; in 1876 by William Harris; and in 1877 by W. J. Phillips. In 1874 the church was admitted to the conference of Colorado, Wyoming, and Montana, and remaining until 1878, when the Colorado conference was formed. In 1878-9 the church was enlarged, handsomely finished, and refurnished.

Hammond, the first missionary of the methodist church in Denver, returned to the Kansas conference, was reappointed in 1860, and died before starting. J. M. Chivington was made presiding elder of the district of Colorado, and, there being no preacher, filled the Denver pulpit until 1861, when he ceased to war against irreligion and went out to fight southerners as major of Gilpin's 1st Col. reg. of volunteers. Upon Chivington's resignation, a Mr Dennis preached for a year, and the 3d year Oliver Willard. Meetings had been held wherever room could be obtained—in a building on Larimer, between 12th and 13th streets, in the second story of the court-house, in Henry C. Brown's carpenter-shop, and in the people's theatre, on Larimer street. The first methodist conference of Colorado was held at Denver in 1863, Bishop Ames presiding, who urged the members present to erect a church, offering to give $1,000 toward it, and also to erect a seminary. The conference appointed Willard presiding elder, and George Richardson preacher. A site for a church was selected on Lawrence street, and the corner-stone laid in 1864. The seminary being first completed, was used as a meeting-house until the church was completed in 1865, and William M. Smith made pastor. He was succeeded in 1866 by B. T. Vincent; in 1868 by John L. Peck; in 1870 by Thomas R. Slicer; in 1872 by himself; in 1874 by J. R. Eads; and in 1877 by Earl Cranston. In 1872, the membership increasing with the spread of the city, a branch church was built on California street. The following year

to $500,000.   The Holly system of water supply was
introduced and over sixty artesian wells bored, some
of which have a flow of 100,000 gallons a day, and
it was in contemplation to erect a reservoir on high

a German methodist church was erected at the suggestion of Conrad Frick,
and Mr Reitz, members of the parent organization.   It was constructed of
brick and stone, and cost $14,000.   The first pastor was Philip Kuhl, also
the first German protestant preacher in Colorado.   He was succeeded by J. G.
Leist and M. Klaiber.   In 1874 St James methodist church, in the southern
part of Denver, was erected at a cost of $5,000.   In 1877 Ex-gov. Evans
erected a small but handsome chapel of Morrison stone, in the south-western
part of the city, which was intended as a memorial edifice to his daughter
Mrs Elbert.   The colored methodists of Denver completed a substantial
brick church on Stout street in 1879, mainly by the efforts of Seymour, an
enlightened and active preacher.
    The begining made by Kehler of the episcopal church has been men-
tioned.   He continued to hold services in the school-house, until during war
times he was crowded out by an excited public, which had made a reading-
room of it which they frequented on all days of the week.   He then removed
to a building owned by Byand, a vestryman, on the site of the American
house, and thence to Appollo hall, a log house in the rear of the present *News*
office, thence to where Taylor's museum now stands, and again to the district
court-room at the corner of 18th and Larimer streets, the rector having his
residence in the upper story of the court-house.   Finally, in 1861, the small
brick church of the southern methodists was purchased and rededicated as St
John's Episcopal church, and the congregation found a home.   In 1862 Father
Kehler, being chosen chaplain of the 1st Colorado regiment, followed whither
Chivington had gone, remaining with the regiment during its term of service;
nor did he ever return to church duties, being well advanced in years.   H.
B. Hitchings was the 2d pastor of St Johns, and remained until 1869, being
succeeded by Bishop Randall, who advocated establishing boys' and girls'
schools.   Wolfe hall, a girl's school, named after a lady patroness, was begun
in 1867, and the main building completed in 1868.   It was enlarged in 1873,
and again in 1879, and cost about $50,000.   The corner-stone of the boys'
school was laid Sept. 23, 1868, at Golden.   This building was named Jarvis
hall, after George E. Jarvis of Brooklyn, N. Y., who gave liberally towards
its erection.   Before it was completed it was blown to pieces in a tornado,
but immediately rebuilt.   A theological school in connection with Jarvis hall,
was erected in 1871-2 by Nathan Matthews of Boston, and called Matthews
hall, and which was formally opened Sept. 19, 1872.   Jarvis made a second
contribution of $10,000 to be invested until the principal reached $20,000,
when the interest should be applied to the education of young men for the
ministry.   In April 1878 Jarvis and Matthews halls were destroyed by fire.
Randall, to whom the inception of these educational movements was due, died
in 1874, beloved and regretted, *Randall, Biog.*, MS., 1-33, and was succeeded
by Bishop John F. Spaulding, and P. Voorhees Finch became rector of St
John's, who was succeeded in 1879 by H.Martyn Hart, of England.   Randall
was a man of great self-sacrifice and abilities.   He was a son of an able jurist
of R. I., in which state he was born in 1809.   He was a graduate of Brown
university and of the theological seminary of New York.   Trinity Reformed
Episcopal church, was organized in Denver, Nov. 16, 1879, by Thompson L.
Smith, J. R. Smith, and J. W. May, wardens.   The congregation secured
a small but elegant church erected by unitarians, at the corner of California
and 17th streets.   The first vestrymen were Currie T. Frith, J. Johnson, W.
A. Hardinbrook, James Creighton, Samuel Copping, Thomas L. Wood, and
Lewis.   In the same year the convocation of Wyoming and Colorado was
formed.   In 1875 Trinity Memorial chapel was erected.   In 1876 Emanuel

ground, and make the water from artesian wells supply the city in the future. The drainage of the city
is good, much attention being given to promote the
healthfulness of the metropolis by the board of

chapel in West Denver was built. Connected with it was All Saints' mission
of North Denver. In 1879 Jarvis hall was rebuilt at Denver. The episcopal cathedral erected since 1879 is a beautiful church, costing $100,000. The
value of episcopal church and school property in Denver in 1886 was
$250,000.

The baptists sent a missionary, Walter McD. Potter, to Denver in 1862 to
spy out the ground, and in the following year appointed him missionary. He
held his first meeting Dec. 27, 1863, having a congregation of 14 persons.
Little advance was made before March 1864, when a Sunday-school was formed
and held its sessions in the U. S. court-room, on Ferry street. On May 2d,
the first Baptist church of Denver was organized, the members being Miss
Lucy K. Potter, Francis Gallup, Henry B. Leach, Mesdames A. Voorhies, L.
Burdsall, L. Hall, A. C. Hall, and Miss E. Throughman. The flood of 1864
having washed away, soon afterward, their place of meeting, they next
resorted to the People's theatre, where they continued to meet during that
year, removing to a school-house on Cherry street in 1865. In Dec. Potter
was compelled by ill health to cease his pastoral labor, and soon after died.
In May 1866 Ira D. Clark became pastor for one year, preaching in the U. S.
district court-room on Larimer street until Dec. In the meantime a church
had been commenced at the corner of Curtis and 16th streets, which, in an
unfinished state, was used for a lecture-room, but which was never completed.
In May 1868 A. M. Averill became pastor for a year, after which the church
was without one until Nov. 1870, when Lewis Raymond succeeded to the
charge for a short time, followed by another season of silence in the pulpit,
though the members kept up their organization. In 1872 Winfield Scott
assumed charge of the church, and began energetically to labor for the erection
of a suitable edifice. Francis Gallup having received some lots on the corner
of Curtis and 18th streets, in payment for some favors done the Baptist home
mission in the matter of land preëmpted by Potter, and bequeathed to the
mission, presented these lots to the church, and on this site was erected in
1872 a church costing altogether $15,000. In 1875 Scott resigned, and was
succeeded by T. W. Green and A. J. Frost the same year, and by F. M. Ellis
in 1876. In 1879 the membership was 330, and church property worth $25,-
000. Since that time a large and handsome church has been erected by this
denomination. There were in 1866 two colored baptist churches in the city:
Zion church, on Arapahoe street near 20th, and Antioch church, at the corner of Wazee and 23d streets. Samuel Shepard was the first pastor of
Antioch church. Neither were so well off financially as the colored methodist church.

Denver had no congregational organization before 1865. In that year
Mrs Richard Sopris and daughters, Irene and Indiana, Mrs Davis, Mrs Zolles,
D. G. Peabody, E. E. Hartwell, Samuel Davis, and Mr Haywood formed
themselves into a church. Mr Crawford preached; Mrs Davis was organist
at their meetings, and the Misses Sopris sang in the choir. At first the meetings were held in the U. S. district court-rooms, and among their temporary
preachers were Norman McLeod, and Mr Blanchard of Wheaton college, Ill.
In 1868, lots were purchased on the corner of Curtis and 15th streets, and a
church edifice erected in 1869–70. The first pastor was Thomas E. Bliss. In
1873 Bliss, with a part of the congregation separated from this church and
established St Paul's church, at the corner of Curtis and 20th, which subsequently became presbyterian. After the secession of Bliss, Julien M. Sturde-
vant, Jr, took charge for 4 years, during which the church prospered. He
was succeeded by Charles C. Salter, who preached two years, and by S. R.
Dimmock. A congregational chapel was built at the corner of Larimer and

health, under the superintendence of the state board,[12] established in 1877.

Arapahoe county, and more particularly Denver, is the largest manufacturing district in the state. The iron and brass foundries and machine-works turned out in 1886 products worth $685,000; the flouring-mills about $1,738,000; the breweries $938,000; the wagon and carriage shops $113,000; the canneries $35,000; the clothing manufactories $790,000; the furniture factories $195,000; sash and blind factories $280,000; manufactories of iron fences $14,000; of harness and saddles $83,000, besides a great variety of lesser manufactures.

The total product of Denver's manufactures in 1886 was $24,045,000, of which $12,334,143 was in bullion produced by the smelters, of whom there were in that year three large and several smaller ones. Denver

31st streets in 1879, George C. Lamb pastor. The parent church afterward erected a handsome edifice. These are all the early protestant churches of Denver standing in 1886.

The catholics were the first to erect a house of worship here, as in most new towns in the west. When fathers Joseph P. Machebeuf and J. R. Raverdy came to Denver in 1860 they set themselves to work to finish what had been begun, and soon they had raised subscriptions enough to proceed with the work. Theirs was the first bell, and the first pipe-organ. This early church on Stout street was the root of the present cathedral. It was but 30 by 50 feet in size at first. A small house was added for the bishop's residence, which in 1871 was replaced by a brick residence. The following year the church was enlarged, and in 1873 it had grown into a cathedral. As early as 1864 the academy of St Mary was established on California street, and placed in charge of three sisters of the order of Loretto in Ky. The buildings were enlarged from time to time until they presented an imposing appearance, and accommodated many pupils and teachers. Branch schools have been planted in other towns under the care of this order. There was in 1886 a parish school adjoining the cathedral. A catholic hospital was opened in 1872, under the care of the sisters of charity. It was situated on Park avenue, and was a substantial brick structure, 45x75 feet, and three stories high. According to their usual premeditated plans of acquiring valuable property, the catholics of Denver and Colorado have become possessed of excellent sites in this and all the towns. *Denver Hist.*, 268–84; *Denver Tribune*, Jan. 4, 1880; *Descriptive America*, May 1884, p. 17; *Colo Gazetteer*, 1871, p. 133–40; *Corbett's Directory of Mines*, 64–5; *Hart's Boy-Education*, pp. 37–41; *Chivington's The Prospector*, MS., 3; *Howbert's Ind. Troubles*, MS., 8; *Chivington's First Colo Regt*, MS., 1. Another manuscript of Chivington's, *The Retrospective*, gives also a slight sketch of the M. E. church in the beginnings.

[12] According to law, the county commissioners of any county where no other board exists shall constitute a board of health, with all the duties usually pertaining to that office. Much interesting matter may be found in the *Rept State Board of Health*, 1877 and 1879–80.

is the leading ore market of the state, and in 1886 its smelters and samplers received and handled 180,173 tons of gold and silver bearing ores. The total business of the city in the same year, exclusive of real estate sales, which aggregated $11,000,000, exceeded $56,500,000.

As early as the spring of 1861 a chamber of commerce was organized at Denver, but was soon afterward abandoned. In 1867 another attempt in the same direction was made through the establishment of a board of trade,[13] which, on account of some defect in its general constitution, was also less successful than its promoters desired. This being recognized, early in 1854 some of its principal members formed a permanent and effective organization, with which the old board was consolidated. The first officers of this new chamber of commerce were R. W. Woodbury, president; M. J. McNamara and J. F. Mathews, vice-presidents; Frank Hall, secretary; and William D. Todd, treasurer. Good and efficient work has from the first been done by this organization in directing the enterprise of Denver, while advancing and protecting its business interests. Its annual reports are models of statistical compilation, and to them I am much indebted for the facts concerning the business growth and development of Denver and the state at large. Under the auspices of the then-existing board of trade was established the national mining and industrial exposition, which made its first exhibit in 1882,[14] erecting a group of buildings which covered seven acres, situated in the midst of

[13] I find in *Extracts from Early Records*, MS., 7, the names of the officers of the Denver Board of Trade. They are taken from a pamphlet published by the board, entitled *Colorado*. John W. Smith pres., William N. Clayton and John Pierce vice-pres., Henry C. Leach sec., Frank Palmer treas., Henry M. Porter, J. S. Brown, V. J. Salomon, D. H. Moffat, Jr, H. H. T. Grill and Joseph E. Bates directors.

[14] The board of commissioners of the exposition, appointed by the board of trade in 1884, consisted of W. A. H. Loveland pres., R. W. Woodbury vice-pres., A. E. Pierce treas., Irwin Mahon sec., Joseph C. Wilson supt of space, R. G. Webster, B. P. Broshear, B. F. Woodward, and E. B. Light.

a tract of forty acres.[15]   The object of the exposition
was primarily to draw the eyes of the world upon
Colorado and Denver, in which effort the enterprise
was successful, the mineral museum, containing specimens from every mine in Colorado and many camps
in the adjacent states, being of itself sufficient to entitle
the exposition to particular notice.   The design contemplated an annual exhibit, but after the third had
been held in 1884 the project fell to the ground by
reason of an unfortunate conflict of interests among
its managers and supporters.

At the first session of the forty-seventh congress a
bill was passed making Denver a port of delivery for
dutiable merchandise;[16] and another bill at the same
session, admitting articles to the Denver exposition
free of duty, provided that none of these articles
should be sold or consumed without paying revenue.
A bill was also passed making provision for the erection of a government building in Denver for the
accommodation of the United States district and cir-

---

[15] The main building was a substantial and handsome cruciform structure of brick, 500 feet long by 310 in width. The floor, with its towers
and angles, contained nearly 100,000 square feet of space, and the galleries
half as much more. The exhibit in the hall of arts in 1882 was estimated to
be worth $200,000. The departments which offer premiums are, first, minerals
and metals, and their products, including ores of gold, silver, copper, lead,
and iron; coal, anthracite, bituminous, cannel, and lignite; cabinets of minerals of all kinds; fire-clay, manufactured; porcelain ware; hydraulic cement;
lime, brick, etc.; marble, lithographic stone, soapstone, gypsum, precious
stones, native chemicals; bullion, gold, silver; pig-lead, pig-iron, steel-rails;
iron-rails, nails, bar-iron, sheet-lead, and lead pipe. The second department
comprises 73 kinds of machinery used in mining and agriculture; third department, 18 kinds of vehicles; fourth department, 34 kinds of leather goods
and leather, and 8 kinds of furriers' goods; fifth department, miscellaneous
manufactures, comprising 93 articles. The sixth department included horses
of 10 classes; the seventh, cattle, in 13 classes; the eighth, sheep, in 5 classes;
the ninth, swine, in 7 classes; the tenth, poultry; the eleventh, grain, vegetables, and miscellaneous farm products; the twelfth, fruits; the thirteenth,
dairy products, and domestic or pantry articles; the fourteenth, apiarian
products; after which followed the art and floral departments, attached to
which, as a sign of progress, there was also considerable interest.   Except in
San Francisco, which has the advantage of being a seaport town, no other
city of the United States, at the age of little more than twenty years, has
been able to make a similar exhibit. *Catalogue National Mining and Industrial Exposition,* 1884.

[16] *U. S. Stat.,* 13, 47th cong., 1st sess.; *U. S. H. Jour.,* 217, 590, 659,
720, 730, 753, 47th cong., 1st sess.

cuit courts, post-office, land-office, and other federal offices, the cost not to exceed $300,000.

Banking has always been a profitable business in Denver. There is no usury law, borrower and lender fixing such rates of interest as they agree upon. In times of excitement three per cent a month might be asked and given. Twelve per cent per annum was the usual bank rate in 1886, but real estate loans could be had for eight or ten per cent. The first bank building of any pretensions was a part of National block, on the corner of 15th and Blake streets, and was occupied by the First National bank, organized by Jerome B. Chaffee, and of which he was president until 1880.[17] Various banking institutions which, calling themselves savings banks, sequestering the savings of the people to their own uses, rose and flourished for a time. In 1885 there were six banks in Denver, five of which were national, their combined capital amounting to $1,708,000; deposits $8,060,000; cash and exchange $3,963,000; loans and over-drafts $4,634,000.[18]

Until the erection of the Tabor opera-house in 1880 Denver had nothing at all elegant in the way of a theatre.[19] It had then one unsurpassed in any

[17] The business was purchased from Clark & Co., private banker. George T. Clark was cashier in 1865, and was elected mayor the same year. D. H. Moffat, Jr, became cashier in 1866. *Hist. Denver*, 213.

[18] *Descriptive America*, May, 1884. In 1881 David H. Moffat, Jr, was president of the First National bank, Samuel N. Wood cashier; of the City National bank William Barth was president, John B. Hanna cashier; of the Colorado National bank Charles B. Kountze was president, William B. Berger cashier; of the German National Bank George Tritch was president, W. J. Jenkins cashier; of the Merchants' National bank Henry R. Wolcott was president, Samuel N. Wood cashier. *Compt. of Currency Rept*, 1881-2, 709–11. The State National bank took the place of the Merchants' bank. The Union bank completes the list.

[19] Apollo theater, erected in October, 1859, by Charles R. Thorne, was situated on Larimer street, between 14th and 15th streets. Thorne had a travelling company on the plains, which was giving entertainments at military posts—at Leavenworth, Kearny, and Laramie, and thence he came to Denver. Platte Valley theater, at the corner of 16th and Lawrence streets, was the next. It was opened in 1860. Both were burned. The next was a building erected by the Governor's Guards as an armory building, at the intersection of Curtis and 15th streets. It was called Governor's Guard hall, and was used until Sept., 1880, when the Tabor opera-house was

of the states for tasteful decoration and comfort, the designs being entirely original and suitable.   In 1882 the academy of music was completed.

It seems tautological to remark, after recounting what the people of Denver have accomplished in less than a third of a lifetime, that they are as a people above the average in intellectual force and superiority of culture.   How much is due to the stimulating influences of their high and dry climate it would be a nice point to determine, seeing that there is a sliding scale of altitudes in Colorado, and that everywhere in the state prevails great mental and physical activity.   That there was a good class of settlers to begin with is undoubted, and upon this tree has been grafted all the choicest fruits of an age of progress.[20]   Yet

opened.   There is still a small theater opposite this called the Walhalla. *Byers' Hist. Colo*, MS., 73–4.   Turner hall, on Holladay street, is the German temple of art, and a commodious one.

[20] Free-masonry was active in 1858–9, when members of the order met informally in a cabin of Auraria, that they might know and assist each other. They had in 1881 10 lodges, representing every degree, and for many years had met at the corner of Holladay and 15th streets.   The Knights of Pythias had 3 lodges.   The Odd Fellows had 9 lodges, and a hall on Lawrence street. The Good Templars had two lodges, and there were two of the Red Cross. There were twelve benevolent societies of various names, and 18 other organizations, such as medical and historical societies, and industrial and other associations.   Croffutt, *Grip-sack Guide*, 32; *Trans. Med. Soc.*, 1883.   There were 37 hotels and public boarding-houses in 1884.   The St James, Windsor, New Albany, American, and Inter-Ocean, can each shelter and feed 600 guests; the Alvord, Lindell, and New Markham, each 200; the New York, 150; and the Brunswick and Charpiot's, 100 each. *Catalogue National Mining and Industrial Exposition*, 15.   There were, besides, 60 restaurants, 47 bakeries, 6 breweries, 6 flouring-mills.   The quality of the flour made in Denver is excellent, and since the first shipment in 1874 to the east, has been in demand in Boston, New York, Buffalo, and Chicago, and also Richmond, Va. *Dept of Agriculture*, 1872, 449.   The names of the principal mills are the Hungarian, Crescent, Davis, and White Rock.   Wheat is brought here from Utah to be made into flour.   The first millers had difficulty in separating the bran, but the true process was discovered by Luther A. Cole of Watertown, Wis., who engaged in milling here in 1870.   The secret was in moistening the hull before grinding the wheat, which prevented crumbling, and enabled him to part the bran from the flour.   It was done by a system of spraying before the wheat went to the hopper. *Byers' Centennial State*, MS., 21.   The Denver City Steam Heating company was incorporated Dec. 15, 1879, to supply steam by the Holly system, or any other, to factories, shops, stores, public or private buildings, for mechanical or heating purposes.   Steam was turned on Nov. 5, 1880, and was found to be a saving in many ways.   The company's capital was $500,000.   Among the incorporators were the pioneers E. F. Hallack, J. W. Smith, and George Tritch.   There was a movement made to organize a fire department July 15, 1862, but the difficulty of procuring machines stood in the way for a time, during which several fires occurred.   Hook and

Denver has not been without its vices, its vicious class, or its unpleasant episodes.[21] Gambling has been from the first a prominent evil. The city council in 1861 prohibited three-card monte, but no other games. The territorial legislature in 1864 passed an act prohibiting gambling-houses, and making it the duty of sheriffs and constables to arrest the keepers and destroy the furniture of such places. But the next legislature yielded to the arguments of those who lived off the gain of games of chance; and after enacting that no person known to be a professional gambler or keeper of a gambling-house should be eligible as a juror, repealed so much of the former act as affected Denver, and permitted that city to control this mat-

Ladder Company No. 1, organized in March, 1866, was for several years the only fire company in the city. Its first officers were George W. McClure, foreman; Frank W. Cram, asst foreman; C. C. Davis, 2d asst; H. L. Rockwell, 3d asst; Hyat Hussey, treasurer. A truck and apparatus was ordered from Cincinnati, and arrived in the autumn across the plains. A brick building 24 by 60 was erected on a lot purchased by the city council, the same occupied later by Central station, which was then called Pioneer station. No other company was organized until the spring of 1872, when the James Archer Hose company was organized, named after the president of the Denver Water company, and located on Curtis street. Soon after the Joseph E. Bates Fire and Hose company was organized, named in acknowledgment of the aid rendered the department by Bates. In July of the same year the Woodie Fisher Hose Company No. 1 also organized, named after a member of the Hook and Ladder Company No. 1, killed in attempting to stop a runaway team. In March, 1874, the Denver Hook and Ladder company was formed, having their station at the corner of Curtis and 26th streets. Tabor Hose Company No. 5 was organized and stationed on 15th street, north Denver. It was named in honor of Lieut-gov. Tabor. Of military companies Denver had three in 1880. The Governor's Guard organized in April, 1872, the Chaffee Light Artillery in January, 1878, and the Mitchell Guards, an independent Irish company, which was formed in 1873. The National Guard was created by the legislature of 1879, and supported by a direct tax. Denver had to make application to congress to be permitted to purchase land for cemetery purposes. *Cong. Globe*, 1871-2, pp. 2206, 2949, 3313, 3338, 3682. There were three burial places, the latest and only one to which much attention has been given up to 1886 being Riverside cemetery, three miles down the Platte, which has a beautiful site.

[21] On Sunday, the last day of October, 1880, there was a riot in Denver, the object of which was to affect the presidential election, and prevent the usual republican majority. The disturbance began with the interference of a few of our drunken Irish patriots in a game of pool played between a white man and a Chinaman at a public resort on Wazee street. Having forced the Chinese to defend themselves, they then treated them as the offending party, assailed them without mercy, driving them into hiding, hanging one of them to a lamp-post, and destroying their property. The mob increasing, a Committee of Control, consisting of 500 citizens, was formed; the city council gave the chief of police authority to muster a special force of 100 to patrol

ter by its own ordinances.[22] The revised ordinances
of Denver, passed in 1881, prohibit both gambling
games and houses of ill-fame, the law-makers apparently forgetting that these excrescences of society
have existed from time immemorial, and probably will
continue till the millennial day; also, that it is the
people who make the gamblers and prostitutes, and
not they who make the people. The urban population of Arapahoe county is nearly all in and about
Denver. Littleton, twelve miles south, is considered as a suburb. Porter's sulpho-chalybeate spring,
in the outskirts of the city, is also a popular resort.[23]

the streets and guard the polls on Monday, and the fire department was kept
in readiness all day to fly at the tap of the bell. Every saloon was closed,
and the city guarded at every point. A number of the rioters, having been
arrested and sent to jail, were promptly bailed out by Ex-delegate Patterson's hench-men, and allowed to vote. The district attorney had a part of
them rearrested on a charge of murder, and so the struggle went on all day;
but the law-and-order men triumphed, and the election was finally as quiet
as the faces of the guardians of the peace were stern and set with determination. *Denver Tribune*, Nov. 2, 1880.

[22] The city attorney elected in 1883 was Mason B. Carpenter, a native of
Vt., born in 1845. He served two years in the union army when between 16
and eighteen years of age, being mustered out as acting sergeant-major. He
graduated at the university of Vermont, studied law, and was admitted to
practice at St Albans; was official reporter of the house of representatives in
1867, and secretary of the senate from 1869 to 1873. In 1874 he married
Fannie M. Brainard, and removed to Colorado in 1875. He was elected from
Arapahoe, to the house of representatives in 1881, and a member of the senate in 1884. The *History of Denver*, from which I have frequently quoted,
is a quarto volume of 652 pages. Its authorship is mixed, and the greater
portion anonymous, but bears evidence of having been the performance of
local writers well acquainted with their topics. It contains articles on a
great variety of subjects, and many biographical sketches. It is on the same
plan as *Clear Creek and Boulder Valley History* and the *History of Arkansas
Valley*. Other authorities consulted are *First Annual Report of Denver
Chamber of Commerce*, by Frank Hall, containing tables, etc., showing general condition of the state; *Porter's West Census of 1880; Colorado Notes*,
MS.; *Graff's Colorado; Pitkin's Political Views*, MS.; *Dixon's New America*,
as seen through English eyes in 1866; *McKenney's Business Directory*, 1882–3;
*Meline's Two Thousand Miles on Horseback; Faithful's Three Visits to America;
Leading Industries of the West*, August, 1883; *Williams' Pacific Tourist and
Guide; Denver Rocky Mountain News*, June 6, 1870; *Denver Tribune-Republi-
can*, Oct. 10, 1884; *Early Days in Denver*, by John C. Moore. He was born
in Tenn. in 1835, and came to Colorado in 1859. He describes Denver and
also Pueblo in the early days. *Sopris' Settlement of Denver*, MS., is another
excellent authority treating of first things.

[23] Argo is the seat of Hill's reduction works. Other settlements in 1886
were Bear Creek Junction, Bennett, Bird, Big Timber, Box Elder, Brighton,
Burnham, Byers, Cherry Creek, Deer Trail, Henderson Isle, Hughes, Gravel
Switch, Island Station, Jersey, Junction, Kiowa, Living Spring, Magnolia,
Melvin, Petersburg, Platte Summit, Pooler's Rancho, Poverty Flat, Rattle-

snake, Reduction Works, Schuyler, Vasquez, and Watkins. One of the pioneers of Arapahoe county whose name is found in the public prints is Caleb
B. Clements, who came to Colorado in 1859, and was from the first identified
with Denver, an addition to which bears his name. He was receiver of the
land office when Chilcott was register. He died March 24, 1880. *Denver
Tribune*, March 25, 1880.

C. J. Gross, who also came in 1859, was born in Vt in 1821. He was engaged in business in Fond du Lac, Wis., for several years, and helped to lay
out the town of Boulder in Colorado, after which he settled in Denver, and
was elected from Arapahoe co. to the legislature in 1866. He formed the
Baltimore Mining company, one of the most substantial in the state, and
owned 1,500 acres south-east of Denver. He married, in 1841, a daughter
of H. T. Shepherd of N. Y., who died at Boulder in 1864. The following
year he married Harriet Beecher of New Haven, Ct.

David A. Cheever was a midshipman in the U. S. navy in 1842. At
the close of the Mexican war he resigned, and also came to Cal. in 1849, but
returned to Wis. in 1854, and from there migrated to Colorado in 1859, engaging in real estate business. He was elected to the lower house of the
legislature in 1864, county commissioner in 1873, and was postmaster in
1875-6.

Cyrus H. McLaughlin, born in Pa in 1827, and by trade a printer, came
from Leavenworth, Kansas, to Colorado in 1859 as a messenger for Jones
and Cartwright's express, and to learn the truth of the reports concerning
gold discoveries. On returning to Leavenworth he carried $40,000 worth of
the precious dust. In 1860 he removed to Denver and worked on the *News*
for a time; then tried agriculture and cattle raising, but the flood of 1864 so
damaged his farm that he gave it up and took a situation in the quartermaster's department, which he held for two years. In 1867 he was elected
to the legislature, which met at Golden, and used his influence to remove the
capital to Denver. In 1868 he was reëlected and chosen speaker. He was
afterward receiver in the land office, clerk in the post office, and alderman.
The rule of the Pioneer Association is that those who arrived before 1860
may become members. *Byers' Centennial State*, MS., 38. Among these were
William Z. Cozzens, deputy-sheriff of Arapahoe district in 1860; David K.
Wall, member of the provisional legislature; T. P. Boyd, associate justice
of the supreme court; N. J. Curtis, W. F. Holman; Charles C. Post, member
of constitutional convention of 1859; Nelson Sargent, who was in charge of
the first express line across the plains, known as the Leavenworth and Pike's
Peak Express company, as before mentioned; Philo M. Weston, built the
first house in Granite; John Rothrock, built the 'eleven cabins,' 16 miles
below Denver, on the Platte, in 1858, and was one of the discoverers of Gold
Run, in Boulder co.; Joseph M. Brown, miner and cattle raiser, built
Brown's bridge over the Platte, elected county commissioner in 1863 for 3
terms; Samuel W. Brown, miner, merchant, farmer; Samuel Brantner, farmer; his daughter was the first child of the settlers of Arapahoe, born four
miles from Denver; Caleb S. Burdsall, miner, smelter, surgeon of the 3d
Colo reg., discovered the soda lakes near Morrison, named after him; Joseph
W. Bowles, miner, sheriff of Nevada mining district in 1860-1, farmer near
Littleton, twice elected county commissioner; Hiram J. Brendlinger, tobacco
merchant, member of the city council 1861-3, mayor in 1864, member of the
legislature 1865; John W. Cline, miner, farmer; Henry Crow, miner, organized the City National bank in 1870 and was president six years, afterward
in stock raising and mining; A. B. Daniels, vice-president of Denver and
New Orleans railroad, died April 9, 1881; Daniel J. Fulton, miner, farmer;
George C. Griffin, farmer and stock raiser; G. W. Hazzard, miner, farmer,
banker, stock grower, owned 20,000 acres of pasture lands, died Feb. 9, 1878,
leaving a wife and four children; Alfred H. Miles, farmer; John McBroom,
farmer, elected to the state legislature in 1876; John Milheim, banker and
capitalist; John H. Morrison, lumber merchant, miller, collector of internal
revenue, agriculturist, died July 21, 1876; Jasper P. Sears, merchant with

C. A. Cook, banker, government contractor, and real estate dealer; Thomas Skerritt, miner, farmer; L. A. Williams, lumber manufacturer, farmer, stock raiser.

Hiram J. Brendlinger, a native of Pa, came with a stock of cigars to Denver in 1859, opening a store on Blake street in a log cabin in June 1859. In 1861 he erected a two-story frame building, which was burned in April 1863. Six months previous he had erected a brick warehouse, in which a large part of his stock was saved, with which he started business again, with a branch at Central City. In 1864 he established a branch at Virginia, Montana, in 1866 at Cheyenne, in Wyoming, and in 1877 at Deadwood, in Dakota. He was a member of the city council, mayor, and member of the legislature.

Daniel Witter, born in Ind., became a miner in Tarryall district, South park, where he worked in 1859-60, and was chosen a member of the house from his district the following year. In 1862 he was appointed postmaster at Hamilton, and soon after asst int. rev. collector and afterward was receiver in the land office, dealer in real estate and stock raiser. He originated the Denver Safe Deposit and Savings bank, of which he was treasurer until 1877. He was vice-president of the Denver Water company from its organization for many years.

David H. Moffat was born in N. Y. in 1839, and came to Colorado in 1860. He started a book and stationery business at Denver, in company with C. C. Woolworth, which became large and profitable, and from which he retired at the end of six years to take the position of cashier of the 1st National bank of Denver, of which he was elected president in 1880, and which owes much to his administrative ability. He was elected to the presidency of the D. & R. G. R. in 1887, and has been prominently connected with all the leading railroad enterprises since 1869, when he with Gov. Evans built the Denver Pacific to Cheyenne. He was one of the organizers of the syndicate which built the D. & S. P. R. R., and helped to build the D. & N. O. R. R. He is also interested in mines in nearly every county in Colorado, and justly ranks as one of the mining kings of the centennial state. He paid Tabor $1,600,000 for his interest in the Little Pittsburg at Leadville, even then making money out of the investment. His residence in Denver cost over $80,000. *N. Y. Financier*, Oct. 17, 1885; *Moffat's Sketch on Banking*, MS.

Bela M. Hughes, a native of Nicholas co., Ky, was born in 1817, and removed to Clay co., Mo., in 1834. He studied for the law, and was admitted to practice in 1841, and in 1845 was appointed receiver of public moneys for his district, which position he held four years, when he removed to St Joseph, where he remained until he came to Colorado in 1861, as president of the Overland Mail company, which office he filled for two years, and for six years afterward that of solicitor of the same company. In 1869 he began the general practice of law in Denver. He was democratic candidate for governor in 1876, though not elected.

Frederick Jones Bancroft, M. D., born May 25, 1834, at Enfield, Conn. On the paternal side he came from the Bancrofts and Heaths of Conn., and on the meternal side from the Bissells and Walcotts, prominent New England families. He was educated at Westfield academy, Mass., and Charlotteville seminary, N. Y., and studied medicine in the medical department of the university of Buffalo, graduating in 1861. His first practice was in Penn. Then he entered the army, and after the war attended lectures in Phil., removing to Colorado in 1866, and practised medicine in Denver, where he became medical referee for several insurance companies, and surgeon of three different railroad companies, as well as member of the Denver Medical society, of which he was president in 1868, of the Colorado Medical association, and American Medical association, and president of the state board of health. He was also an early and active member of the Colorado Historical society, and has been an officer in many societies, particularly educational, and is authority upon such topics. He married a daughter of George A. Jarvis, of Brooklyn, N. Y.

James Moynahan was born in Wayne co., Mich., in 1842. He entered the army as a private in 1862, remaining in it through the war, being twice wounded, and made a captain in 1863. In 1866 he married Mary Moynahan, of Detroit, and set out for Colorado with an ox-team, leaving his wife, who followed him in 1867. He resided in Park co. until 1884 when he removed to Denver to educate his children. In merchandising, mining, and stock raising, he fast accumulated property. He was elected to the state senate in 1876, and again in 1882.

Charles Hallack, born in N. Y. in 1828, came to Colorado in 1867 from Kansas, and settled in Denver in the business of a lumber dealer. In 1884 he was elected president of the State National bank, of which he was one of the organizers.

Job A. Cooper, born in Ill. in 1843, removed to Denver in 1872, where he practised law for four years, and was elected vice-president of the German bank. In 1877 the bank was reorganized under the name of the German National Bank, when he was elected cashier. In 1877 he purchased 300 head of cattle, on a range near the Neb. state line, but sold them and bought 15,000 acres of land in Weld co., on which he had in 1886-7, 500 head of cattle. He was president of the Colorado Cattle-grower's association, a wealthy organization.

D. H. Dougan, born in Niles, Mich., in 1845, removed to Ind. at the age of 15 years, and became a clerk in a bank at Richmond, studying medicine in his leisure hours. He subsequently studied at Rush medical college, Chicago, and at Bellevue hospital, New York, graduating in 1874, and coming to Colorado the following year. He resided in several parts of the state temporarily until 1878 when he went to Leadville, where he became mayor in 1881 and 1882. He was the first president of Carbonate bank, and remained a director while living in Denver.

John C. Stallcup, born in Ohio in 1841, came to Colorado for the benefit of his health in 1877, and remained. He was nominee of the democratic party for state senator in 1878, and was again nominated for attorney-general of the state in 1880. He was elected city-attorney of Denver in 1881, and was retained as city counsel afterwards in cases then pending. In 1884 he sold most of his city property, and invested in land in Arapahoe co., 17 miles from Denver, which was being stocked with cattle.

Stephen H. Standart, born in Ohio in 1833, and brought up on a farm, came to Colorado in 1879 to engage in cattle-raising. He started in business with 1,200 head, about 60 miles from Denver. He was one of the organizers of the Western Live stock co. in 1880, and of the American Cattle company in 1883, of 400 members, the two companies owning over 20,000 head in 1885.

For congressional and legislative references I have found matter in *Pac. R. R. Rept*, i. 17–19; *U. S. Sen. Jour.*, 808, 38th cong., 1st sess.; *U. S. H. Jour.*, 241, 38th cong., 2d sess.; *Zabriskie's Land Laws*, sup. 1877, 49; *Hollister's Mines of Colo*, 292–4; *Cong. Globe*, 1864–5, 316, 753, 1404; *U. S. H. Ex. Doc.*, i., p. 152, 46th cong., 1st sess., vol. 16, pt 2, 184, 227; 46th cong., 3d sess., and xxv., pt 1, 446; 46th cong., 2d sess.; *U. S. H. Misc. Doc.*, xiii., pt 4, p. 56–9, 124–31, 46th cong., 2d sess.; *U. S. Ex. Doc.*, xxv., 364, 47th cong., 2d sess.; *Gen. Laws Colo*, 1865, 108–11, 117–18, 127, 132, 135, 141, 142; *Id.*, 1877, 180–94, 738; *Sen. Jour. Colo*, 1881, 629–30; *Charter and Ordinances of City of Denver*, 287–309; *Corporations, Rev. Statutes*, 1883.

CHAPTER XII.

BENT COUNTY—INDUSTRIES, TOWNS, AND PEOPLE—BOULDER COUNTY—
EARLY SETTLERS—QUARTZ MINING—COAL AND IRON—CHAFFEE COUNTY
—DISCOVERIES AND DEVELOPMENT—CLEAR CREEK COUNTY—EARLIEST
SMELTING—STAMP MILLS—CONEJOS COUNTY—COSTILLA—CUSTER—MEN
AND TOWNS—MINING—DELTA, DOLORES, DOUGLAS, EAGLE, ELBERT, EL
PASO, AND FREMONT COUNTIES—THE GREAT RAILROAD WAR—CAÑON
CITY AND ITS INSTITUTIONS.

BENT county, separated from Arapahoe by Elbert county, lies on both sides of the Arkansas river, and occupies the country of which Bent's fort was in ante-mining days the seat of such civilization as was found on the east slope of the Rocky mountains. It was organized in 1870, and named after the Bent family. It occupies an extent of territory larger than the state of Massachusetts, but is comparatively uninhabited, being almost entirely appropriated to the uses of the great cattle companies and owners, a single one of whom owns forty miles fronting on the river.[1] Boggsville was the first county seat, which later was west Las Animas, the rendezvous of cattle owners and purchasers. East Las Animas, a few miles below, is another similar point. Both are on the railroad. La Junta, at the junction of the Pueblo branch, is a prosperous town. Besides these there

---

[1] J. W. Powers, before mentioned. He came to Colorado in 1858 a poor young man, made his first money cutting the native grasses for hay, and selling it to the government at Fort Lyon. He finally became a merchant and banker, and owner of 20,000 cattle.

are few worthy of note.[2] The Arkansas valley is adapted to agriculture, but the population of about 2,000 is devoted to the grazing interest to the exclusion of farming. The county of Greenwood was created at the same time that Bent was established, and occupied a part of its present territory, with Kit Carson for the county seat ; but it was abolished in 1874, and the present boundaries decreed, at which time the county of Elbert was set off.

Boulder, one of the original seventeen counties established by the first legislative body of Colorado territory, contains 794 square miles, and combines mining with agriculture in a proportion which renders it a peculiarly favored section of the state. It was first settled by a portion of a train which arrived in 1858 by the Platte route, which on coming to the confluence of the St Vrain, determined to take a course directly leading to the mountains. Among them were Thomas Aikins and son, S. J. Aikins, a nephew, A. A. Brookfield and wife, Charles Clouser, Yount, Moore, Dickens, Daniel Gordon and brother, Theodore Squires, Thomas Lorton, Wheelock brothers, and John Rothrock. They pitched their tents on the 17th of October at Red rock, at the mouth of Boulder cañon. They were joined by others in the course of the autumn. On the 15th of January, 1859, the first gold was discovered at Gold Run by a party consisting of Charles Clouser, John Rothrock, I. S. Bull, William Huey, W. W. Jones, James Aikins, and David Wooley. Out of this gulch was taken by the hand-rocker that season $100,000. The second discovery, on south Boulder, was the Deadwood diggings, by B. F. Langley, about the last of

[2] Alkali, Apishapa Station, Arapahoe, Benton, Bent's Fort, Blackwell, Caddoa, Carlton, Catlin, Cheyenne Wells, Dowlings, First View, Fort Lyon, Granada, Hilton, Holley, Iron Springs, King's Ferry, Kiowa Springs, Kit Carson, Main Rancho, Meadows, Monotony, Nine-mile Bottom, Point of Rocks, Prowers, Red Rock, Robinson, Rocky Ford, Rush Creek, Salt Springs, Sand Creek, The Meadows, Tuttle's, Well No. 1, and Wild Horse, are the settlements in Bent co.

January; and the third at Gold Hill,[3] in February. Soon after David Horsfal discovered his famous mine.

In February the town of Boulder was laid off, ten miles from the gold diggings, by H. Chiles, Alfred A. Brookfield being president of the town company.[4] The first seventy houses on Pearl street were of logs. It soon had a population of 2,000, which so exalted the expectations of its shareholders that they turned away customers by their high prices. Efforts were made by bridging the Platte, and by other means, to draw immigration to that point, but without marked success.[5]

[3] Some of the pioneers of Gold Hill were P. M. Housel and wife, George W. Chambers and wife, Charles Dabney and wife, Charles F. Holly, Miles Jain, John Wigginton, William Fellows, James Smith, E. H. N. Patterson, W. G. Pell, James A. Carr, W. A. Corson, Henry Green, L. M. McCaslin, and family, Richard Blore, John Mahoney, Cary Culver, Hiram Buck, George Zweck, Alph. Cushman, Mrs Samuel Hays, William and John Brerly and families. The first child born in Gold Hill was Mamie McCaslin, who became Mrs J. C. Conlehan of Boulder.

[4] Brookfield was born in Morristown, N. J., in 1830. His father was a merchant, and he was his partner. He was afterward mayor of Nebraska City. He came to Colorado in 1858. Henry Wilson Chiles was born in Va in 1828, and came to Colo from Neb. in 1858. He served in the civil war, and returned to Colo at its close.

[5] Some of the men of Boulder were: Thomas A. Aiken, born in Md, 1808. He came to Colorado in 1858, and settled four miles from Boulder City. He died in 1878.

Samuel J. Aikins, born in Ill. in 1835, came to Colorado in 1858, and settled on a farm on Dry creek, five miles e. from Boulder City. A. J. Macky, who erected the first frame house in Boulder, was born in N. Y. in 1834. He came to Colorado in 1859, in company with Hiram Buck. He mined, worked at his trade of carpentry, and kept a meat market in company with Buck. He erected the first brick house in Boulder, and the first building with an iron front. He was postmaster, county treasurer, justice of the peace, member of the school board, clerk of the dist court, and deputy int. rev. collector. For eight years he held the office of sec. Boulder County Industrial association. In 1872 he was elected town clerk and treasurer, which office he retained for about ten years. He at one time kept the Boulder house. In 1865, in company with Daniel Pound and others, he constructed the Black Hawk and Central City wagon road, and the following year built the Caribou and Central City road. He was influential in securing the state university for Boulder, and aided all worthy enterprises.

Alpheus Wright, born in N. Y. and educated for the law, came to Colorado in 1859. He was a member of the legislature in 1865, and was elected county attorney. He made a comfortable fortune at mining operations.

Samuel Arbuthnot was born in Pittsburg in 1836, and came to Colorado in 1859. He mined at Gold Hill, at Russell gulch, and in California gulch. In 1863 he settled on a farm on Left Hand creek, Boulder co., and helped to organize the Left Hand Ditch company, of which he has been president. He was also clerk of the school board.

About this time men went wild over quartz, until they found, upon protracted trial, that they could not extract the gold   I have already spoken of that era, and its effect on the country.   Then they were driven to other pursuits, especially farming   Boulder organized the first county agricultural   society in 1867. Grist-mills were erected, and a farming community grew up at the confluence of the north and south Boulder creeks, with a thriving centre called Valmont.[6]   Boulder became the grain-milling as well as grain-growing country[7] of the territory.   In time, also, its mines were developed, until its annual production of the precious metals reached half a million,

George F. Chase was one of the Central City and Boulder valley toll-road builders, county commissioner, town trustee, farmer, and stock raiser. George W. Chambers was a miner, farmer, county commissioner, and justice of the peace.   Andrew Douty erected on South Boulder creek the first grist-mill completed in Colorado.   He also built a mill at Red Rock, near Boulder City, in 1866.   In 1867 he erected the first flouring mills at St Louis, in Larimer co., where he died in 1874.   Douty was from Pa.

Tarbox & Donnelly erected the first saw mill in Boulder in 1860, using the water power at the mouth of the cañon.   J. P. Lee built the second the same season a few miles from Gold Hill; Tourtalotte and Squires a third in Boulder City in 1862.   Samuel Copeland erected the first steam saw mill in Four-mile cañon in 1863.

Edward W. Henderson was the purchaser of the Gregory mine, and had many vicissitudes of fortune.   He was connected with the Western Smelting company, in charge of affairs; was treasurer of Gilpin co.; and receiver of the U. S. land office at Central City 1873-9.

T. J. Graham brought the 3-stamp mill in 1859 which was set up on Left Hand creek, near Gold Hill.   He continued to reside at Boulder.

Other men of Boulder in early times were William Arbuthnot, miner and farmer; August Burk, baker and farmer; Norman R. Howard, miner and farmer; Thomas J. Jones, miner, merchant, and farmer, built the large hotel at Gold Dirt in 1860; Henry B. Ludlow, miner and farmer; Holden R. Eldred, freighter and merchant; William Baker, farmer; Thomas Brainard, freighter and farmer; John Reese, carpenter, miner, and farmer, elected assessor of Boulder co. in 1871; Jay Sternberg, miller and proprietor of the Boulder City flouring mills; William R. Howell, twice elected sheriff of Boulder co.

[6] The first cheese factory was established at Valmont.   This town was laid off by A. P. Allen, his sons, G. S. and W. H. Allen, and his son-in-law, Holden Eldred.   Near Valmont were settled, with their families, W. B. Howell, once sheriff, now a large land owner, John Rothrock, Henry Buck, P. A. Lyner, William A. Davidson, H. B. Ludlow, J. J. Beasley, projector and builder of the Beasley irrigating canal; Jeremiah Leggett, Edgar Sawdey, Hiram Prince, E. Leeds, J. C. Bailey, Stephen H. Green, and George C. Green, his son.

[7] A. and J. W. Smith of Denver, erected a grist-mill at White Rock Cliffs, on Boulder creek, six miles from the mountains; P. M. Housel and John D. Baker built one near Valmont.   Housel was twice elected county judge.

chiefly in silver, and the assessable valuation of the county is considerably over four and a half millions.[8] The coal production of the county in 1883 was 45,500 tons.[9] Iron is one of the valuable productions of this county;[10] and also stone for building purposes, and lime manufacture. Boulder county in 1870 received the addition to its early population of a company of persons organized in Chicago, under the name of the Chicago-Colorado colony, of which Robert Collyer was president, C. N. Pratt secretary, and William Bross treasurer. With so much ability at the head it should have made itself a history. The land, selected by W. N. Byers, consisted of 60,000

[8] The principal mining districts of Boulder are Caribou, in which are situated the well-known mines of Native Silver, Seven-Thirty, Ten-Forty, Poorman, Sherman, No Name, and the Caribou, which shipped in 1881 $227,982.88 in silver bricks. Ward district contained the Ni Wot, Nelson, Stoughton, Celestial, Humboldt, and Morning Star, free-milling gold mines. In Central district were the smuggler, John Jay, Last Chance, Longfellow, and Golden Age. The Gold Hill, Grand Island, Sunshine, Sugar Loaf, and Magnolia districts had good mines, which up to 1886 worked up to their greatest point of productiveness. Placer mines were neglected. *Smith's Rept on Development of Colorado*, 1881-2, 30, being the annual report of the state geologist. There were, in [1880, 9 mills, running 185 stamps, at work in Boulder county. *Fossett, Colorado*, 260.

[9] The coal of Boulder county is a free-burning lignite, of jet black color and high lustre. Coal was first developed here in 1860. In 1864 Joseph W. Marshall, one of the owners, after whom the coal-mining town of Marshall was named, William L. Lee, Mylo Lee, and A. G. Langford erected a small blast-furnace at this place, and made 200 tons of pig-iron from the red hematite ores which abound in the locality. The Marshall mine was worked for several years on a small scale; but when the Golden, Boulder, and Caribou railroad was completed, in 1878, the output immediately increased to 50,000 tons annually. *Tice's Over the Plains*, 86–7; *Rocky Mountain News*, May 6, 1868; *Clear Creek and Boulder Val. Hist.*, 421. Louisville is another coal-mining town on the Colorado Central railroad, 12 miles from Boulder. C. C. Welch of Golden conceived the idea of boring for coal at this place, where it is found 200 feet below the surface. The town was named after Louis Niwatany, a Polander, who had charge of the explorations. This mine was sold to Jay Gould, of the Union Pacific R. R., in 1879, with all its equipments. Louisville has a population of about 600. Among the permanent settlers in Coal Creek valley are the pioneer families of David Kerr, Robert Niver, W. C. Hake, first president of the South Boulder and Coal Creek Ditch company, G. W. Eggleston, A. M. Wylam, and James Minks. Niver, who is a well-to-do farmer, was the projector of the South Boulder and Coal Creek Ditch company, of which he was superintendent and stockholder, the benefit of which to the valley has been great.

[10] The Davidson Coal and Iron Mining company was incorporated in 1873, with a capital stock of $160,000, organized by William A. Davidson, Jonathan S. Smith, George W. Smiley, Charles B. Kountze, and William B. Berger. The company owned 8,000 acres on the line of the Colorado Central railroad, 8 miles from Boulder.

acres in the valleys of Boulder, St Vrain,[11] Left Hand, and Little Thompson creeks, including foot-hill lands with timber, building stone, water, iron, and coal convenient to railroad transportation. A location was chosen for a town about thirty miles due east from Long's peak, the view of which gave it the name of Longmont. The founders of the colony did not find it an Arcadia, but taking it all in all, it proved a good investment. The town, which was incorporated in 1873, had in 1886 1,800 inhabitants, excellent schools, local journals, several churches, important agricultural and milling interests, and a railroad connecting it with the Erie and Canfield[12] coal banks, and was on the line of the Colorado Central railroad.

Boulder City, the county seat of Boulder county, was incorporated in November 1871,[13] and had in 1886 a population of 6,000, railroad communication with Denver[14] and the other principal towns of northern Colorado and the main line of the Union Pacific, sampling and smelting-works, and flouring mills,[15]

[11] In St Vrain valley still reside some of the settlers of 1859, namely: Coffman, Pennock, Allen, Hamlin, Affalter, Peck, Isaac Runyon, B. F. Franklin, John C. Carter, Lyman Smead, David Taylor, Harrison Goodwin, Perry White, Richard Blore, Weese brothers, Thomas McClain, C. C. True, George W. Webster, Fred, George C., and Lawson Beckwith, Alf. and Wash. Cashman, John Hagar, Powell, Ripley. Mason, Manners, and Dickson.

[12] Canfield is another coal-mining town on the Denver and Boulder Valley railroad, 12 miles from Boulder. There were three mines, two owned by the Star Consolidated Coal-mining company, and another, opened in 1879, called the Jackson.

[13] Its mayors have been James Ellison, James P. Maxwell, Charles G. Van Fleet, and John A. Ellet. Maxwell was born in Wis. in 1839, and came to Colorado in 1860, settling first in Gilpin co. at mining and lumber dealing. He removed to Boulder in 1872, and engaged in farming and stock-raising. He was elected to the territorial legislature in 1872 and 1874, to the state general assembly in 1876 as senator, and in 1878 was chosen president of the senate pro tem. He was also elected co. treas. in 1880. Charles C. Brace, elected in 1885, came to Colorado in 1876 from Grand Rapids, Mich., where he was born in 1849. He studied medicine in the Hahnemann medical college of Chicago, coming direct to Boulder after graduating. He was chosen president of the Colorado State Homeopathic Medical society.

[14] While the population was only a few hundred the citizens subscribed $45,000 to secure a branch from the Denver and Boulder Valley R. R. Before it was completed the Colorado Central had reached them.

[15] The sampling-works were erected by N. P. Hill, manager of the Boston and Colorado Smelting co., the smelting-works by J. H. Boyd, in 1874. The Boulder City flouring-mill was erected in 1872 by Jay and D. K. Sternberg; the Colorado state mill in 1877 by Mrs E. B. Yount.

which purchased most of the wheat grown in the county. The business of the town and vicinity supported several banks.[16] It had a good system of water-works, erected in 1874 at a cost of $50,000, a fire department organized in 1875, excellent public schools,[17] newspapers, churches,[18] various benevolent societies, a public library,[19] and the state university. This last distinction was obtained from the legislature of 1861 and the corner-stone laid September 17, 1875. The preparatory and normal departments were opened in 1877, since which period it has increased and prospered.[20] There are few towns of importance in the county.[21]

[16] The Boulder bank was established in 1871 by George C. Corning of Ohio; discontinued in 1877. The National State bank was founded in 1874 by Charles G. and W. A. Buckingham of Ohio, but did not take the present name until 1877. The First National bank of Boulder was opened in 1877 by Louis Cheney.

[17] Boulder built the first school-house in Colorado in 1860, costing $1,200. It was occupied until 1872, when a large public school edifice was erected, costing $15,000, and the graded system was adopted. Since that period additions have been made as required.

[18] The churches of Boulder were founded as follows: methodist in 1860, by Jacob Adriance; congregational in 1864, by William Crawford; presbyterian in 1872, by J. E. Anderson; protestant episcopal, 1873, by Henry Baum; reformed episcopal, 1874, by James C. Pratt; catholic, 1876, by A. J. Abel; baptist, 1872, by J. G. Maver. After these came the christian and adventist churches, liberalists, and spiritualists.

[19] The library was founded by Charles G. Buckingham.

[20] Robert Culver and Charles F. Holly were active in influencing the location. The first board appointed consisted of D. P. Walling, J. Feld, A. O. Patterson, A. A. Bradford, William Gilpin, Edwin Scudder, C. Dominguez, Bryon M. Sanford, William Hammind, J. B. Chaffee, B. F. Hall, Amos Steck, Jesse M. Barela, G. F. Crocker, J. S. Jones, and M. Goss. Colo, Sess. Laws, 1861, 144–8. The first meeting of the board was held in Jan. 1870, when it was duly organized. The citizens had donated 61 acres of land, valued at $10,000, but there was as yet no cash found available. Application was made to the legislature, which not until 1874 appropriated $15,000, conditional upon an equal amount being subscribed in Boulder, and $16,656.66 being raised, the contract was immediately let to McPhee and Keiting of Denver. A second appropriation by the legislature was sufficient to furnish and start the institution. Provision was made for the permanent support of the university by the annual assessment of one fifth of one mill on the valuation of the state, and also for the election of regents by vote of the state. The first board elected were L. W. Dolloff and Junius Berkley of Boulder, George Tritch and F. J. Ebert of Denver, W. H. Van Geisen of Del Norte, and C. Valdez of Conejos. They chose Joseph A. Sewall president of the university. The regular collegiate course began in 1878, and in 1880 there were 121 pupils in attendance. The college edifice was placed on high ground overlooking the city, and surrounded by well cultivated and ornamented grounds. It was built of brick, three stories high, and surmounted by an observatory. The library, furnishing, and finishing were all that could be expected of a university school while in its infancy, and shows that Boulder has done well in selecting this one of the state institutions for its own.

[21] The towns and settlements of Boulder county not mentioned are Altona,

Chaffee county was created out of the southern portion of Lake in February 1879.[22] Its area is about 1,189 square miles, situated between the Musquito range and Arkansas hills on the east, and the great divide on the west. It is peculiarly a mining region. The districts of as yet comparatively undeveloped Chalk creek, one of the earliest discoveries on the east side of the range, Granite,[23] Monarch, south Arkansas, Cottonwood, and Hope are the most extensively developed. The discoveries at Leadville, and consequent railroad building, were the first causes of the recent developments in Chaffee county, as they were of its organization. The Monarch district, lying twenty-six miles west from the town of Salida, contains some of the most remarkable mines in Colorado. They are lead carbonates or argentiferous galena ores, and yield from 20 to 1,500 ounces of silver, and forty to sixty per cent of lead to the ton.[24]

Balarat, Blue Bird, Brownsville, Burlington, Camp Tellurium, Cardinal, Cove Creek, Crisman, Davidson, Eagle Rock, Erie, Four-mile Creek, Highland, Jamestown, Jim Creek, Lakeside, Langford, Left Hand, Logan Mine, Magnolia, Marshall, Mitchell, Modoc, Nederland, Nerkirk Mill, Ni Wot, North Boulder, Orodelfan, Osborn, Pella, Pleasant Valley, Queen City Mills, Rockville, Salina, Springdale, Sugar Loaf, Sumnerville, Sunbeam Gulch, Sunnyside, Sunshine, Tellermin, Ward District, White Peak, Williamsburg. Charles Dabney settled in Boulder in 1860 at mining and blacksmithing. He was postmaster in 1861-2, justice of the peace, and in 1863 county commissioner. In 1878 he engaged in mining and brokerage, and added real estate and lumbering. John J. Ellingham, miner, cattle-dealer, and owner of a quartz-mill, settled same year. Also William H. Dickens, farmer; and Porter T. Hinman, son of Anson Hinman, Alleghany co., N. Y., of which he was judge. He resided in Ohio and Iowa before coming to Colorado, and was assistant in the U. S. land office at Des Moines. He secured a farm of 320 acres on Left Hand creek.

[22] It was first allowed to retain the name of Lake, that portion of the original organization north of it, and containing Leadville, being named Carbonate. But the Leadville people protested—they were permitted to retain their county name of Lake, Carbonate was abandoned, and the new organization was called after a favorite senator. *Colo Sess. Laws*, 1879, 4.

[23] Stephen B. Kellogg, a pioneer of 1859, and who was one of the discoverers of Chalk Creek mines in 1860, was born in Vt in 1816. He had been in South America and Cal. before coming to Colorado. He changed his residence often afterward, but without leaving the state. He was a member of the provisional legislature, has been police justice, and has held several other official positions. *Arkansas Val. Hist.*, 520. Of Granite and its early history I have already spoken.

[24] The large-paying mines of Monarch district were Madonna, Silent Friend, Wilson, Oshkosh, Fair Play, Monarch, Eclipse, Rainbow, Little Gem, Denver, Wonder, Michigan, and Silver King. *Descriptive America*, May 4, 1884. In Chalk Creek district the Murphy mine yielded 50 or more tons of ore daily

The Madonna mine, discovered by the Boon brothers, had cut 300 feet, in May 1884, through solid ore
of this description without finding the end of the
deposit. Other districts contain copper and silver,
some gold and silver, and some free-milling gold. The
bullion product of the county in 1883 was about
$300,000, nearly half of which was in gold.

The Calumet iron mine, the most valuable in the
state, was a deposit of magnetic and hematite ore containing between seventy and eighty per cent pure
iron. Ten car-loads daily were taken by railroad to
Pueblo, where it was smelted and manufactured by
the Colorado Coal and Iron company, who owned it.
The other mineral resources of the county are numerous. Poncho hot springs and Wellsville hot springs[25]
are extensively known for their medicinal qualities.
Charcoal-burning is an important industry, being
made from the piñion which covers the foot-hills.
Lime, also made in large quantities, is used as a flux
at the smelting works of Leadville and Pueblo,
twenty-six car-loads daily going to those places.[26]
Marble is also quarried near Salida, black, white, and
colored, of excellent quality, and granite as fine as
that of New England. Coal deposits just being
opened in 1885 promised well. Agriculture, while

worth $60 per ton, net value. The Columbus, in the South Arkansas district,
was one of the largest silver mines in the state, and yielded 100 ounces to the
ton. These are only named as samples of the best mines in the county. The
Hortense mine, on Mt Princeton, though of low grade ore, was one of the best
developed and most productive.

[25] Poncho Hot springs are 6 miles southwest from Salida. They are 13 in
number. Alongside of them are cold springs. Sulphur and soda predominate,
although it is said that 60 different mineral waters are flowing constantly from
these fountains, with wonderful curative qualities. At Cottonwood creek,
north of Salida, are similar springs. Horn's Rept on Mineral Springs of Colo,
in *State Board of Health Rept*, for 1876, p. 62.

[26] These statements are furnished by W. W. Roller of Salida, who has
contributed his *Colorado Sketches*, MS., to my library. He was born at Tona-
wanda, Erie co., N. Y., in 1842, and came to Colorado in 1877. After spending two years at Colorado Springs as a furniture-dealer, he removed to Salida
and went into the more remunerative business of cattle-dealing. Roller is
supplemented by *E. H. Webb's Salida and its Surroundings*, MS., which deals
more particularly with the town. Webb was born in N. Y. in 1844. He
came to Cleora, Colorado, in 1878 to engage in mercantile pursuits, but removed to Salida when it was founded, and opened business there in 1880, as
the pioneer merchant.

still unrecognized as of importance, exists and increases, the soil being rich and warm in the valleys.[27] The great San Luis valley in the adjacent county of Saguache furnished in 1886 a convenient grazing ground for cattle.

[27] In 1863, when Chaffee was part of Lake county, Frank Mayol took land claim 8 miles north of Buena Vista, where he raised potatoes at 50 c. per pound, realizing $5,000 from 5 acres. He soon accumulated a fortune. George Leonhardy leased the farm in 1871, and purchased it the following year, paying $3,750. He also opened a 'cut-off' into South park, which became the mail route. A post-office was established at his place called Riverside. Leonhardy added to his land from time to time, and being engaged in other business became wealthy. In 1864 Andrew Bard and Frank Loan took up land near where Buena Vista now stands, which they watered from Cottonwood creek, and which produced large crops of hay and vegetables, all of which found a ready market. The next settlers were Benj. Schwander, William Bale, afterward sheriff, John McPherson, and J. E. Gonell, who took claims on the creek, and in 1865 Cottonwood was made an election precinct, and Bale, Bard, and Gonell were appointed judges of election. The same year Galatia Sprague, R. Mat. Johnson, Matthew Rule, and John Gilliland settled at Brown creek, where the agricultural and mining town of Brownsville grew up. Gilliland, John Weldon, and G. M. Huntzicker were appointed judges of election in that precinct, which extended from Chalk creek to the south end of the county. In 1866 John Burnett, with Nat. Rich and others, settled near the present town of Poncho Springs. Soon another election precinct was declared, embracing the county south of Sand creek, and Burnett, Rich, and W. Christison were appointed judges of election. At the election this year the county seat was removed from Oro to Dayton, near the upper Twin lake. Leonhardy, Bale, and Peter Caruth were county commissioners. At their first meeting in Dayton the Trout creek road was declared a public highway, and the following year a road was opened from the summit of the divide at Poncho pass to the Arkansas river above Trout creek, via the claim of George Hendricks and Brown creek. This gave communication between the north and south portions of the county, and was a difficult piece of work, as the road passed through the narrow defiles of the Arkansas river. Granite was made an election precinct in 1867. In 1868 R. B. Newitt took a claim on the divide, since known as Chubb's rancho, which became the centre of a mining camp, and Charles Nachtrieb erected a grist-mill on Chalk creek, which was proof of the grain capabilities of this region, although when transportation from Denver and other business centres became easier, wheat-raising was abandoned for other cereals. In 1868 Granite was made the county seat, and continued such until after the separation of the northern portion from what became Chaffee. Cache creek, where placer mining had been carried on since 1860, 300 persons being gathered at that camp previous to the rise of Granite, became again in 1865 active, the claims having been purchased by a company with means to work them by hydraulic process. The company obtained government patents to 1,100 acres of placer ground, from which they have taken over $1,000,000. Lost Cañon placer mines, owned by J. C. Hughes, were discovered in 1860, and lie in the mountains of that name at an elevation of from 11,009 to 12,000 feet. Red Mountain district, on the head waters of Lake creek, was discovered in 1864, and created a great excitement, the mineral belt being very extensive, although the ore was f a low grade. It took its name from the color given to the quartz by the decomposition of the sulphurets of iron. Other richer districts soon drew away the mining population. La Plata district, discovered in 1867, embraced the country on the head waters of Clear creek, and all the territory between the Arkansas river and the heights along the stream. Finding less gold than lead and other

Salida, that is to say junction, twenty-eight miles south of Buena Vista, was laid out in May 1880 by Ex-governor Hunt, who owned the land, and was at that time connected with the Denver and Rio Grande railroad.[28]   When it was three months old it had 1,000 inhabitants.   It was for a short time the terminus of the railroad, which was being extended to Leadville, and was the shipping-point of freight and passengers for the Gunnison country, and points beyond.   With the completion of the road to these points much of

metals for which they were not searching, the district was abandoned by its discoverers.   In 1860 a revival of interest took place, the town of Vicksburg was laid off on Clear creek at the entrance to the cañon, and several farms located.   Cottonwood district, on Cottonwood creek, is a silver-producing region of more recent development, with some rich mines on the north-east side of Mt Princeton, and on Jones and Fox mountains.   Trout creek district was discovered after the Leadville mines, and includes Chubb's settlement before mentioned.   It contains both gold and silver mines.   Buena Vista, the county-seat, founded by the Buena Vista Land company, at the junction of the Railroads, is on Cottonwood creek, six miles east of Mt Princeton, in the midst of a plain surrounded by lofty peaks, and having a finely tempered climate.   The company has made many improvements in the way of parks and irrigating ditches, and has donated land for school purposes.   The town was incorporated in 1879.   The population in 1884 was 3,000.   There were good schools, several churches, and two newspapers, with a considerable and growing business.   Cleora was founded in the interest of the Atchison, Topeka, and Santa Fé railroad, when it was expected that this road would have secured the right of way through the Grand cañon of the Arkansas river, which was finally granted to the Denver and Rio Grande company.   Having refused any patronage to the bantling of its rival, the latter company laid out the town of Salida, two miles above Cleora, to which the inhabitants and business of the abandoned town immediately removed.   Smith, in his *Statement*, MS., says: 'When Cleora was deserted, two brothers called Raglin went to Oriental, where they discovered a mine, near where Villa Grove now is... Fletcher Taylor went to Bonanza, in Saguache co.   Dr Brien went to the Monarch district...Judge Hawkins built a hotel (at Cleora) which prospered until the town was abandoned...In 1879 Capt. Blake was one of the prominent merchants in Cleora.   There were three lumber yards in Cleora, one belonging to Allen & Mack, who afterward moved to Salida.'

[28] Miss Millie Ohmertz, in her *Female Pioneering*, MS., states that she went to the Arkansas valley, 6 miles above Salida, in 1878, and for three years lived on a farm; but in 1881 moved to Salida to take charge of Gov. Hunt's real estate, he having left the Rio Grande company to undertake the development of extensive coal mines near Laredo in Texas, and to assist in the Mexican National railroad enterprise.   In 1884 George Sackett, from Ohio, came to Salida and invested in real estate in and about the town, all of which he placed in Miss Ohmertz' hands as his agent.   She is also manager of the landed interest of several Denver owners.

J. W. O'Connor, county physician of Chaffee co., was born in Ill. in 1852, and educated at the Rush medical college, Chicago, graduating in 1879.   He came immediately to Denver, where he was appointed resident physician of the Arapahoe co. hospital.   In 1880 he removed to Chaffee co., and the following year was appointed surgeon of the railway.   He superintended the construction of the railroad hospital at Salida.

the business of the place was removea, and its growth
was thenceforth slower. The railroad company in
1886 had extensive buildings and works; the town
was well watered, and had a bank, an opera-house,
churches, schools, good hotels, a public reading-room,

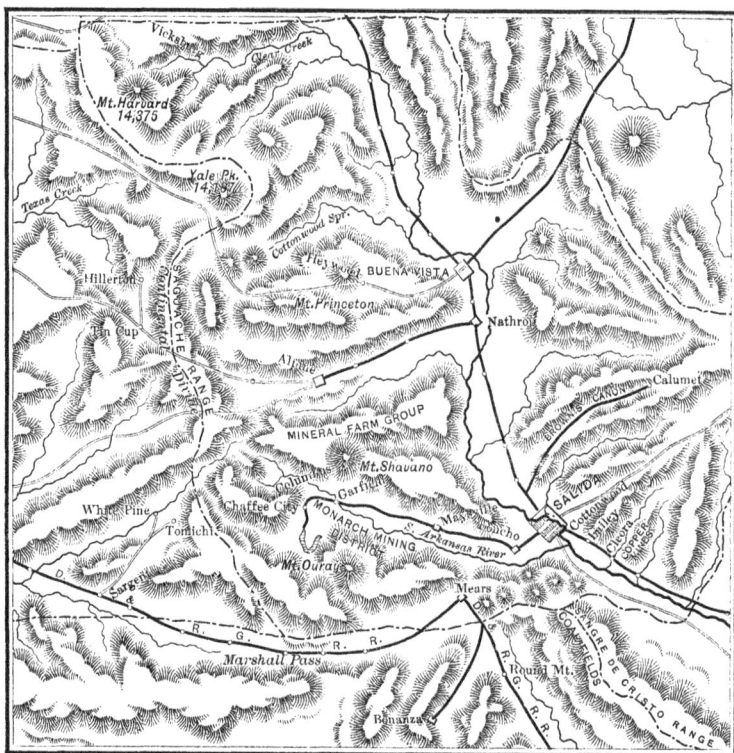

SALIDA AND VICINITY.

pleasant drives, and was generally prosperous, being
in the centre not only of rich mining districts, but of
a good farming region, which was being rapidly settled.[29]

[29] In Ohmertz' *Female Pioneering*, MS., 2, it is said that a large oat-meal
mill would be erected in 1865 by M. Sackett, and that a large smelter was
talked of by other capitalists. A coal mine, 6 miles below Salida, owned by
Davis, Carstarphan, and Craig Brothers, was about to be opened. J. H. Stead,

Clear Creek county, not large, but important, was the scene of some of the earliest mining discoveries after the slight indications of Cherry creek, and one of the original seventeen counties organized by the first legislature. The early history of this portion of Colorado has been quite fully given.[30] Its name was taken from the creek which flows through it, the highlands along which for thirty-seven miles are filled with veins of silver. Another silver belt extends from Idaho springs up Chicago creek to Argentine

born in Albany, N. Y., in 1827, came to Colorado from Chicago in 1880, locating at Maysville, and remaining there for 4 years, when he removed to Salida. He was engaged in mining and merchandising. In a manuscript by him entitled *Town-building* are the following notes on Chaffee co. and Salida; ' Near Salida is the Sedalia copper mine, producing silver and copper, a very valuable mine. In Chalk creek district, 15 miles from Salida, is the Mary Murphy mine, valued at $3,000,000, besides several others of prospective great value.' On Monarch hill he mentions the Monarch, the Madonna, producing 100 tons per day, owned by the Pueblo and Colorado Mining and Smelting company at Pueblo, the Magenta, the Eclipse, Paymaster, Silent Friend, Robert Wilson, Fairplay, and Lexington. He represents the Arkansas valley between Salida and Maysville as being a fine agricultural region, with many valuable farms growing all kinds of grain, apples, and small fruits, while the mesas or table-lands north of them are also productive along the streams, which means that they only need irrigation to become fertile.' See also *Frank Earle's Salida, its Mineral, Agricultural, Manufacturing, Railroad, Resources, Location, Society, Climate, Business,* etc., a pamphlet containing a map and a directory: *Colorado, The Press and People,* MS., a dictation taken from M. R. Moore, postmaster of Salida in 1884. Moore was born in Indiana, in 1846, and came to Colo from Kansas in 1875, locating himself in San Juan co., whence he removed to Salida in 1880. He published a number of newspapers which will be mentioned elsewhere, and established the *Mountain Mail* at Salida. L. W. Craig came to Salida in 1880 and engaged in merchandising for five years. In 1885 he sold out and opened a private bank, known as the Continental Divide bank. He had previously made a fortune in the cattle business in Montana, and was owner in some Colorado mines. There were several other aspiring new towns in Chaffee county, in 1886, all owing their existence primarily to mining, but gradually developing other resources of the country. These were Alpine, Arborville, Americus, Arkansas, Columbus, Chaffee, Carmel, Cascade, Centreville, Chalk Mills, Cove Rock, Crees Camp, Crazy Camp, Divide, Foose's Camp, Forrest City, Free Gold, Garfield, Green Gulch, Hancock, Herring's Park, Helena, Hortense, Junction City, Knoxville, Kraft, Lake Fork, McGee, Mahonville, Mears, Midway, Nathrop, North Fork, Pine Creek, Sharano, Silverdale, Spaulding, St Elmo, Taylor Gulch, Trout Creek, Wellsville, Winfield. The population of the county in 1884 was 10,000.

[30] O. E. Lehow was discoverer of the Spanish bar diggings, and sold his mine for $4,000, receiving his pay in cattle and horses with which he began stock-farming on Cherry creek. In 1860 he located with his brother, C. L. Lehow, a rancho at Platte cañon where he resided until 1870, securing in the mean time 1,600 acres in San Luis valley, which he fenced and stocked with cattle. Then he became a resident of Denver, with an interest in mines at Silver Cliff, in Custer county.

pass. The principal gold district was immediately surrounding Empire, in the vicinity of which there were also some rich silver mines. Clear Creek county was the scene of the first successful milling and smelting of silver ores, as well as of the manufacture of the first silver brick by Garrett, Martine, & Co.[31]

[31] Among the stamp-mills so freely introduced from 1860 to 1864 was the What Cheer mill at Georgetown, arranged at first for the crushing and amalgamating of auriferous quartz. When it was ascertained that no supply of free-milling ores were to be found in that district, the mill was leased to Garrett, Martine & Co. for 5 years, who introduced Bruckner cylinders for roasting and revolving barrels for amalgamating silver ores. In spite of the many difficulties to be overcome, this firm saved 80 to 85 per cent of the silver treated. This was in 1867. In 1868 they sold to Huepeden & Co., but the superintendent, embezzling the funds of the firm. Palmer & Nichols next came into possession of the mill, and failed. In 1873 the Pelican company purchased the property, and having renovated and added to its machinery, made several thousand bars of silver from the ores of the Pelican mine. In 1877 the mill was leased to Ballou, Napheys & Co., who operated it for 10 months at a loss, after which it was used as sampling-works by the Boston and Colorado Smelting co. The next experiment, by Prof. Frank Dibdin of the International Mining co., began in 1868, at East Argentine, 8 miles from Georgetown, and has already been spoken of. This mill ran for 4 years on the company's ore, mixed with the lighter ore from the Belmont and Harris mines, under the superintendence of P. McCann. At the same time the Baker Silver Mining co., Joseph W. Watson, superintendent, erected a mill at West Argentine, which was destroyed by fire. Meanwhile, J. Oscar Stewart, of Georgetown, was experimenting with a small reverberatory furnace, and two amalgamating pans, erected in 1867, and achieved sufficient success to induce eastern capitalists to furnish money to erect a $100,000 mill, which was modeled after his experimental works. But the ores that could be reduced soon became scarce, and while he had thousands of tons of tailings on the dump, containing 40 ounces of silver each, he could not extract this without loss. Next the Arey and Stetefeldt furnaces were tried, which gave too little time for thorough roasting, then a smelting furnace for getting rid of the lead, and many variations and adaptations of the reverberatory furnace, and of the Hunt & Douglas leaching process, but all in vain. In the meantime the mill was twice burned, and a total failure was the result. In 1870–71 a mill was erected at Masonville, 4 miles below Idaho springs, which also failed after a short time. A mill was started in 1872 at Georgetown by Judd & Crosby, who soon abandoned the attempt at making it pay. J. V. Farwell purchased it, took down the patent furnaces, and placed in their stead Bruckner cylinders and amalgamating pans, which, under the management of S. J. Learned, saved a high percentage of the ores treated. The Clear Creek company, by using a modification of the Hunt, Douglas, & Stewart leaching process, made a successful specialty of treating low-grade ores. In this costly school was the knowledge acquired which was to benefit the future miner.

Among the early experiments was that of smelting for lead. The first effort was made by Bowman & Co., negroes from Missouri, who knew something about lead-mining in that state, and thought to put their knowledge to practical use. They erected a small smelter a mile above Georgetown, on Leavenworth fork. It consisted of a rude water-wheel, a bellows, and a 10-foot stack. It was charged a few times with antimonial galena from their mine, the Argentine, but this class of ore soon gave out, and their smelter became worthless. Caleb S. Stowel tried the Scotch hearth with no better results. In 1867 the Georgetown Smelting company erected a lead smelter

Although the county had produced between 1864 and 1884 bullion to the amount of $28,447,400, few of

with a large stack, and the most approved roasters, which produced a few bars of base bullion, and suspended. The Brown Silver Mining company, which owned two productive mines, the Brown and Coin, also erected, about the same time, a mill and smelting-works at Brownsville. By the aid of galena, iron pyrites, and fluxes secured from other districts, the company were enabled to keep their mill going for a year, when it was closed. In the course of their experiments they shipped a large amount of silver to Phil., one mass weighing 1,800 pounds. Subsequently the mill was leased to three different parties, each of which realized a profit from working over the refuse slag. Lead-smelting in Clear Creek co. has been abandoned, the galena ores being sent to Golden or Pueblo in Colorado, or to Omaha, Chicago, St Louis, Wyandotte, Pittsburgh, or Newark for reduction. Richard Pearce, Samuel Wann, and Hiram Williams attempted the smelting of gold and silver ores with the same results as above, the refractory nature of the silver ores preventing their success. But what can be done in other places can certainly be done here as well, when the facilities are provided. The first concentrating mill was introduced in 1870 by the Washington Mining association which had first tried smelting unsuccessfully. The Krom machines for dry concentration were tried, but the mill was burned before a fair test was made. The Clear Creek co. had in 1886 a fifty-ton mill which used Krom's improved dry concentrators with profit, on low-grade ores. Rude Cornish hand-jigs and buddles had been in use from the discovery of silver; but George Teel first systematized their working in 1873, when, as sup't of the Terrible mine, he induced the company to erect a 25-ton mill using the Hartz jigs, settling-tanks, and slime-tables. Teel, Foster, and Eddy erected the Silver Plume mill in 1875, which finally failed and was sold to Franklin Ballou. W. W. Rose & Co., in 1875, built a concentrating mill to reduce the ores of the New Boston mine on Democrat mountain, which failed on account of poor ore. John Collom, after 10 years of experimenting, had a mill built from designs of his own, at Idaho. The Dunderberg co. erected at their mine, in 1878-9, a concentrating-mill of 40 tons capacity, with 5 Hartz jigs, and improved machinery; and A. P. Stevens erected a 20-ton mill at Lawson. Several inventions have been introduced from time to time, but none that have been able to save all the silver, and some of which have failed entirely. The Freeland Mining co. erected at Idaho springs, in 1879, the best appointed concentrating-mill in the state at that time, with a capacity of 115 tons daily. It used 12 Hartz jigs for separating the worthless rock from the ore, and a rotary circular buddle for dividing the latter into pure ore, seconds, and tailings, and saved by means of a second stamp-mill all that the rock contained; but the ore of their mine ran two thirds gold to one third of copper, silver, iron, sulphur, and arsenic. Then there were the Farwell reduction-works, and Pelican reduction-works at Georgetown; the Colorado United Mining company, the Hukill company of Spanish Bar, the Miles company of Idaho, wet concentrating-mills; the Sunshine of Idaho, the Pioneer, Knickerbocker, and Bay State of Empire, raw gold ore amalgamators. The ore-sampling, buying, and shipping firms were: at Georgetown, Rocky Mountain mill, Matthews, Morris & Co., established in 1876, burned, and rebuilt in 1877; Washington mill, Olmstead & Ballou, 1872; G. W. Hall & Co., 1871-2; Clear Creek company, 1876; J. B. Church, 1874; P. McCann, Georgetown and Lawson, 1877-8; Silver Plume, Ballou & Co., 1875; Harry Montgomery, Idaho Springs, 1876. The number of men directly employed in mining, milling, and handling ore in Clear Creek co. was estimated by Fossett to be 2,000. The mines have returned an average of $3 per day for the men thus employed, and have at the same time been advanced nearly or quite an equal amount in value by each day's labor, the mining property of Clear Creek co. being estimated at $20,000,000, which was what the county had produced in gold, silver, lead, and copper down to 1880.

the mines were down to any great depth. The Terrible, situated on Brown mountain, three miles from Georgetown, had reached a depth of 1,300 feet. The ore at this depth yielded 200 ounces of silver to the ton. Twenty-five or thirty other large mines in Silver Plume district were the producing mines of the county, though the Dumont, Idaho springs, Fall river, Chicago creek, Atlantic, and Daily districts were promising, and some yielding well. Not more than half a dozen mines used pumps. The deeper mines were growing richer. Hence the inference that this country has before it a long and prosperous career at mining. The population in 1880 was about 8,000. Georgetown, the county seat, is situated at the head of a level valley, with mountains towering above it covered with pine and veined with silver. It has a population of 3,500. Higher, and at the foot of Republican, Sherman, and Leavenworth mountains, are the mining towns of Silver Plume and Brownville, with 1,800 and 1,000 inhabitants respectively. Notwithstanding the altitude of Georgetown, 8,504 feet, the mountains rise so much above it that half the day's sunshine is cut off except in midsummer.[32]

[32] Thomas Cooper, born in Kent, Eng., migrated to the U. S. in 1852, and after several removes and a visit to his native land came to Colorado in 1859, engaging in placer mining with success, making some valuable discoveries. He became one of the owners of the Champion.

Frank J. Wood, another of the men of 1859, was born in Ohio in 1839, and came to Colorado from Iowa. His first location was at Central, where he remained at mining for five years, making considerable money which he lost in speculation. He then set himself up in merchandising at Empire, but in 1867 removed to Georgetown, where he opened a drug store. After a time he sold out and went into the book and stationery trade.

F. J. Marshall, who organized the Marshall Silver Mining company, which sold its property to the Colorado Central Consolidated Mining company, and has been connected with some of the most celebrated mines in the county and state, was born in Va in 1816. He founded Marysville, on the Big Blue river, Kansas. He was a member of the first and second legislatures of Kansas. In the struggle of 1855 he was elected by the legislature brigadier-general of militia, and afterward promoted to be major-general and commander-in-chief of the Kansas militia. In 1856 he was elected governor under the Lecompton constitution, but retired to private life in 1857. Two years afterward he came to Colorado, and after a few years settled himself at Georgetown.

Charles P. Baldwin, a mining man of Georgetown, was born in Maine in 1835. On the breaking out of the rebellion he raised a company and enlisted in service of his country, being promoted until he reached the rand of briga-

The only other towns of any note in the county are Idaho springs,[33] Freeland, Empire City, Bakerville, Dumont, and Red Elephant.

dier-general. He was president of the board appointed to audit war claims at Richmond after Lee's surrender. On being mustered out in 1866 he came to Colorado, selecting Georgetown for a residence on account of the silver mines. After prospecting and mining for a time he purchased the Comet lode, which in a few months yielded $10,000, but could never be made to repeat this production. In 1879 he came into ownership of the Magnet, which for a long time was a rich and productive property. In 1884 he was appointed manager of the Terrible group of miners. He was a man of good ability and commanded the respect of all.

Russell J. Collins, who came to Georgetown in 1866 fresh from the army, in which he had served as surgeon of an Ill. regiment during the war. He was born in N. H. in 1828, and graduated from Berkshire college in 1851, afterward practising in Grand Rapids, Mich., and in Ill.

George W. Hall, born in N. Y. in 1825, came to Colorado in 1860, engaging in lumber dealing at Central and at Empire, but removing finally to Georgetown in 1868. In 1878 he engaged actively in mining, and became manager of the Colorado Central Consolidated Mining company's mines, which produced $500,000 in one year.

[33] Idaho Springs was the first settled town in the county. It was within its limits that the first mining was begun in 1859 on Chicago bar. About 200 miners were attracted thither, many of whom remained over winter, and in 1860 the town was perceived to be a fixed entity. A hotel was opened in a log cabin, kept by F. W. Beebe, which was the precursor of the present Beebe house. Among the pioneers of 1859 who still remained in 1880 were William Hobbs, John Needam, and A. P. Smith. A. M. Noxon, E. F. Holland, R. B. Griswold, John Silvertooth, M. B. Graeff, John W. Edwards, and others, settled in 1860. In 1861 religious services began to be held by an itinerant preacher nicknamed the Arkansas Traveller, whose real name was Bunch, intermitted with sermons by another preacher named Potts. In 1860 the Hukill quartz mine was discovered, and in 1861 the Seaton quartz mine and the first stamp mill erected. And in this year the county was organized, and the county seat located at Idaho Springs. It was not until 1863 that any attention was given to improving the hot soda springs, when E. S. Cummings erected a small bathing house. In 1866 Harrison Montague purchased them and began to prepare for the reception of visitors and invalids. Their medicinal qualities and nearness to Denver have made them a popular resort and the chosen residence of a number of wealthy families. The temperature ranges from 70° to 110° Fahr. in the several springs, which is tempered to use by water from Soda creek. The altitude of the springs is 8,000 feet, the scenery attractive, and the climate agreeable. In 1873 a government patent was obtained for the town-site, and a board of trustees organized, with R. B. Griswold president. It was not until railroad facilities reached it that the town began to make any rapid progress. The population in 1884 was between 800 and 900.

This history of Idaho Springs is only a proper introduction to the history of the present county seat and metropolis, Georgetown. In 1859 George F. Griffith and D. T. Griffith, his brother, while prospecting for gold, followed the windings of South Clear creek to the foot of the mountains, where Georgetown now stands, and discovered the Griffith lode, which runs into the town-site. Like most of the silver fissure mines, it showed gold at the top, and was rich. Griffith mining district was organized June 25, 1860, after a number of discoveries had been made in the neighborhood of the first. George F. Griffith was the first recorder, and James Burrell first president. About the same time the town was laid off, and named Elizabethtown, after a sister of the Griffiths. A rude water-mill, with 12 wooden, iron-shod

Conejos county, first named Guadaloupe by the legislature of 1861, and changed during the same ses-

stamps, pounded out the gold from the Griffith, Burrell, Corisannie, and Nancy lodes, which soon, howev.r, betrayed that refractory character which paralyzed mining for a time. For two weeks in 1863 John T. Harris was the sole denizen of the town, the population having run after the better paying discoveries at Idaho, Spanish bar, and Empire, leaving Georgetown to desolation. In 1864-65 a company formed in the east erected a mill, which, on trial, was a failure, and the discovery that this was really a silver district coming about the same time, started on again the car of progress. In September 1864 Ex-provisional Governor R. W. Steele, James Huff, and Robert Layton discovered the Belmont lode, in East Argentine district, which, on being assayed, as I have related, established the argentiferous character of the region about Georgetown. From this time its prosperity was assured, In 1867 it was resurveyed and platted by Charles Hoyt, under direction of the citizens, and the name changed to Georgetown, by vote at a mass meeting held a the corner of Rose and Mary streets. At the general election of this year it became the county seat, and was incorporated in Jan. 1868. Under its municipal organization its first police judge was Frank Dibdin. The selectmen of the 1st ward were W. W. Ware and Charles Whitner; of the 2d ward, H. K. Pearson and John Scott. The *Colorado Miner* newspaper was established the same year, by J. E. Wharton and A. W. Barnard, the office being in a 12 by 14 building in the lower town. About the same time the public school was organized, Miss L. H. Lander being the first teacher. She was drowned in Clear creek about the last of June, 1867, slipping from the foot-log used as a bridge. In 1870 the mining camp of Silver Plume, two miles above Georgetown, was first settled, and named after the mine, which has since become famous and given its name to the district, which contains many of the most important mines in the county. The richness of the Dives, Pelican, and other mines provoked cupidity, and consequent litigation, which for years netted a rich profit to the legal fraternity. The Terrible was at length sold to an English company, which has liberally aided its development. Georgetown receives the benefit of the immediate neighborhood of these mines, besides being the seat of most of the reduction-works of the county. Unlike the more modern towns of Colorado, little care was bestowed upon streets or buildings, although the character of the latter soon improved. It had an excellent public school, and several churches. The methodists organized in 1864, B. T. Vincent, preacher at Central City, officiating. They erected a church, costing $8,000, in 1869. The presbyterian church organized in 1869, and erected a stone edifice in 1874. The episcopalians first organized in 1867, F. W. Winslow rector, and built a small church in 1869, which was destroyed by a hurricane soon after its completion. It was rebuilt, and in 1877 received a large pipe-organ, the first in Georgetown. The catholics, as usual, secured a valuable block of land when the town was first laid out, Thomas Foley being their first pastor. In 1872 they built a small wooden church, and in 1875 a brick edifice, costing $12.000. Georgetown possesses a good system of water-works. The company was organized in 1874. The town has also a fire department, consisting of several companies. At a tournament, held under the auspices of the state association, at Georgetown, the Alpine hose company won the first prize, consisting of a silver tea-set and a brass cannon. In a contest with a Denver company the same year, the Bates hose company of Georgetown were victorious. In 1879, with the other Georgetown companies, they took the first prize of $150 at both the hose and hook-and-ladder races, and later in the year, at the state tournament in Denver, again took the first prize in the hose race. The Star hook-and-ladder company has also won a long list of prizes. Among them are a silk flag, presented by the women of Georgetown, and two silver trumpets. At the state tournament at Georgetown, in 1877, they were victorious, and at a tourna-

sion to Conejos, was until the advent of the railway
inhabited almost exclusively by a Spanish-American

ment at Cheyenne, in July 1878, they won $50. In August of the same year
they took the champion belt at the state tournament held at Pueblo, and $75
in gold. Georgetown has a public hospital, and a number of secret and benevolent orders and societies. The man who sawed the lumber to build the
first frame houses in Idaho Springs was William F. Doherty. He was born
in Me in 1837. He learned the trade of an iron-moulder, working thereat,
and making occasional voyages to sea. In 1862 he enlisted in the 1st R. I.
cavalry, was in several important engagements, and carried the colors in
Sheridan's famous ride, in Oct. 1864. He was mustered out in Feb. 1865,
and came to Colorado in May following. After mining at Black Hawk one
year he settled at Idaho Springs, where, as miner and lumberman, he resided
continuously. In 1884 he purchased the Spa hotel.

F. F. Obiston, born in England in 1843, came to the U. S. as secretary of
the Washoe Mining company of Reno, Nev., in 1864, where he remained two
years. He was afterward supt of different mines on the Comstock, and came
to Colo in 1879, when he purchased, in company with J. W. Mackay, the
Freeland mine, which produced, in the 6 years following, $2,000,000. He
also purchased, with Mackay, the Plutus, another valuable mine. The two
mines together produced $20,000 per month. The Freeland mine, in 1855,
had two miles of tunnelling. The property is over a mile in length, and is
situated on South Clear creek, 4 miles from Idaho springs, and two miles
from the Colorado Central raildroad.

B. D. Allen, born in Ohio in 1845 came to Colorado in 1880. He was
auditor of the express company until 1884, when he purchased, with Matthews & Webb of Denver, the sampling-works at Idaho Springs, of which
he became manager, doing a business of $100,000, and handling 1,500 tons
of ore per month, or about three fourths of all the output of the district.

The only other town in Clear Creek county in 1886, with a history, was
Empire. In the spring of 1860 a few prospectors from Spanish bar, a small
district contiguous to Idaho springs, namely, George Merrill, Joseph Musser,
George L. Nicholls, and D. C. Skinner, temporarily organized Union district
for placer mining, and founded a settlement, Merrill and Musser erecting the
first cabin. Dr Bard, after whom Bard creek is named, drove the first wagon
into the new town. About August 1st Edgar Freeman and H. C. Cowles
came across the mountains from Central. Prospecting on Eureka mountain,
they picked up some bits of wire gold, and, stimulated by this discovery,
continued with others to search for mines of gold and silver in the district.
In Sept. D. C. Dailey & Co. discovered a lode which they believed to be silver, naming the mountain where it was found Silver mountain, and the lode
Empire. The Keystone lode was discovered about the same time. The miners at once proceeded to complete the organization of the district, electing,
in Dec., Henry Hill pres., H. C. Cowles miners' judge, D. J. Ball clerk and
recorder, James Ross sheriff, and George L. Nicholls surveyor, all of whom
remained in office until the organization of the territory. Some further development of the mines in Union district showed them to be auriferous, and
population flowed in from the adjoining districts. The settlement took the
name of Empire City, and was surveyed and laid off in lots and blocks by
G. L. Nicholls, H. C. Cowles, D. J. Ball, and Ed. Freeman. The enthusiasm
of the first set-to at quartz-mining received a check when the owners of lodes
had come down to pyrites, and the flush times of Empire were over in 1865;
but ever since the art of mining properly and profitably began to be mas-
tered, the mines about Empire have steadily yielded a golden return. The
town, albeit it is a prettily situated spot, has never returned to the anima-
tion of its first days, and remains but a miners' camp.

Lawson, a mining camp six miles below Georgetown, named after Alexander Lawson, owes its existence to the Red Elephant group of mines, discovered in 1876. Dumont, two miles below, was formerly known as Mill

or Mexican population, which, while they sent members to the general assembly, maintained little communication with the United States Americans to the north of them.[34]

City, but in 1880 had its name changed in honor of John M. Dumont, one of the pioneers of the county. The other settlements are Bakerville, Baltimore Tunnel, Bear Creek, Big Bar, Brook Vale, Burleigh Tunnel, Camp Clifford, Downerville, Dry Gulch, Elephant, Fall River, Floyd Hill, Freeland, Gilson's Gulch, Grass Valley, Green Lake, Hukill, North Empire, Seaton Hill, Silver Creek, Silver Dale, South Clear Creek, Spring Gulch, Stephensville, Stevens' Mine, Swansea, Yankee Bar, and York River.

[34] An exception to the rule was Antonio D. Archuleta, born in Taos, N. M., in 1855, and removed to Conejos co. in 1856. He was sent to Denver in 1870 to be educated, where he remained 4 years, when he returned to Conejos to act as clerk in his father's store, and became a partner. He was elected to the general assembly in 1882, and in 1884 to the state senate. The boundaries of the county have been several times changed and diminished, but it still contains a large area, much of which lies in the fertile San Luis valley. The principal industries in the ante-railroad period were wheat-raising, wool-growing, and cattle-raising. The farming productions found a ready market in the San Juan mines to the west, but such was the race prejudice of the Mexicans that when the active American population began to invade this region, many abandoned it. Those who were left were chiefly employed as freighters. In 1879 a colony of Mormons settled at Manassas, on Conejos creek, and these will probably affect the agricultural output of the county favorably. An immigration of Scandinavians was invited to this section in 1882, which will add to the farming population a valuable element. Irrigating ditches are being constructed, which will bring a large body of land under cultivable conditions. Its mineral wealth is very little developed. The original county seat was at Guadaloupita, but was changed to Conejos, a Mexican town, and has a good local trade. Alamosa is, however, the principal town, having connection with Santa Fé, Pueblo, and the San Juan country. It is situated on the west side of the Rio Grande del Norte, almost in the centre of San Luis park, at an elevation of 7,492 feet, with a panorama of mountain views skirting the plain on every side. Aside from its fine situation it is a thriving place. It was founded in June 1878. In the first six months the sales of merchandise reached $600,000. The population at the end of a year was 500. A large amount of freighting was done in wool, pelts, hides, machinery, and bullion. *Colorado Condensed*, 6-7. This is a pamphlet collated in 1883 by the editor of the *Rocky Mountain News*, which furnishes a few paragraphs on the several counties, chiefly with regard to their present condition. *Fossett's Colorado*, 85-6, also furnishes a few hints of the recent advancement of Conejos county, and the *Colorado Gazetteer* of 1871 portions of its earlier history, but the whole is incomplete, owing to the avoidance of the Americans by the Mexicans, and the little known of the latter by the former. Pagosa Springs is a government reservation withheld from sale on account of the great hot basin of medicinal waters, which is found here. The spring is situated west from Alamosa, on the south side of the San Juan river, near its headwaters. Its altitude is 7,084 feet, the country about it is fertile, and the climate agreeable, a combination of advantages which, united with scenic and other attractions, promises to make this a noted resort whenever the required improvements are made for the accommodation of visitors. Antonita is a town which had a rapid growth. The lesser towns and settlements of Conejos co. are Amargo, Antonio, Camp Lewis, Capulin, Carracas, Chama, Cockrell, Coxo, Codyville, Cumbres, Ephraim, Fuertecitos, Gato, Juanita, Jackson, La Jara, Lava, Los Brazos, Los Pinos, Los Rincones, Los Serribos, Navajo, Osier, Piedra, Price,

Costilla county was originally larger than at present.[35] Its characteristics and history are similar to those of Conejos, having a Mexican population, and embracing a portion of the San Luis valley or park. A part, also, of the county is claimed as belonging to the Sangre de Cristo, or Beaubien grant, and is unsurveyed.[36]

Rincones, Rio Grande, Rivane, San Antonio, San José, San Rafael, Serro Largo Servilleta, Sheldon, Shultze Rancho, and Spring Creek.

[35] For earlier county boundaries, see *Gen. Laws, Colo*, 1861, 52-7; *Id.*, 1864, 68-9; *Id.*, 1877, 186-216.

[36] The history of this grant is given in a manuscript by Cutler, of the Denver *Journal of Commerce*, in my possession, as follows: A few years before the Mexican war two Canadians, Charles Beaubien and Miranda, settled at Taos, then a state of the republic of New Mexico, under the dictatorship of Santa Anna. The local governor of Taos was Armijo, a Mexican of culture and liberal ideas. He had for a secretary and confidential adviser Charles Bent, the same who was made military governor of New Mexico by Gen. Kearny when the U. S. acquired that territory, and who was killed in the massacre of Taos not long after. The Frenchmen above named obtained by purchase a large tract of desert country, lying north of Red river, the chief consideration being their promise to induce an immigration from Canada and France, an obligation which they never fulfilled, although the grant was approved by the Mexican government, and signed and sealed by Santa Anna. Lucien Maxwell married the daughter of Beaubien, and purchased of his father-in-law for a small sum all that part of the grant lying north of Red river, and between that stream and the Raton mountains. He erected a fine house on the Cimarron, where he entertained in good old feudal style, surrounded by his dependents, and owning immense herds of cattle, sheep, and blooded horses, employing as herders all the Cimarrons. About 1869 Wilson Waddington, Jerome B. Chaffee, and George M. Chilcott purchased the Maxwell grant for an English syndicate, each of them making a fortune out of it. The English company bonded the land in Holland as security for a large amount of money, and when the loan became due allowed it to be sold. But the Dutch proprietors in a few years tired of their useless possessions, and the land was sold year after year for taxes. Their agent in New York was Frank Sherwin, who bought in the shares of the Holland firm as he could obtain them until he became proprietor, and then he laid claim to a wide belt of land on the north-west border of the grant, extending over the Raton mountains into Costilla county, Colorado. Mining in this county is of late beginning, but promises well. Its iron mines include some of the largest bodies of that metal yet found in the state, the ore taken from here being smelted at Pueblo and Denver. The first county seat was San Miguel, changed to San Luis, the principal town in the county. The only other town of any note is Placer. Antonio A. Salaza, born at Abiquiu, N. M,, in 1848, began herding sheep at 10 years of age, remaining at that occupation 6 years, when he went to work in a general store in San Luis, becoming clerk, then treasurer of the county for two years, next, a stock-raiser and a merchant. He was elected to the general assembly in 1880, and to the state senate in 1882. He never spent a day in school, and acquired his education by night study. The following are the settlements in the county : Big Bend, Big Hill, Charmer, Conlon's Ferry, Costilla, Elkhorn, Fort Garland, Garland City, Grayback, La Trinchera, Lojeta, Medano Springs, Mountain Home, Orean, Russell, San Accacio, Sangre de Cristo, San Pedro, Spalding, Underhill, Upper Culebra, Valles, Wayside, Wilcox, Williams.

Custer, formerly a portion of Frémont, from which it was cut off in 1877, is a small county, lying on the east slope of the Sangre de Cristo range. It contains the El Mojada or Wet mountain valley, an elevated basin with an undulating surface, sentineled by lofty peaks, and offering some of the finest scenery in the state. The extent of the valley, which is watered by Grape creek, a tributary of the Arkansas river, is twenty-five miles in length by ten in width. Its elevation, from 6,500 to 7,000 feet, does not prevent it being a good farming region, although the lower and smaller Hardscrabble valley, twenty miles east, is more productive, with a shorter and less severe winter season. Wet mountain valley was for some years overlooked or neglected, owing to the difficulty, or rather, impossibility, of taking wagons through the cañons of Oak and Hardscrabble creeks leading into it; and although it was prospected for minerals in 1863, it had not a single settler before 1869. It was selected about this time for the seat of a German colony numbering 367 souls, who settled there in 1870.[37]

[37] The first prospectors in the valley were S. Smith, Melrose, and Wetmore, of Pueblo. The first settlers, in 1869, were Voris, Home, and Taylor, who took land claims that year. *Brinckley & Hartwell, Southern Colo,* 99. The history of the Colfax Agricultural and Industrial Colonization company is as follows: Prof. Carl Wulsten, impelled by a desire to ameliorate the condition of persons of his own nationality, 'condemned by a cruel fate to work in greasy, ill-ventilated, and nerve-destroying factories of the great city of Chicago,' formed a colony of about 100 families, and brought them to Wet Mountain valley, in his eyes a paradise of beauty, fertility, and health-giving air. But the colonists, used to city habits, and at a loss what to do in a naked country, however beautiful, proved ungrateful for the favor conferred, and in 6 months the organization had collapsed, every man following his own devices. It was doubtless best so, for every one of the colonists was in a few years in good circumstances, and the benefit aimed at was achieved independently of organization. About 30 families took land claims, which speedily became productive farms; the others went to different parts of the territory, but all remaining in it. William Ackelbein, John and William Knuth, O. Groeske, Carson Kunrath, William Shultz, Ruester, father and son, Dietz, Menzel, Klose, John and Frederick Piorth, Kettler, Philips, Katzenstein, Henjes, Falkenberg, and others were among those who remained. Abstract of an account of the colony, by its founder, in *Brinckley and Hartwell's Colo,* 106-7. Roads were made, farms opened, and the colonists, being joined by others, soon made this portion of Fremont county blossom as the rose. But had it remained purely an agricultural community, its separate organization as Custer county might not have occurred. The ubiquitous prospector, in the persons of Daniel Baker and C. M. Grimes, from Black Hawk, discovered a

Delta is a new county, cut off from Gunnison in February 1883, lying on both sides of the north fork of Gunnison river. What has been said of the leading features of the Gunnison country in a previous

crevice containing metal in 1871. Grimes was a pioneer, and had been a leading man in Gilpin co. as sheriff and territorial representative. He was of that genial, liberal, merry making disposition which secured for him the affectionate appellation of 'old Grimes,' according to mountain custom. Wulsten, in 1869, took to Chicago pieces of rock from the vicinity of later discoveries at Gold Hill, which assayed 1¾ ounces in gold, and 37 ounces in silver, per ton. The Black Hawk mine, later called the Senator, began to pay in 1873; the Pocahontas and Humboldt in 1874. These were the initial point in the mining district named Hardscrabble, in which more than 600 locations were made previous to 1874. Mining was carried on, and some small smelters introduced, but no excitement was created for some years. Meantime, the mining town of Rosita had grown up, overshadowing the pioneer settlement of Ula, situated on Grape creek, in a location thought favorable to future greatness. Joseph A. Davis was the first settler at Ula, in Sept. 1871. Soon after he erected the Ula hotel, and kept a store in it. The town grew, and the people having petitioned for a post-office, it was established, under the name of Ula, at Davis' store. The Wet Mountain Valley Library association was founded in 1874 by R. S. Sweetland and Dr Richter, who was one of the original colonists. The interests of the district and valley seeming to demand it, the legislature created the county of Custer in March 1877, and the commissioners, R. S. Sweetland, H. E. Austin, and T. W. Hull, named Ula as the county seat, but it was removed soon after, by election, to Rosita. This step in advance was greatly hastened by the remarkable discovery of the Maine gold and silver mine, by Edmund C. Bassick, who named it after his native state. This was in many respects a phenomenal mine, consisting of a chimney of circular form, filled with boulders, and from six to 25 feet in diameter. The ores, both of gold and silver, were new to mineralogists. They consisted of a true conglomerate, the kernels of which were trachytic, prophyry, and quartz, encased in a cement of a telluride of gold and silver, exceeedingly rich. For instance, a lump 12 inches long and wide and six inches in thickness weighed 43 pounds, and assayed $7,000 per ton. *Engineering and Mining Journal* in *Yankee Fork Herald*, Oct. 18, 1879. The proportion of gold and silver was 70 per cent of the former to 30 of the latter. Some of these nodules had the telluride coating covered with crystallized blende and copper pyrites. Altogether, the Bassick mine was a discovery of much interest to the scientific world, as it was of profit to its finder, for it sold for over $1,000,000 when it was down nearly 300 feet. Its yearly yield after 1880 was nearly $1,000,000. The Bassick mine, as it is now called, was situated on the top of a conical hill, two miles and a half north-west from Rosita; and it appeared as if it might have been at some period of the earth's history a geyser which had built this mound. The suggestion led to prospecting in the direction of other similar eminences, and the discovery, three miles westerly from Rosita, of the Golden Eagle, a true fissure vein in black granite, carrying from two to five ounces of free gold per ton.

In 1878 a miner named Edwards, while passing by a long sloping hill which from its abrupt termination at one end was called the cliff, knocked off a piece of rock, which he had assayed, and which returned twenty-seven ounces in silver per ton, not enough to pay the expense of smelting. He thought no more of it for several months, when, weary of unfruitful prospecting, he returned with his partner, Powell, to the cliff, and soon found rock which assayed $1,700 per ton. Taking in another partner, Spoffard, they made further investigations, and located the mines later celebrated as **the** Racine Boy, Horn Silver and Plata Verde situated on the mountain which

chapter pertains also to this division. The town of Delta is the county seat. Escalante and Dominguez are two other new towns.

Dolores county was established in 1881. It contains in its eastern part the great carbonate district

they called Silver Cliff. This district soon bade fair to rival Leadville, the ores being chlorides, which needed no roasting. In 1879 the discovery mine was sold in New York to Senator Jones, of Nevada, and James Keene, and stocked for $10,000,000. The other two sold equally well. Other chloride mines were soon after discovered, and more recently a second mine, like the Bassick, called the Bull Domingo. I have not space to mention the many important mineral discoveries which have made the new and small county of Custer notable and prosperous among its older neighbors. Its most important towns are Rosita and Silver Cliff, besides which there are several busy mining camps. Rosita. that is to say, little rose, was founded early in 1873, as the capital of the mining district of Hardscrabble, organized Nov. 15th of the year previous. The miners gathered in the district at this time were the Remine brothers from Central City, Jarvis and son from Georgetown, Schoolfield brothers from Mill City, Jasper Brown from Fort Garland, Hedges, V. B. Hoyt, James Pringle, William J. Robinson, Charles Ragnan, Nicholas Mast, Thomas Barrett, and John Palmer. When the town was laid off Frank S. Roff was the first blacksmith—he was afterward mayor of Silver Cliff—Frank Kirkham and Lewis Herfort, storekeepers, James Duncan and Charles Nelson, carpenters, James A. Gooch, afterward postmaster, George S. Adams, the first lawyer, J. M. Hobson, Woodruff brothers, Alexander and Thomas Thornton, Charles Fisher, keeper of the first meat market, and livery stable, Ed C. Smith, saloon keeper, John Hahnenkratt, boarding house keeper for the Hoyt Mining company, who afterward built the Grand View hotel, A. V. Temple, who surveyed the town site, Malcolm C. Duncan, and others. In the autumn of 1874 the town consisted of 400 houses, with over 1,000 inhabitants. It had by this time several stores and hotels, a newspaper, the *Rosita Index*, owned by Charles Baker, and edited by Lane Posey, and a bank, owned by Boyd and Stewart. These bankers claimed to have secured an interest in the Pocahontas mine, which was in possession of Herr brothers, and, aided by the superintendent, Topping, assumed tne management, Topping retaining most of the miners, and keeping a reserve of rough characters to fight, if fighting it came to, in the struggle for mastery. The leader of this gang was one Graham, an ex-convict. James Pringle having been wounded by one of Graham's men, without provocation, a committee of safety was organized, the roads guarded to prevent escape, and the mine surrounded. Graham appearing, armed, was ordered to surrender, but turning to fly was shot down. The remainder of the gang attempted to escape in a body, but were intercepted, and being much frightened at the attitude of the citizens, displayed a white flag, and were finally permitted to leave town. Boyd, who had been seized and confined, was also permitted to depart. Stewart had already fled. It was later discovered that he was a forger, being sought by the police of New York, having served a 20 years' term in the Sing Sing state prison. Thus ended an attempt at the piracy of a mine. The same property was embarrassed by litigation, in which Ballard of Ky figured, but ultimately emerged from its troubles to be a good property. There were the usual unsuccessful attempts at the reduction of ores, but the Penn. works situated in the town, erected to treat the Humboldt ores, performed the same for other mines. The richer ores were sent to Cañon City or Pueblo. The Denver and Rio Grande extended a branch to Silver Cliff in 1881, which facilitated their transportation. The population in 1880 was 1,200. Elevation of the town 8,200.

of the San Juan country already described, and in its western part good grazing grounds, which, if irrigated, would be cultivable. Rico is the county seat, and the seat of the smelters erected to reduce the rich ores of the district to bullion. The population in 1883 was 2,000, of which 750 were at Rico. Bowen, Narraquinep Spring, and Dolores are rising towns. The assessed valuation was $552,310, and the bullion production $200,000. Besides silver and gold mines, some of the best coal in the state is found here.

Douglas county was organized by the first territorial legislature, since which time it has lost the larger portion of its area. It resembles Arapahoe, which it adjoins, and is principally occupied by a grazing and farming population, with dealers in lumber and building stone, which find a ready market in Den-

Silver Cliff took root with the erection of the first house in Sept. 1878 by McIlhenney and Wilson, and grew so surprisingly that when it was a year old it had 1,200 inhabitants and houses for their accommodation, with all the usual concomitants of comfortable living, and some of the luxuries of older communities. The town site was patented Dec. 8, 1879. The population was at one time 4,000, but since the rush has passed has settled back to 1,500. Mills and reduction works are being introduced. In 1882 the Silver Cliff mines were under a cloud from the difficulty of finding the exact processes for the deeper ores, none, however, except one, being down more than 700 feet, the Humboldt being 1,800. At this time there was a 40-stamp mill in operation on the property of the Silver Cliff Mills company, treating 100 tons daily of the Racine Boy ore. The sampling establishment of the Milling company, with a capacity of 50 tons daily, adjoined the mill. The Plata Verde also had a 40-stamp mill near the town, which was the base of supplies for these works. The town was incorporated in 1879. Its first mayor, elected in Feb., was J. J. Smith; recorder, G. B. McAulay; trustees, Frank S. Roff, Walter B. Janness, Mark W. Atkins, Samuel Baeden. In April Roff was chosen mayor; Webb L. Allen, Samuel Baeden, Samuel Watson, and O. E. Henry, trustees. In April 1880 S. A. Squire was chosen mayor; C. D. Wright, recorder; O. E. Henry, John Dietz, William French, and Alfred Wood, trustees. In 1881 H. H. Buckwalter was elected mayor; George W. Hinkel, recorder; R. Rounds, W. T. Ulman, William Feigle, and E. Meyers, trustees. In 1882 Oney Carstarphen was elected mayor, and re-elected in 1883 and 1884. Carstarphen was born in Mo. in 1844, came to Colorado in 1879, and settled at Silver Cliff. He was elected to the state legislature in 1884, and became interested in various mining properties. Querida is a town which has grown up about the Bassick mine, with a population of 400. Dora is another little place built up about Chambers' concentrator, 6 miles N. E. from Silver Cliff, which has a capacity of 20 tons daily. Blackburn is 12 miles from Silver Cliff. Westcliff and Bassickville are also mining camps. Other settlements are Benton, Blumenau, Colfax, Comargo, Govetown, Hardscrabble Cañon, Hollan Springs, Millville, Round Mountain, Silver Circle, Silver Creek, Silver Park, South Hardscrabble, Wetmore, Wet Mountain Valley, Wixon Park.

ver. Castle Rock is the county seat. Sedalia was founded and fostered by the railway corporation. The settlements in Douglas county not named above are Acequia, Bear Cañon, Divide, Douglas, Franktown, Glen Grove, Greenland, Huntsville, Keystone, Larkspur, Mill No. 1, Mill No. 2, Parker, Perry Park, Pine Grove, Platte cañon, Plum, Rock ridge, Spring valley, Stevens Gulch, and Virginia Rancho.

Eagle county, organized in 1883, was cut off from Summit, and contains a rich mineral district, of which Red Cliff is the metropolis and the county seat. It is broken by high mountains and lofty peaks. The population in 1884 was 2,000, confined to the southeast portion. The assessed valuation of the county in 1883 was $338,454; the yield of the mines—one group—was $940,000. Besides Red Cliff, which had at this time 500 inhabitants, there were the towns of Gold Park, with 400 population, Holy Cross, Cleveland, Lake, Mitchell, Rock Creek, Taylor, and Eagle.

Elbert, organized in 1874, and large enough for a kingdom, is one of the great stock-raising counties of Colorado. The western portion, which joins Douglas, is well watered, and considerably cultivated.[38]

El Paso, one of the original seventeen counties, is reckoned among the agricultural divisions, and, as such, is one as yet unrivalled for resources. Its assessable property in 1885 was nearly $5,000,000,

[38] There is also a large supply of pine timber in this end of the county. But the principal capital of its business men is in stock cattle. The population, at the census of 1880, was 2,500, and the valuation of assessable property $1,202,052. This gives about double the usual amount of property per capita in farming districts. The county seat is at Kiowa. Moses R. Chapman, born in N. Y. city in 1844, was brought up in Ill. In 1859 he came to Russell's gulch, and was afterward about Central City. Becoming discouraged, he borrowed money enough in 1865 to take him to Elbert co., where he engaged himself as a herder, and gradually worked himself into the stock business. In 1874 he married Laura A. Danks. In 1882 he was elected to the general assembly, having been county commissioner for 14 years. He owned, in 1886, a large farm and over 1,000 head of cattle. The towns and settlements of Elbert county are Agate, Arroyo, Bellevue, Boyero, Brown & Dods, Buzzards & Sharretts, Cameron, Cedar Point, Clermont, Cochran's Rancho, Elbert, Elbert Station, Elizabeth, Fork-in-Creek, Gebhard, Godfrey, Gomer's Mills, Hugo, Lake, Lake Station, Long Branch, Middle Kiowa, Monatt's Mills, Ranch, River Bend, Rock Butte, Running Creek.

divided between farm improvements, cattle, and other stock, and town property. Immense coal deposits exist in the eastern portion of the country. Pike's peak, by which Colorado was long known, is situated in this county. In an earlier chapter I have given a narrative of its first exploration and settlement, when Colorado City aspired to be the leading town of the territory, and of the causes of its failure. The principal city of El Paso is now Colorado Springs, already world-famous as a health resort.[39]

[39] When Gen. William J. Palmer in 1870 organized the Denver and Rio Grande railway company, he likewise projected a number of auxiliary organizations to develop town-sites, coal lands, and other resources of the region through which the railway was expected to pass. Among these was the Colorado Springs co., which acquired about 10,000 acres of land near the base of Pike's peak and on both sides of Colorado City, including a large level tract through which the railroad would run, and where it was proposed to build the principal city of this region. On July 31, 1871, the first stake was driven, and the city named Colorado Springs because of its proximity to the famous soda springs at the entrance to Ute pass, which were also owned by the company. The region developed more rapidly than was expected, and early in 1872, a hotel had been erected at the springs and a little village there started, named at first La Font, but soon changed to Manitou, the Indian name of one of the springs. The president of the Colorado Springs co. was William J. Palmer. Its executive director was Henry McAllister, Jr, who was born in Wilmington, Delaware, in 1836, and won the title of major by his services in the army during the rebellion. At the close of the war he was elected secretary of the American Iron and Steel association, which position he resigned after seven years' service. He was at once elected president of the National Land Improvement co., organized to develop the lands lying along the Denver and Rio Grande railway. He was also made executive director of the Colorado Springs co. At the time Colorado Springs was started, the success of the Union and other colonies in Colorado had popularized this method of town building, and hence was formed the Fountain colony, which had no legal existence, but was simply an instrument of the Colorado Springs co. in the development of its property. From the beginning this company and its associate colony pursued a liberal and far-sighted policy. The profits accruing from the sale of two thirds of its property were constituted a fund for general and public improvements. Early expenditures from this fund were $44,000 for an irrigating canal, and $15,000 for the purchase and planting of 7,000 trees upon the town-site. During the first five years of the company's history, about $272,000 were thus expended. A lot was presented by the company to each of the Christian denominations, and ample reservations were also made for a public school and for a college. The officers of the colony were Robert A. Cameron vice president, William E. Pabor secretary, E. S. Nettleton chief engineer, William P. Mellen treasurer, and Maurice Kingsley assistant treasurer. The trustees were William J. Palmer, Robert H. Lamborn, Josiah C. Reiff, Robert A. Cameron, W. H. Greenwood, William P. Mellen. The temperance question was given prominence in the organization of the colony by the insertion in every deed given by the company of a clause forever prohibiting the manufacturing, giving, or selling of intoxicating liquors as a beverage in any place of public

Frémont county, a portion of whose early history
has been given, has remained in a backward condition

resort. As might be expected, this clause was soon and repeatedly violated; but the cases were decided in favor of the company in the state
supreme court in 1876, and the lands forfeited. On appeal to the U. S.
supreme court in 1879, this judgment was affirmed. The public sentiment
of the city has always sustained prohibition. *Fountain Colony of Colorado,
Prospectus; Denver Tribune*, June 29, 1871; *Faithful's Three Visits*, 146–50;
Graff's Colorado, 41–6; *Buckman's Colorado Springs; Roberts' Colorado Springs
and Manitou; Colorado Springs*, by H. H.; *Raper & Co.'s Directory of Colorado Springs; Selections from the Enclycopedia of the New West*, 5.

Colorado Springs became the ideal city of the Arkansas valley, if not of
the entire Rocky mountain region, by reason of its wonderful and beautiful
surroundings, its healthfulness and orderliness, its temperance, education,
and refinement. Its growth from the first was healthful and uniform. At
the close of the first year of its history, 277 town lots had been disposed of
at a valuation of $24,700, 159 houses erected, and the population was esti-
mated at 800. The value of the buildings erected by private individuals was
placed at $160,000. Two church edifices were built, and a weekly newspaper
was established. An enterprise most fruitful in benefit to the new city was
the building in 1871 of a good wagon road through the Ute pass to the mining region of South park. The trade of a growing section was thus secured,
contributing from the beginning no little to the commercial importance of
Colorado Springs. When Leadville arose in 1878, this road became one of
the chief highways to that great camp, and made Colorado Springs a principal supply point. When the railroad reached Leadville in 1880, this trade
ceased, but it had sufficed to establish the commercial interests of Colorado
Springs on a sound basis. At one time during the palmy days of Leadville
freighting, 12,000 horses and mules were employed in transportation over
the road. During 1876–7, the city suffered from the depression then general throughout the country, and also from a visitation of grasshoppers,
which caused great devastation to the Rocky mountain region. Prosperity
was fully restored in 1878, in which year a complete system of water works
was constructed, the supply being taken from one of the sparkling streams
flowing down the sides of Pike's peak, at a distance of seven miles from the
city, and at a point 1,200 feet above its level. Gas works costing $50,000
were built in 1879, in which year also new buildings to the value of $200,000
were erected. The growth of the city has since been continuous, and with
slight exceptions uniformly rapid, till in 1886 it had attained a population
of about 7,500, the assessed valuation of its property was $2,248,300, and its
business, exclusive of real estate sales, aggregated nearly $3,000,000. Acces-
sions to the population were largely of health seekers, to accommodate a
portion of whom was begun in 1881 the Antler's hotel, a handsome Queen
Anne structure costing $200,000, and ranking among the most noted of
Rocky mountain hostleries. The public spirit of three citizens, Irving
Howbert, B. F. Crowell, and J. F. Humphrey, gave to Colorado Springs a
beautiful opera house, seating 750, and costing $80,000, which was opened
April 18, 1881.

The public schools of Colorado Springs have always been adequate and
of high grade. In 1871, Mrs Gen. Palmer established the first school, giving
her services voluntarily and without compensation. In 1874, a handsome
school building was erected costing $25,000. By 1879, this had become
crowded, and two frame buildings were added. In 1884, a large modern
brick school-house was built at a cost of $20,000, and in 1886 two others
were completed. Colorado Springs is the seat of Colorado college, founded
by the Colorado association of congregational churches, on the general plan
of New England colleges, but with modifications. T. N. Haskell, formerly of
the state university of Wisconsin, was selected as financial agent. The prepar-

for reasons which will appear hereafter.   In natural
resources it is rich, especially in an excellent quality

atory department was opened in May, 1874, with Jonathan Edwards, graduate of Yale, as principal.   A frame building was temporarily erected, in
which the school remained until 1880.   A department of mining and metal-
lurgy was established about 1877, of which in 1880 William Strieby, a graduate of Columbia college, was in charge.   This department met with such
success that for its better accommodation a wing was erected on the north
side, contributed by William J. Palmer, who also offered to add a south wing
if the college were first freed from debt.   This promise inspired the friends

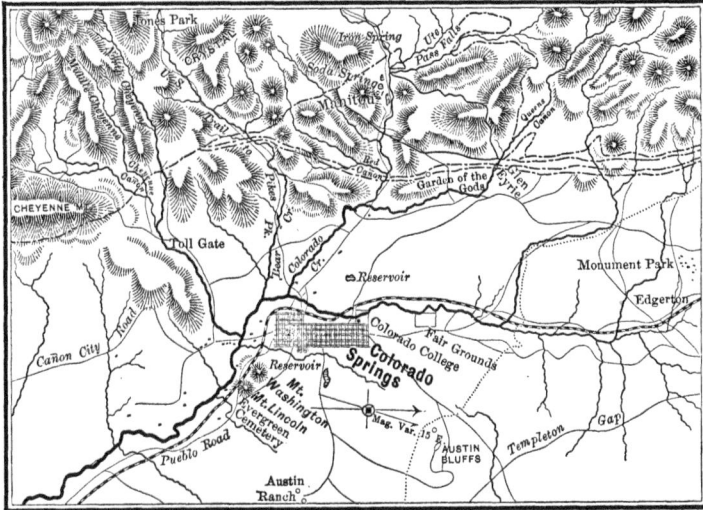

VICINITY OF COLORADO SPRINGS.

of the college to make the requisite effort, and the building now presents a
handsome front of over 100 feet.   The library embraces 6,000 volumes, including 1,000 contributed by the El Paso county library association.   A
collection of natural science specimens and an herbarium of native plants
has made a promising beginning.   President Tenney did much by his writings and personal efforts, to make both the city and college known in the
east.   Friends came to the rescue, and in 1886 it was in a fair way to be
extricated.   Its officers in 1886 were: William Strieby chairman of faculty,
W. F. Wilder vice-president, G. H. Parsons secretary, J. H. Barlow treasurer, and George N. Marden financial agent.   The territorial legislature of
1874 located an institute for the education of deaf mutes at Colorado Springs,
appropriating $5,000 for immediate application to that purpose, and pro-
viding a permanent fund by instituting a tax of half a mill on all the assessable property in the territory.   A house was rented and the institution
opened with a dozen pupils.   To this, also, the Colorado Springs company
donated 12 acres of land, title to be given whenever suitable buildings should
be erected thereon.   Thus prompted, the trustees raised $5,000, and started
the building.   At its next session the legislature appropriated $7,000, inde-
pendent of the tax, and additions were made.   Subsequently that body
added to the institution a department for the blind, $20,000 more being

of coal, of which the amount is practically unlimited.
Petroleum has also been found. It has gold and sil-

appropriated for improvements. The institution is in a prosperous condition and doing a noble work.

The first religious services were held in the winter of 1871, by the Rev. Edwards, rector of the episcopal church at Pueblo. From this time till 1873 services were held at irregular intervals, conducted by Bishop Randall or by J. E. Liller as lay reader. In 1873, Grace church parish was organized, and soon afterward a church built at a cost of $12,000. The First presbyterian church was organized in 1872, previous to which time services had been held in various places. The M. E. church, which was organized in Colorado City very early in the history of that place, was in 1873 transferred to Colorado Springs. In 1881, an edifice costing $12,000 was built in a central location. The First baptist church was organized in 1872. The congregationalists, Cumberland presbyterians, Roman catholics, christians, and African methodists established congregations at later dates. Of the various secret and benevolent organizations, the masons and odd fellows early established lodges in Colorado Springs, and were followed by the knights of pythias, good templars, knights of honor, united workmen, and others. In 1886, there were 20 lodges and encampments of the various organizations.

Previous to 1878, there was no fire department worthy of the name, the only protection against fire being a hook and ladder company, a Babcock engine, and the water from a few wells. When in that year the system of water works was introduced, the organization was begun of a volunteer fire department that for efficiency has no superior in the country. The first bank was established in 1873 by William S. Jackson, C. H. White, and J. S. Wolfe, and called the El Paso. Soon afterward J. H. Barlow became connected with it. This was followed the next year by the First National, organized by W. B. Young, B. F. Crowell, C. B. Greenough, G. H. Stewart, F. L. Martin, and others, and two years later James H. B. McFerran started the People's bank. All are sound and prosperous institutions, and in 1886 had deposits of $500,000. The history of journalism in El Paso county began in 1861 with the publication of *The Journal* at Colorado City. It was edited by B. F. Crowell, and was issued weekly for about a year, when publication was discontinued. After that the county possessed no newspaper until 1872, when the first number of *Out West* was issued by J. E. Liller. About the same time, Judge Eliphalet Price began the publication of the *Free Press*. In January, 1873, *Out West* became the *Colorado Springs Gazette*, and about a year later the *Free Press* was merged into the *Mountaineer*. In 1878, the *Gazette* became a daily, as did also the *Mountaineer* in 1881 under the name of the *Republic*. The *Gazette* and *Republic* continue the leading newspapers of the county. Various weeklies appeared from time to time, prominent among which was the *Hour*, started in 1885. Monument, a town in the northern part of the county, has had at times a weekly paper since 1878.

William J. Palmer, to whom Colorado Springs owes its existence, and the state in large measure its present condition of development, was born in Philadelphia in 1836. Receiving a fair education, he early became confidential secretary to J. Edgar Thompson, then president of the Pennsylvania railroad, in which position he evinced marked ability, and at one time was sent to Europe to study methods of iron manufacture and railroad management. On the breaking out of the rebellion, he raised the Anderson cavalry, of which he was, till the close of the war, the commander. Meantime Thompson and his associates had become interested in the Kansas Pacific railroad, and on Palmer's return from the war he was made managing director of that enterprise, and superintendent of construction. While thus engaged, he made the famous survey of transcontinental routes along the 32d and 35th parallels. Failing to induce the Kansas Pacific management to adopt one of these, and impressed with the resources of the Rocky mountain region, in 1870, as-

ver mines, not yet much developed, also copper, lead,
zinc, mineral paint, marble, alabaster, valuable building stone, potters' clay, and one of the few jet mines
in the world.[40]

sociated with William A. Bell and others, he organized the Denver and Rio
Grande railway company. In the face of difficulties, physical and financial,
he pushed this great enterprise to completion, after first building the Denver
and Rio Grande Western, of which he was president until 1883. He was at
the head of a majority of the companies organized for the development of
southern Colorado, the most prominent among which was the Colorado Coal
and Iron company. A few years later he retired from the presidency of the
Mexican National, though still remaining at the head of the construction
company. He is also president of the reorganized Denver and Rio Grande
Western railway company, which is becoming a very important factor in the
railroad system of the Rocky mountains.

Doctor William A. Bell, prominently associated with General Palmer in
the building of the Denver and Rio Grande railway, was born in Clonmel,
Ireland, in 1841. He studied at the London hospital, and took a medical
degree at Cambridge in 1865. In 1866-7 he visited the United States, and
in the latter year joined the 35th parallel surveying expedition, which
brought him into close personal and business relations with Palmer. Returning in 1870 from a visit to England, he joined him in the organization of
the Denver and Rio Grande railway company, and was its first vice-president.

M. L. De Coursey, who had much to do with the building up of Colorado
Springs, was born in Philadelphia in 1842, and served in the civil war in
which he was captain. In 1871 he joined his former cavalry commander,
General Palmer, in Colorado, and held prominent positions in the national
land and improvement and other companies. He afterwards engaged in the
real estate business.

The growth and permanent prosperity of Colorado Springs has been very
marked. Among the publications that have made known to the world its
scenic wonders and famous climate, as well as the merits of its mineral waters,
are Charles Dennison's *Rocky Mountain Health Resorts*, a treatise on pulmonary
diseases and their cure; *Colorado Springs*, a descriptive and historical pamphlet relating to the city of that name and its vicinity, by George Rex Buckman; *Health, Wealth, and Pleasure*, a treatise on the health resorts of Colorado and New Mexico; *Glenwood Springs*, a descriptive pamphlet; Mrs Simeon
J. Dunbar's *Health Resorts of Colorado Springs and Manitou*, descriptive;
S. Anna Gordon's *Camping in Colorado*, descriptive and narrative. Dr S.
Edwin Solly, of Colorado Springs, has done much by his pamphlets to call
attention to the curative value of Colorado's climate and mineral waters.
He graduated in London in 1867, and in 1874 came to Colorado Springs,
where he has since been engaged in the practice of his profession. He is a
member of the royal college of surgeons, England, and of various other medical and scientific societies, both in England and America.

The villages and settlements in El Paso county are Aroways, Bassett's
Hill, Bierstadt, Big Sandy, Bijou Basin, Cheyenne Peak, Chico Basin, Colo-
rado House, Costello's Rancho, Crystal Peak Park, Easton, Edgerton, El
Paso, Florissant, Fountain, Four-mile Creek, Franceville, Franceville Junc-
tion, Granger, Gwillemville, Highland Rancho, Hursley's Rancho, Husted,
Jimmy Camp, Lake Station, Little Buttes, McConnellsville, Monument, O.
Z., Petrified Stumps, Quarry, Sidney, South Water, Suffolk, Summit Park,
Table Rock, Turkey Creek, Twin Rocks, Weissport, Wheatland, Widefield,
Wigwam, Winfield.

[40] It has ranked mainly with the agricultural counties, but it is not emi-
nent in that class, although its altitude of less than 6,000 feet gives it a
climate better suited to corn than most other counties in the state. In 1883

The chief town and county seat is Cañon City, with a population of about 3 000 in 1884. The Col-

it raised considerable grain, and had 15,000 head of cattle, besides 5,000 other animals, produced $625,000 worth of coal, and $20,000 in bullion. It had 108 miles of railroad within its boundaries, and its population was 4,730. This was not a flattering exhibit for one of the oldest counties with these natural resources. But the hindrance to development had been, first, the want of railroads, and secondly, a war between railroads for possession of the Grand cañon pass through the Rocky mountains. This wonderful and awful defile of the Arkansas was the gate of the mountains, its eastern end being situated in the neighborhood of Cañon City, named in reference to it. To secure the exclusive right of way through this passage involved a long struggle between two companies, first in personal encounter, and lastly in the courts, where the Denver and Rio Grande prevailed against the Atchison, Topeka, and Santa Fé company.

The first organized effort to secure a railroad was made in the autumn of 1867. This was done by a committee consisting of B. M. Adams, B. F. Rockafellow, and Thomas Macon, who appointed A. G. Boone, about to visit Washington, a special commissioner to confer with John D. Perry, president of the Kansas Pacific railroad, in reference to the Arkansas valley transcontinental route. Perry promised that his engineers should look into the matter, and the Fremont county people were hopeful. At that time General Palmer was managing director of the Kansas Pacific, and had charge of its construction, and W. H. Greenwood was its chief engineer. Palmer organized and commanded an expedition which surveyed the proposed route. His report, which was made in 1868, recommended that the route from Ellsworth, Kansas, westward should deflect to the south of its former survey, and follow the one by the Arkansas river to its headwaters, and thence via the San Luis valley to intersect the thirty-fifth parallel transcontinental route. This road, had it been built, would have given an outlet eastward to the richest mineral and some of the best agricultural country in Colorado. But the eastern managers decided to build to Denver, a decision which finally threw them into the hands of the Union Pacific. When the Kansas Pacific was about completed, Palmer, remembering what he had seen on his surveys, originated the plan of a narrow-gauge railway, which should run southward from Denver along the base of the mountains. Disappointed in their expectations of a direct road to the east, the people of Fremont county welcomed the thought of communication with Denver and connection with the Union Pacific, and voted the Denver and Rio Grande company—the narrow-gauge line—$50,000 in county bonds, the first contribution of the kind received by them, and which through some technicality was finally lost in the courts.   In the mean time the Denver and Rio Grande had constructed its road to Pueblo, with a branch to the coal mines at Labran, eight miles from Cañon City, which was completed in October, 1872, and without going to Cañon City, as was expected, was pushing south with the design of reaching the extensive fields of coking coal at El Moro, near Trinidad, and of ultimate extension to the city of Mexico, via Santa Fé and El Paso, which latter was, of course, regarded as an achievement of the somewhat remote future. Thereupon, there was a movement made inviting the Atchison, Topeka, and Santa Fé to come to Cañon City and occupy the route formerly suggested to the Kansas Pacific. For this purpose a public meeting was held at Cañon City in Jan., 1873. But the A., T., & S. F. co. proving slow to act, and the people being impatient, the county again voted its bonds to the D. & R. G. co., this time for $100,000, after an exciting canvass, there being a majority of only two in favor of the gift, and the county commissioners refusing to issue the bonds. In 1874, however, on demand of the D. & R. G. co., Cañon City voted $50,000 in bonds, and in addition gave deeds to $25,000 worth of property, and the road was soon afterward completed to

orado penitentiary is located here, and was in charge
of the general government until 1874, when the ter-

that place. The next movement in the way of increased railway facilities
was in Feb., 1877, when the Cañon City and San Juan railway co. was organized, with C. T. Alling president, B. F. Rockafellow secretary, James Clelland treasurer, and H. R. Holbrook chief engineer. Alling soon resigned,
and was succeeded by Frederick A. Reynolds. Meantime the new Leadville
mining region began to attract attention, and was seen to offer a promising
field for railroad enterprise. Stimulated by this, and it may be also by the
appearance of a rival in the field, the D. & R. G. co. proceeded, on April
19, 1878, to resume work on its line from Cañon City westward and towards
the Leadville region, and on that day took possession by its agents of the
narrow portion of the grand cañon, known as the Royal gorge, with the
avowed intention of constructing its road upon the line of the surveys made
in 1871-2, right of way over which had, as it claimed, been secured to it by
acts of congress of June 8, 1872, and March 3, 1875. But during the night
of April 19, 1878, the board of directors of the C. C. & S. J. co. were convened, and elected William B. Strong and A. A. Robinson respectively
general manager and chief engineer of the A., T., & S. F. co., to similar
positions in the C. C. & S. J. co., giving conclusive evidence that the
great Santa Fé co. was behind the local enterprise. These officials made
preparations to take immediate possession of the grand cañon on behalf of
their company, which was done as early as four o'clock on the morning of
April 20th, at which time a small party of men, under the charge of an
assistant engineer, swam the Arkansas river, and in the name of their company took possession of the cañon. That party was followed the same day
by a large force of workmen under the control of Chief Engineer Robinson.
The war was now commenced. Each side had from 500 to 700 men at work.
Fortifications were erected by each, beyond which the other was not permitted to pass, and for a time the spilling of blood seemed inevitable.
These movements were succeeded by a suit instituted the same day in the
state court in the name of the C. C. & S. J. co. against the D. & R. G. co.,
in which an injunction was obtained, afterward sustained by Judge Hallett of the U. S. district court, restraining the latter company from occupying or attempting to occupy the cañon for railroad purposes, and from
interfering with the C. C. & S. J. co. in the construction of its own road
therein. By virtue of this decision the C. C. & S. J. co. proceeded with
the work of construction through the grand cañon, and completed during
the following ten months the 20 miles from Cañon City, being as far as it
was permitted under its charter to build. The work in the grand cañon was
difficult, requiring engineering skill of the highest order. In places the
blasting could be carried on only by suspending men by ropes down the
rocky walls 2,000 feet in height; in others the chasm was so contracted
that the road itself was suspended over the river by a hanging bridge, supported from above by braces fixed in the rock and raised in the middle on
the principle of an arch. About the time the C. C. & S. J. co. had finished its 20 miles of road, the D. & R. G. co., under stress of the decision
against it and the financial troubles which this had served to bring to a
climax, executed a 30 years' lease of its entire completed line to the A., T.,
& S. F. co., which took possession in Dec., 1878. The right of way through
the grand cañon was expressly excluded from this lease, the A., T., & S. F.
co. taking the ground that this was the property of the C. C. & S. J. co.,
and that a lease thereof from the D. & R. G. co. would be of no effect.
    In April, 1879, the U. S. supreme court, to which the case has been ap-
pealed by the D. & R. G. co., reversed the decision of the lower court, and
confirmed to the D. & R. G. co. its prior right to the grand cañon. The
possession of this prior right, however, was not to be understood as preventing the C. C. & S. J. co. from afterward building a parallel road of its

ritory assumed its support. In 1877 it consisted of one cell building with forty-two cells. The state now owns thirty-six acres, five of which are enclosed by a wall of stone twenty feet in height and four in thickness, with good buildings, and cell-room for over 400 inmates,[41] a boot and shoe factory, lime-kilns, stone-

own through the cañon, where the latter was wide enough to admit of two, nor from using the D. & R. G. tracks in common with that company, in the narrow places where but one road could be built, these rights having been generally conferred by act of congress of March 3, 1875. Complications then arose in the affairs of the A., T., & S. F. and D. & R. G. companies which kept them in constant litigation. The latter company, now that its rights in the grand cañon had been restored to it, and in view of the great business revival, due to the discovery of new and rich mining regions, naturally desired to regain possession of its road. It charged the lessee with non-observance of contract in certain particulars; but the case turned on the point that there was no Colorado law which would permit a foreign corporation to operate a railroad within the state. The prayer of the D. & R. G. co. was granted, and a writ issued by the court, copies of which were placed in the hands of sheriffs in the principal places along the line, the effect of which was to restore the road to the D. & R. G. co. These were served simultaneously at Denver, Colorado Springs, Pueblo, Cañon City, El Moro, and Alamosa, and possession taken in each place by the officers and agents of the D. & R. G. co. Immediately after possession had been gained, on June 15, 1879, Judge Bowen, on application of several of the D. & R. G. bond-holders, appointed one of the company's solicitors, Hanson A. Risley, its receiver. He took possession of the road and operated it for one month, during which time his receivership was attacked in several courts and finally terminated by Chief Justice Miller, who ordered the discharge of the receiver, and enjoined him to restore the road to the D. & R. G. co., and that company in turn was directed to restore it to the A., T., & S. F. co., in accordance with a writ previously issued by Judge Hallett and not at that time obeyed. When all this had been done, Judge Hallett further ordered that, till the equities of the several parties could be determined, both companies be restrained from further work in the grand cañon, and appointed L. C. Ellsworth as receiver, to take possession of the property of the D. & R. G. co., and operate it under the direction of the court. While this warring had been going on, the Pueblo and Arkansas valley railroad company, a local corporation of the A., T., & S. F. system, had begun to build westward from the 20-mile point where the Cañon City and San Juan company had stopped, and had succeeded in completing about two miles, when the D. & R. G. co. arrested further progress by erecting stone enfilading forts and keeping them manned, besides mining the position in readiness to send the enemy skyward at a moment's notice. Meantime Judge Hallett had appointed a commission to determine what parts of the grand cañon would admit of the construction of but one line of railway. In accordance with the report of this commission, the court, on January 2, 1880, issued a decree giving to the D. & R. G. co. the exclusive right of way through the grand cañon from Cañon City to South Arkansas—the present town of Salida—and to the Pueblo and Arkansas valley railroad the right of way from South Arkansas to Leadville, either company having the right to build a separate road between the latter points. This practically ended the war, and the two companies, after having spent $500,000 in carrying on the fight both in and out of the courts, concluded a treaty of peace. In accordance with an agreement entered into, all suits were withdrawn, and the A., T., & S. F. co. bound itself for a term of ten years

quarries, and brick-yards, in which the convicts are employed. The Colorado collegiate and military institute is located here. It was established by a stock company of citizens in 1881, under the supervision of E. H. Sawyer.[42] There is also a large silver smelter, and a copper smelter. The Arkansas river offers abundant water power; the town is supplied with water works; there are cold and hot mineral springs, and other scenic attractions, all of which promise a not unimportant future for this place when the surrounding country shall be made to yield its corn and wine, its coal, gold, silver, and copper.

not to build either to Leadville or Denver, while the D. & R. G. co. for a like period was to be restrained from building within a specified distance from Santa Fé. The D. & R. G. co. purchased the 20 miles of road constructed through the grand cañon by the C. C. & S. J. Co., paying therefor, according to the *Denver Tribune*, of April 2, 1880, the sum of $1,400,000. In the same month Receiver Ellsworth was discharged by the court, and the property turned over to the D. & R. G. co. Construction had meanwhile been pushed with all speed, and in July, 1880, Leadville was reached, and the golden stream of wealth started which has ever since continued to flow. Thus ended Colorado's most serious railroad war, and one waged for the possession of a prize well worth the struggle.

William H. Greenwood, so conspicuous in railroad affairs in Colorado, was born at Marlboro, N. H. He had purchased property in Cañon City when he made his survey of the grand cañon. After the railroad war was ended, he settled there with his family. In the summer of 1880 he was employed by the D. & R. G. to go to Mexico, and while near Rio Hondo was assassinated by an unknown person. The Mexican government exhibited much feeling, and made every endeavor for the apprehension of the murderer, but in vain.

[41] New buildings were added for the second time in 1883. Fowler remarks that there are over 400 convicts confined here, 'and more life-prisoners among them, in proportion, than elsewhere in the world.' This may be accounted for by the further statement that there are throughout the state drinking-saloons in the proportion of one to every 67 inhabitants—only a little behind Nevada, which has one to every 56—and the prevalence of gambling.

[42] The board of trustees consisted of F. A. Reynolds pres.; D. G. Peabody vice-pres.; W. R. Fowler sec.; J. F. Campbell treas.; E. H. Sawyer, J. L. Prentice, A. Rudd, Samuel Bradbury, and J. J. Phelps. It had besides a 'collegiate committee,' and a 'military committee.' E. H. Sawyer was president, commandant, and professor of moral, mental, and military science and engineering. The other instructors were H. S. Westgate, Frank Prentiss, J. M. Willard, and C. Uttermochlem.

CHAPTER XIII.

COUNTIES OF COLORADO CONCLUDED.

1859-1886.

GARFIELD county was organized in February 1883 out of Summit, one of the original divisions of 1861. At that time the county seat was temporarily located at Parkville, but removed soon after to Breckenridge. On the organization of Garfield and Eagle counties little of Summit remained, and the county seat of the former was located at Carbonate, near the eastern boundary. It lies wholly on the western slope of the Rocky mountains, and is chiefly an agricultural and grazing region, but has mines of silver and enormous deposits of coal. It was vacated by the Utes as late as 1882, and has little history. Carbonate was one of the earliest settlements, and Glenwood Springs,[1]

[1] The springs at Glenwood are notable both for their enormous flow and the large percentage of their mineral constituents. The largest of the group has a flow of 2,000 gallons per minute, while that of the entire group of ten large and several smaller springs reaches 8,000 gallons. The solid constituents amount to 1,250 grains per gallon, 1,000 grains of which are composed of chloride of sodium, constituting these the strongest hot saline springs upon the continent. Their temperature is 125° F. Strangely enough these springs are not mentioned by Hayden in his U. S. geological survey reports, not shown upon his maps. A possible explanation of this omission is that the locality may have been visited during a season of high water, and the Grand river for the time submerged the springs, all of which are upon its

located at the junction of Roaring fork and Grand
river, with its mineral waters and rich tributary region, is becoming the commercial centre of north-
western Colorado.

The population is between 300 and 400.   The other
towns are Axial, Gresham, Barlow, and Ferguson.
The valuation of the county in its first year was
$136,781.

Gilpin, named after the first governor has an area
of twelve by fifteen miles.   It is purely a mining
region, and not exceeded in mineral productions
except by the county of Lake.   Within its limits
mining has been carried on for twenty-four years, during which time it has produced $43,208,988 in bullion,
of which $38,500,000 was in gold, being about one-
fourth of the production of the state in precious metals.   In a previous chapter I have sketched the
beginning of Gilpin's history, when John H. Gregory
there discovered gold, and was followed by a rush of
miners, who soon exhausted the surface deposit, and
after impoverishing themselves in milling experiments
abandoned mining or sought new fields of exploita-
tion.   The gold-bearing lodes occupy an area one mile
wide and four miles long, in the midst of which are
the closely allied towns of Black Hawk, Central, and
Nevadaville.   The silver belt extends across north
Clear creek and other hills from York gulch to Dory
hill.   It was not discovered until 1878.

The first improvement of the gold district was by
the construction of the Consolidated ditch in 1860.
More than 100 small mills were taken to Gilpin county
in its early years.   In 1868 there were over thirty

margin. Walls of masonry now protect them from such overflow. The
tract covering the springs was secured by Isaac Cooper and others, immediately upon extinction of the Indian title effected in 1882. Settlement was
begun the following year, and in 1885 the town of Glenwood Springs was incorporated with a population of 200. The growing importance of the mines
at Aspen on the Roaring fork, 25 miles above Glenwood, the value of which
was first recognized about 1882, drew the attention of capital to this virgin
portion of Colorado. The history of its rapid advance will be given elsewhere in this volume.

mills at work operating 700 stamps. In 1874 mining was dull. Soon after large operators began purchasing small mines and consolidating, by which means a new impulse was given to this industry. The gold ores of Gilpin are of a low grade, and do not pay for any other treatment than by stamp-mill or smelting. There are fewer mills of larger capacity than formerly, and although the increasing depth of the mines makes the extraction of the ore more expensive, the returns are satisfactory. The entire bullion output of 1883, for instance, was $2,208,983. The assessed valuation of the county for that year was $1,871,244, and its population 7,000.[2]

Central City,[3] which, next to Denver, has been the seat of money, political influence, and brain power,

[2] Some account of the earlier and later operations in this county seems imperative, although it should but repeat the experiences of others. In 1859 several arastras were constructed to pulverize quartz. A miner named Red fixed a trip hammer, pivoted on a stump, the hammer pounding quartz in a trough. His invention was called the Woodpecker Mill. Charles Giles, of Gallia, Ohio, made a 6-stamp wooden mill, run by water power, in Chase gulch, which pounded out $6,000 in a season. T. T. Prosser imported the first mill not home made. It was a 3-stamp affair, and was set to work in Prosser gulch in Sept. 1859. Coleman & Le Fevre brought in a 6-stamp mill the same season, which was run with the Prosser mill on Gunnell quartz, saving from $60 to $100 per ton. Ridgeway next set up a 6-stamp mill on Clear creek, below Black Hawk, and soon after Clark, Vandewater, & Co. imported a veritable foundry made, 9-stamp mill at the junction of Eureka and Spring gulches, where now is the centre of Central City. This was all accomplished in 1859. The Gregory lode has maintained its preëminence. The Bobtail was reckoned second; the Gunnell third. There are several mines on each of these. They all have a history, but for which I have not space. Few of the mines are down more than 1,500 feet; but this depth requires tunnelling, of which a good deal has been done. The British-American tunnel, beginning on south Clear creek below Fall river, extends 4 miles northerly, through Quartz hill to the silver district, and is not yet finished. The Union tunnel cuts through Maryland mountain. The European-American tunnel begins a mile below Black Hawk and runs westerly, being incomplete. There are numerous other shorter tunnels. The first iron-works set up in Colorado was by Langford & Co. of Denver, in May 1861, who manufactured iron from the bog ore found 16 miles north-west of Denver. After making the trial they removed their works to Black Hawk, where they continued to make iron and manufacture mining machinery.

[3] Although early settled, Central City was not surveyed into lots until 1866, when George H. Hill laid it off. The town-site act of congress authorized the location of 1,280 acres where there were over 1,000 inhabitants, and Central being entitled by population to half that amount, obtained it, less a little over 50 acres already patented to mines. The question of superior rights necessarily arose for settlement, the town being upon mining ground. Theodore H. Becker contested the claim of the city to a strip of surface ground 50 feet wide lying through the centre of town, on the supposition

which was at one time the capital of the territory, and is the county seat, is the principal of the three towns

that the prior record of his mine would secure him in his claim. The secretary of the interior decided adversely to Becker, but referred the case to the courts. The city obtained its patent without reservation of the ground claimed by Becker, but with a proviso again referring the question to 'existing laws.' The existing laws granted mining patents in towns, excepting all rights to the surface, or anything upon it, which decision was finally established and order restored. Black Hawk was incorporated in 1864. The first post-office in the Rocky mountains was located here, in 1860, and designated Mountain City, to distinguish it from another Central City in Kansas, of which Colorado was then a part. The name was dropped when the territory was organized. The second land office in Colorado was opened at Central City in 1868, for the district composed of Clear creek, Gilpin, and parts of Jefferson and Boulder counties, Irving Stantan register, and Guy M. Hulett receiver. The first application for a patent was for the Compass and Square lode, in Griffith mining district, Clear Creek co. The first express company which extended its line to Central City was the Central Overland and Pike's Peak express, in the spring of 1860. It came into the possession of Holladay in 1861, and in 1865 was transferred to Wells, Fargo, & Co., after which it passed into the hands of the Kansas Pacific Railroad company in 1871, when that road was completed to Denver. It was then known as the Kansas Pacific Railroad Express company, but later became the Pacific Express company.

The telegraph line was completed to Central City Nov. 7, 1863, by the Pacific Telegraph company, which two years later was merged in the Western Union company.

The first newspaper started in the county was the *Rocky Mountain Gold Reporter and Mountain City Herald*, published in 1859, by Thomas Gibson, at Gregory point. It suspended the same year. The *Miners' Register*, published by Alfred Thompson, was the second, in 1862, which went through several changes, and suspended in 1873. In 1876 the *Post*, democratic, was first issued at Black Hawk, by William McLaughlin and W. W. Sullivan. It soon came into the hands of James R. Oliver.

The first banking in Central City was done by the private firm of Kountz Brothers. In 1866 the Rocky Mountain National bank was organized, Joshua S. Reynolds president. In 1874 the First National Bank of Central City was organized, which succeeded the private banking house of Thatcher, Standley, & Co., successors of Warren, Hussey, & Co. Hanington & Mellor organized a banking house in Central City in 1875. There is also at Black Hawk a private banking house, owned by Sam Smith & Co., established in 1880.

Public schools were organized in Central City in 1862, Daniel C. Collier superintendent; first teachers, Thomas J. Campbell and Ellen F. Kendall. Schools were organized the same year in Black Hawk and Nevadaville. The first public school-house erected by the county was completed in 1870, at a cost of $20,000, at that time the best school building in Colorado.

Religious services were held in the open air in 1859, at Gregory Diggings, by Lewis Hamilton, resulting in the formation of a union church, composed of all denominations. The hall over the post-office at Central City was used as a meeting house. In 1862 Hamilton went as chaplain to a Colorado regiment, and the records of the church were lost. G. W. Fisher, methodist, also held open-air meetings in 1859, and organized a church in 1860, afterward holding meetings in a public hall. A lot was purchased in 1862, but no church edifice was completed before 1869, when the first methodist church at Central was dedicated by Bishop Calvin Kingsley. The society in due time had a church, costing $20,000, and a membership of over 300. Its first settled pastor was Mr Adriance. A methodist church was also organized

before mentioned as occupying the heart of the gold
district.   It was named in reference to its central

at Black Hawk in 1862, and a small church edifice erected. The first settled pastor was D. H. Petfish. It was not until after 1872 that a church
was built for the Methodist society at Nevadaville. The first woman to
arrive in the gold district of Gilpin county was Mary York, afterward Mrs
William Z. Cozzens, in 1859. She was a catholic. There were plenty of her
faith in the mines, and services began to be held in the following year in a
public hall by J. P. Machebeuf, afterwards bishop of Colorado. In 1862 a
building was purchased and converted into a church, which continued to be
used until the present large edifice was erected, the corner-stone of which was
laid by Bishop Machebeuf in 1872. It was first used for religious services in
1874, though still incomplete. During this year an academy was opened on
Gunnell hill by the catholics, under the charge of the sisters of charity. The
presbyterians were organized into a church in 1862 by Lewis Hamilton,
before mentioned, under the name of First Presbyterian church of Central
City, George W. Warner, missionary, being its first pastor, succeeded by
William Crawford, Theodore D. Marsh, Sheldon Jackson, J. G. Lawrie, H. B.
Gage, J. P. Egbert, W. L. Ledwith, R. M. Brown, J. W. Johnstone, J. H.
Bourns, and Otto Schultz, covering a period of about 20 years. The church
building was erected in 1873. The First Presbyterian church of Black Hawk
was organized in 1863 by George W. Warner. A church was erected the same
year costing $7,500, and dedicated Aug. 28th, Warner pastor. He resigned in
Nov., and was succeeded by T. D. Marsh, Dr Kendal, A. M. Keizer, Albert F.
Lyle, G. S. Adams, and W. E. Hamilton. The church was closed in 1872, and
subsequently rented to the methodists. The congregationalists organized in
1863, under William Crawford's ministrations, as the First Congregational
church of Colorado, being what its name indicated in reality, and wishing to
be general in its efforts to do good. It was incorporated in 1866, however,
as the First Congregational church of Central City. In that year a church
edifice costing $11,700 was erected. Crawford remained with the society
until 1867, when he resigned, and was succeeded by E. P. Tenney, after whom
came S. F. Dickinson, H. C. Dickinson, Theodore C. Jerome, and Samuel R.
Dimock. The church was closed in 1876. A baptist church was organized
in 1864 by Almond Barrelle, a missionary from the American Baptist Home
Mission society, and a house of worship erected, which in 1871 was repaired,
and in 1879 closed, being since occupied as a store and dwelling. The episcopal churches also have closed their doors. Why Central City so often
closes its churches seems to require explanation. Probably the attempt to
support too many in the three contiguous municipalities rendered abortive
the effort to support any. In this matter the protestant churches would do
well to imitate their catholic brethren. In 1866 was organized the Miners and Mechanics' Institute of Gilpin
county, Colorado, which association was chartered in 1867, but did not
remain permanent. The library of 1,000 vols which it collected was sold
to the city of Central at a nominal price, for the use of the public schools.
The school board soon added another 1,000 volumes to the public school
library. The cabinet of minerals and other valuable matter was burned in
1874.
The fire department of Central City was organized in 1869, when the Central Fire company No. 1 was formed, with 78 members, M. H. Root foreman.
The city was not then supplied with water for extinguishing fires, and the
department was otherwise wanting. After the fire of May 1874, which burned
the greater part of the business portion of the town, it was reorganized. The
Rescue Fire and Hose company No. 1 was first formed, N. H. McCall foreman. In 1875 the Rough and Ready Hook and Ladder company No. 1 was
organized, M. H. Root foreman. In 1878 the Alert Fire and Hose company
No. 2, Thomas Hambly foreman. In 1879 the Black Hawk Fire and Hose

position between Black Hawk and Nevadaville. The
other towns are but its suburbs, and together make a

company No. 1 was organized, W. O. Logue foreman. There was soon an efficient fire department, with hydrants at convenient distances, and reservoirs at a sufficient elevation to throw water over any building in the town. There was mustered into service as Colorado militia a military company, known as the Emmet Guards of Gilpin county, in Nov. 1875, James Noonan captain, James Delahanty 1st lieut, T. F. Welch 2d lieut.

Of secret and benevolent orders there are a number in Gilpin county. Nevada Lodge No. 1, of Free and Accepted Masons, was granted a dispensation by the grand lodge of Kansas Dec. 22, 1860, and formally opened for business Jan. 12, 1861. Its lodge-room being burned in the autumn, steps were taken to rebuild, and 80 feet of ground fronting on Main street purchased. Nevada lodge was the first organized in Colorado, but later in the same year John M. Chivington, appointed by the grand master of Nebraska, instituted lodges as follows: Golden No. 1, at Golden City; Rocky Mountain No. 2, at Gold Hill; and Park No. 3, at Parkville; in the counties of Jefferson, Boulder, and Summit respectively. He then called a cenvention at Golden, to institute a grand lodge, Aug. 3, 1861. This action of the Nebraska grand lodge was regarded by the Nevada lodge as an infringement of the privileges of the Kansas grand lodge, under whose jurisdiction Colorado, it was claimed, properly came. The Kansas grand lodge, however, recognizing the Colorado grand lodge, removed the difficulty, and Nevada lodge surrendering its first charter, was rechartered by the Colorado grand lodge as Nevada lodge No. 4. Its building was of stone, brick, and iron, and cost $7,000. Chivington lodge was chartered Dec. 11, 1861. Central City Chapter No. 1, Royal Arch Masons, received its charter from the grand royal arch chapter of the United States, Sept. 9, 1865. Central City Council No. 54, Royal and Select Masters, was chartered by the grand council of Ill., Oct. 23, 1872. Central City Commandery No. 2, Knights Templar, was instituted Nov. 8, 1866, and received its charter from the grand encampment of the United States Oct. 24, 1868. Black Hawk lodge No. 11, A. F. & A. M., was instituted Feb. 17, 1866. The Rocky Mountain lodge No. 2, Independent Order of Odd Fellows, was chartered June 14, 1865. Colorado Encampment No. 1, I. O. O. F., was instituted May 22, 1867. Colorado lodge No. 3, of Black Hawk, instituted May 16, 1866. Nevada lodge No. 6 was chartered Sept. 23, 1868. Bald Mountain Encampment No. 3 was instituted at Nevada March 18, 1871. The first lodge of Good Templars in Gilpin county was instituted at Nevada in August 1860, by A. G. Gill, commissioned by the grand lodge of Kansas. The fire of 1861 having destroyed their lodge-room, the order was reorganized at Central under the name of Central City lodge No. 23, of Kansas, and prospered until the fire of 1874 again destroyed its property. The lodge did not disband, but continued to meet in hired rooms. The first grand lodge of this order was instituted in Washington hall, Central City, March 17, 1868, with 788 members and 11 lodges. Nevada lodge No. 52 was instituted by the grand lodge of Kansas in April 1866; but in March 1868 it applied to the Colorado grand lodge for a new charter, and received the name of Nevada lodge No. 3. It owns a building, and is in good circumstances. The Knights of Honor, Knights of Pythias, Knights of the New World, Foresters, and Red Men have their organizations in Gilpin county, as well as the Scandinavian and other benevolent societies. Not to be behind the rest of the world in amusements, Central is provided with an opera house of stone, 55 by 115 feet, which will seat 500 persons in the dress-circle and parquette, and 250 in the gallery. It is warmed by hot-air furnaces, is finely frescoed, lighted with gas, and cost altogether $25,000. It was begun in 1877, and completed in 1878, and furnishes a strong contrast to Hadley Hall, the large log building, still standing, in the upper story of which, in earlier times, theatrical representations were wont to be given.

population of 5,500. It has excellent schools, and a
generally progressive and refined society. The other
towns and camps in the country are Rollinsville, Russell's gulch, Black's camp, Cottonwood, and Smith
hill.[4]

[4] Among the pioneers of Gilpin county are the following: Corbit Bacon,
who came to Colorado from Pontiac, Mich., in 1858 with a small party consisting of James A. Weeks, Wilbur F. Parker, and Alverson and son.
Arriving late in the year he encamped 30 miles above Denver, and the following spring began mining on Quartz hill. He has continued in the business
in Gilpin county ever since. J. M. Beverly, born in Va, in 1843, came to
Colorado from Ill. in 1859 in company with J. R. Beverly, his father. They
went at once to Gregory gulch, and thence to Nevadaville, where they
erected the first cabin. J. M. Beverly was elected recorder, sheriff, and justice of the peace in the autumn of 1859. During the winter he discovered a
mine, named after him, on the Burroughs lode, which he sold in 1864. He
built the Beverly mill in Nevada gulch in 1862, which he sold after running
it 5 years, and built another. Having accumulated a fortune, he returned to
Chicago, but suffered a loss of his property in the great fire of 1871, and
began the study and practice of the law in that city. Later he invested in
mines in Lake and Gilpin counties. Chase Withrow, born in Ill., in 1839,
came to Colorado in 1860, and settled at Central City, where he followed
mining for two years, after which he engaged in lumber-dealing for 6 years.
He then returned to the study of the law, commenced before leaving Ill.,
was admitted to the bar, and practised until 1875, when he was elected clerk
of the district court, which position he held for 6 years, when he returned to
the practise of his profession. Soon after he was elected city attorney. William H. Beverly, his brother, came to Colorado in 1860, and settled at Nevadaville. Hugh A. Campbell, born in Pa, in 1826, was brought up in Ohio.
In 1850 he joined a party of adventurers going to California, and mined in
Nevada co. 8 years. He had no sooner returned to Ohio than the rush to
Pike's peak began, which he immediately joined, arriving in Central City in
June 1859, where he opened a store with Jesse Trotter, in a brush tent.
During the summer they erected a log cabin, on what is now Lawrence street,
and removed their goods to it. They put a sign over their door with Central
City on it, and so fixed the name, not recognized by the P. O. department.
Campbell discovered the Cincinnati lode on Casto hill; owned 40 acres of
placer ground on the south side of Quartz hill; 30 acres on Pine creek;
the Globe, Progressive, and Centennial lodes on Gunnell hill; Greenback
lode on Casto hill; Inter-ocean and Gettysburg on Quartz hill, and other
mining property.

D. D. McIlvoy, born in Ky, in 1824, was the son of a farmer. He
crossed the plains to Cal. in 1850. He joined a militia company during the
Pah Ute outbreak, and was commissioned a lieutenant by Gov. McDougal.
In 1851 he returned home by sea, meeting at Habana with the filibustering
army of Lopez, recruited at New Orleans, witnessing the shooting of Capt.
Crittenden and 50 men by Lopez, for insubordination and desertion. In
1859 McIlvoy came to Colorado with his family, and settled on Missouri flats
near Central City. Soon after he discovered Lake gulch, and engaged in
mining and farming, having 160 acres of land on the flats.

David D. Strock, born in Ohio, in 1832, raised a farmer, and educated at
Hiram, came to Colorado in 1859, mining at Gregory gulch that summer,
when he returned to Kansas, but finally settled at Black Hawk, in this state,
in 1863, as a millwright and carpenter. He owned 50 feet on the Gunnell
lode, which he leased to the Gunnell company.

Anthony W. Tucker, born in Pa, in 1837, reared in Ohio, a machinist by
trade, came to Colorado in 1859, and mined at Gregory and Russell diggings.

Grand county, organized in 1874, included the North park, and most of the Middle park, and all of

He set up and operated the first engine in Colorado, in Bentley & Bayard's saw-mill at Central City. In 1862 he worked on J. L. Pritchard's quartz-mill at Nevadaville. Afterwards he superintended different mills—D. P. Casey's in Chase gulch, Ophir mill, Clayton mill, Truman Whitcomb mill, and Wheeler & Sullivan mill. In 1877 he leased the Tucker mill in Russell gulch, which was burned in 1879, after which he purchased an interest in the New York quartz-mill at Black Hawk. He was elected county commissioner in 1877. Henry Paul, born in Ky in 1841, and brought up to farm life in Ky and Mo., came to Colorado in 1859, but returned to Mo. the same year, and studied medicine until 1863, when he settled in Gilpin co., where he engaged in mining and farming, varying these pursuits with medical studies. His mining discoveries are the Hazelton, Helmer, Powers, and Searle lodes in Willis gulch in Gilpin county, and Security lode, on Mt Bross, in Park co., and many others in several counties. He was elected to the legislature in 1873, and was chairman of the committee which drafted the mining law of Colorado. He was a delegate to the National Democratic convention at Cincinnati in 1880. He engaged in mining and merchandising.

Joseph S. Beaman, born in Baden, Germany, in 1834, was apprenticed to a brewer. He came to the U. S. in 1851, and learned carpentry at Louisville, Ky, after which he attended school two years. In 1859 he came to Colorado, locating at Central City, where, after mining a few years, he worked at his trade, and finally established himself as a bottler of soda water and liquors.

Lewis W. Berry, born in Brooklyn, N. Y., in 1822, was the son of a ship-carpenter, and learned the trade of painter. He was in New Orleans in 1846, where he raised a company for the Mexican war, and fought under Gen. Scott, as 'captain. Returning to Brooklyn, he remained there until 1859, when he came to Colorado, mining at Central City for 4 years, when he spent two years in Montana, living later at Idaho Springs.

Samuel Copeland, born in Me in 1819, after a youth spent on a farm and at academies in St Albans and Charleston, embarked in mercantile pursuits at several points in Me, N. B., and Mich., and travelled for health and pleasure. In 1860 he came to Colorado, having invested his means in a train of 11 wagons, 28 yokes of oxen, and 4 horses, the wagons being freighted with machinery for a quartz-mill, saw-mill, and shingle-mill. The quartz-mill proved a loss, but the others were set up and profitably operated in Michigan gulch until 1863, when he removed them to Boulder, being the principal lumber merchant there until 1870, and engaged also in mining and merchandising. His energetic course resulted in a fortune.

James B. Gould, born in N. Y. in 1836, was reared in Pa and Iowa as a farmer. He came to Black Hawk in 1860, engaging in freighting about the mines for two years, and afterwards for 7 years between the Missouri river and Denver. He then sold his teams, and purchased a farm in Boulder co., where he secured 440 acres of improved land near White Rock. I have abstracted these biographical sketches from *Clear Creek and Boulder Val. Hist.* The names of C. A. Roberts and Charles Peck occur in connection with mining regulations in 1859, but I have no further information of them. *Hollister's Mines of Colo*, 78. Some facts concerning Central City and Gilpin co. have been drawn from N. T. Bond's *Early History of Colorado, Montana, and Idaho*, MS., containing narratives of discovery and early government.

Clara Brown, a colored woman, born near Fredericksburg, Va, in 1800, after an eventful life as a slave, was liberated in Ky. In her 57th year she removed to St Louis, and again to Leavenworth, joining in the spring of 1859 a party bound for Pike's peak, and paying for her transportation by cooking for a mess of 25 men. She had the first laundry in Gilpin co., and in a few years accumulated $10,000. After the close of the war she went to Ky for her relatives, and established them in Colorado, herself settling in Denver in

what is now Routt county. It now embraces the
Middle park and most of the settlements of its former
territory.[5]

Gunnison county, whose early history has been
given, was organized in 1880. Its development has
been rapid. Over 100,000 tons of coal were taken
out of this county in 1883. It is beginning to be cultivated for its agricultural wealth; its grazing interest is large and increasing; but its gold, silver, copper, lead, coal, and iron mines are still the chief
incentive to settlement. The bullion output in 1883
was $650,000, and the assessed valuation of the county
$3,234,490.[6]

a neat cottage of her own, and being a member in good standing of the presbyterian church. *Clear Creek and Boulder Val. Hist.*, 443.

[5] It contains arable and grazing lands, beautiful mountain lakes, and is a
sportman's paradise. The lack of facilities for transportation have interfered
with its development. The population in 1880 was but little over 400, but
had increased in 1883 to 2,000. One of the attractions of the park are the
hot sulphur springs on Grand river and at Grand lake. Placer mining has
been carried on in this county for twenty years, and coal of good quality is
one of its best known resources. The later mineral discoveries have revealed
gold and silver lodes of great value. Petroleum is another natural production awaiting railroads to be made available. The assessment valuation in
1883 was 353,998. Grand Lake, with a population of 300, was the county
seat. Hot Sulphur Springs had 300 inhabitants, Teller 560, while Fraser,
Gaskill, Lulu, Troublesome, Colorow, Rand, Hermitage, and Canadian had
100 or less.

[6] Gunnison City, the county seat, had in 1886 6,000 inhabitants, and the
county not less than 14,000, distributed among other towns as follows: Pitkin 1,500, Crested Butte 1,000, Gothic 900, Irwin 600, Tin Cup 500, West
Gunnison 400, and the remainder among mining camps and settlements.
There were numerous settlements belonging to Gunnison at that time, namely,
Allen, Almont, Anthracite, Aureo, Barnum, Bellevue, Bowman, Camp
Kingsberry, Chipeta, Chloride, Cloud City, Copper Creek, Crooksville, Cur-
ran, Delta, Doyleville, Drake, Elko, Elkton, Emma, Galena, Haverly, Hiller-
ton, Howeville, Indian Creek, Jack's Cabin, Marom, Montrose, Ohio, Paradox
Valley, Parlins, Petersburg, Pittsburgh, Powderhorn, Quartzville, Red Moun-
tain, Richardson, Roaring Rock, Rock Creek, Ruby City, Rustler Gulch,
Sage, Sapinero, Scofield, Silver Night, Spring, Stevens, Toll Gate, Tomichi,
Turner, Uncompahgre, Virginia, Waller's Camp, Washington Gulch, White
Earth, White Pine, White Sulphur Springs, and Woodstock. Some few of
these have been cut off by the division of the county in 1883.
The Denver and Rio Grande railroad now passes across the county from east
to west, with a branch to Crested Butte, where considerable progress is being
made in the development of extensive and valuable deposits of anthracite,
bituminous, and coking coal. But there is less population in the towns, notably less in Gunnison City, than for the first two or three years of growth, and
when this was the terminus of the railway. The secondary epoch of all mining
and railroad towns is upon it, from which the healthy growth of the country,
which comes later, alone will redeem it. There are some interesting and

Hinsdale county, named after George A. Hinsdale, was organized in 1874, on the discovery of the mines of the San Juan country. Owing to its mountainous character, and lack of transportation, it made

instructive facts given in *Eaton's Gunnison Yesterday and To-day*, MS. 'We have always,' he says, 'lived on eastern capital,' and proceeds to relate that a St Louis company laid gas and water pipes, expending $100,000; erected the La Veta hotel, on foundations abandoned by its projector, at a cost of $212,000; formed a plan for an opera house and a block of stores; organized the Gunnison Steel and Iron company, buying coal and iron lands all over the country, the city raising $20,000 to put in escrow, to be paid over when it should fulfil certain conditions. Furnaces were partially erected when it was discovered that the coal owned by the company was not coking coal, and that the coking coal had been bought up by the Colorado Coal and Iron company. This suspended the business of the St Louis company. A patent smelter, owned by Moffat of Joplin, Mo., was erected in 1882–3, and failed, but was afterward made to work successfully. Shaw and Patrick, young men, also erected a smelter, which when still incomplete was abandoned, presumably for want of capital. An attempt was being made in 1884 to raise money to start the works. These several failures of companies and individuals affected the business of the town, and decreased its population. In the autumn of 1884 a brewery was started, which, with the Moffat smelter, two planing-mills, a cement, and a mineral-paint factory constituted the manufacturing industry of Gunnison.

The first banks of Gunnison were the Miners' Exchange, and the Bank of Gunnison, both owned by private individuals, but afterward made the First National and the Iron National banks, the latter printing drafts with an engraving of the projected steel works in a corner.

A. E. Buck, proprietor of the *News-Democrat*, formerly of the *Spirit of the Times* in New York, laid out an addition to Gunnison town site. The first amusement hall was the Globe theatre, of a low character. It was purchased by the citizens, and converted into an academy of music. In 1882 the Gunnison opera house was erected, and a private theatrical company of the citizens gave entertainments occasionally, varied by the performances of travelling artists. In 1882 Gunnison had two small brick school houses. The following year $28,000 was appropriated by the citizens for the erection of two new school buildings, to be used in connection with the others, and the schools rose to a high order. Six churches were organized by 1886, having their own edifices. A chamber of commerce was started in 1884, for which there appears to have been no urgent demand. It had begun making a collection of minerals.

Hartly C. Eaton, from whose MS. I have taken most of the above suggestive items, was born in Portland, Me, in 1853. He came to Gunnison in 1882, with J. A. Small and A. W. Sewall, to engage in the book and stationery trade. John B. Outcalt, born in New Jersey in 1850, a carpenter by trade, who came to Denver in 1871, and to Gunnison in 1874, with Richardson and William W. Outcalt, and who secured, with his brother, 1,100 acres of meadow land and town property enough to make them wealthy, also furnished me the result of his observations on Gunnison county and city, in *Grazing in Gunnison*, MS. See *Gunnison Sun*, Oct. 13, 1883; *Gunnison Review*, Jan. 1, 1883. The principal reliance of Gunnison is in coal and iron, to promote manufactures, which are still in their infancy, a fine grade of anthracite being found within twenty-five miles. Sandstone, granite, and marble are abundant in the neighborhood; also fire clay and materials for cement. But the place lay long under the ban of the railroad, to whose tyrannies men and municipalities must ever submit. Archie M. Stevenson, born in Scotland in 1857, but brought up in Wis. and educated for the prac-

little progress. Lake City, the county seat, had in 1886, 800 inhabitants. It lies in a sloping valley, at an elevation of 8,550 feet, surrounded by mountains ribbed with mineral veins. The principal mining districts are Engineer mountain, Lake, Park, Sherman, and Cimarron. The first development attained to was due chiefly to the firm of Crooke & Co., eastern capitalists, who purchased a number of mines, and erected concentrating and smelting works near Lake City, which were completed in 1878. The product of their mines the first year was $85,498 in silver, $23,698.27 in lead, and $2,925 in gold.[7]

Huérfano county was organized in 1861 with the county seat temporarily at Autobes. It was removed to Badito subsequently, and is at present at Walsenburg, a railroad and coal-mining town. Huérfano is principally a grazing and agricultural district. There were in the country in 1883, 20,000 cattle, and 100,-000 sheep. No mining except for coal was being done there, although it is known to have mines of gold and galena. The coal product of 1883 was 100,000 tons, from the mines of the Colorado Iron and Coal company. The population at that date was over 5,000, and the assessed valuation $1,321,826. Walsenburg had in 1886 400 inhabitants.[8]

Jefferson county, besides being one of the earliest

tise of the law, came to Colorado in 1880, locating first at Pitkin, but removing to Gunnison after being elected to the state senate for 4 years, in 1882. He formed a law partnership with Stevenson and Frankey.

[7] Two smelters were also erected at Capitol City, in 1880, under the management of George S. Lee. The mines of the county best known are the Little Annie, Golden Queen, Ute, Ulé, Belle of the West, Ocean Wave, Emperor, Fairview, Scotia, John J. Crooke, El Paso, Inez, Palmetto, and Hotchkiss, which are but few of the many good mines. Capitol City, Antelope Springs, Sherman, Burrows Park, and Argentum, have from 125 to 200 inhabitants each. There are a few other settlements, and mining camps: Antelope Park, Barrett's Station, Belford, Clear Creek, Crooke City, Hudson's Rancho, Lost Trail, San Juan, Sparling's Rancho, Tellurium, and Timber Hill.

[8] Lesser settlements are Apache, Butte Valley, Chabez Plaza, Cucharas, Dickson, Dixolt, Fabian Plaza, Gardner, Garzia Plaza, Hager's Mill, Hamilton, Huerfano, Huerfano Cañon, La Veta, Malachite, Meaz Plaza, Mining Camp, Mule Shoe, Ojo, Park's Mills, Piedras Animas, Quebec, Quinland, Rito de Gallina, Sangre de Cristo Station, Santa Clara, Santa María, Spanish Peaks, Tirneros Plaza, Turkey Creek, Veta Pass, Wahatoya, Walsen's Springs, Walsen Station.

settled and first organized, enjoys the advantage of a
nearness to the metropolis and a variety of products
to take to that market.   While not strictly a mining
county, it contains in its western portion gold, silver,
copper, lead, zinc, iron, mica, coal, mineral paint,
petroleum, alabaster, fire clay, potters' clay, limestone,
marble, building stone, timber, and other productions
which enter into manufactures.   Its coal mines are
extensively worked.   It is one of the foremost agricultural and horticultural counties, and has a greater
variety of industries than almost any other.   The
population in 1883 was 8,000, and the assessed valuation $2,746,498.   Golden is the county seat, with
2,500 inhabitants.   There are a number of smelters
located here for reducing the ores from other counties, besides flouring mills and factories of various
kinds.[9]

[9] The towns of Arapahoe, Mount Vernon, and Golden Gate were mining
camps in the spring of 1859, the second at the mouth of Table Mountain
cañon, and the latter at the mouth of another cañon called the Gate of the
Mountains.   Golden City on Clear creek, was settled at the same time by W.
A. H. Loveland, John M. Ferrell, Fox Deifendorf, P. B. Cheney, George Jackson, Hardy, Charles M. Ferrell, John F. Kirby, T. P. Boyd, William Pollard,
James McDonald, George West, Mark L. Blunt, Charles Remington, E. B.
Smith, J. C. Bowles, David McCleery, I. B. Fitzpatrick, and W. J. McKay.
A part of this number belonged to the Boston company of 8 members who
crossed the plains together, arriving in June, among whom were Henry Vallard
and A. D. Richardson and Thomas W. Knox, the celebrated correspondents of
the *N. Y. Tribune*.   George West, a Bostonian, was president of this company.
They decided that the temporary settlement at the crossing of Clear creek
was the proper site for a city, and accordingly they, with Loveland, Kirby,
J. M. Ferrell, Smith, H. J. Carter, Mrs Williams, Stanton & Clark, F. W.
Beebe, J. C. Bowles, E. L. Berthoud, and Garrison selected 1,280 acres on
both sides of Clear creek and laid out a town.   F. W. Beebe surveyed 320
acres that season, but the survey was completed in 1860 by Berthoud.   By
the close of the year, with the help of a saw and shingle mill, Golden had
grown to a town of 700 inhabitants.   Robert L. Lambert erected a log store
in the winter of 1859, between the seasons of mining.   He became a wealthy
cattle and sheep raiser in Las Animas co.   Many farms were taken up.   I. C.
Bergen settled in Bergen park, where he kept a hotel.   In the autumn Mc-
Intyre and McCleery organized a company to construct a wagon road from old
Fort St Vrain to South Park, via Golden, Bergen Park, Cub Creek, etc.,
which was located in the following spring.   On the 7th of Dec., 1859, the
Western Mountaineer issued its first number, George West publisher.   The
first county election under the provisional government was held Jan. 2, 1860,
when the votes for county seat gave Golden a majority over Arapahoe of 401
to 228.   Baden, later Aleck, received 22 votes.   Joseph C. Remington was the
first sheriff elected.   There was a public sale of town lots in February, prices
ranging from $30 to $120.   A school was also opened in the spring by M. T.
Dougherty, with 18 pupils.   At the first municipal election, held April 10, 1860,

Lake county was first organized in 1861, when California gulch was in its first flush period, with the county seat at Oro. On the discovery of silver at a later date the legislature cut off the northern end and

J. W. Stanton was chosen mayor; S. M. Breath, recorder; W. C. Simpson, marshal; W. A. H. Loveland treas.; R. Barton, J. M. Johnson, R. T. Davis, D. G. Dargiss, O. B. Harvey, A. B. Smith, W. J. Smith, J. Kirby councilmen. In August a weekly mail was established. A period of slow progress, and in 1883 Golden was made the capital of Colorado, but the legislature did not meet there until 1866-7. In 1867 the county voted $100,000 in bonds in aid of the Colorado Central and Pacific railroad to Cheyenne and to Denver. Golden had now two flouring-mills, a brewery, and a paper-mill, and was making fire-brick. In 1868 ground was broken for the first Colorado railroad, and the following year the road-bed was made ready for the rails 10 miles, from Golden to the eastern boundary of the county. On the 26th of Sept., 1870, the first locomotive reached Golden. In April a narrow guage railroad, the first west of the Mississippi, had been begun, which was finished to Black Hawk late in 1872. In March 1873 a narrow guage to Floyd Hill was in running order, and in April the Golden and Julesburg branch of the Colorado Central was completed to Longmont. Still later in the year the Golden and South Platte railway was graded 18 miles to Plum creek. Then came the panic of 1874-6, when railroad building was interrupted. In 1877 the narrow guage to Georgetown was completed, and the line from Black Hawk to Central in the spring of 1878. The Colorado Central also, when completed, belonged to the system of railroads which contributed to the prosperity of Golden, 34 trains leaving and arriving daily. They carried away coal, stone, hay, grain, and flour, and brought ore, coal, coke, lumber, grain, and groceries. Golden built three flouring-mills, five smelting and reduction works, two breweries, a paper-mill, six coal shafts, three fire brick, pressed brick, and drain-pipe factories, three perpetual lime-kilns, and two quaries, with a variety of minor industries. The smelters turned out from $1,200,000 to $1,500,000 annually. It has seven churches, good schools, and an intelligent press. The state school of mines was placed at Golden. It was established by act of legislature in 1870, making an appropriation for that purpose. It was reëstablished by another act in 1874; and in 1877 still further placed on a permanent footing. It now occupies a fine brick edifice, and is an ornament to the town. It is supported, like all the other state institutions, by a direct tax of so many mills on the dollar. A signal-office has been maintained in connection with it. Here are taught analytical and applied chemistry, mineralogy, metallurgy, assaying, civil and mining engineering, geology, and mathematics. The state industrial school is also located at Golden by an act of the legislature of 1881, the old school of mines building being used for a beginning; but by an act of 1883 an appropriation of $15,000 was made for new buildings. The whole appropriation for industrial school purposes in that year amounted to $60,000, to be applied to its maintenance, machinery, and material for industries, and a library. The lesser towns and settlements of Jefferson are Ahlstrom's, Anchor Station, Archer's, Arvada, Bartlett's Lake, Bear Creek, Beaver Brook, Beeson Mill, Bellville, Big Hill, Brownville, Buffalo, Buffalo Creek, Buffalo Tank, Chimney Gulch, Church's, Clear Creek, Copperdale, Cottonwood Falls, Creswell, Crossons, Crosson's Camp, Deansbury, Deer Creek, Deer Creek Mines, Dome Rock, Eagle Brook Park, Elk Creek, Emperor Rancho, Emperor Springs, Enterprise, Ford Lake, Forks Creek, Forks of Clear Creek, Gallagher Camp, Gilman, Glen Plym Rancho, Grotto, Guy Creek, Hildebrande, Hines Rancho, Huntsman, Hutchinson, Jefferson, Jefferson Park, Johnson's Crossing, Jones Siding, Last Resort, Leahow Island, Lee Siding, Little Station, Littleton, Memphis Camp, Morrison, Mount Carbon,

called it Carbonate county, with the county seat at Leadville, while the southern portion retained its former name. At the same session, however, the name of Lake was restored to the silver region, and that of Chaffee given to the remainder.[19]

Olio, Oxeville, Park Siding, Pine Grove, Platte Cañon, Platte River, Ralston, Ralston Creek, Shingle Mill, Smith Hill, South Platte, Spruce Park, Steven's Gulch, Stewart's Rancho, Thompson's Mill, Troutdale, Turkey Creek, Turtle Pond, Ute Trail, Vermillion, Webber's Saw-mill, Welters Wood Camp, Willowville, Wilson's Saw-mills.

Andrew H. Spickerman, born in New York in 1820, came to Colorado in 1859, and settled on Turkey Creek in 1862, where he has continued to reside. Reuben C. Wells, born in Ill. in 1833, came to Colorado in 1859 from Moline, of which his father was one of the founders. He returned the same year to Ill., but finally settled at Golden in 1869, where he is engaged in making paper. David G. Dargin, born in Me in 1835, came to Colorado in 1859, settling at Golden City, and opening the second store, Loveland having opened the first. He afterward spent some time in other parts of the union, but returned in 1879 to Golden, where he improved his town property, and opened the Monster lode in Clear Creek co., where he secured several mines.

[19] These changes were made in Feb. 1879. It is a small county, and noted only for its mines, of which I have already given an account. Its history is summed up in the brief statement that it produced in gold, silver, and lead between 1860 and 1884, $79,934,647.69. Of this amount about $13,000,-000 was in gold, and $55,000,000 in silver. Lake county is the largest lead producing district in the U. S. A variety of the less common minerals and metals is found in these mines, among which are zinc, antimony, bismuth, tin, copper, and arsenic. The official reports for four years give $15,025,153 for 1880, $12,738,902 for 1881, $16,531,853 for 1882, and $15,691,200 for 1883, with better prospects for 1884. There are 13 smelters at Leadville, and 231 steam-engines employed in the mines, with an aggregate horse-power of 5,454. Other business is proportionately active. The population of Leadville is 20,000. Adelaide and Malta have together 1,000 inhabitants, besides which there are the villages of Twin Lakes, Eilers, Alexander, Alicante, Soda Springs, and a number of small settlements. They are Bird's Eye, Buckskin, Clark Rancho, Crane Park, Crystal Lake, Danaville, Dayton, Evansville, Fifteen-mile House, Hayden, Henry, Howland, Keeldar, Oro, Ryan's, Union Station. Soda Springs, five miles from Leadville, is a popular health resort; and Twin lakes, on which a steamboat was placed in 1880, a famous pleasure resort.

Among the pioneers of Lake county are the following: George L. Henderson, born in northern Ohio in 1836, came to Colorado in 1859, and resided at Central City and California Gulch. He was the first postmaster of Leadville, and claims to have suggested its name. His business is general merchandising.

Emmet Nuckolls, born in Va in 1842, migrated to Nebraska City while a boy, and thence to Colorado in 1859, engaging in cattle-trading. He removed to Leadville on the discovery of silver, where he engaged in selling stock. wagons, hay, and grain. He was a member of the board of aldermen.

Rufus Shute, born in N. Y. in 1837, removed to Wis. at an early age, and thence to Colorado in 1859. He mined for a year, and returned east, and did not again visit this state until 1877, when he located at Leadville in the lumber trade. In 1879 he sold out and went into stock-raising. He served as alderman one year.

N. C. Hickman, born in Mo. in 1844, was the son of a physician, and left Davenport, Iowa, with his father in 1859 for Colorado. In the following year his father died at Central City, and young Hickman returned to Iowa

La Plata county is the south-west division of the state, was organized in 1874, but its development has not been rapid. In the south-west corner of the county are found many of the cliff-dwellings,[11] whose history

college to complete his education, after which he came once more to this state and located at Central as merchant and miner. In 1867 he sold out and spent several years in Kan. and N. M., but returned in 1879 to settle at Leadville, where he became a merchant and miner again on a larger scale than before. He was elected alderman in 1880, serving for two years.

[11] Of the remains of that ancient civilization and long extinct race which once overspread an area of fully 150,000 square miles in the south-western portion of the U. S., the most interesting and remarkable in many respects are the so called cliff-dwellers' ruins in south-western Colorado, and adjacent portions of Utah, New Mexico, and Arizona. These curious structures, built like swallows' nests in niches and crevices, high up in perpendicular cañon walls, are found scattered over the region drained by the Rio San Juan, and comprising an area of about 20,000 square miles. The most distinctive cliff-dwellings yet discovered are found in the cañon of the Rio Mancos, in the extreme south-west corner of Colorado. The first authentic account of any remains bearing a resemblance to these was contained in the report of Lieutenant J. H. Simpson, of the U. S. topographical engineers, who, while accompanying a military expedition against the Navajos in 1849, traversed portions of the Chaco and Chelly cañons, in northern New Mexico and Arizona respectively, and examined some of the more important groups of ruins which they contain. *Simpson's Jour. Mil. Recon.* In my *Native Races*, iv. 651, 661, I have given an account of this expedition and of the discoveries then made. A more thorough and careful examination of the cañons in question was made in 1875 and 1877 by W. H. Jackson, of the photographic and naturalist division of the U. S. geographical survey, whose detailed reports, illustrated from photographs, remain to the present day the most complete and valuable authority upon this a region of supreme interest to the ethnologist and antiquarian. See *Tenth Annual Report U. S. Geol. and Geog. Survey*, 420–450. Mr Jackson characterizes the ruins of the Chaco cañon, in particular, as 'preëminently the finest examples of the numerous and extensive remains of unknown builders to be found north of the seat of the ancient Aztec empire in Mexico.' They are for the most part the ruins of great communal structures, in shape somewhat like the largest of those occupied by the Pueblo Indians of the present day, but unlike these, built of stone, dressed and fitted with great nicety, and showing in their construction a much higher intelligence and skill. The Pueblo Bonita, the largest of the great piles of architecture which line the Chaco cañon for a distance of 25 miles, is 544 ft long and 314 ft wide; while the pueblo of Chettro Kettle, the next in size, has dimensions of 440 by 250 ft, and was surrounded by a wall which contained about 315,000 cub. ft of masonry. The larger number stand upon level ground in the bottoms of the cañons, and as a rule extend back to their perpendicular walls, rendering them impregnable from the rear. A few were built on ledges of rock in the sides of the cañons, and often as high as 100 ft from the bottom, access being gained in some cases by stairways cut in the almost perpendicular rock. With the exception of one skull found by Jackson in the Chaco cañon, and some broken pottery, no remains of the ancient builders other than their habitations were found in these cañons, no extended attempts at exhumation having been made.

Proceeding northward and crossing the line into Colorado, we come to the regions of the cliff-dwellers proper, and find in the Mancos cañon in particular the most wonderful illustrations of their altogether unique architecture. This cañon, together with those of the Hovenweep, McElmo,

must be relegated to the indeterminate and unrecorded past.

Montezuma, La Plata, and Las Animas, was first visited by W. H. Jackson in the summer of 1874, and his report, though the record of a hurried and incomplete examination, was nevertheless of supreme value, and excited great and widespread interest in the subject. *Report of U. S. Geol. Survey*, 1874, 369–381; *Bancroft's Native Races*, iv. 718–733. The Mancos river has cut its way through the great Mesa Verde for a distance of about 40 miles, forming a cañon which, from the peculiar character of its walls, was especially adapted to the purposes of the cliff-dwellers. These walls range from 1,000 to 2,000 ft in height, and in them occur numerous horizontal crevices, formed by the more rapid erosion of the strata of shale and clay which lie between the harder sandstones. It was in these crevices, and on the very brink of precipices often a thousand feet deep, that the strange habitations were built, generally of squared and faced stone cemented to the ledge of rock forming the base, and occasionally to the overhanging cliff as well. The largest and most perfect structure discovered by Jackson at this time consisted of two stories, was twelve ft high and ten wide, and was perched on the edge of the cliff at the height of 700 ft, perpendicularly above its foot. The Mancos

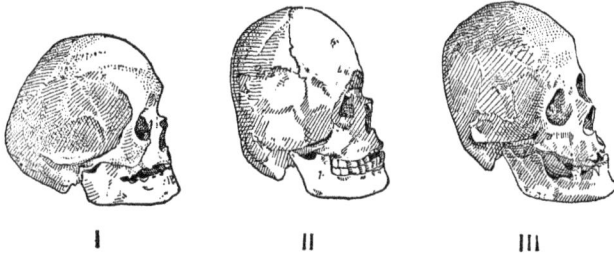

I   **II**   **III**

SKULLS FOUND IN CLIFF-DWELLINGS, MANCOS CAÑON, COLO. NO. 1. SIMILAR TO THOSE FOUND IN CHACO CAÑON, N. M. NOS. 2 AND 3. PROBABLY COMMON TYPE CLIFF-DWELLERS.

cañon was again visited in 1875 and 1876, this time by W. H. Holmes of the geological survey, who gave to its entire 40 miles of length a more careful and painstaking examination. Scores of cliff-houses were discovered and accurately described; the largest of which, known as the 'Sixteen Windowed House,' had a length of 60 ft, and a depth of 15 ft, and stood 800 ft above the bottom of the cliff. Only slight attempts at exhumation were made by Mr Holmes; but a small collection of stone and bone implements, a few whole articles of pottery, and numerous fragments from which successful restorations have been made, were nevertheless obtained. *Tenth Annual Report U. S. Geol. Survey*, 391–399.

From the remoteness and inaccessibility of the cliff-dwellers' region, and the fact that the greater part of it lies in the Ute Indian reservation, it has been visited by few explorers; and till recently the accounts given by Simpson, Jackson, and Holmes were the only sources of accurate information concerning it, their hasty examination, for no other was possible, precluding any serious attempts at exhumation. On Nov. 1, 1888, however, a party of eight men, fully equipped and provisioned, led by Charles McLoyd of Durango, and Richard Wetherill, the owner of a ranch near the Mancos river,

Larimer county was organized in 1861, with the county seat temporarily at Laporte, and belongs to

set forth for the cliff-dwellers' country. During the succeeding four months these men made a most thorough exploration of the Mancos cañon, and emerged on March 10, 1889, laden with a priceless collection of antiquities yielded to their diligent search. They found that the most extensive remains of the cliff-dwellers' architecture were not in the main cañon, but in its short tributary arroyas, and generally at the heads of these, where they first break down from the flat table-land or mesa through which the cañon has been cut. At such points there are commonly large semi-circular sweeps, or amphitheatres, of perpendicular rock-wall, from 1,000 to 2,000 feet in height; and in these the ancient builders erected their largest and finest structures. On Dec. 8, 1888, Richard Wetherill discovered, in one of the forks of Cliff cañon, a tributary to the Mancos, the most notable ruin thus far found, and to which the appropriate name of 'Cliff Palace' has been given. This great structure, which both in size and architecture and in the constructive skill which it evidences, may well take rank with the finest

FROM CLIFF-DWELLINGS, MANCOS CAÑON. CORRUGATED JAR, STONE AXES, ETC.

of the Chaco cañon pueblos, and with the additional interest which attaches to it from its remarkable location, occupies a crevice in the perpendicular rock-wall fully 1,000 feet above its base. The building is 425 feet long, and has a height of 80 feet in front. Its depth in the centre is about 80 feet, and 124 rooms were counted on the ground-floor. It was built of faced stone, first course of which was firmly cemented to the rock forming the base. Within it was finished with a smooth layer of plaster.

Of the collection made by this party, and which has become the property of the State Historical Society of Denver, little can be said by way of description that will convey an idea of its value. It contains 18 perfect skulls, one of which shows the same peculiar flattening of the upper posterior portion which gave a distinctive character to the skull found by Jackson in the Chaco cañon. There are also 18 large coiled or corrugated water-jars, the largest about 16 inches high and 14 inches in diameter, the whole forming the most complete collection in existence of these curious vessels which seem to be examples of a stage of the potter's art anterior to that which produced the

HIST. NEV. 40

the agricultural divisions, although it has mines of
copper, silver, and gold in its mountainous parts. Its
facilities for irrigation from the Cache-la-Poudre and
Big Thompson rivers are gradually extending the
cultivable area.[12]

common smooth ware of to-day. The large number of bowls, basins, and
jars, of the ordinary glazed ware, are chiefly interesting in their decorations,
which, severely plain and quite elegant, are in striking contrast with those
seen in modern Pueblo pottery, which abounds in grotesque animal figures
and designs far from beautiful. The glazing of this ancient pottery is likewise superior; and some articles which were found must have served an
ornamental purpose only. The skeletons, or mummies, of two infants were
exhumed, and have a place in the collection. These were found wrapped
first in the curious feather-cloth which seems always to have been put to
mortuary uses, and this in turn was enclosed by a number of small wooden
rods, strung together with cords after the fashion of a Venetian blind. Stone
axes, many of them with handles complete; stone knives in great abundance;
bone implements of various kinds, including needles with eyes; baskets
woven with great skill; fillets or head-bands, plaited of yucca or reeds, and
ornamented with the Grecian fret, and which were used for carrying water-
jars and other burdens—these are a few of the objects to be found in this
wonderful collection. And in one of the houses of that valley, which for
long centuries has known no occupant, the explorers found some dried grasses
and reeds, which had been tied in bundles with utmost precision, and laid
carefully away against the day when they should be needed.
   As to the race which once inhabited these strange dwellings it might be
idle to speculate. That the cliff-dwellings themselves were the last refuge
of a people harassed by savage foes, is the generally received opinion; to
which the frequent occurrence of circular structures, for which no other use
than that of watch-towers can be assigned, lends additional weight. The
date of their final abandonment is conjectural and opinions differ widely.
Holmes thinks it was comparatively recent, 'certainly subsequent to the
Spanish conquest.' Cushing would assign a much earlier date. That the
mysterious builders were the ancestors of the Pueblo Indians of the present
day is confidently asserted by Holmes, and has been generally accepted as
true; but it seems probable, in the light of the later discoveries, that a closer
relation will be found to exist between them and the modern Moquis, if indeed
these are not the identical race which once inhabited the ruined cliff-dwellings
of the San Juan region. It is well known that the Moquis, while classed
broadly with the Pueblos, differ from them in many essential particulars—
in language, in physique, in the manner of carrying burdens, and in their
myths relating to their origin and destiny. So far as can yet be determined,
the points in which the cliff-dwellers differed from the modern Pueblos seem
to be those in which these latter differ from the Moquis. The Moquis, moreover, have a legend that they once lived in the Cosnino cañon, where ruined
cliff-dwellings abound; and a Ute Indian who acted as guide to Messrs Chapin
and Howard, members of the Appalachian club of Boston, visiting the Mancos cañon in the summer of 1889, strongly objected to their excavations
among the cliff ruins, giving as a reason that 'digging Moquis make men
Utes, squaw Utes, all Utes heap sick.' In view of these facts, it would seem
that the Moquis present a most inviting field for ethnological research, which
might result in clearing up much of the mystery which surrounds both the
Pueblos of the present day and that strange race which once, like very birds
of prey, built their lofty eyries among the cliffs.
   [12] The principal productions are hay, wheat, oats, barley, rye, corn,
roots, melons, and vegetables, which grow to great perfection, and with cattle

Las Animas county was organized in 1866, and comprises a large extent of country in the south and south-eastern part of the territory. It is an agricultural and coal-producing district, and excellent in both.[13]

and sheep form the wealth of the county, which in 1878 was assessed at $1,502,330, but which increased after the irrigation canals were completed to $3,012.040, in 1883. The population in 1880 was 5000; in 1883, 7,500. Fort Collins, the county seat, is situated on Cache-la-Poudre river, thirty miles above its junction. It has some small manufactures, several churches, good schools, two local newspapers, and about 1,300 inhabitants. The buildings of the State Agricultural society and college are located here. There are no important towns besides, the population being widely scattered on farms.

Andrew Armstrong, born in Ireland in 1825, immigrated to the U. S. in 1839, residing in New York city until 1873, when he came to Colorado on account of failing health. He settled at Fort Collins, which at that time had 200 inhabitants, bought real estate, and realized satisfactory returns.

Charles P. Miller, born in Mich. in 1853, graduated from the medical department of the state university as a homeopathic physician in 1877, and removed to Colorado the following year, there to practise his profession. The towns and settlements are as follows: Ada Spring, Berthoud, Box Elder, Branch Cañon, Buckhorn, Burns Station, Chambers, Colorado Junction, Cow Creek, Crescent, Elkhorn, Elkhorn Rancho, Estes Park, Fall River, Farrar House, Ferguson Rancho, Fossil Creek, Home, Horse-shoe Lake, Hupp's Rancho, Lamb's House, Laporte, Lily Lake, Little Thompson, Livermore, Lone Pine, Loveland, McGregor Hotel, McLaughlin Rancho, Michigan, Moraine, Mugen Gulch, Namaqua, North Fork, Otis, Pinkhamton, Pinewood, Pollock's, Raw House, Round Butte, Rustic, Sprague's House, Spring Cañon, Spring Gulch, St Louis, Taylor, Timber Creek, Tyner, Virginia Dale, Walden, Wheatland, Whyte Rancho, Willow Park, and Winonac.

[13] The wheat yield exceeds 150,000 bushels annually, corn 110,000, and oats 200,000 bushels. It has 60,000 head of cattle, 142,762 sheep, 6,210 horses and mules, the value of which exceeds one million dollars. The county was assessed in 1883 on $3,654,987, without its mines, mining land, and crops. Its coal-field is 50 miles square, and the coal of the best quality for heating or cooking purposes. As much of the coal found in other parts of the state does not coke, this is in demand, and the coke-ovens of El Moro and Trinidad furnish large quantities to the smelters of Pueblo, Denver, and Leadville. The production of the mines in 1883 was 370,680 tons, worth about $833,000. There were produced 136,000 tons of coke, and 20,000 tons of iron ore, which is worked by the Colorado Coal and Iron company at Pueblo. Limestone, hydraulic lime, building stone, cement, grind-stones, and silica are among the mineral deposits of the county. The population is 10,000. Trinidad, with 3,500 inhabitants, is the county seat. Its altitude is 6,005 feet. It is an old Mexican town, but much modernized. The business houses are of stone and brick; it has schools, churches, secret orders, hotels, banks, and newspapers like any American city. El Moro, five miles from Trinidad, has a few hundred inhabitants. Barela and Starkville have each 400, and Apishapa 200.

Casimero Barela, a member of the mercantile house of Barela and Wilcox at El Moro, and of the house of C. Barela & Co. at Trinidad, is a man of note in Las Animas county. Born at El Embuda, Rio Arriba co., N. M., in 1847, he received his education from Bishop Salpointe of Mora, and at the age of 20 years came to Colorado in search of something to do, having already married Josefa Ortiz. He began life as a freighter. In 1870 he was elected assessor of Las Animas county; in 1872 and 1874 he represented the county

Mesa county was organized in 1883, from the western portion of Gunnison, bordering on Utah. It is for the most part an agricultural and grazing country, with large beds of coal. As a fruit-growing region it is likely to surpass the counties east of the Rocky mountains, and has already extensive nurseries. Grand valley, supplied with water from the Grand river, in irrigating ditches, is an extraordinarily rich region, 70,000 acres of which were made cultivable by irrigation in 1882-83. The climate is delightful, the altitude being 4,500 feet. Large herds of cattle and sheep are pastured in the county, which had a population of about 3,000 when organized.[14]

Montrose county, organized at the same time, out of the south-west corner of Gunnison, is drained by the Rio Dolores, San Miguel, and other affluents of the Grand and Gunnison rivers. Its eastern portion contains extensive beds of coal, and probably other minerals and metals. The Uncompahgre valley is a fine agricultural district, bordered by the lofty mesas which are a distinctive feature of western Colorado. The valuation of property in this county in 1883 was estimated at $575,448, and its population at about 2,800. Montrose, the county seat, had then 300 inhabitants, Cimarron 100, Brown 100; and there

in the territorial legislature, being also elected sheriff in the latter year. In 1875 he was chosen a member of the constitutional convention, and in the following year was elected to the first state senate, drawing the long term. Being a democrat in politics, he was chosen delegate at large to the democratic national convention at Cincinnati in 1880, and again elected to the state senate. In 1881 he was elected treasurer of Las Animas county. He became a member of one of the largest stock companies in the state, with the largest herds and the best breeds. The minor settlements are Alfalfa, Apishpa Station, Barnes, Bent Cañon, Carriso, Chilelila, Cordova, Davis, Dodsonville, Earle, Eagle, Gonzales, Grinnell, Hoehne's, Hog Back, Hole in Prairie, Hole in Rock, Las Tijeras, Linwood, Lucero, Morley, North Siding, Pedros Coloradus, Placita, Purgatoire, Pulaski, Raton, Red Rock, San Francisco, San Isidro, San José, San Pedro, Spring Valley, Stockville, Stonewall, Strange, Tejara, Terrichero, Thatcher, Toll Gate, Tyrone, and Vigil.

[14] The county seat is at Grand Junction, which has had a rapid growth, and is destined to be an important railroad centre. In 1883 it had 2,000 inhabitants, two weekly newspapers, five churches, three schools, and other features of advanced society. The use of brick in building gives an air of permanency to the improvements. The assessable property of the county in 1883 was $965,144. Fruita had between 300 and 400 inhabitants, Mesa 150, Arlington 100. Whitewater, Kahuah, and Bridgeport were railroad stations.

were a few other incipient towns, but the population is chiefly bucolic.

Ouray county, organized in 1877, at which time it comprised a large extent of territory, has been cut down, and had its boundaries changed, until it now occupies a small portion of the eastern part of its former domain. In 1881 Dolores was set off. In 1882 Uncompahgre was taken, partly from the eastern side of Ouray, and partly from Gunnison.[15]

Park county, organized in 1861, covers nearly 1,000 square miles in the geographical and metal-producing centre of the state. South park, which it includes, has an elevation of 8,842 feet, and the average altitude of the whole county, which embraces a number of high peaks, is 10,000 feet. It contains ten or more mining districts, each differing from the other, some containing fissure veins, some contact lodes, others blanket or bedded deposits. The mineral belt is twenty-five miles long by five in width. Placer mining has not failed in this county, where the hydraulic process has yet to be applied to placer ground. Besides gold and silver, copper, lead, iron, coal, and salt are produced.[16]

[15] In 1883 Uncompahgre county was changed to Ouray, and Ouray to San Miguel. Ouray is altogether a mining county. The population in 1883 was 2,800, and assessable valuation $402,903; but in 1884 the local newspapers predicted a bullion output of $5,000,000. Red Mountain district produced $1,000,000 in 1883, about one third of which was gold, and the greater portion of which was from one mine, the Yankee girl. The districts of Poughkeepsie Gulch, Mount Sneffles, Uncompahgre, and Imogene Basin were also largely productive. Coal mining had only begun about this time. Ouray was the county seat, with 500 inhabitants. It is named after the Ute chief, for whose friendship the white people were grateful, at a time when his word might have precipitated war. Its situation, at the western end of the Uncompahgre cañon, is on the Pacific slope of the continent, at an elevation of 7,640 feet, in a round park, with rocky heights all about it of exceeding grandeur and startling wildness. Three miles below Ouray the valley is cultivable. In all respects this mountain-walled town is like the cities of the plains, with stores, churches, schools, newspapers, quartz-mills, smelters, sampling-works, and concentrators. It is reached by a branch from the Denver and Rio Grande from Montrose. There are hot sulphur springs a few miles from Ouray. About one mile south is the famous mineral farm, which has already been mentioned, discovered in 1875. Red Mountain City had about the same population in 1883 that Ouray had; Ophir 200, Ironton 150, Portland 100, Mount Sneffles 100; Aurora, Hoffman, Windham, and half a dozen hamlets, less.

[16] Salt was made from saline springs in Park county, which contain from

Pitkin county, named after Governor Pitkin, was organized in 1881, being set off from Gunnison, with a fair division of the indebtedness of the elder county. It embraces the mining region about the headwaters of Roaring fork of Grand river, which produced between 1879 and 1884, $550,000 in gold and silver.[17]

Pueblo county was organized in 1861, and much of its history appeared in previous chapters. Its first commissioners were O. H. P. Baxter, R. L. Wooten, and William Chapman. At the first county election Chapman was chosen probate judge, and John B. Rice sheriff.[18] The first term of court in the county

6 to 14 per cent salt. They were first located and improved by Charles L. Hall, who manufactured salt in 1861–3. A company was formed in 1864, J. Q. A. Rollins at the head, and Hall superintendent. Works costing $25,000 were erected, and the manufacture carried on until the completion of railroads, which transported salt more cheaply than it could be made in Colorado, caused the works to be closed. This information is taken from N. T. Bond's *Early Hist. Colorado, Montana, and Idaho*, MS., 21–2. As a history of Park co. it is very complete. The Hartsel mineral springs, named after their discoverer and locator, are noted for their healing qualities. From 40,000 to 50,000 cattle, 5,000 horses, and 10,000 sheep are grazed in South park. The bullion output of 1883 was $400,000, many of the mines being idle. The county was assessed, not including mining property, at $1,911,166. The population was 5,000. Fair Play, the county seat, has 800 inhabitants, Alma 900, Como 550.

Abraham Bergh, born in Milwaukee, Wis., in 1835, came to Colorado in 1859, locating himself in South park. He erected the first house in Fair Play, where he has been a hotel-keeper and merchant, as well as miner and owner in valuable mining property. He was elected to the general assembly in 1882, and again in 1884. The towns and settlements of Park county not named above are Alma, Arthur, Astroville, Bailey, Bentley's, Bordenville, Buffalo Springs, Como, Dudley, East Leadville, Estabrook, Fairville, Garo, Grant, Guirds, Guyrand's Park, Hamilton, Hall Valley, Hartsel, Holland, Horse Shoe, Hubbard, Jefferson, Jones Saw-mill, Kenosha, Lone Rock Rancho, Mountaindale, Mullenville, Park, Park Place, Platte Crossing, Platte River, Platte Station, Rocky, Sacramento, Salt Works, Spring Rancho, Slaght, Sulphur Springs, Summit, Tie Siding, Webster, Webber's Saw-mill, and Weston.

[17] The valley of Roaring fork is also a good grazing country. Absence of the means of transportation has retarded the development of the mines, one of which, the Smuggler, is widely known. The population in 1883 was estimated at 2,500, and the assessed valuation of the county $319,107. Aspen, the county seat, is situated at the confluence of Castle, Hunter, and Maroon creeks with Roaring fork. It had a population of 750 in 1883, and was a thriving business centre for the county. Ashcroft, above it on the river, had about 500 inhabitants, and Independence 250, Sparkhill 100; besides which there were Highland, Massive City, and Sidney.

[18] Stow, in his *General View of Colorado*, MS., says that one of the original town company, J. F. Smith, was the first police magistrate, and that Ned Cozzens, a cousin of Fred S. Cozzens, author of the *Sparrowgrass Papers*, was another. William H. Young and William H. Green were also of the company. Duell and Boyd were the surveyors.

was held by A. A. Bradford, in a house belonging to A. G. Boone, on the lower end of Santa Fé avenue, Pueblo. An adobe building was subsequently erected on the same avenue near Third street for a court-house. No jail was erected until 1868, when a stone building was rented to the county by R. N. Daniels for that purpose, which served until the commissioners soon after erected a brick jail on Court-house square, which was in use until 1880, when the present prison was completed.[19]

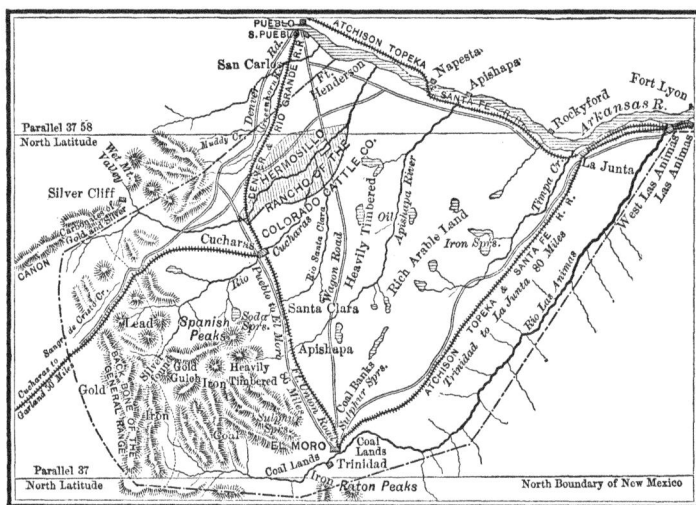

LAS ANIMAS GRANT.

[19] Pueblo county has no mines except of coal, and is therefore classed with the agricultural counties. Its inhabitants in its earlier years lived by grow-ing provisions, which they sold to the miners outfitting for the mountains. At present stock-raising is followed equally with farming. The beautiful Hermosillo rancho of the Colorado Cattle company, covering 91,000 acres, lies in this county, twenty miles south of Pueblo City. It belongs to an or-ganization of eastern capitalists, and grazes an immense number of cattle. This rancho is a part of the Las Animas grant. It was obtained by Ceran St Vrain and Cornelio Vigil, of the governor of New Mexico in 1844, and com-prised all the country north of the Beaubien grant in N. M. as far as the Arkansas river, and between the Las Animas and the St Charles tributaries. The U. S. government reduced the grant subsequently to 11 leagues. A part of it was called the Nolan grant, and was sold to the company which laid out south Pueblo. There is still some question as to the rights of heirs of the original grantees. The amount of wheat raised in Pueblo county in 1883 was 10,696 bushels, which placed it in the fifth rank of wheat-producing

Rio Grande county was established in 1874. It is situated on the west side of San Luis park, and is

counties, Boulder, San Miguel, Larimer, and Jefferson, in the order here given, being the leading wheat-growing districts. In corn-growing Pueblo ranked third, Weld and Boulder taking the lead. Pueblo had 213,781 acres of pasture-land, being only a little less than El Paso, Weld, and Elbert; but it had 92,422 acres under irrigation, which was more than other county, and irrigation is likely at any time to change pasture into farming lands. The county contained 50,000 cattle, 75,000 sheep, and 5,600 other domestic animals. The population has increased from 7,617 in 1880 to 20,000 in 1883, and the total assessable valuation was $7,286,422. Like almost every county in the state, it has hot mineral springs.

The town of Pueblo, the county seat since 1861, had a population in 1880 of 3,317, and south Pueblo, on the opposite side of the Arkansas river, 1,443, or 4,760 altogether. Together they had, three years later, four times that amount of population, and were practically one city, although still keeping up separate municipal governments. Old Pueblo is handsomely laid out, with an abundance of water and shade-trees, churches, schools, newspapers, banks, a board of trade, places of public amusement, founderies, mills, smelting-works, water-works, gas-works, and street railroads. The county buildings are among the best in the state. The state asylum for the insane is located here. I have a dictation from P. R. Thombs, who is superintendent of the insane asylum. He was in Colorado before the settlement, and acquainted with the famous traders and guides, Bridger, Carson, and others. He is a man of fine physique, medium size, fearless and genial. He gave me some bits of early history in his *Mexican Colorado*, MS., which I have incorporated in my work. The legislature of 1879–80 authorized the establishment of the asylum, making the necessary appropriation for their support by a tax of one fifth of a mill upon all taxable property. Previous to this date each county had taken charge of its own lunatics, for which they were reimbursed by the state. Pueblo obtained the location by donating the land required—40 acres. The board of commissioners appointed, James Macdonald, Theodore F. Brown, and J. B. Romero, purchased the residence of George M. Chilcott, near Pueblo, which served for a beginning, but the next legislature appropriated $60,000 for the erection of a new building, which not being sufficient, $80,000 was appropriated in 1883 to enlarge and furnish the asylum. A part of old Pueblo was entered under the act of congress of March 2, 1867, by Mark G. Bradford, probate judge of Pueblo co., in trust for the occupants. On Jan. 19, 1869, the present title to that portion was derived from the United States through him. Another portion was entered by the county at the same time. The town was incorporated March 22, 1870. The trustees appointed were: George A. Hinsdale, M. G. Bradford, James Rice, H. C. Thatcher, and H. H. Cooper. The first town election was held in April. It was merged in a city organization in March 1873. The first city election was held April 7th of that year, when James Rice was elected mayor, and G. P. Hayslip, O. H. P. Baxter, H. M. Morse, and Weldon Keeling aldermen. In 1871 the county voted $100,000 in bonds to aid the D. & R. G. R. R., rather than have it go south via Cañon City, which was threatened. In this same year the U. S. land-office was opened at Pueblo, with Wheeler as register, and M. G. Bradford receiver. The Pueblo *People* was also first issued this year in Sept., with Hinsdale editor, the office being the n. e. corner of Fourth and Summit streets. Its material was sold in 1874 to the proprietors of the *Chieftain*, its successor. The county court-house was completed in 1872, and was paid for from the sale of lots in a quarter-section of land preëmpted by the county authorities, and filed as an addition to the city, costing the tax-payers nothing. The successors to Mayor Rice were John R. Lowther, M. D. Thatcher, W. H. Hyde, and George Q. Richmond. In 1874 the present Holly system of water-works was completed, at a cost to the city of $130,-

watered by the Rio Grande river. The western portion of the county lies in the San Juan mountains, in

000, the contract being let to the National Building company of St Louis. Soon after a fire department was organized, consisting of two hose companies and a hook and ladder, W. R. Macomb chief. In 1875 the Pueblo and Arkansas valley railroad, connecting with the Atchison, Topeka, and Santa Fé, was completed to Pueblo, giving it a road to the east. The county subscribed $350,000 to this road, and its opening was the occasion of a monster excursion from all parts of Colorado, and from Kansas, the rejoicings lasting for two days. The first handsome public school building was erected in 1876, the district voting $14,000 in bonds. The trustee, after realizing the money, left the country, and the county was $14,000 poorer. Mather & Geist erected large smelting-works in 1878, which treat ores from all parts of the state, and employ about 500 men. The methodist church south began in 1884 to organize a college at Pueblo, which is meeting fair encouragement.

South Pueblo is a manufacturing town, the seat of the Colorado Coal and Iron company's works, one of the most extensive of the kind in the United States, where iron and steel manufactures are carried on. The works cover 40 acres of area, and the other buildings of the company 400 acres more. The town was founded by the Central Colorado Improvement company, whose officers were the officers of the D. & R. G. Co., and which was subsequently merged in the Colorado Coal and Iron company. According to M. Sheldon of south Pueblo the D. & R. G. Co. agreed to build a station on the north side of the river should the county vote the required amount in bonds to help construct the road. Having an opportunity, in 1872, to purchase 48,000 acres of the Nolan grant, they took the name of Central Colorado Improvement company, founded a town on the south side, and removed the terminus of the railroad to that site. Sheldon was born in Trumbull co., Ohio, in 1844. He came to Colorado in 1872 for his health. *South Pueblo,* MS. There are 1,000 acres laid out in town lots, with wide streets, bordered with trees, which are irrigated by tiny canals. The town has a mayor, board of aldermen, newspapers, and post-office of its own. The only thing shared in common between the towns is gas, the new town illuminating from the gasworks of north Pueblo. Taking them together as one, Pueblo is the natural centre of commerce and railroads for south-eastern Colorado, the depot of merchandise, and convenient seat of manufactures for an immense region. These advantages, with the resources already named, are sufficient to maintain a large city. There are no other considerable towns in the county. *Stone's Land Grants in Colo,* 4–6; *Gray's Colo,* 47–51; *Inter-Ocean,* Jan. 10, 1883; *Rocky Mtn News,* May 7, 1870; *The Pueblos, and Pueblo Co., Colo,* being a history of the twin cities; south Pueblo *Pueblo Collegiate Institute, Prospectus.* W. W. Strait, born in Pa in 1839, came from Min. to Colorado in 1876, and kept the Grand Central hotel in south Pueblo for a year and a half. From him I obtained a manuscript, *The Pueblos.* James Rice, born in Vt in 1830, came to Colorado in 1868, locating himself at Pueblo, engaging in the book and stationery business. From him, also, I gathered some interesting details. *Politics in Pueblo,* MS. The towns and settlements not named are Agate, Anderson's Rancho, Andersonville, Barry Rancho, Baxter, Beulah, Booneville, Cactus, Chico, Cody Rancho, Cook Rancho, Dog's Rancho, Doyle's Mill, Dry Rancho, Fosdick's Rancho, Four-mile Rancho, Goodnight, Graneros, Greenhorn, Holliday Rancho, Horn Rancho, Huerfano, Jackson, Jones' Rancho, Juniata, Langley Rancho, McClellan's Rancho, McIlhaney's Rancho, Meadows, Mace's Hole, Merrie's Rancho, Mexican Plaza, Muddy Creek, Nada, Nepesta, Old Fort Reynolds, Osage Avenue, Parnassus Springs, Peck's Rancho, Piñon, Pond, Robinett's Rancho, San Carlos, Skeeter Rancho, Spring Lake Rancho, St Charles, Sulphur Springs, Swallows, Table Mountain, Taylorville, Undercliffe, Walker Rancho, Wilson's Rancho, Wood Valley, a rich mineral region. Its resources are about equally divided between mining and agriculture. The Sum-

Peter K. Dotson, born in Va in 1823, crossed the plains from Independence, Mo., in 1851, intending to go to Cal., but stopped at Salt Lake, where he was employed a few months in running a distillery for Brigham Young. The following year he was engaged by an express and mail company as agent, which position he held for 9 years. In 1855 he was commissioned U. S. marshal for Utah, but being ordered away from the territory by Heber Kimball in 1857, he went to Washington, and came with the army of Johnson to Utah. He came to Colorado in 1860, and settled at Fountain City, (now Pueblo) and commenced the business of cattle-raising. I took a brief dictation from him called *Dotson's Doings*, MS. One of the pioneers of Pueblo county is here briefly mentioned: J. W. Lester, born in Pa in 1828; owns 240 acres of land on the Arkansas river below Florence.

Jacob A. Betts, born in Md in 1830, was a tailor by trade. He went first to Central City on coming to Colorado, but after roving from gulch to gulch for some time, stopped for three years at Greenhorn in Pueblo co., and was sheriff of the co. in 1864 and 1865. Subsequently he removed to Pueblo, where he was in the grocery trade. He settled in the adjoining county of Fremont, and became the owner of 740 acres of land, and herds of horses and cattle.

Alva Adams, born in Wis. in 1850, came to Colorado in 1871, and worked at first on the railroad at common labor. At Colorado Springs he helped to erect the first house, remaining at that place three years, when he removed to south Pueblo and engaged in hardware business for two years, selling out there and establishing a hardware store at Del Norte, Rio Grande co. In 1876 he started a branch business at Alamosa, returning in 1878 to Pueblo, leaving the branch stores in charge of others, and commencing a wholesale business in hardware at this point. He was elected a member of the first state legislature from Rio Grande co., was chosen a member of the first city council of south Pueblo, and later elected governor.

Alfred W. Geist, born in Boston in 1848, graduated from the scientific department of Yale college, and went from there to Mexico, travelling throughout the west, studying ores, smelting them, and looking for a place to locate a smelting establishment. In June 1878 he broke ground at Pueblo, starting with one furnace. The following year two more were erected. The business increased faster than his capital, compelling the formation of a stock company. The works are the largest in the world, requiring 1,000 tons per day to keep all the furnaces at work. They employ 400 men, and the company paid the railway for freight in 1884, $750,000. Ores from every part of the country are purchased, and the product goes to all points from San Francisco to New York.

Henry M. Fosdick, born in Boston in 1822, was educated a civil engineer. He came to Colorado in the spring of 1859, and assisted to lay out the streets of Denver. He was chairman of the vigilance committee in the autumn of that year. In 1861 he purchased a section of land in El Paso county, and laid off the town of Colorado City, but afterward sold the land to A. Z. Sheldon. He was with Chivington in the Sand creek fight, and justifies his course. In 1864 he went to Pueblo, and assisted in laying off that town. In 1866 he purchased 1,000 acres in Pueblo co., and became a farmer and stockraiser.

James N. Carlile crossed the plains with an ox-team in 1859. After a few days at Denver, he went to South park, where he mined for a few years. He then engaged in freighting between Denver and St Joseph, Denver and Montana, and Denver and Utah. Then in 1868, in partnership with William Moore, he became a railway contractor, and subsequently went to farming and stock-raising, which resulted in the ownership of large ranchos in Pueblo co., stocked with horses and cattle, with a residence in south Pueblo.

mit district is one of the most important in southern Colorado for gold mining. There are several stamp-mills in the district, which have produceb for several years from $200,000 to $400,000 per annum. The mines furnish an excellent market for the farm pro-ductions of the fertile San Luis valley.[20]

Routt county in the north-west corner of the state was cut off from Grand in 1877, but made small prog-ress until the removal of the Utes in 1882. The population the following year was 500. It is a graz-ing and agricultural district, with some placer mines and unworked quartz lodes. The assessed valuation in 1883 was $241,564, principally in stock cattle. Steamboat springs, and half a dozen hamlets, were

I. W. Stanton was born in Pa in 1835. At the age of 20 years he migrated to Pawnee City, Kan., and was there when the first Kansas legislature met, in 1855. The following year he removed to Iowa, remaining there until 1860, when he came to Colorado, driving a team. From Denver he went to Russell gulch, and later to California gulch, returning to Denver in the autumn, where he entered a store as clerk. In the spring of 1861 he walked to Cañon City, but finding nothing to do there returned to Denver, and was employed as clerk in the post-office. He enlisted in the 2d Colorado infantry in 1862, and was ordered to Leavenworth, serving until 1865. When mus-tered out he went to Washington, where he remained until he obtained the appointment of register in the land-office at Central City in 1868. In 1871 he was transferred to the land-office at Pueblo. In 1881 he was appointed postmaster at Pueblo.

[20] There were in 1883, 30,000 cattle, 40,000 sheep, and 20,000 horses and mules in the county. The population was 3,000, and the assessed valuation $1,013,417. Del Norte, the county seat, was first settled in the winter of 1871-72. The population in 1883 was 800. It is situated at a point where the mountains from the north and south approach so closely to the river as to leave only an elevated bench, a quarter of a mile in width between their rocky cliffs, on the southern margin. The view of the San Luis valley, the tree-fringed river winding below, and the snow-crowned peaks of the Sangre de Cristo range, make the situation delightfully picturesque. Del Norte has a good trade, several fine, large blocks of stores, built of stone, where whole-sale and retail merchandising is carried on, good county buildings, schools, a local newspaper, and wide streets, shaded by rows of trees, irrigated after the prevailing custom of the mountain towns. In the suburbs and surround-ing country there is a considerable Mexican population, which is domiciled in houses built of adobe. Timber is abundant in the mountains, and there are a number of saw-mills in the county run by water-power, of which there is an abundance.

Twenty-nine miles west of Del Norte is the romantic summer resort of Wagon-wheel gap, where there are hot sulphur springs; altitude 8,459 feet; climate healthful. The name comes from a narrow pass of several miles through a range of mountains, with vertical cliffs from 500 to 1,500 feet in height, of reddish-gray sand stone, with only room between them, as it was supposed, for the river and a wagon-road. Summitville in Summit mining district had in 1886 a population of 400. Jasper, Adams' Springs, La Loma del Norte, Lariat Piedra, and South Fork are small villages.

all the settlements at this time.   Hahn's peak is the county seat.

Saguache county was organized in 1866.   Its bound-aries have been several times altered, its present area comprising 3,200 square miles, the principal part of which is agricultural and grazing land.   Notwith-standing its favorable situation in the centre of the state, and embracing the northern portion of the San Luis valley, it is very little developed.[21]

San Juan county, organized in 1876, has been quite fully spoken of in a previous chapter.   The discoveries in Lake county, which followed immediately after the San Juan country had taken its first grand start, with-drew a large portion of its population, and diverted capital to Leadville.   Its original area has also been curtailed, until it is now one of the smallest counties in the state, and strictly devoted to mining, although lumbering, and every kind of milling might be profit-ably carried on here, timber and water power being abundant.   The bullion output of 1883 was $418,954, a small yield for a county with so many good mines. The assessment valuation, which excludes mining property, was $1,045,597.   The population of the county was 5,000.   The town of Silverton had 1,750 inhabitants, and Animas Forks 450.   Eureka, Min-

[21] This neglect was owing to its being partly covered by a Spanish grant, which was sold to Europeans who had not attempted to make it profitable. According to Wallihan's *Colorado Gazetteer*, 58, Ex-governor Gilpin sold a portion of Saguache county for $2,500,000.   It is, however, settling up with farmers, who sold in 1883 $300,000 worth of agricultural products.   The cat-tle and sheep in the county were valued at about $485,000, and other prop-erty at $911,931.   From the mines in the Kerber creek district $100,000 in bullion was produced. The population of the county was estimated at 6,000. Saguache is the county seat.   It has a fine location on the San Luis river. There were 900 inhabitants in 1883.   Bonanza, situated in Kerber district, had a population of 500.   Carnero, Claytonia, Crestone, Iron Mine, Alder, Marshalltown, Sedgwick, and Shirley were villages of 100 or 150 inhabi-tants.   The list of settlements comprises Bismarck, Blakeville, Bonanza, Bonito, Burnt Gulch, Camp Sanderson, Cebolla River, Cedar Creek Mines, Christione, Cochetopa, Cotton Creek, Cottonwood, Elkhorn Rancho, Ex-chequer, Franklin, Frisco, Garibaldi, Garner Creek, Gray Siding, Hauman, Jackson, Kerber Creek, Kimbrell, Kerberville, Los Pinos Agency, Marshall Pass, Milton, Oriental, Plaza, Poll Creek Mines, Rito Alto, River Meade, Rock Cliff, Sangre de Cristo, San Isabel, Sargent, Sheep Mount, Silver Hill, Silvery City, Star Branch, Uncompahgre, Venerables, White Earth, Willow Dale.

eral Point, Howardsville, Poughkeepsie Gulch, Congress, Cunningham Gulch, Del Mine, and half a dozen other small villages were all the settlements worth mention.

San Miguel county, set off from Ouray in 1883, comprises all of the former county of Ouray, except that part drained by the Uncompahgre river and its tributaries, which is still known as Ouray. The boundaries are so loosely described in the act establishing these counties that it would be impossible to say how much of the mineral discoveries being already developed went with the county of San Miguel. But it is safe to say that its new name cannot have deprived it of its established character as a mineral region. The name of the county seat, Telluride, is indicative of the resources upon which it depends. The population, at the period of its establishment, was 2,000, and its valuation $449,856. Telluride had 400 inhabitants, and Placerville 125.

Summit county, established in 1861, extended in its earlier form to the boundary of Utah. Its former territory was divided up into Garfield, Routt, and Eagle, leaving only its eastern end, resting on the western slope of the Park range, to sustain its ancient name. In 1882 it ranked fourth among the bullion producing counties, whereas, after the excision of Eagle county, it ranked only as the eleventh.[22]

---

[22] It contained 73 silver mines, which produced, in 1882, $459,550, and placers which yielded $51,000; but the following year the whole yield of the mines was no more than $350,000. The assessable property of the county was valued at $1,026,352, divided among a population of 5,000. The county seat was temporarily located at Parkville, but removed to Breckenridge. The town, although among those founded in 1860, was not incorporated until 1880, at which time it had 1,628 inhabitants. Breckenridge is situated on Blue river. Like all the Colorado towns, it has churches, schools, an opera-house, theatre, banks, and newspapers. Like all mining towns it has stamp-mills and smelting-works. Robinson has a population of 500, Racine 350, Frisco 250, Montezuma 250, Kokomo, Taylor, and Chihuahua each 200, Lincoln City 125, Swan, Wheeler, and Argentine each 100. Remaining settlements in Summit co.: Adelia, Argentine, Astor, Belden, Blue River, Blue River Valley, Buffalo Flats, Carbonateville, Chihuahua, Cliff Spring, Clinton Gulch, Conger, Cooper, Crocker, Decatur, Defiance City, Delaware City, Delaware Flats, Dillon, Eagle City, Farnham, Fisk's Hotel, Fort McHenry, Genera, Golden City, Golden Gulch, Gold Run, Haywood, Hill's Camp,

Weld county, occupying the north-east corner of the state, was organized in 1861, and named in honor of Secretary Weld. It is exclusively an agricultural and grazing county, although it has for a foundation extensive beds of coal. An account of its great irrigation companies has been given, and of the Greeley colony's acequias. Of a somewhat later date, about 1871, was the South-western, sometimes called the Tennessee colony, although its members were from several western and middle states. This association purchased a large tract of land in the Platte valley, and selected a town site near Fremont's orchard, twenty-five miles below Evans, on the Denver Pacific railway, which they named Green City, after D. S. Green of Denver. A considerable portion of the colony's lands needed no irrigation, being on the Platte bottom; but 8,000 or 10,000 acres had to be brought under cultivation, which was done by means of ditching, as in the former instance. All these improvements have made the western portion of Weld a great grain field, while the sheep and cattle ranges in the eastern half are sufficiently watered for that purpose by the numerous branches of the Platte.[23]

Hugh Flat, Inferno, Intermediate, Junction City, Lake, Loveland, Lower Swan River Valley, Mill Rancho, Monument Toll-gate, Park City, Rexford, St John, Sulphur Spring, Summit City, Surles, Swan, Tariff Mine, Timothy, Warren Camp, Webster Rancho, Wheeler, White River, Williams Fork. This list embraces most of the settlements existing in Eagle, and some in Garfield, or in Summit, previous to the late change of boundary.

A late-comer to this region was H. H. Eddy, who was born in Milwaukee, Oregon, in 1855. He removed to Watertown, N. Y., in 1866, and was educated for the law, being admitted to the bar in Rochester in 1877. He then migrated to Topeka, Kan., and thence to Colorado in 1878. After a few months at Leadville, he removed to Summit co., locating at Chihuahua. He was elected to the state senate in 1880, and again in 1884. He secured mines and lands in the co., where he made his residence.

[23] The wheat crop of 1882 was 370,000 bushels, worth about as many dollars, and all the other crops, including hay and potatoes, were valued at $900,000. The population of the county was 8,000, and the assessed valuation $7,907,145. The county seat was first temporarily located at St Vrain, but was finally established at Greeley, which had, in 1883, 1,500 inhabitants. Evans, Erie, and Sterling had each 400. There are the following minor towns and settlements in Weld co.: Akron, American Rancho, Athol, Baker Coal Bank, Barrie Rancho, Beaver Creek, Beaver Station, Big Bend, Blair, Blakeville, Boulder Valley Coal Bank, Brush, Buffalo, Cap Rock, Carr, Corona, Corona Station, Cottonwood Spring, Crystal Spring, Divide, Eckley, Fleming Rancho, Fort Morgan, Fort Sedgwick, Gard Rancho, Geary, Godfrey's Bluff,

Such is the extent and variety of aspect and resources of Colorado that each division has required
a separate history, which, at the best my space allows,
remains too brief. To sum up the condition of the
state in 1883-6, when it had only fairly entered upon
a career of settled industries, we have the following : Wheat produced from 114,000 acres, 2,394,000
bushels ; corn produced from 21,287 acres, 532,100
bushels ; oats produced from 41,250 acres, 1,209,000
bushels ; potatoes, 1,000,000 bushels, and large crops
of hay, which with minor productions were not reported, the approximate value of which was about
$4,000,000. The value of cattle on the ranges was
$37,500,000 ; of sheep, $10,000,000. The output of
coal was nearly $6,000,000. The iron and steel prod-

Hadfield Island, Hall, Hillsborough, Hopkins Coal Bank, Howard Spring,
Hudson, Hyde, Iliff, Johnson, Julesburg, Junction House, La Salle, Latham,
Lemons, Lone Tree, Manchester, Meadow Island, Mitchell's Coal Bank, Mor-
gan, New Liberty, Old Fort St Vrain, Old Julesburg, Pawnee Creek, Pierce,
Platte Valley, Platteville, Pleasant Plains, Pleasant Valley, Riverside,
Sarinda, School-house, South Platte, Spring Hill, Sterling, Stewart, Summit,
Valley Station, Weld, Weldon Valley, Wild Cat Creek, and Wray.

One of those who freighted across the plains before the railroad era was
Jared L. Bacon. He was born in Ohio in 1837, removing to Iowa in 1857, and
to Colorado in 1859. After mining two years in Russell's gulch he engaged
in the transportation of goods from the Missouri river to Denver until the
completion of the Union Pacific. Then he turned to stock raising in Weld
co., and had, in company with J. L. Routt, 3,000 acres of land, with an extensive range, and 32,000 head of cattle. He was elected sheriff of Weld co. in
1872, and to the general assembly in 1877, and again in 1879. He was also
appointed brig.-gen. of the state militia for 4 years, and was chairman of the
board of county commissioners for 6 years.

Samuel Southard, born in Ohio in 1846, enlisted in the army at the age of
15 years, serving through the war. He came to Colorado in 1866, remaining
unsettled for several years, but going into mercantile business at Era, in
Weld co., in 1872. In 1877 he was elected county treasurer and removed
to Greeley, being reëlected in 1879, and chosen county clerk in 1881. Later
he became a merchant at Greeley.

Jesse Hawes, born in Me in 1843, migrated to Ill. at the age of 16 years,
and enlisted in the army in 1861, serving through the war. He then commenced the study of medicine and graduated from Michigan university in
1868, after which he spent two years in the Long Island hospital, and two
years in European hospitals. On returning to the U. S. he came to Colo.,
settling at once at Greeley. He was surgeon of a railway co., and president
of the State Medical Society, as well as of the State Board of Medical
Examiners.

Henry B. Jackson, born in N. Y. in 1848, came to Colorado in 1872,
locating himself at Greeley, and beginning his money-getting by hewing ties
for a railroad company. In 1877 he started a small store, but was burned
out in 1883. The same season he built the Jackson Opera house block at a
cost of $16,000.

uct was about $3,000,000,   The gold, silver, lead, and copper amounted to $26,306,000, as nearly as it could be estimated, an increase of $3,000,000 since 1885, but a slight falling off from 1882.   According to census returns in 1880, the capital employed in 599 different manufactories, not including smelting, reducing, and refining works, was $4,311,714.   The census returns prepared for publication at each decade are really prepared the previous year, and therefore this estimate gives the amount of capital employed in manufactures in 1879, when they were in their infancy.   Without any exact figures to demonstrate the fact, it is evident that in 1883 the amount of money in use in manufactures, of the nature of iron and steel works, brass founderies, machine and car shops, flour and lumber mills, wagon and carriage factories, furniture, clothing, saddle and harness, and boot and shoe factories, breweries, meat packing, brick making, cigar making, printing, and other establishments to the number of over 600, great and small, must have quadrupled the census figures of 1880; besides which there were 175 smelting, stamping and reduction works in operation.   The whole product of the entire manufacturing industries of Colorado exceeded $35,000,000.

At the close of 1883 there were eighty-three banking houses in Colorado, of which two were national banks, with a capital of $1,640,000, deposits of $11,-171,734, and business to the amount of $16,704,-165.90 ; fourteen state banks and trust companies, with capital of $615,754 and $2,433,417 deposited; and forty-seven private banks, with $774,735 capital and $2,423,305 deposited. The fire insurance companies had policies out on $32,817,015; the life insurance companies on $29,374,019 ; and accident companies for $1,036,981.   The state debt consisted only of state warrants, which there was money in the treasury to meet, and a surplus of $372,961.   The constitution prohibits the bonded indebtedness of the state,

The biennial expenditures and receipts very nearly balance each other, and average $558,000. The amount raised by taxation in 1883 was $295,104.44, the assessed valuation being $110,729,756. A poll-tax of fifty cents was levied on 27,700 polls. The state tax was four mills on the dollar. The amount of internal revenue raised in 1880, with less than 200,000 inhabitants, was $168,259.

There were 370 school-houses, valued at $1,235,-491, and a school-fund for distribution amounting to $45,000, but which the improvement and leasing of the school lands was rapidly improving. The state supports by a special tax the state university school of mines, agricultural college, mute and blind institute, state industrial school, insane asylum, and penitentiary. The industrial school had 129 inmates, and the state prison 341 convicts. There are a state board of health, a state historical society, a state library, and a historical and natural history society maintained by legislative appropriation. Other state societies, depending on their members for support, are maintained by the medical or other professions to which they belong. These intelligent organizations to which the legislature and the people in their homes give their attention, illustrate the prevailing character of society in Colorado. Not without blemishes or errors, the young commonwealth stands out a shining example of mental, moral, and physical progression rare to find in the first twenty-five years of a nation's political existence. The laws are liberal; public gambling is not prohibited, and drinking saloons are numerous. According to the census of 1880, the whole number of inhabitants was 194,327, with an excess of 65,196 males; 154,-537 were native born, 39,790 foreign born, 2,435 were colored, 612 Chinese, 154 Indians. The population is largely drawn from New England, but is thoroughly cosmopolitan. Since the 10th census was taken Mormons have commenced colonizing in this

state, their number amounting to 1,578.   The Chinese,
though in the main well treated, have been driven out
of some of the mining towns.   The most remarkable
feature of Colorado is the number and size of its corporations; and the question to be solved in the future
is how far they are beneficial or detrimental to a state,
particularly in the form of money preponderance and
monopoly.   Possibly they will be crippling to individual enterprise, and enslaving to independent will and
thought; in which case the most republican of our
young states will have taken a backward step in
republican principles, and directors of wealthy organizations be able to dictate to the producing classes as
to their bondsman.[24]

[24] For yield of metals, see *Descriptive America*, May 4, 1884; Hall, *Ann.
Rept to Chamber of Commerce*, 1883, 147; *Farmer Resources of the Rocky Mts*,
17–40; *Farrell's Colorado as it is*, 1868, 15–46; *Stone's Hist.*, MS.; *The Rocky
Mtn Gem, Corbett's Legis. Manual*, 1877, 316; *Hayden's Great West*, 116–27;
Rocky Mtn Herald, Dec. 18, 1875; *Gunnison Sun*, Jan. 5, 1884; *N. M.
Pointers on the Southwest*, p. 46; *S. F. Call*, Jan. 12, 1885; *Rept of State Geol-
ogist*, 1881–2, 126–49; *Colorado Condensed*, 1881–82, 39–40; *Id.*, 1883, 25–34;
Burchard's Productions of Colorado, 1881, 132; *Rept Director of the Mint*,
1882, 14; *N. Mex. Revisita*, 1883, 279, *Elliott & Co.'s Hist. Arizona*;
Tucson Fronterizo, Jan. 27, 1882, 2; *N. Mex. Mining World*, Feb. 1, 1884,
93; *The Mines and Miners*, 507, 509–10.   On other subjects, see *H. Misc.
Doc.*, 47th cong. 2d sess., 98, 100; *Galveston News*, Dec. 1, 1884; *H. Ex.
Doc.*, 47th cong. 1st sess., vol. 15, 708–13; *Colo. Sess. Laws*, 1881, 31; *Id.*,
1883, 23–4; *Denver Tribune*, Jan. 13, 1880; *Colo. Gen. Laws*, 1877, 557–9;
Colo. Sess. Laws, 1883, 23–4; *Denver Hist.*, 240–1; *Transactions of State Med-
ical Soc.*, 1884; *Hawes' Charlatanism in Colorado*; Reprint from Transactions
of State Medical Soc. for 1883; *Shinn's Mining Camps*, 280; *Mining Rights in
Colo*, by R. S. Morrison; *Mining Code*, by M. B. Carpenter; *Gen. Laws Colo*,
1865, 71–2; *Fowler's Around Colorado*, MS., 8; *Leadville Democrat*, Jan. 1,
1884; *10th Census*, vol. 1, 378–447; *Porter's The West Census*, 1880, 392;
Hall's Ann. Rept Chamber of Commerce, 1880–3, 128; *Corbett's Directory of
Mines*, 1879; *Rept Sec. Int.*, ii. 319, 43d cong. 1st sess.   In regard to society,
see *Harper's Mag.*, vol. lx. 542–57; *Bird's Lady's Life, etc.*, being the observations of an early traveller in Colorado, 40–296; Bancroft, *Colo Notes*,
MS.; *Sac. Record-Union*, April 7. 1884; *S. F. Post*, Nov. 15, 1884; *Denver
Tribune*, Oct. 17, 1880.   The Chinese were driven from Como in 1879, *Denver
Tribune*, Nov. 13, 1879, and from other places at different times, and always
by the other foreign populations, led by political demagogues, who, whether
right or wrong, were never governed by a regard for the public welfare, but
sought rather to make capital for themselves by pandering to the base
instincts of our low and ignorant foreign voters, or their sympathizers or
dependents.

CHAPTER XIV.

LATER EVENTS.

1886-1889.

ELEMENTS OF GREATNESS—MINING VERSUS AGRICULTURE—LAND AND WATER MONOPOLY—MATERIAL PROGRESS—RAILROADS—DEVELOPMENT OF DENVER—ELECTION CAMPAIGN—LEGISLATION—EXCELLENCE OF STATUTORY, INSTITUTIONAL, AND SOCIAL REGULATIONS—CHARACTER OF PUBLIC MEN —BIOGRAPHICAL.

THE elements of a great commonwealth were in Colorado from the beginning. Like all the mid-continent states, it was misunderstood. From being a desert, according to early explorers whose experience was of heavily timbered countries, it was at length discovered to be a land rich in minerals, but it was not regarded as a farming, or even a grazing, region until accident revealed its capabilities in these directions. After thirty years of settlement, farming was hardly secondary, though the mining and grazing interests overshadowed it. The era of neglect of this industry was attributed to the scarcity of water on the surface, and the dryness of the atmosphere. Then came the water-grabbers, and fenced off the rivers from the common use of the people; or water companies constructed miles of canals, carrying water through immense tracts, which were thereby greatly augmented in price. They condescendingly sold the water which belonged to the people to the farmers along their route, and charged them with a "royalty" upon their land—that is, they exacted a bonus for benefiting the land irrigated in addition to the water rent.[1] Another

---

[1] The question was mooted in the legislature of 1887 whether the companies should not be denied the right to own water, and be treated simply as com-

abuse was the practice of aliens in taking up large tracts of land in the state for grazing or for speculative purposes. The legislature of Colorado, following the example of congress, passed an anti-alien law, to prevent English capital from fastening upon state lands. Mining property was not guarded in the same manner, but was owned to a considerable extent by aliens. Foreign capitalists, however, had not the same success in securing returns that American owners enjoyed, owing, perhaps, to the fact that they paid large prices for the undeveloped mines, and reserved too little capital with which to work them.

After a period of depression from 1883 to 1885, Colorado entered upon a career of great prosperity, which has since been steadily maintained. The immigration which for years had been pouring into Kansas, Nebraska, and Dakota had at length reached Colorado, giving a decided impetus to the development of her resources. A considerable proportion of the new-comers were farmers, who set at naught every agricultural tradition of the country by locating in the eastern part of the state, and attempting to farm, without the aid of irrigation, the arid plains which had been esteemed as of little value except to the stock-raiser. The north-eastern portion of the state, and particularly the great county of Weld, was the first to be thus invaded, and the records of the land-office at Denver are evidence of the rapidity with which settlement progressed.[2] In a similar manner,

mon carriers—a principle undoubtedly correct, for the water in the streams which they robbed belonged to the people, and they could do no more than convey it to the points where it is required. The legislature passed an anti-royalty bill for the relief of the farmers. At the same time a company from the neighborhood of Boston was planning an aqueduct to be 175 miles long, and to irrigate a large area east and south-east of Denver. The ditch was to be 10 feet wide and 3 or 4 feet deep.

[2] The entries and filings in the Denver land district, embracing the north-eastern portion of Colo, were, in 1885, 942,389 acres; 1886, 1,495,650 acres; 1887, 1,764,310 acres. At the election held in November 1886, there were over 3,200 votes polled in the precincts covering this territory, in which at the beginning of 1888 it was estimated that 4,000,000 acres remained unappropriated. *Report of Denver Chamber of Commerce,* 1887, 93.

and only a little later in point of time, settlement was begun in the south-eastern portion of the state, and principally in the broad valley of the Arkansas river.[3] As a result of this immigration, a large number of new towns sprang up and had a surprising growth. The principal of them were Akron, Yuma, Hyde, and Lamar; while Julesburg, Sterling, Fort Morgan and others, which had previously been insignificant way-stations on the railroad, became thriving and prosperous settlements.[4] It is probably too soon to determine whether agriculture without irrigation can be made permanently successful in eastern Colorado; it may, however, be safely affirmed that, while the agricultural possibilities of the region were formerly held in too light esteem, they have since been as greatly over-estimated.[5] Meantime the reclamation of large portions of the state by the building of irrigating canals has steadily progressed, and in 1889 there had been constructed, according to the state engineer's report, 5,000 miles of main canals, with their complement of smaller ditches and laterals, covering

[3] In the Lamar land district, comprising the greater part of south-eastern Colorado, a total of 1,583,360 acres were filed on in 1887. During the same year the filings in the entire state aggregated 4,318,770 acres, more than three fourths of which were comprised in the agricultural settlements of eastern Colorado. Id., 94.

[4] The following is a partial list of new towns of about the same age: Armour in Pueblo co.; Battle Mountain and Clinton in Eagle co.; Rogers and Kingston in Arapahoe co.; La Salle in Weld co.; Orson in Mesa, a new county in west Colorado; Otis and Red Lion in Weld co.; Parkville in Saguache co.; Parma in Rio Grande co.; Rangely in Garfield co.; Romley in Chaffee co.; San Antonio in Las Animas Co.; Sunnyside in Hinsdale co.; Woody and Emma in Pitkin co.; McMillan and Butter City in Bent co.; Prospect in Gunnison co.; Abbott, a farming settlement, in Arapahoe co.

[5] The settlement of eastern Colorado by farmers has been watched with great interest. The settlers were chiefly from eastern and central Kansas and Nebraska, where they had converted the so-called arid plains into productive farms, and when these became valuable, sold them and went 500 miles farther west to repeat the operation. The crops in 1886 were very fair, but in the two succeeding years were deficient in most localities. The theory that the rain-belt moves westward with the breaking and cultivation of the soil has been abundantly disproved by the extended observations of the signal service. That there are localities here and there on the Colorado plains where the natural rainfall and moisture will suffice to raise crops admits of no doubt; but it is equally true that extensive systems of irrigation, involving the construction of storage reservoirs, will be necessary to bring the region as a whole under successful cultivation.

a total of 2,000,000 acres, of which about one half had been brought fully under cultivation.[6]

The growth of Colorado during the period from 1886 to 1889 was further evidenced by the continued and rapid division of its larger counties. During this time no fewer than fifteen new counties were thus created, of which all but two lie in the eastern portion of the state, and upon the great plains where but a few years before the buffalo, and in their turn unnumbered herds of cattle, held undisputed possession.[7]

The rapid settlement of the state and the development of its resources gave a great impetus to the growth of its cities and towns, and particularly of those lying on the eastern slope of the mountains. Denver has easily kept in the lead, and its increase in population and wealth has been remarkable. In the three years following 1886 it grew from a city of 75,000 inhabitants to one of 125,000, and its trade, which in 1886 amounted to $67,000,000, exclusive of $12,000,000 produced by its smelters, had increased two years later to $127,750,000, to which the smelters added a further contribution of $16,000,000. The sales of real estate show the same surprising increase. In 1886 they amounted to $11,000,000; in 1887, $29,000,000; in 1888, $42,000,000; while during the first nine months of 1889 they reached a total of $44,000,000. Values rose with amazing rapidity, and this advance was not merely speculative, but was

[6] The first ditches were built in northern Colorado, and took their water from the streams that issue from the mountains north and west of Denver. Since 1882 extensive irrigation works have been constructed in the southern part of the state, and particularly in the San Luis valley and on the Arkansas river, in the vicinity of Las Animas. More than 200 miles of main canal have been built in the San Luis valley alone, at a cost of $500,000. The chief promoter of these enterprises was T. C. Henry, who secured for them large investments of eastern capital.

[7] The legislature of 1887 created the counties of Logan and Washington from territory formerly embraced in the large county of Weld, in the northeastern corner of the state. In 1889 all previous efforts in this direction were surpassed by the creation of thirteen new counties as follows: Baca, Cheyenne, Kiowa, Kit Carson, Lincoln, Montezuma, Morgan, Otera, Phillips, Prowers, Rio Blanca, Sedgwick, and Yuma. The county of Archuleta had been set off from Costilla in 1885.

accompanied by substantial improvements.[8] Prominent among them were the state capitol building,[9] upon which satisfactory progress is being made, and a federal court-house and post-office, the first to cost $1,000,000, and the latter half that sum.

Denver was also directly benefited by railroad building, which has been continued almost without interruption, till in 1889 the aggregate exceeded 4,000 miles of road, reaching out to the gulf of Mexico and the Missouri river on the one hand, and to the Pacific ocean on the other, together with local roads, that, scaling the mountain-sides, sought to bring the remotest mining region into communication with commercial centres.[10] Colorado railroads produced dur-

[8] The handsome building of the Denver Club, and a methodist church costing $40,000, were among the local improvements in Denver for 1886, in which year a total of $2,000,000 was expended in building operations. Each succeeding year has witnessed a large increase in building, especially of massive and elegant business blocks. The architecture of these, as well as of the better class of dwellings, is in the main of a high order. Colorado is rich in building stone, and its granites, trachytes, and sandstones of various colors are being utilized with good effect in its more important cities and towns. A masonic temple, costing $350,000, new buildings for the Wolfe and Jarvis halls, costing with the land $425,000, and a new opera-house, the Metropolitan, were completed in 1889. In the preceding year Denver spent $6,000,000 for new buildings, among which was Trinity methodist church, costing $275,000. The mercantile library of the chamber of commerce was opened in 1886 with 3,000 volumes. It owes its existence chiefly to R. W. Woodbury, then president of the chamber, and its support to that institution. It is free to the public, and has grown to a well-selected library of 16,000 volumes. Charles R. Dudley, a graduate of the Yale law school, is librarian. The State Historical Society, organized in 1879, of which Dr F. J. Bancroft is president, is doing a good work in its chosen field. In 1889 its museum was enriched by the purchase of a most interesting and valuable collection of articles obtained from the ancient cliff-dwellings in south-western Colorado. Early in 1887 Gen. Sheridan visited Colorado to select a site for a permanent military post, and a point seven miles from Denver was chosen. The government appropriation of $100,000 sufficed only to commence the improvement of the 640 acres, for which the citizens of Denver had paid $31,000. In 1888 an era of cable railway construction was begun, and in less than two years 30 miles of road had been put in operation, and the system was being extended in all directions. *Reports of Denver Chamber of Commerce*, 1887 and 1888; *Report of State Historical Society*, Jan. 1889.

[9] The style is of the Corinthian order. The main pediment will have an allegorical group representing the wealth, progress, and promise of the state. A magnificent rotunda will light the halls and corridors. The dimensions of the building north and south are 294 feet, or with its projections 383 feet, and it will contain 160 rooms. It will be built entirely of granite from quarries about six miles north of Gunnison. The stone is said to have no superior either as to beauty or durability among granites found elsewhere in the United States.

[10] The cost of these roads, and the wealth added to the state by railroad building in 1887, was $16,000,000. The increased value given to property

ing one year a revenue from freight shipped from the
east of $7,600,000, and from competitive passenger
traffic $3,000,000, while the traffic of the strictly
local roads amounted to $3,000,000 more. The im-
portance of the state and its geographical position
invited, and must ever invite, the transcontinental
roads to make connection with its local roads, if not
to send lines direct to its business capitals. Denver
is the railroad centre—Denver, "Queen City of the
Plains," as her people have been pleased to name her,
because she sits at the foot of the mountains, whence
she looks eastward over a vast expense of gently
sloping savannas. Behind her rise the majestic
heights of the great continental range. All about
her are bright landscapes, over her skies of summer
azure. In her lap is wealth, on her brow peace and
honor. Let no one dispute her royal right to preside
over and receive the homage of her sister municipalities. Young, beautiful, strong, worthy of all praise,
let her be called Queen.

Pueblo, destined from its location to become the
principal manufacturing centre of the Rocky Mountain region and the commercial metropolis of southern
Colorado, but whose growth was long retarded by
numerous causes, has since 1886 made rapid strides
toward realizing its possibilities. The consolidation
in that year of the three municipalities,[11] which had

along the lines could not be estimated. The Missouri Pacific extension into
Colorado opened a large grazing and agricultural area from the Kansas line
to Pueblo, a year later the Rock Island also built across the plains and made
its terminus at Colorado Springs. Meanwhile both the Colorado Midland and
the Denver and Rio Grande had built to Aspen and Glenwood Springs, opening
a region rich in the precious metals, in coal, and in agricultural possibilities.
The Denver and Rio Grande completed a branch to Ouray in Jan. 1888, and to
Lake City, one of the oldest mining towns in the San Juan region, in July
1889. The Denver, Texas, and Fort Worth, by bringing tide-water a thousand miles nearer to Colorado, is destined to revolutionize commerce with
the Atlantic seaboard.

[11] The consolidation of Pueblo, South Pueblo, and Central Pueblo was
effected April 19, 1886. The idea was first publicly agitated in 1882 by the
board of trade, and was favored by a majority of the influential citizens on
both sides of the river. Opposition came chiefly from the south side, and in
particular from the Colorado Coal and Iron Co., whose influence, then dominant in South Pueblo, would necessarily be lessened by the change. Chiefly

grown side by side as rival towns, marked the beginning of a new era in the history of the city on the Arkansas, and placed it in position to play its part in the general development of the state. The final completion of the Denver, Texas, and Fort Worth railroad in 1887 was of great benefit to Pueblo; but perhaps the greatest stimulus to its growth was the decision of the Missouri Pacific to extend its line thither, and make the southern metropolis its Rocky Mountain terminus. The assurance of this important connection was followed, during 1888, by a very marked increase in values as well as in the city's area. In the summer of 1889 buildings to the value of $2,000,000 were in course of erection, and every department of trade and manufacture gave evidence of healthful activity and substantial growth.[12]

Colorado Springs likewise shared in the general progress. In 1889 it had grown to a city of 10,000 inhabitants, and the assessed valuation of its property had doubled in three years. A prominent cause of its prosperity was the construction of the Colorado Midland railway,[13] which, starting westward from

through the exertions of Gov. Pitkin, an enabling act was secured from the legislature of 1885, and the matter brought to a successful issue the following year.

[12] The population of Pueblo in 1889 was 25,000. It is rapidly becoming the principal smelting point in Colorado, and its furnaces had reached in 1889 a capacity of 1,000 tons of ore daily. The output of the Colorado Coal and Iron Co. in 1888, was 20,800 tons of pig iron; 8,000 tons of steal rails; 5,300 tons of bar iron; 1,300 tons of cast iron pipe; 46,400 kegs of nails and spikes, together with 730,000 tons of coal, and 135,800 tons of coke produced by its mines in various parts of the state. It paid in wages for the year a total of $1,250,000. Pueblo has four national banks, which had in Dec. 1888 deposits aggregating $1,036,500. In addition there are two private banks, and a fifth national bank, with a paid-up capital of $125,000, began business in 1889. An opera-house, with a seating capacity of 1,700, and costing $300,000, is in course of erection, Pueblo has had since 1882 a board of trade, which at times has done effective work in furthering the city's interests. In 1887 it was reorganized, and has since acquired property worth $35,000. Its officers in 1889 were A. B. Patton, president; Andrew McClelland, vice-president; Charles W. Bowman, secretary; and J. D. Miller, treasurer.

[13] The Colorado Midland is a Colorado Springs enterprise, and originated in the belief that the Ute Pass afforded a short central route to Leadville, the Elk Mountain mines, the valley of the Grande, and Salt Lake City. The company was organized in 1883 by H. D. Fisher, J. F. Humphrey, and Irving Howbert, to whom, and particularly to the first named, belongs the credit of carrying the enterprise past its preliminary stages and well on

Colorado Springs in 1886, pushed its standard-gauge track over Ute Pass and across South Park to Leadville, and thence over the main range of the Rocky Mountains by a tunnel 2,164 feet long, and at an altitude of 11,530 feet above the sea, to Aspen and Glenwood Springs, which were reached in the autumn of 1887. The building of this railroad formed a turning-point in the history of Colorado Springs, since that city was thereby brought into closer communication with the largest wealth-producing districts of the state, and its place upon the direct line of transcontinental travel was more distinctly marked. Already two trunk lines of railway have crossed the plains, seeking this gateway of the mountains, and more must follow.[14]   But while Colorado Springs' increasing importance as a commercial centre has been in

toward success. In the following year Orlando Metcalf became interested in the project, and a year later J. J. Hagerman, who had but recently come to Colorado, accepted the presidency of the company, and pushed the enterprise to completion.   Jerome B. Wheeler, who had acquired large interests at Aspen and Glenwood Springs, and in adjacent coal lands, was also prominently identified with it.   The Midland was the pioneer railroad in north-western Colorado, its building compelling the Denver and Rio Grande to extend thither, and compete for the traffic of an immense region, rich in the precious metals and in coal.   In the latter part of 1889 the Midland and Denver and Rio Grande built jointly a line of railway down the Grande river from Glenwood Springs to Grand Junction, giving the former a transcontinental connection, and the latter an easier line than that by way of Marshall Pass and the Gunnison valley.

J. J. Hagerman, to whom is largely due the credit of making the Colorado Midland an accomplished fact, was born in Port Hope, Canada, March 23, 1838, and at an early age removed to Michigan.   Working his way through the university of that state, and graduating in 1861, he engaged in the iron business in Milwaukee, and later developed the famous iron mines of the Menomonee range, in which latter enterprise he amassed a large fortune.   Ill health compelled retirement from business, and several trips were taken to the Rocky Mountains and to Europe before location was finally made at Colorado Springs in the winter of 1884-5.   There, with improved health, he again engaged in active business, and in addition to his work in connection with the Midland railway, became largely interested in the development of north-western Colorado, in the improvement of real estate in Colorado Springs, and in extensive irrigation enterprises in the Pecos valley, New Mexico.

[14] The Atchison, Topeka, and Santa Fé accomplished in 1887 its long-threatened paralleling of the Denver and Rio Grande from Pueblo to Denver, and established close relations with the Midland at Colorado Springs.   When the Colorado extension of the Rock Island system was determined upon, the claims of Denver, Pueblo, and Colorado Springs as the terminus were fully considered, and a decision reached in favor of the last, to which the line was completed in Nov. 1888.

no small measure the occasion of its growth and prosperity, yet its chief attractions continue to be, as they have been from the beginning, such as appeal to invalids and valetudinarians, who, in ever-increasing numbers, here find the climate for which they have sought the world over, and the social order incident to a refined and cultured community.[15]

To George Rex Buckman, one of the most public-spirited citizens of Colorado Springs, and long identified with its interests, I take this opportunity of acknowledging my obligations for a large amount of recent and valuable material touching the counties,

[15] During 1888 nine additions to the city were platted, and buildings costing a total of $750,000 were erected, including two church edifices costing respectively $35,000 and $45,000, though not completed till the following year. The assessed valuation of the city in 1889 was $4,373,935. Its three banks had aggregate deposits of $1,200,000, and its business, exclusive of real estate, reached a total of $4,500,000. A complete system of sewerage was introduced, and its water system, which has cost a total of $280,000, was extended and enlarged. Colorado College was free from debt in 1889, and under the presidency of William F. Slocum, a graduate of the Johns Hopkins university, entered upon a career of higher usefulness. The building of the Sisters of Loretto hospital, the Bellevue sanitarium, and the Glockner memorial home testified to a generous spirit of charity.

The Colorado Midland railway was also the direct cause of the resurrection of Colorado City, once the capital of the territory, and one of its cities of promise, but long fallen into decay. In 1889 it had become a prosperous and growing town of 2,000 inhabitants, with glass-works and other manufactures, and with at least two independent municipalities, of which the principal is Calvert Heights, pressing hard upon its borders. Manitou has likewise gained steadily in population and substantial improvement, and in reputation as a spa and fashionable resort. Water from one of its famous springs is bottled in large quantities, and made an article of commerce. The idea of a railway from Manitou to the summit of Pike's peak was early entertained. In 1883 a local company completed the survey of a line of ordinary traction railway 30 miles long, and with maximum grades of 316 feet per mile. About $100,000 was spent in construction, when the project was abandoned hrough failure to secure necessary capital. Early in 1889 a strong company was organized, with John Hulbert president, and R. R. Cable vice-president, to build a cog-wheel railway on the Abt system, construction of which was actively begun in October of the same year, under contract requiring completion June 15, 1890. The line is 8.7 miles long, with about equal lengths of 10, 16, and 25 per cent grade respectively, the steepest being at the summit. It is being built in the most substantial manner, with grade 15 feet wide and track of standard gauge. The ascent of nearly 8,000 feet is to be accomplished in an hour and a half, the motive power being 25-ton locomotives, which, as well as the cars, are furnished with every safety appliance. The cost of the road will be $500,000. Cascade, Cañon, and Green Mountain Falls are new suburban resorts in Ute Pass, made available by the Colorado Midland railway, and from the first of them a carriage-road has been constructed to the summit of Pike's peak, over which 2,500 persons made the ascent during the season of 1889. *Colorado Springs Gazette*, Jan. 1, 1888, Jan. 1, 1889.

settlements, railroads, industries, institutions, and other matters included in the annals of his adopted state.[16]

Trinidad, for long years a sleepy semi-Mexican town, has been awakened into vigorous life and growth largely by a realization of the fact that the cheap fuel at its doors must make of it an important manufacturing centre. The older valley towns of northern Colorado have continued to grow steadily, if less rapidly, than those in other sections. Leadville early reached the limit of its growth, and has for a decade remained almost stationary, while continuing to add from its mines an average of $18,000,000 yearly to the world's wealth. The mineral yield of the state had increased quite gradually, indicating a healthy growth throughout the mining regions; but in 1888 a long step forward was taken, the output exceeding that of the preceeding year fully 30 per cent, and reaching $35,317,823. Nearly the whole of this great increase came from the Aspen district, one of the many treasure-filled regions, and the latest to be unlocked in the great storehouse of the mountains.[17]

[16] A native of Philadelphia, where he was born Nov. 26, 1853, Mr Buckman is on the father's side of English descent, among his mother's ancestors being one of the pilgrim fathers who landed from the *Mayflower*. After graduating, in 1871, at the Central high school, Phil., he learned the trade of a machinist with the firm of Wm Sellers & Co., with whom he remained till Jan. 1879, when, on account of failing health, he removed to Colo Springs. His health restored, he engaged in active business and also in literary pursuits, his contributions to magazines, newspapers, and other current literature largely assisting to make known the resources of Colo, and especially the attractions of Colo Springs.

[17] In 1889 Aspen had grown to a city of 7,500 inhabitants, and had two railroads, two banks, five churches, two daily and two weekly newspapers, and a handsome opera-house, the Wheeler Grand. The mineral yield of the district, which was $505,300 in 1886, and $857,400 in 1887, jumped in 1888 to $7,954,000, realizing at a bound all the expectations that had been formed regarding it, and placing it in the front rank of the great producing regions of the state. The ore is found in contact fissures between brown and blue lime-stone, and much of it is of a very high grade, running from 5,000 to 10,000 oz. of silver per ton. Among the most noted mines are the Aspen, Emma, Vallejo, Durant, Edison, Celeste, and Mollie Gibson. Mining operations were retarded for several years by extended litigation, growing largely out of the difficulty of construing the mining laws with reference to the geological peculiarities of the regions. The most famous suit, that of the Durant against the Aspen, Emma, and others, and which involved the apex question, was settled by compromise after having been in the courts for about three years.

The election campaign of 1886 was a hardly contested one, the democratic party throughout the United States having a revival, and the republicans being divided by the 'mugwump' faction and the prohibitionists. Three tickets were in the field in Colorado, the prohibitionists drawing their strength mainly from the republicans. However, all the republican candidates for state officers were elected, except the governor, Alva Adams, who, from being a hardware merchant of Pueblo, came to be elected chief of his noble young state by a plurality of 2,418, his competitors in the race being William H. Myers, formerly lieutenant-governor, and W. H. Fishback, prohibitionist. His predecessor was Benjamin H. Eaton. N. H. Meldrum, formerly secretary of state, was elected lieutenant-governor, succeeding P. W. Breene, elected state treasurer; and James Rice became secretary in place of Melvin Edwards, or, more correctly, after Edward R. Hanley, appointed in place of Edwards, resigned. D. P. Kingsley was

The development of the Aspen region, as well as of the coal-fields adjacent to Glenwood Springs, is largely due to the foresight, energy, ability, and capital of Jerome B. Wheeler, a New York merchant, who began in 1882 to make investments in mining properties and coal-lands in Pitkin and Garfield counties. As early as 1883 he organized a company which began the purchase and smelting of the ores of the Aspen district, thereby affording a much-needed encouragement to the miners, and making it possible for development to be prosecuted. It was in the search for cheaper fuel for the smelter that Mr Wheeler acquired the large areas of coal-lands in Jerome Park and in the Grand valley near Glenwood Springs, which, as a result of vigorous development by the Grand River Coal and Coke Co., of which Mr Wheeler is president, are rapidly becoming the most extensive and valuable coal properties in the state. Of the 2,000 acres of coal-land owned by this company, a single tract of 160 acres has been estimated to contain 56,000,000 tons, one of the nine parallel veins measuring 45 ft in thickness. The capacity of the mines is 2,500 tons of coal and of the ovens 150 tons of coke per day. In addition to these large mining and smelting interests, Mr Wheeler was one of the chief promoters of the Colorado Midland railway enterprise, and was the first vice-president of the company. He also established a bank and built an opera-house in Aspen, and is interested in the development of Glenwood Springs as a sanitarium. Born in Troy, N. Y., Sept. 3, 1841, he enlisted on his twenty-first birthday in the sixth New York cavalry, and served with distinction till the close of the war. Engaging in commercial pursuits, he finally became a partner in the firm of R. H. Macy & Co., New York, in which he remained till Jan. 1888, withdrawing at that date to devote his whole attention to his western interests. Mr Wheeler has invested several millions of dollars in Colorado, and his ventures have been uniformly successful.

elected state auditor, and L. S. Cornell state school-superintendent. Attorney-general Charles Thomas was succeeded by Alvin Marsh, and George G. Symes was elected congressman, running against Myron Reed democrat, and Murray prohibitionist, beating them by a plurality of 866. On the organization of the legislature, in January 1887, George M. Chilcott was chosen president of the senate, and T. B. Stuart speaker of the lower house. The republican majority in the senate was ten, in the assembly one.[18]

Two years later the republicans were returned completely to power in the state offices, Job A. Cooper, a highly respected lawyer and banker of Denver, being elected governor; W. G. Smith, lieutenant-governor; James Rice, secretary of state; W. H. Brisbane, treasurer; L. B. Schwanbeck, auditor; Samuel W. Jones, attorney-general; Fred Dick, superintendent of public instruction, and Hosea Townsend, of Custer county, member of congress. E. O. Wolcott was elected by the legislature of 1889 to succeed Thomas M. Bowen in the United States senate.

The legislation of Colorado has never been disgraced by violence, by wanton waste of the people's money,[19]

[18] Mention was made by the president of the senate of the death of two state senators since the last session—Tilford and Elkins; and Gov. Eaton in his farewell message regrets the demise of ex-U. S. representative Jerome B. Chaffee and ex-gov. Frederick W. Pitkin.

[19] There was, in 1887, when the legislature met, some embarrassment from the financial condition of the state. The total amount in the treasury at the close of Gov. Eaton's term of office was, in cash and securities, $834,579.05, out of which to make the various appropriations for the support of state institutions, and to pay salaries to state officers. This deficiency was not the result of bad management, or extravagant outlay, but came from the too common practice of assessing property below its value. For instance, the property of the state was actually worth $400,000,000, yet was assessed at $120,000,000, whereas the railroads alone were selling in the market at a valuation greater than that, although they were assessed at only $23,696.666. The constitution required that the property of the state should be rated for taxation at its true value, and it was manifest that a low tax on a full valuation should be more satisfactory than a high tax on a low estimate. The legislature took up this subject in 1887, and provided for the taxation of mining property, the opinion of the courts having first been obtained as to the constitutionality of the bills offered. All mines producing more than $1,000 per annum in mineral were made assessable, and in case of a mine which was not patented being sold for taxes, the title, under the laws of Colorado, should be good and valid. A list of all the producing mines was

or by disrespect of the constituted authorities. If its statutes are not perfect, neither were they for whom they were made, nor the makers themselves. It is enough that an effort at excellence in statutory regulations, as in institutional and social affairs,[20] is a feature of the centennial state. Notable, not notorious, the character of her public men is an example to the younger states, and blends harmoniously with her many charms, material, natural, and inspired by art. Colorado is the flower of a peculiarly western civilization, in which is mingled the best blood of the north and the south, the virile sap of New England and the Carolinas—a truly American state.

The close of this record leaves Colorado still on the flood tide of prosperity. In the rapid increase of her population, in the vigorous and successful development of the plentitude of her resources, in the growth of material wealth, and of those institutions whence flow the higher riches of education and enlightenment,

to be furnished by the county clerk to the county assessor. An attempt was made to correct railroad abuses and encroachments by statute, and a law was enacted creating a supreme court commission. The persons appointed under the act were atty.-gen. Marsh, ex-senator Rising of Custer co., and Thomas Macon of Fremont co.

[20] The new county of Archuleta, which had not more than 150 voters, rebelled against the authority of the county commissioners (republican) in July 1887, being led by one E. T. Walker and the sheriff, Height (democrats). The rioters burned the property, and threatened the life of one of the commissioners, Charles D. Scase. The others were intimidated, and forced to resign, and anarchy for a time held sway. The population of this region was Mexican, and two, at least, of the commissioners were Mexican, but were men of wealth and standing. That they should be such appears to have been too much for the democracy to bear, and their ukase was issued as follows: 'If you don't resign, we will kill you and destroy your property.' The legislature sent a committee to inquire into the cause of the terrorism, as it was bound to do, when it appeared that one of the mob which had broken up a meeting of the commissioners had enunciated the doctrine that 'this is a democratic administration, and it shall be run on democratic principles.' Accordingly the ballot-box was stolen, and other democratic practices resorted to, and when the commissioners met to open court they were prevented. The legislature then attached Archuleta co. to La Plata co. for judicial purposes, and the matter was brought before the grand jury; but in the mean time Walker had disappeared. A race war of another sort was the outbreak of the reservation Utes, August 1887, by which some blood was spilled on both sides, ending by the Indians returning to their homes. The trouble arose from the ruling of a new agent that the band must come to the agency to draw their annuities, be counted, and placed on the list. The Utes refused, and went one year without their annuities. The agent then required the sheriff to return them to the reservation; hence the conflict.

she may well challenge the admiration and command
the respect of the nation and of the world.[21]

[21] Leadville elected a democratic mayor in the spring of 1888, who surprised his constituents by ordering the gambling saloons closed, and closed
they were within a month. Colorado had two, if not more, towns where the
public sale of intoxicating drinks was prohibited. But to prohibit by agreement from the start is quite different from saying to a whole community of
gamblers 'depart,' and enforcing the command. Mayor Roche of Leadville
might have been a martyr in the days of the inquisition, and yet have died
profitlessly, like many another martyr.

A conservative estimate of the present population of the state places it
at 405,000, or more than double that of 1880. The state institutions, upon
which upwards of $2,000,000 has been expended, are without exception in
a flourishing condition. The state university at Boulder, under the able
presidency of Horace M. Hale, A. M., LL. D., who in 1887 succeeded Dr
Joseph A. Sewall, is taking high rank among the educational institutions of
the land. The state school of mines at Golden, with a distinguished faculty,
at the head of which is Regis Chauvenet, A. M., meets an educational need
in a region where mining is a principal industry. Its annual reports are valuable contributions to geological and metallurgical science. The success of
the state agricultural college at Fort Collins has been pronounced, both edu-
cationally in its special field and in the conduct of experimental agricultural
stations, two of them being located respectively in the Arkansas and San
Luis Valley; the officers at present are C. L. Ingersoll, director; F. J. Annis,
secy and treas.; A. E. Blount, Jas Cassidy, David O'Brine, L. G. Carpenter,
and Wm McEachran are the professors of the various departments, the faculty
of the college itself at present is C. L. Ingersoll, prest; A. E. Blount, agric.;
J. W. Lawrence, mechanics; V. E. Stolbrand, mathematics; Maud Bell, history,
etc.; D. O'Brine, chemistry, etc.; L. G. Carpenter, physics and engineering;
W. H. Cowles, military tactics; C. S. Crandall, botany, etc.; Grace Patton,
instructor; F. J. Annis, secy. The State Mute and Blind Institute at Colorado
Springs continues its noble work among these unfortunates. The episcopal
church in Colorado has been diligent in founding educational institutions,
and now has school property in Denver valued at $600,000. The baptist
church is also doing good work in this direction, erecting among others an
institute for young women, to be conducted after the model of Vassar college. The generous gifts of Mrs Elizabeth Iliff Warren and Jacob Haish to
the university of Denver have been supplemented by one of $40,000 from H.
B. Chamberlin for the establishment of an observatory with a twenty-inch
Alvin Clark telescope and other instruments for astronomical research.

Prominent also among the citizens of Denver, as one of those who have
have contributed largely to the common good, is Humphrey B. Chamberlin,
a native of Manchester, England. Coming with his parents to the United
States in 1851, when not yet five years of age, he received his education at
the public schools of Oswego, and after serving in the civil war, and afterward engaging in business at Fulton and Syracuse, N. Y., removed in 1880
to Denver on account of failing health. Here he embarked first of all in the
boot and shoe business, and afterward in the insurance and real estate business, his transactions in the latter yielding him a handsome fortune. To him
is due the organization of the Denver, Colorado Cañon, and Pacific railroad,
of which he is vice-president. He is also president of the Denver Chamber
of Commerce, the Young Men's Christian Association, and the State Micro-
scopical Society. The Chamberlin Observatory, to be transferred with its
equipments to the Denver University, he is building at his own expense, its
telescope, an equatorial refractor, with twenty inches aperture, to be the
largest between Washington and the Pacific coast. To churches and charities he is a most liberal subscriber, and while an energetic and successful

business man, is recognized as one of the most moral, progressive, and benevolent citizens of his adopted state.

Among those who are identified with the history of Denver, who have grown with its growth and prospered with its prosperity, is Milo A. Smith, a native of Newark, in central Ohio, and a grandson of Jesse Smith, whose memory is still dear to the citizens of Jefferson county, New York. After graduating at the Troy Polytechnic Institute, Mr Smith entered the service of the U. S. government, was appointed assistant engineer under General Cram, and ordered on lake survey work at the mouth of the Huron river. This accomplished, he engaged in a manufacturing business, and afterward in real estate operations, which he found much more profitable, and also more to his taste. Removing to Denver a year or two before Colorado's admission to statehood, he found in the business atmosphere of that city so much of activity and hopefulness, that he launched out boldly into real estate ventures, and with most favorable results. In 1883, when the cattle interests of the centennial state were assuming large proportions, he invested largely in live-stock and lands, controlling by means of water rights no less than 1,000,000 acres on the borders of Arizona and New Mexico. Within recent years he has laid out and subdivided the sightly addition to the metropolis known as the Eastern Capitol hill, where was built an electric motor railway to connect with the cable road. He also located Arlington grove in partnership with four others, building for himself in 1880 a handsome residence on Sherman avenue. At the time his friends asked him, 'What makes you go out into the country to live?' But meanwhile Denver has grown to be a city with some 130,000 inhabitants, and in the midst of its most fashionable residence quarter is Sherman avenue. Among other enterprises in which he is interested is the University Park Electric railroad, of which he was one of the promoters, and is now the president. He is also president of the East Denver Water Co., whose purpose is to bring a supply of pure water into the city from Sand creek, about 15 miles to the eastward. In morals and religion Mr Smith's faith and works are as pure and unsullied as his business integrity. An episcopalian in belief, and a liberal subscriber to the cause of his church, he is averse to all theologic dogmas and sectarian entanglements. In Denver he is known as a man whose success is by no means the result of accident, but rather of intelligence, hard work, and fair dealing; one possessed of quick perceptive powers and keen penetration; one who never wittingly injured his fellow-man, and who to the rising generation has taught the value of self-reliance and earnestness of purpose, united with the most perfect sense of honor.

Worthy of mention as one to whom is largely due the development of the oil interests of Colorado is Isaac E. Blake, a native of Bolton, Canada, but of American parentage and English descent, his ancestry being traced back to the days of the conquest. Among his ancestors were the great admiral Sir Robert Blake and Major-general John Blake of revolutionary fame. In 1865, after completing the term of his engagement with a mercantile firm at Bolton, Mass., he tried his fortune at Petroleum Center, where two or three years later he became the owner of oil-lands which yielded handsomely, and thus, when only twenty-four years of age, he found himself a rich man. Being now married to Miss Agnes N. Maloney, he removed to Boston, where both acquired a thorough musical education. In 1874, after suffering financial reverses, he turned his attention to Col., where the oil business then offered unusual inducements. Reaching Denver in this year, he devised an ingenious plan of shipment, storage, and distribution, including his 'freight combination oil tank car,' his invention being later adopted all over the United States, and recently introduced into Europe. In 1855 he was appointed president and manager of the Continental Oil and Transportation Co. of California, after consolidated with the Standard Oil Co. In 1888 the company's wells at Florence, Col., produced 42,000 gallons a day, with sales amounting for the year to 4,000,000 gallons, while the output of their wells at Newhall and Pico Cañon, Cal., was on a very much larger scale. The opinion which he expressed on his first arrival in Col., that the state would produce all the oil required for her own consumption, has since been fully justified. In California he has entirely revolutionized the methods of conducting the oil business, and that in the face of determined opposition from some of the strongest men and most powerful corporations in the country. A man of rare executive ability, and with the clearest insight into all business operations and details, he is also one of the most public-spirited citizens of Denver. As a member and musical director of the Trinity Methodist Episcopal church, he has been always most anxious to promote its interests, presenting it with an organ pronounced by critics one of the most perfect instruments in the world, subscribing largely to the building fund for the edifice recently erected, and being equally liberal in his contributions to the churches of other cities. In Denver his reputation is that of a shrewd and successful business man, a lover of music and the finer art, an earnest, practical christian, and one to whom the city and state are greatly indebted for their prosperity, culture, and refinement.